D1597271

Building Anatomy

Other Books in the McGraw-Hill Construction Series

Defect-Free Buildings: A Construction Manual for Quality Control and Conflict Resolution by Robert S. Mann

McGraw-Hill Construction Locator: Building Codes, Construction Standards, Project Specifications, and Government Regulations by Joseph A. MacDonald

Construction Safety Engineering Principles: Designing and Managing Safer Job Sites by David V. MacCollum

Solar Power Systems in Building Design: The Complete Photovoltaics Engineering Resource by Peter Gevorkian

Building Anatomy

An Illustrated Guide to How Structures Work

Iver Wahl

New York Chicago San Francisco Lisbon London Madrid Mexico City
Milan New Delhi San Juan Seoul Singapore Sydney Toronto

The McGraw-Hill Companies

Library of Congress Cataloging-in-Publication Data

Wahl, Iver.
Building anatomy : an illustrated guide to how structures work / Iver Wahl.
p. cm.—(Mcgraw-Hill construction series)
Includes bibliographical references and index.
ISBN 0-07-143213-2 (alk. paper)
1. Structural stability. 2. Building—Details—Pictorial works. 3. Structureal failures—Prevention. I. Title.
TH846.W34 2007
624. 1—dc22
2006036272

1 2 3 4 5 6 7 8 9 0 DOC/DOC 0 1 3 2 1 0 9 8 7 6

ISBN-13: 978-0-07-143213-9
ISBN-10: 0-07-143213-2

The sponsoring editor for this book was Cary Sullivan, the editing supervisor was David E. Fogarty, and the production supervisor was Richard C. Ruzycka. It was set in Times by International Typesetting and Composition. The art director for the cover was Anthony Landi.

Printed and bound by RR Donnelley.

This book was printed on recycled, acid-free paper containing a minimum of 50% recycled, de-inked fiber.

To Kol

ABOUT THE AUTHOR

Iver Wahl is a licensed architect and a professor at the University of Oklahoma where he teaches structures and architectural design. He is certified by the National Council of Architectural Registration Boards and is a member of the Earthquake Engineering Research Institute and the Architectural Engineering Institute. The author has conducted disaster site reconnaissance for over fifteen years, sometimes with the International Center for Disaster Research in the United States or in cooperation with the Disaster Prevention Research Institute in Japan. This work has included forensic analysis of collapsed buildings during or after earthquakes, typhoons, floods, tornadoes, terrorist bombings, riots, and war. He received awards for his vertical rebound theory which offered an explanation for vertically collapsed buildings in the Kobe earthquake.

Contents

9 Arches 105

10 Post and Beam 125

11 Rigid Frames 153

12 Bearing Wall and Slab 171

13 Trusses 191

14 Space Frames 215

Preface

Most architecture schools slowly reveal the secrets of building technology over the first three years of their programs. At the University of Oklahoma a clear decision was recently made to reveal the conceptual aspects of building technology in the first year with the math aspects following along in a more traditional manner. This has allowed students to immediately integrate structural behavior into their first design studio. The motivation for this text was born of that change. This is a book about technical concepts, alternatives, and choices directed at those just beginning their study of architecture, engineering, and construction. Initially basic structural fundamentals are introduced. Next traditional "families" of structures are described. Finally some assistance is offered to the young designer in selecting a structure from these alternative families. Since a traditional solution may not always be appropriate, an additional chapter concerning structural creativity has been provided. Because structure is a "life support" system, a chapter encouraging quality assurance was chosen to conclude this text.

This book is intended to be read from beginning to end, rather than used as a reference book. Later chapters will build upon the knowledge gained in previous chapters. Important words have been emphasized, and are grouped together in a "vocabulary" section at the end of each chapter. A set of study questions is also provided at the end of each chapter. All sources, end notes, and recommended readings have been collected in a single bibliography at the end of the text, rather than at the end of each chapter.

Where appropriate, photos of failed structures have been provided as illustrations. These have been collected by the author during disaster site reconnaissance over the past fifteen years.

Acknowledgments

As a young student I was grateful to Harry Parker, Mario Salvadori, Robert Heller, P. A. Corkill, H. Puderbaugh, and H. K. Sawyers for making the technical world of structures exciting and understandable. More recently James Ambrose, Dimitry Vergun, Stephen Tang, Edward Allen, Fuller Moore, J. E. Gordon, Rod Underwood, Michele Chiuini, Matthys Levi, Elmer Botsai, Henry Lagorio, Daniel L. Schodek, and Robert Brown Butler have greatly extended this same effort. Their continuing impact on my understanding will be evident in this text to all who are familiar with their important work. This book has been greatly enriched by knowledge personally gained from Dr. Roberto Quaas, Dr. Ayala, and many other seismic researchers at UNAM and CENEPRED in Mexico City. Mentoring, support, and insights gained from Raymond Yeh, Dr. Yoshi Sasaki, Dr. Junji Katsura, and many friends at the Disaster Prevention Research Institute in Japan have made fifteen years of direct observation of structural failures an important part of this book. Much is owed to my father Iver William Wahl, FASCQ, for the credibility of the final chapter in this book, and a good deal more. Without continuing support and release time granted by James Kudrna and the College of Architecture at the University of Oklahoma, a work of this type would not have been possible. Throughout this text the reader will see the excellent work of many of the students within that college. It is much richer because of them. The effective copyright research and pursuit of appropriate releases by Ms. Kasha Preston made the final publishing schedule possible. Finally, without the guidance, friendship, and encouragement of Terry and Jenny Patterson this book would never have seen completion.

Building Anatomy

Figure 1-1

Guell Park by Antonio Gaudi in Barcelona Spain. Notice the structural logic of sloped columns.

1 Overview

DEFINITION OF STRUCTURE

Building *structure* is the ordered (or controlled) flow of physical force through conduits (or routes) formed by resistive materials in order to shelter three-dimensional space. The pattern or layout of the routes along which the forces flow is the basis used to name alternative structural systems, and from which a designer will normally choose.

IMPORTANCE OF STRUCTURE

Structure is one of the life-support systems in a building. Only design decisions concerning fire have equally grave implications. People die from errors in structural design. The design of structures is personally enjoyable, visually and technically significant, and professionally satisfying; however, it will always be a deadly serious business. It has life and death consequences.

COMPONENTS OF A BUILDING STRUCTURE

A building must maintain its shape and position by resisting widely changing physical forces in the context of its given site. In resisting these dynamic forces, it is essential to consider five components of a structural system (Fig. 1-2).

1. *Loads* are the physical forces acting on a building.
2. The *superstructure* is the part of the resistive building frame above the ground line.
3. The *lateral support system* resists horizontal loads such as wind.
4. The foundation is the part of the force resistive frame below the ground line.

Figure 1-2
1. Loads 2. Superstructure
3. Lateral Support System
4. Foundation 5. Geology & Soil.

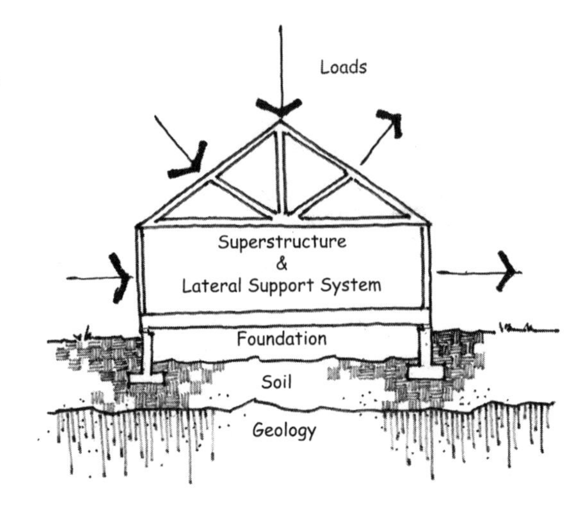

5. *Soil and Geology are* the material into which all the loads must ultimately be dissipated.

While each component may be considered separately, it is critical that the interaction of all five components must also be jointly and conceptually considered in order to assure a safe design. Also, understand that only some of the choices in a structural system are under the designer's control. Seismic loads, winds, and underlying geology exist beyond a designer's control.

CLASSIFICATIONS OF LOADS

Loads, the first component of a structural system, are classified in several different ways. Internal and external, vertical and lateral, dead and live, equivalent, uniform, point and distributed, impact, inertial, and static loads will all be discussed in a separate subsequent chapter (Fig. 1-3).

TRIBUTARY AREAS

Loads are said to fall on, or act on, a *tributary area*. One foot of snow on 10 square feet of roof produces 10 times the load of one foot of snow on one square foot of roof. A more full discussion of tributary areas is provided in the chapter on "post and beam" systems, but for now it is important to appreciate that the size of tributary area is as significant as the size of the load that is placed upon it. If this were not so the sail size on a boat would have no importance.

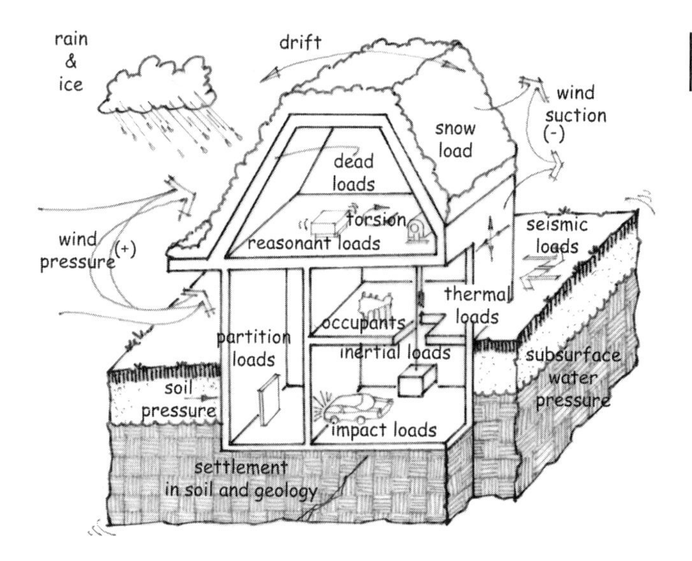

Figure 1-3
Common types of loads.

FORCES AND VECTORS

Loads on a building must be converted into *forces* in order to be mathematically analyzed. They may be further visualized by converting the forces into *vectors* (Fig. 1-4). Such graphic and mathematical analysis is beyond the scope of this book, but it is useful to have a conceptual understanding of forces and vectors at this time. Conceptually, vectors use graphic arrows to provide a visual representation of a force's:

Axis of action—indicated by the path of the line

Magnitude—shown by the length of the line

Sense—indicated by the end on which the arrow is placed

Direction—given with reference to the standard graphic zero position

Point of application for a force—indicated by the point of the arrow

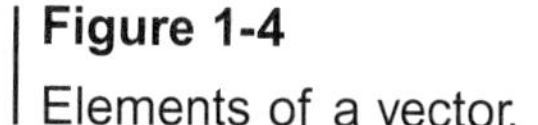

Figure 1-4
Elements of a vector.

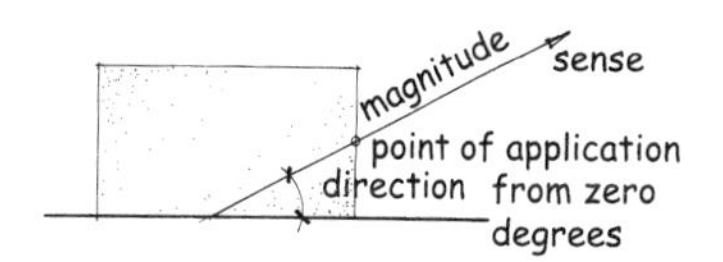

LOAD PROPAGATION

Loads are physical forces that are applied to a building and resisted by the rest of the structure system. The superstructure collects and conducts these forces down to the foundation, by converting them to *stresses* inside of the members, joints, and materials of the structural system. The foundation mitigates between the forces transmitted through the superstructure, and the resistance of the soil and geology upon which the building rests. The forces flow through the elements of the structure, similar to the way in which water flows through a plumbing system. The flow of these forces down through the structural system is called *load propagation*. The system of paths, or routes, used to control the ordered flow of load propagation defines the alternative families of superstructure and foundations from which we normally choose. This book dedicates several subsequent chapters to description of such alternative traditional superstructures and foundations; however, innovation beyond these conventions is often necessary. A chapter on structural creativity has been included to assist in these circumstances. The results of such activities often produce structural hybrids (which combine more than one traditional alternative) and exotics (which are one of a kind).

LOAD SCENARIOS

Load combinations

On any given site, load conditions are continuously changing. The effects of the various loads must be combined in a systematic way. While we must understand each independent load fully, it is the joint effect of combined loads that normally leads to structural failure. For example, the weight of snow on a roof can combine with the dead load of a building during an earthquake to cause a collapse that none of the three could have caused separately. For this reason, building codes require systematic consideration of all load combinations. Building elements will be sized based on the worst case combined loading scenario.

Construction loads

One of the most vulnerable periods in a structure's life is during its construction. Unique, one-time forces may act on members and joints of a structure during a building's construction process. The live loads placed on a building structure during construction are radically different from those it is designed to resist once completed. For example, a floor designed to carry office furniture after completion may have to carry the masonry for the exterior walls of an upper floor during a brief period in its construction. These continuously varying construction load conditions are made more dangerous since only a portion of the total final structure is in place at any moment during construction.

SUPERSTRUCTURE

Classification system

There are several methods used for classifying alternative types of superstructure. Many are more sophisticated and rational than the one used in this book. However, the "common language" method used in this book makes use of terms most often used and understood during preliminary design in an architectural office, or in conversations between constructors and architects.

Common alternatives

Using this "common language" classification method, the following types or families of superstructure will be addressed: cable systems, arches, post and beam, bearing wall and slab, trusses, space frames, vaults, domes, shells, folded plates, tents, and pneumatics. In addition, hybrid combinations and exotic systems will be briefly addressed.

Structural creativity

A designer will need to be capable of doing more than selecting an appropriate alternative from this list of common alternatives. For that reason, some selected methods of structural creativity will also be briefly outlined.

LATERAL SUPPORT SYSTEM

Many types of superstructure have a configuration that will inherently resist *lateral* (horizontal) loads such as winds and earthquakes. For those types of superstructures that do not have the inherent ability to resist lateral loads, a separate *lateral support system* is required. There is a wide range of lateral support configurations. The most common alternatives include shear walls and various types of bracing. To more fully address this important subject, a separate chapter has been offered in this text. It must be noted that some lateral support is also needed below the surface of the ground, due to such forces as soil and hydrostatic pressure. These issues will be more fully addressed in subsequent chapters on geology, soil, and foundations.

FOUNDATION

Foundations are crudely classified as *shallow* (such as a slab-on-grade), and *deep* (such as piles and piers). The appropriate selection of a foundation system must recognize its simultaneous "fit" between both the superstructure above, and the specific type of soil and geology below.

SOIL AND GEOLOGY

Soil is the weathered and/or transported subsurface rock (geology) upon which it rests. These issues and those of surface and subsurface water must also be more fully considered in a subsequent chapter.

STRESS AND STRAIN

General discussion

When loads are externally applied to a structural member (such as a beam), stresses are developed inside the member. The load is trying to tear or crush the material from which the member is made, but the molecular bonds in that material are providing resistance. This struggle is known as *stress*. This conversion of external loads to internal stresses in members is the necessary mechanism by which forces "flow" down through the structure (known as *load propagation*). *Strain* is the extent to which a member measurably yields or changes shape due to stress.

Simple stresses

There are only two simple stresses:

1. *Tension:* Simple straight line (or axial) pulling. When a string is pulled at both ends, simple tension stress is developed.
2. *Compression:* Simple straight line (or axial) pushing. When a straight stick is directly pressed at both ends, simple compression stress occurs inside the member.

Complex stresses

Tension and compression can be combined in many ways to form complex stresses. *Shearing*, *bending*, *buckling*, and *torsion* are all complex stresses that will be discussed in greater detail in the subsequent chapter on post and beam superstructures.

STRUCTURAL DESIGN GOALS

Safety

In their implications some of the following principles are only philosophical, some are economic, but some address occupant safety. Beauty is not the highest demand of architecture, safety is. At the absolute minimum, architecture should not bring harm or death to its occupants. A more appropriate standard is that architecture should provide positive shelter and protection from harm to its occupants. In an earthquake, an occupant should throw himself into a building for protection, not out of a window in order to escape. The bare minimum in case of structural failure is to give ample warning and to buy adequate "escape time" for the occupants.

Value

While cost will be discussed in more detail later, it is usually unwise for a professional to speak with a client only in terms of isolated cost. *Cost* is what you pay for a thing in time and money. *Value* is a comparison of what you get, for what you pay. It is, therefore, often more appropriate to discuss value than just cost.

Fitness

The structure should "fit" the conditions on its specific building site, and programmatic requirements of its internal circulation and functions.

Compatibility

The structural system must be successfully integrated with the envelope, mechanical, and electrical systems internally, and natural systems externally.

Flexibility

Structures have a life span. The longer the predictable life span of a building, the more unpredictable the future functions and site context become, and the more flexible the structure should be.

BIG CONCEPTUAL DESIGN DECISIONS

While more detail is given to these questions in the next chapter, some of the most typical and significant preliminary structural design questions are:

1. What functions must be supported and sheltered?
2. What forces must be resisted?
3. Upon what geology and soil must my design rest?
4. How long must it stand up?
5. Which (if any) of the common superstructures is most appropriate?
6. Which (if any) of the common foundation types is most appropriate?
7. What materials should be used?
8. How will the total system behave under all probable loading scenarios?
9. Roughly what size will the structural system and its components be?
10. What are the probable modes of the systems failure?
11. How should we put this thing together?
12. How will time change this building?
13. What is "plan B" if the structure fails?

STRUCTURAL DESIGN GUIDANCE

Formal and informal background

In addition to the tools and methods (i.e., codes, precedent, specialized references) discussed in the next chapter on "process", the following will assist a young designer in making these important conceptual structural decisions:

1. *Personal practice:* Experience is a great teacher. As a designer builds experience through professional practice, structural decisions become easier.
2. *Education:* Very few professionals attempt structural design without an appropriate formal education. Architects and engineers require years of formal study in these subjects.
3. *Standard Practice:* Architects, engineers, and related design professionals continuously evolve and improve standard methods and procedures in the design of structures. Law requires conformance to these minimum standard professional procedures.

Principles

Experienced practicing professionals have evolved a few very important principles to guide young design professionals. It is wise to measure your conceptual design decisions against these useful principles. In 15 years of disaster site reconnaissance it has become clear to the author that more of the buildings studied collapsed from conceptual flaws in the six following principles, than from incorrect math calculations. They are among the most important information provided in this book.

1. *Logic:* The principle of structural logic expresses two simple concepts:
   a. Big members carry big loads, and small members carry small loads.
   b. Loads should be directly opposed on the same axis of action if possible.
2. *Integrity:* Structural integrity has two faces:
   a. *The issue of honesty*: The structural means by which loads are truly resisted should be honestly expressed visually. An arch applied as a false face on a simple bearing wall is a deceit, and a violation of this principle.
   b. *The issue of wholeness*: If a bite is taken out of the wholeness of a structural system, this is a violation of this principle. All of the system is not there. For example, if a piece is cut from a dome in order to join it to another form, this principle is violated. Pragmatically, stresses will build up in load propagation at the edges of such bites.
3. *Economy:* This principle asserts four things:
   a. Loads should be minimized where possible.
   b. Heaviest loads should be placed as near the bottom of the building as possible.
   c. Structural complexity should be avoided to the extent possible. Keep it simple.
   d. Do not unnecessarily oversize the structure beyond true load requirements.
4. *Continuity:* Clean, smooth, direct, uninterrupted paths for forces must be provided for load propagation down through the building all the way into the bearing soil and geology.
5. *Redundancy:* This principle stresses the safety gained by providing multiple supports, or alternative routes for load propagation in a structure. In this way if one fails, the others may carry the load. On its face, this principle seems directly opposed to that of structural economy. However, early space

missions had a backup for all life-support systems. Remember building structure is a life support system.

6. *Priority:* The sequence of structural failure must be controlled. Generally it is better to fail in a member than in a joint, and better to fail in a horizontal member, than in a vertical member. This controlled sequence of failure gives warning, buys escape time, and has fewer tendencies to lead to a broader or more global collapse of the structure.

SELECTION OF A STRUCTURAL SYSTEM

The following is not a full checklist: however, some of the following discussion may assist the young designer in evaluation of structural alternatives:

Functional footprint

This is the functional area that can be sheltered by the structure. Obviously a two-lane bowling alley requires a very different "footprint" than 12 people doing a round dance. Each common type of superstructure can be associated with its implied "footprint" (Fig. 1-5).

Figure 1-5
Note the shaded building footprint.

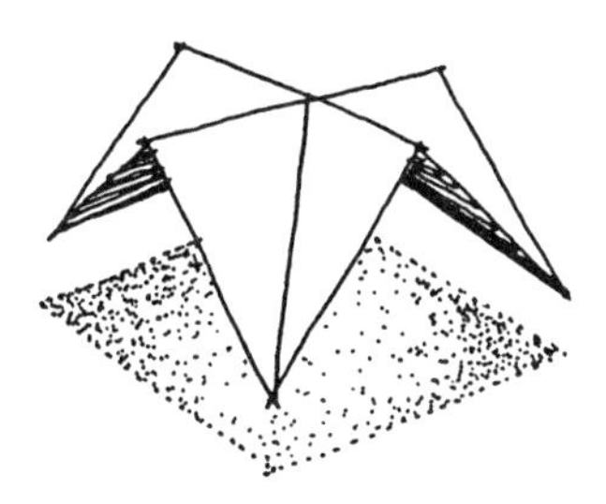

Spans

Function and other issues may dictate the minimum distance between vertical supports. The distance between these supports is called the "span". Each alternative type of superstructure not only results in a characteristic "footprint", but will be limited in the "span" it can economically sustain.

Aesthetics

Buildings send messages, just as they house functions. Each type of superstructure also offers characteristic aesthetic opportunities. The extent and manner of structural expression must match the appropriate "message" that the architect wishes the building to send.

Cost

The amount and type of material to be used in a structure will affect its *initial cost* of construction. All types of structural material may not be used to fabricate all types of structural systems. In most industrialized nations, the amount and type of labor required will even more profoundly affect the cost of a structure. Generally well evolved traditional structural systems are often, but not always, cheaper to design and build than radically innovative ones. Repetitive structural details will also normally lower cost. Lots of unique and custom details will have the opposite impact on costs. Also, do not omit consideration of the *lifetime cost* of maintenance, repair, replacement, and salvage of the structure.

Constructability

The structure will usually be fabricated in part in an industrial context, and in part on the actual building site. It directly depends on the type of structural system selected. Any limitations in local availability of equipment, labor, and construction experience, must be anticipated. Structures that cannot be realized are not designs, they are dreams.

Security

Normally, the preeminent concern of all structure is safety. That includes safety during its construction, during the buildings use or operation, and even during its failure or demolition.

Reuse

With today's awareness of sustainability in design, potential reuse and salvage of a structure is an important concern. Direct reuse of the structure may be possible, or more likely reuse with modifications may be possible. Any reuse or salvage may arise in the total structure, its components, or at least its materials.

PRELIMINARY LAYOUT OF STRUCTURAL SYSTEMS

Module matching

Different functions have predictable recurring dimensions. For example a library has a module based on the common size of bookshelves and the aisle distance between. Building envelopes also have a predictable module. For instance, bricks and other masonry units come in predictable sizes. Finally, different commonly available structural elements have also evolved into a limited number of standard sizes. Coordination of these different modules is one aspect of structural design. In a very large building, such as a high rise, huge savings can be realized by attention to this deceptively small issue.

Functional patterns

Circulation patterns may be axial, concentric, radial, and the like. Similarly, the sequence and appropriate adjacencies of the buildings functional activities and spaces are predictable, and have an optimum configuration. Such functional patterns are a common concern of architects in preliminary building design, and structure is normally configured to accommodate it. This is not always the case. When structural challenges such as very long spans are more urgent than the functional tailoring required, such as a vast exhibit area, then structure may drive functional adaptation.

Structural optimums

An optimum or *funicular* system configuration is sought. That configuration will be the most economical use of material for that type of structure. It is the configuration of that structural type that uses the least volume of structural material. Although this optimum structure may not always be used, there is never an excuse for ignorance of its existence.

Production and transportation constraints

The size and weight of the structural units that may be industrially fabricated, transported, and placed in the building at the site is affected by such obscure constraints as road widths, underpass clearances, site access, and availability of site storage areas.

Structural recognition of critical details

Typical structural details are those that will be repetitively used in a given design project. Since such details are used many times, they deserve early resolution. It is more difficult for a young designer to recognize *critical structural details*. Critical details often occur at:

1. Points where propagation discontinuities exist. These are usually sharp turns or breaks in the route of forces flowing through the structure to the ground.
2. Points of potential *stress reversal*. At these locations internal stresses may change or reverse (i.e., compression to tension).
3. Points where non-structural members (i.e., gypsum board wall surfaces) may potentially receive structural loads under certain unusual conditions (i.e., earthquakes).
4. Joints where large thermal expansion potential exists.
5. Points of significant load concentration.
6. Joints that are exposed to weather, fire, or tampering.

Recognition of structural problems

A beginning designer also needs to know when special structural concerns are likely to be present. They often occur if any of the following conditions are present:

1. Very heavy or unusual loads
2. Very long spans
3. Very long, or thin, or tall walls, columns, or struts
4. Long members that meet in small joints
5. Unanticipated loads or stresses
6. Probability of the building changing occupancy or functional use

SPECIAL STRUCTURAL SITUATIONS

A number of special structural situations will also require additional focused study by designers. Most common among these are:

Long span structures

Spans in excess of about 60 feet begin to have special problems. Ponding scenario failure during a rainstorm, extreme leverage of long members against small joints, profound thermal expansion, and generally large tributary areas are common concerns.

Special approaches are sometimes appropriate. Two design teams working completely separately, on the same structure is one way to be more certain that the final structure is safe.

Special emphasis on selected principles may also be appropriate. In sports arenas, long spans imply occupancy by large numbers of people, and use of only a minimum number of vertical supports so that everyone can see. This is a glaring violation of the principle of "redundancy."

Seismic resistance

Our understanding of seismic forces, and the available means of resistance to those forces, has grown significantly in recent years. Any current understanding in this area will soon be obsolete. Continuous study is therefore required.

Wind resistance

During the last decades of the twentieth century, meteorologists have similarly advanced our understanding of strong winds. Only recently has that quest for knowledge focused on the boundary layer of storms. Since this is where buildings are located, we can anticipate growth of knowledge parallel to that of seismic design in the near future.

Tall buildings

High-rise buildings present behemoth loads, but also behave differently than equal size horizontal buildings. Lateral loads become more important than vertical loads. Whole floors are given over to mechanical/electrical equipment leading to potential load concentrations and propagation discontinuities. The "p-delta" effect, which will be discussed later, becomes a critical concern. The "drift" (or swaying) of the top portion of such a tall building can become so profound that office workers in upper floors may experience motion sickness. Such issues demand specialized study similar to that required for long span, wind, and seismic resistant structures.

Temporary structures

Temporary structures are needed during the construction process. Shoring and underpinning, temporary fences, temporary buildings or shelters, temporary lifting structures, scaffolding, and the like are often no less sophisticated than final building structures, but often receive less professional consideration. A partially completed building structure is itself a temporary structure. Partially completed building structures require the same degree of structural concern as those that are completed. Indeed most structural failures take place during a state of partial completion. Some common concerns in temporary structures are:

1. Transient loads are temporary loads that may only exist for a few seconds.
2. Incomplete lateral support is a common condition in partially constructed buildings.
3. Temporary structural discontinuities may exist in a partially constructed building that will not exist once the building has been totally completed.
4. Impact construction loads resulting from dropped materials or equipment are particularly destructive.
5. Partial strength and stiffness of materials and connections is a wide spread condition particularly when concrete is being used.
6. The temporary distribution of construction loads can lead to short term imbalances causing brief but disastrous moments of instability.
7. Building and construction equipment interaction accidents such as cranes "bumping" a building, can not only have direct results, but may initiate a chain of profound events.
8. Temporary loss of structural support may be as small as a ladder collapsing under a single worker, or as monumental as the failure of major underpinning or shoring.
9. Weather damage to the structure can alter the structural condition or contextual circumstance of a partially completed structure. A typical example is the onset of a storm with significant winds during the erection of a partially completed roof.

Figure 2-1
London City Hall by Foster and Partners.

2 Process

STRUCTURE AND ARCHITECTURAL DESIGN

It is traditionally accepted that architecture includes function, technology, and aesthetics. It includes the building, its site, and its interior. Architecture not only houses current functions, but also sends visual messages to all who see it. Buildings must both resist and exploit the unique environmental forces that currently exist on its specific building site. The structure of the building will be required to accommodate all of these aspects of the building's existence, and it must do so for some predictable duration or life span. However, a considerable degree of uncertainty exists in predicting changes to future functional needs, site forces, and future aesthetic appetites. Design of a building's structure is usually conducted simultaneous to the design of all the other aspects of the building.

MAIN CONCEPTUAL DECISIONS

Early conceptual design decisions have a profound impact on the final building, therefore it is important for the reader to immediately identify some typical examples of the types of conceptual decisions that are commonly confronted early in the structural design process.

Relative design priority

Structure is only one of many systems that comprise a finished building. Heating, ventilation, plumbing, electrical, and other building systems will also vie for design, time, and attention. The relative importance of structural system in comparison to other design decisions will vary from one project to another. Structure for a long-span stadium will be given more design, time, and attention than the roof of the garage for a private residence. However, because structural failures threaten life and property, it can never be treated as trivial in any building design project. Site conditions, such as steep topography, poor soil, and high water table, can further increase the design priority placed upon structural decisions, compared to other design issues. The aesthetic intentions of the architect may conflict, accommodate, exploit, or ignore structural realities. This relationship may often be traced to the role and responsibilities shouldered by the different participants involved in the design process. The sophistication of the local construction industry may also generate the need for additional attention to structural issues. For example, the erection of a major structure where heavy equipment and strong materials are not present is a very different problem from the same project if staged in a sophisticated industrial setting.

Accommodation of internal function

Buildings house function: Structures must support and facilitate the central role of function. Therefore, structure should not interrupt function, such as columns that block the view of an audience in a theater.

Type and magnitude of design loads

Building codes are usually embraced at the municipal level. They assist the structural designer in estimation of design loads; however, remember that these code values only define the absolute minimum legal acceptable standard. This does not necessarily lead to an adequate structural design standard.

Components of the structural system

All five of the components of the structural system must be conceptually addressed (both separately and jointly) during preliminary design. The reader is asked to recall these five components. They are loads, superstructure, lateral support system, foundation, and soils and geology.

Structural materials

Choices of a superstructure and foundation are related to, but different from, the choice of a structural material from which the system will be fabricated. When asked what structural system the building will have, "concrete" or "steel" is not an answer. Concrete and steel are structural materials not structural systems.

Interaction with external systems

Structure interacts directly with other systems that are both internal and external to the building. Externally, the structure interfaces with natural systems such as winds, earthquakes, surface water runoff, snow, ice, soil movement, and movement of a seasonal water table.

Interaction with internal building systems

Internally the structural system gains part of its design importance because it provides the supporting frame for the building envelope, facilitates the internal circulation system, and accommodates mechanical and electrical systems. Other than the large point loads caused by transformers, the electrical system seldom profoundly affects the choice of a structural system. However, the raw size of heating and cooling ducts and other equipment will usually require close coordination with the structural system. While water, vents, and sanitary sewer pipes are not as large as ducts, they require a consistent slope that can effect structural decisions. The structural designer must not neglect consideration of impact, vibration, or weight of such equipment as chillers, pumps, storage tanks, and elevator lift mechanisms.

Cultural and economic setting

Legal constraints such as building codes, zoning ordinances, and construction budget constraints will profoundly affect the design of all structures. Design development decisions rarely have the profound legal and cost impact of earlier conceptual design decisions. Failure to accommodate the realities of cost and code early in a structural design can bring an abrupt stop to a building project.

Specific significant structural opportunities and problems

It is critical that designers identify special opportunities and problems at the earliest possible point in the design process in order to prevent unnecessary loss of design, time, and money. Every project is absolutely unique. Earlier experience may inform the current project design process, but it is never a substitute for it. Assumptions of this type can be disastrous.

Scope of structural innovation needed

Every design decision requires some mix of both tradition and innovation. While most structures are aggregated from existing alternatives that have already been developed, this is not always the case. The designer should initially identify the type and degree of innovation inherently justified by the specific project that he/she is confronting. Considerable effort has been made in this text to acquaint the reader with commonly used structural alternatives; however, a structural designer must be capable of more than "shape shopping" from traditional types of structure.

Preliminary configuration, sizes, and materials for the structure

Once a superstructure and foundation have been selected and placed upon the topography, soil, and geology of the site, it becomes necessary to give a relatively crude configuration and size to the structure and its major components. To do this crude initial sizing of the system and its components, simultaneous choice of a structural material is required.

Coordination of envelope and structure

The weather proofing skin of buildings has its own modular sizes. Coordination of functional module, structural module, and envelope module is an important early conceptual consideration.

Defined contribution of selected structure to building aesthetic

Collaboration, rather than conflict, is a clear measure of the sophistication of a designer. Structural systems and building aesthetics should not be conceptually developed without interactive consideration.

Fabrication and erection process and feasibility

Local industry, labor, materials, equipment, and experience limit the design latitude available to a given project. Equally important, it must be accepted that the site is a factory for the production of a building. The final form of structure is designed; however, the specific construction procedure must also be designed.

Cost feasibility of the structure

Just as different types of automobile vary in cost, so do building structures. Just as certain types of autos are beyond a personal budget, so are some types of building structures beyond a client's budget. Know it early, accept the constraint, define the full latitude of choice, and make the design wonderful because of that reality.

SEQUENCE OF DESIGN ACTIVITIES

Architectural design, to include structural design, is normally executed in a series of design phases. All the participants on the design team coordinate their actions within a series of phases. During the *project organization phase,* assets are identified and allocated to a unique design problem. Those assets are usually time, money, and talent. Then during the *research phase,* raw data are collected. Project precedent, design loads, local conditions, and client needs dictate selected types of data that must be collected. Important products of this phase include a performance specification, a site inventory, preliminary costs and budgets, and code and zoning ordinance searches. The *analysis phase* is used to make meaning from the raw data collected during research. A clear set of design goals, principles, and priorities should be developed and shared at this time. The *synthesis phase* is separated into lesser steps. Schematic synthesis explores the buildings' behavior (or how it will act) not how it will actually look. The products of schematic design are often referred to as "bubble diagrams." During conceptual synthesis, the physical appearance and how they will actually be built are developed. The product of conceptual design is usually a set of "freehand, roughly to scale drawings." Tradition or precedent usually guides the basic structural configuration, while rules of thumb, tables, and certain types of software are used to establish preliminary sizes. The focus of this text ends at this point, but the sequence of design activities does not.

The next phase, *design development*, leads to the production of the final construction documents. These consist of working drawings and specifications which will guide the final construction of the building. The working drawings move the freehand conceptual drawings to very detailed, measured, mechanical drawings. It is at this time that math methods are required in order to give sufficient definition to allow measured details.

Several other activities lie beyond the scope of this book. During *bidding*, additional design definition may be required to sufficiently describe the structure for competent construction cost estimating by competitive constructors. Small design changes often become necessary during the *construction phase* once the bid is awarded to an individual general contractor. During the construction phase, the building is actually erected. *Post construction evaluation* is rapidly becoming a more spread activity after the completed building has been occupied by the client for a while. While this phase happens well after conceptual design, which is the focus of this book, the general issue of quality assurance has conceptual significance during all design phases.

PLAYERS AND RESPONSIBILITIES

During the above sequence of design activities, several "players" will participate. While that list varies from one project to another, and is directed by the contracts that bind them, a general understanding of the common contribution of each participant may be helpful to the reader. The *client* initiates the project, establishes most of the requirements, and defines the budget. Though not advisable, the client has often already purchased the building site before contacting the architect. The client does not control some design requirements. *Local government* is tasked with protection of public health, safety, and welfare. Structural requirements of this type (and they are many) are controlled by local government. Design requirements within this scope are contained in building codes and zoning ordinances. Traditionally an *architect* will usually lead the design team, coordinate and guide the work of consultants, and play a leading role in quality control on behalf of the client. Integration of the structural system with other systems is a central responsibility of the architect. As the primary consultant on the structure, the *structural engineer* supports the architect in design decisions requiring special structural expertise. This professional will do most of the math related to the structural design. The wise architect involves the structural engineer at the earliest possible moment. It is inappropriate to complete a building design, and then dump it on the engineer to sort out. It is a naïve but common misconception that the structural engineer will relieve the architect of legal responsibility for the safety of the structure. By contract, the engineer is usually a consultant or agent of the architect. It is wiser to anticipate that if serious structural problems are encountered, the architect, engineer, and constructor will probably, uncomfortably, face litigation together. A similar consulting relationship exists between the architect and the *soils/foundations engineer*. As a specialized professional, this engineer will conduct appropriate investigations of the soil and geology at the selected building site, and analyze the results in a lab. This will result in a report that will describe site conditions, interpret the design significance of those conditions, and provide specific guidance to the foundation selection and design. Once again it is best to involve the counsel of this professional at the earliest possible moment, preferably as part of the site selection before purchase. In many contemporary contracts the *constructor* becomes a member of the initial design team. This is useful because the constructor has specialized knowledge of cost and construction activities. Even when involved only at, and after bidding, it is the constructor who exercises direct control of cost and construction means.

PRODUCTS OF THE DESIGN PROCESS

As a result of the work of the professionals listed above, several products come into existence by the end of the conceptual design phase. Some of the most common are:

Code search

This document has a sufficiently standard content to allow it to be reduced to a checklist. It is wise to develop such a checklist if it is not already a standard practice within an architectural firm.

Load estimates summary

It is wise to collect all load estimates, with the basis utilized for each estimate, into a single document. This should be retained in the permanent project file along with the code search. If a structural failure occurs at any time during the building's life, these will become critical legal documents.

Precedent research

It is always wise to begin where others left off, not where they started. This is particularly wise in the design of structures. A significant portion of structural design is empirical (based on past experience) as well as analytical (based on math calculations). A completed structure that has withstood the forces of the environment for many years has a credibility that complements a new math model in a computer. It is proven that time is well invested in learning from 5000 years of completed structures. Some caution is needed in precedent study:

1. Be certain to collect information beyond the earlier design, often widely available, to the actual subsequent performance of that design, which is often not widely available.
2. Formally note what is similar, and what is different between any case of precedent that is to be used, and the design circumstance immediately at hand.
3. It is a common fault, and a pointless exercise, only to collect data on earlier structures without making meaning from these data. Analyze the data, draw usable conclusions, and act on that new understanding.

Schematic drawings

By the end of the design development phase (beyond the scope of this book), a complete set of carefully measured hard line drawings will ultimately be developed to include: plans, sections, elevations, axonometric, and perspective drawings. However, they will all begin with "bubble diagrams" showing only behavior, not physical reality. These are the schematic drawings.

Conceptual drawings

The schematics will be matured into crude visual reality in that set of freehand, roughly to scale drawings known as the conceptual drawings. Firms retain all drawings both schematic and conceptual, at least until the project is completed, and they have been paid for their work.

Typical and critical details

In their early thinking, it is difficult for a beginning designer to consider more than one item, or scale, at one time. In reality, "global" conceptual decisions carry "detail" implications that should be studied simultaneously. Similarly, the design of small individual details during late design development often has global implications for the total structure. For that reason, the development of critical details is often done parallel to the development of the total conceptual structural frame.

SPECIFIC DESIGN METHODS AND TOOLS

Use of checklists

Many prefabricated checklists have been developed to assist designers in their work on structures. Some are widely published, while others are only the result of standard procedures developed within a given firm. When available, acquire and retain such checklists. However, understand that they are never fully adequate or fully appropriate for the current design project at hand.

Use of rules of thumb

Several rules of thumb also exist to give a crude initial guess at structural span capabilities, span depth ratios, and approximate preliminary sizes for major components of each common structural system. They are only suitable for crude initial estimates.

Use of tables

Tables can give a more visual understanding than rules of thumb during early conceptual design; however, they are not more accurate. One of the most widely used sources of this type is the *Architects Studio Companion* by Edward Allen.

Schematic and conceptual graphics

These are powerful tools that have been previously discussed and are widely used.

Study models

While rapidly constructed and unrefined in finish, the thought behind these models is not unsophisticated. Since models are three-dimensional, they are often more efficient than a series of similar drawings. Since they have a physical reality, they may be more informative than computer models. To be specific, they may be difficult to build or fall down. The computer model cannot.

Mining of standard references

Load tables, lists and views of common structural alternatives, common details, and considerations will be on hand in most schools and firms. *Architectural Graphic Standards* initiated by the late authors Charles Ramsey and Harold Sleeper, *Time Saver Standards for Architectural Design Data* edited by John H. Callender, the *Standard Handbook for Civil Engineers* edited by Frederick S. Merritt, and *Design* by Elwyn E. Seelye are all widely used examples of such sources. A collection of building codes will also be found in most schools and firms. The American National Standards Institute (ANSI) Code has been widely used in the estimation of loads. The Uniform Building Code and the newly developed International Building Code are typical, and widely used, examples of building codes. While it is good practice to study the requirements of several codes, be certain that at least the one required in the city where the project to be built is one of them. While the design must conform to the local building code legally, many designers will study and compare many codes, then use the most stringent requirement identified to guide the final design, even if higher than locally required.

Computer software

Recently, computer software has been developed and made widely available that may individualize initial structural estimates in a specific design project a bit more than is possible with rules of thumb and tables. One of the best current software packages accompanies the *Standard Handbook for Architectural Engineers* by Robert Brown Butler.

Figure 3-1
Column failure in the 1985 earthquake in Mexico City.

3 Structural Failure

DEFINITION OF STRUCTURAL FAILURE

Any time that a structural system falls short of expectations or needs in even the smallest way, it may be termed a structural failure. Based upon the information offered thus far, several types of structural failure should be immediately apparent. A structural system that interrupts the flow of function within a building is a structural failure in functional fitness. A structural system that inappropriately interfaces with its site context might be termed a failure in contextual fitness. Designs for structures that violate "logic", "economy", "integrity", "continuity", and "redundancy" are failures in principle. Structures that become too expensive to build or maintain are cost failures. A structure that cannot accommodate some future change is a failure in structural flexibility. A structure that is unsatisfying to view, or that visually sends some inappropriate message is thought to be a failure in structural aesthetics.

This book focuses on failures in structural safety. Death and physical injury are by far the most important structural design concerns. The most serious failures lead to loss of life and property. Because of their central importance, this chapter that follows will explore failures in structural safety in greater detail.

GOALS RELATED TO STRUCTURAL FAILURE

There are two great guiding goals in structural design. The first, and most important, goal of structural design is to prevent physical injury, and loss of life. The second most important goal of structural design is to prevent or minimize threats to, or loss of property. Goals related to cost, aesthetics, ease of construction and maintenance are less important than these two goals.

FAILURE AS AN EVENT IN TIME

Sudden failures without warning are the most dangerous structural failures. These are sudden catastrophic events that take place without any warning. These collapses are often the direct result of some natural or man-made disaster such as earthquake or war. They can be the result of temporary occupant, or construction overloading. Occasionally they result from inadequate designs. These failures give no opportunity for escape.

Sudden failures with warning are only slightly less dangerous. These are sudden events that provide warning. A building structure that groans, cracks, sags, sways, or deforms can give sufficient warning that occupants may escape before collapse.

Structural failures that proceed very slowly are known as creeping failures. In the beginning these very slow failures may go unnoticed. Slow settlement of a building into the soil upon which it rests is a typical example of a creeping failure. Providing that owners observe, respect, and respond to these changes, they may only face threats to property and have considerable time to resolve the problem.

A progressive failure also initially proceeds very slowly, with only minor movement; however, it increases in pace or severity as it advances. Rain ponding on a long span structure (discussed in the chapter on loads) is a common example of a progressive failure.

BENEFITS OF STRUCTURE FAILURES

Of course the most important impact of a failure is the threat to life and property. In this matter, failures are to be avoided at all costs. However, study of failures has been critical to our continually growing understanding of structural behavior. Structural failures, both large and small, provide clear visual evidence of the forces that were at work during the failure. Forensic study of structural failure is essential once a failure has taken place. Every effort must be made by a committed design professional to directly view every possible structural failure. An intuitive insight can be built in this way that is not possible using any other method.

COMMON CAUSES OF STRUCTURAL FAILURE

In a recent government study the following were the most common issues of structural failures:

1. Communication and organization in the construction industry
2. Inspection of the construction by the structural engineer
3. General quality of the design
4. Structural connection design details and shop drawings
5. Selection of architect and engineers
6. Timely dissemination of technical data

"Structural Failure in Public Facilities", House Report # 98-621, Committee on Science and Technology, US Government Printing Office, Washington, DC: 1984. Page 4–7.

GENERAL MODES OF STRUCTURAL FAILURE

Beware, the "cause" of a failure (why it happened) is different than its "mode" of failure (how it happened). There are three general modes of structural failure:

1. *Stability failures* involve sliding, rotating, sinking, buckling, or other types of movement.
2. *Strength failures* involve such failures as crushing, breaking, and tearing.
3. *Stiffness failure* is the excessive deforming, changing size, or shape of a structure.

Stability failures

To be certain that the materials, members, and joints of a structure are fully utilized, they must remain fully stable. For example, a person lifting weights in a gymnasium may lose balance and fall over long before his/her maximum lifting capacity is reached. A structure that doesn't move (fail in stability) is said to be static. This necessary stability gives its name to the important area of structural knowledge known as "statics".

Stability can be lost if the shape of the structure cannot be sustained. More commonly it can be lost by translating in each of the three axes, and by rotating in each of the three axes. Therefore there are 6 degrees of freedom in which a structure may fail through instability (movement) (Fig. 3-2).

Strength failures

Two Sources of Structural Strength

A structural member or joint gains its ability to resist forces from two general sources:

1. *Material properties* provide that part of strength that arises from the type of material selected for the structure. Typical structural materials are concrete, steel, and timber.

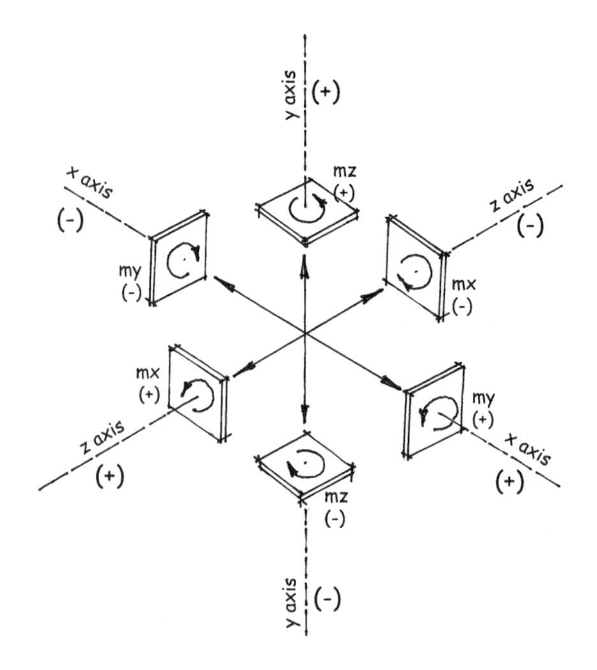

Figure 3-2
Six degrees of freedom.

2. *Sectional properties* are rooted in the size and shape of the members and joints into which a structural material is formed. Together these two areas of knowledge are the basis of a field of study known as "strength of materials". Poor design, weathering, poor maintenance, unauthorized changes and modifications, and fire can lead to diminished capacity and strength failures.

Types of Stress

A given member (with its inherent material and sectional strength) may fail in any of the previously discussed types of stress. The strength of a given structural element differs in its compression, tension, bearing, shearing, bending, and torsion strength.

Stiffness failures

Stiffness vs. Strength

Stiffness also results from both material properties and sectional properties, and will also be studied in the area of knowledge known as strength of materials. To understand how it differs from strength, compare a common rubber band to an old dry ginger snap cookie. Under a load the stale cookie changes shape by very little (stiffness), but will break even under a very little load (strength). Excessive beam deflection is one of the most common examples of a stiffness failure, and will be discussed in greater depth in a later chapter on post and beam structures. The rubber band deforms much but doesn't break.

LOCAL VS. GLOBAL FAILURE

A local failure involves only a single structural member or joint in a system. (Fig. 3-3). A global failure involves the total structural system. Both local and global failures may result from inadequate stability, strength, or stiffness.

One great concern in structural failure is that a local failure may become a global failure. There is a common empirical rule among engineers that states "It is better to fail in a beam than a column, and a member instead of a joint". Why is this so? Failure of a member may stay "local", but failure of a joint has a greater tendency to "go global" (lead to the collapse of the total system). Similarly failure of a beam may stay local, but the collapse of a ground floor column will probably lead to the collapse of every floor above it (Fig. 3-4).

Figure 3-3
Local failure in a single truss member.

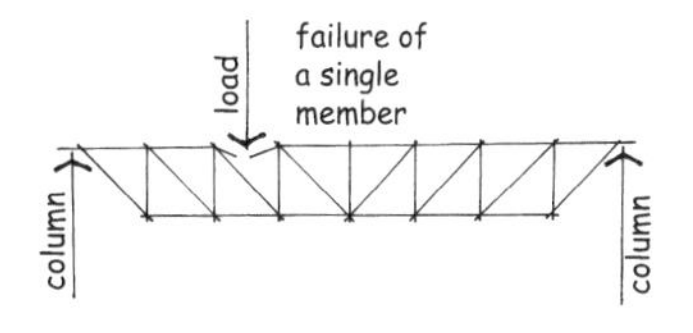

Figure 3-4
Global failure of the total truss.

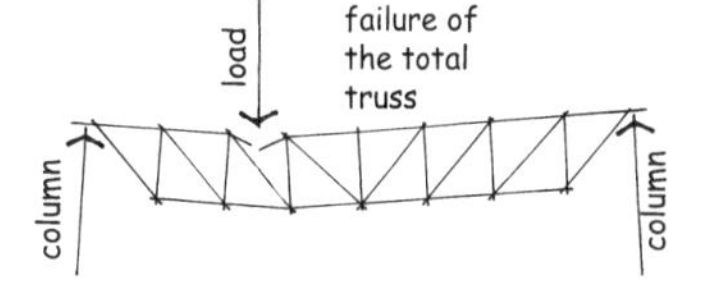

FAILURE SCENARIOS

Insights from disaster reconnaissance

During 15 years of personal disaster site reconnaissance and architectural forensics, two issues have emerged:

1. Very few buildings fall down due to incorrect calculations. Most catastrophic building failures result from unanticipated conditions, and/or conceptual design flaws.
2. We must not stop with analysis of only a single joint and members, but begin to think in probable failure scenarios. This is now possible due to the speed and computational power of computers. Why is this new proactive scenario approach necessary, or potentially useful?

Role changes

During the process of collapse, individual members and joints change structural roles. They receive unconventional (but predictable) loading. The functional role of a structure changes once total or partial collapse has begun. For example, the structure may have the initial function of supporting and sheltering a set of offices prior to collapse; however, at the time of collapse its new and more important role becomes "fall-cushioning". An individual office may become a survival bunker, and could become an escape pod. The structure should become its own collapse warning system. The structure becomes a new living and moving "creature" that undergoes metamorphosis, or at least is forced to assume a more stable position. If the collapse is sufficiently slow and controlled, the building can become an alternative lowing system similar to an improvised elevator. Although unplanned, occupants on upper floors have survived global collapses of fairly large buildings. Finally, the structure becomes an excess energy absorbing system. Why is this so?

The work/energy budget

Potential energy is converted to kinetic energy during a collapse. Physics tells us that a big steel beam resting on the ground contains less potential energy, than it will when elevated to its final position in the 92nd floor. In a collapse, this embodied energy comes back out of the beam (becomes kinetic). In the collapse of a high-rise building such as the World Trade Center, the profound release of energy becomes visible to the naked eye. As structural materials bend, tear, and are crushed, work is done by this energy. When the work/energy budget is balanced, the debris comes to rest in a new static equilibrium. Therefore, due to conservation of matter and energy during a collapse, a beam in a one story building has less destructive energy locked in it than that same beam elevated 1100 feet, but it has the same energy dissipating capacity when it bends, tears, or is crushed (Fig. 3-5).

Figure 3-5
Structural elements fallen from high in the World Trade Center terrorist attack.

SUMMARY

As an aid to systematic consideration, it may be useful at this time to summarize some of the main issues involved in structural failure in a single matrix (Fig. 3-6).

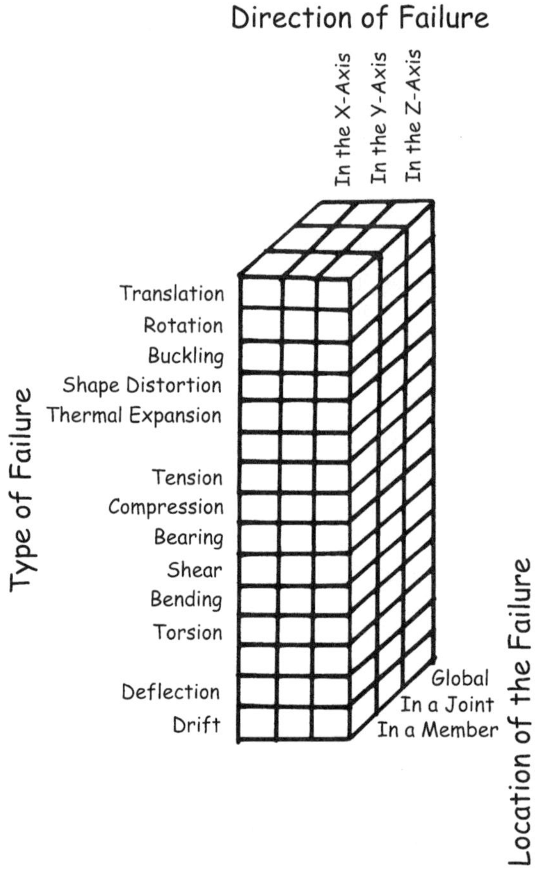

Figure 3-6
Failure matrix.

Figure 4-1

Dr. Roberto Quaas with two story "shake table" at the Centro Nacional de Prevencion de Desastres in Mexico City.

4 Loads

LOAD PREDICTION

As previously mentioned, the prediction of loads on any single building is a guess. Such guesses are guided by experience, codes, and evolved accepted professional methods. They usually require some mathematical computation; however, they are still just guesses. Early *preliminary design* decisions addressed in this book are based on a conceptual understanding of loads, load effects, and the response of different types of structural systems to loading. Only very crude relative load magnitudes are normally needed during this early phase in the design process. Later in the *design development phase* much more exacting load prediction is required. It is critical to remember that building codes, calculations, testing, and the involvement of appropriately trained and qualified engineers must be used to proceed beyond early preliminary design.

COMMON LOAD ESTIMATION TOOLS

During early preliminary design load estimation at least four tools of crude estimation are often consulted. *Rules of thumb* are the crudest empirical guesses based on an engineer's past experience. The *Studio Desk Companion* by Edward Allen has become a widely accepted source used in this role. The International Building Code (IBC) and Architectural Graphic Standards have *tables* of loads, which are usually based on a more extensive and systematic database than empirical rules of thumb. Codes like the IBC also contain *maps* of snow, seismic, and wind loads, depending upon the location of the building site. These cannot be used in unmodified form for final design load determination, but are occasionally used to guide crude preliminary design decisions. More recently commercial computer *software* has become available to assist in preliminary load estimation. The *Standard Handbook of Architectural Engineers* by Butler contains an excellent example of such software.

CONSERVATIVE LOAD ESTIMATION

Designers will find varying estimates when using different sources and methods. Even within a single source a range of estimated load values is often encountered. It is generally a good practice to embrace the worst, or most severe, load that is identified. When maps are used to assist in preliminary load estimates, some designers "interpolate" between available values shown on a map. However, a more conservative designer might just use the higher value of the two. It is also important to remember that these loads are crude empirical guesses that often demand an additional margin of safety. One day an occupant will buy a waterbed, piano, or another heavy object that was never mentioned during design. (Fig. 4-2)

Figure 4-2
Typical wind load map (based on drawing by Robert Butter Brown 1998).

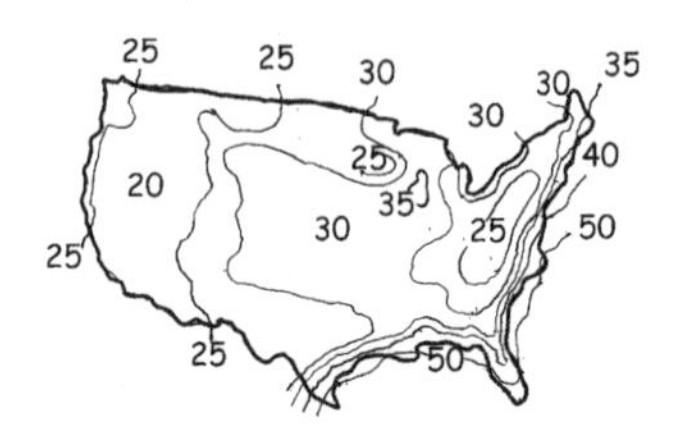

LOADS IN PERSPECTIVE

When beginning to design structures, a given load is just a number. Later, experience will give perspective to that number. Is it an unusually large and threatening load, or a laughably insignificant one? How can an inexperienced designer know? At least the relative significance of different load types may normally be directly understood from a simple visual inspection of load estimation tables and maps. A novice designer should notice the highest, lowest, and mean or median on charts, tables, or maps. By noticing these, a better perspective of the significance of the particular load indicated for the specific project of immediate interest, is gained; therefore, a more relevant conceptual response can be made. If the snow load for your site is near the highest value found on a map or table, then the roof on your project should show significant response to that reality.

PARTIAL LIST OF SIGNIFICANT BUILDING LOADS

Building codes usually provide guidance, and demand consideration of a wide range of loads. Some of the more important are:

1. *Dead loads*: These are usually of all the building materials used in the building (i.e., brick or concrete).
2. *Occupant loads*: These include the weight of people in the building, depending upon the functional use of the building. (Remember that during a fire, occupants may become tightly packed together in a small floor area. With this in mind the values will look more reasonable.)
3. *Equipment loads*: These include the weight of permanent equipment in the building (such as chillers, lift motors, and pumps etc).
4. *Partition loads*: These are used if temporary or moveable office partitions are anticipated.

5. *Snow loads*: These are the weight of snow anticipated at that building site. Ice may also be an issue in this load. Snow loads on a sloped roof are projected upon a horizontal surface (Fig. 4-3).
6. *Roof load*: Even if snow loads are insignificant at a given site, a minimum roof load is required for roof maintenance and other movement of people on a roof.
7. *Wind loads*: Prevailing wind, hurricane, and tornado loads are all considered.
8. *Seismic loads*: These include all loads, both vertical and horizontal, resulting from earthquakes.

Figure 4-3
Snow load is measured on a "horizontal projection".

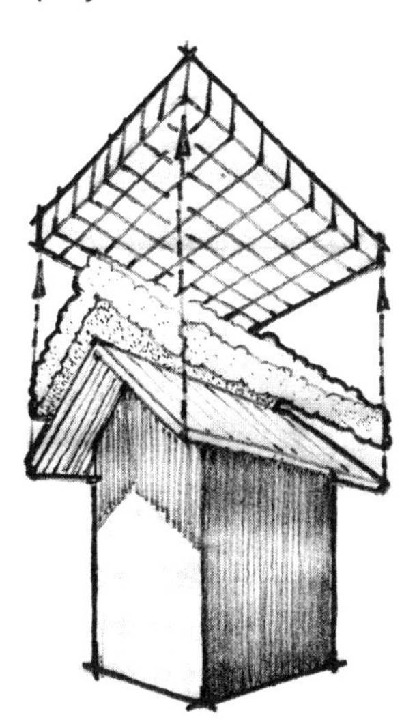

TYPES OF LOADS

The loads listed above may be grouped into several different classifications. A given load may simultaneously belong to more than one classification. Here are the most common load classifications:

Internal and external

Snow, wind, and other *external loads* are applied to the outside of the building. Building occupants, moveable partitions, and mechanical equipment, and other *internal loads* are applied inside the building.

Vertical and lateral (horizontal)

V*ertical loads* may be internal or external. A building occupant standing on the floor inside the building, and snow outside on the roof, both exert a downward *gravity load* on the building's structure. Not all vertical loads are downward. Wind can lift a roof upward, just as water in the soil under a building can force the structure upward out of the ground. Wind and earthquakes place horizontal forces on the building structure, and are called *lateral loads.*

Dead and live loads

Any load that is permanent is called a *dead load*. Dead loads include the weight of the building itself. *Live loads* are temporary or transient. Wind may blow for a time, and then stop. A heavy snow on the roof will ultimately melt. Such transient forces are called live loads.

Equivalent uniform load

Because we cannot fully predict many exact actual loads such as the number of people in a room at any given moment, or the force of gusting wind on the wall, building codes make use of a substitute value called an *equivalent uniform load.* It is considered to be a safe substitute value based on the experience.

Point, distributed, and uniformly varying

Whether vertical or horizontal in direction, loads may be applied on a concentrated area (also called a *point load*) or it may be distributed evenly across a large surface called a uniform or *uniformly distributed load.* Occasionally a load may be applied in a predictably varying amount across a broad surface. This last loading is called a *uniformly varying load.*

Impact, inertial, static, and resonant

Loads may also be classified by their duration. A suddenly applied load such as dropping a heavy object on the floor is called an *impact load.* The surge of force on a structure by the rapid acceleration of a high-speed elevator is an *inertial load.* Most loads are treated as gradually applied, or more specifically as not moving. Their significance is not increased by inertia. These are called *static loads*, and form the basis for one of the oldest and most important fields in the study of structures. Wind, earthquakes, and some types of mechanical equipment can impart *resonant loads* to a structure. Under resonant loads, a structure may begin to oscillate at a regular interval called its *fundamental period.* If the oscillating earthquake or machinery matches the fundamental period of the structure, each cycle of oscillation will become larger. This can ultimately lead to a total collapse of the structure under relatively small loads that only progressed due to very unfortunate matching of cyclical timing.

PRELIMINARY SIZING

In preliminary decision making, a designer may occasionally jump beyond crude load estimation, and directly give crude dimensions to a selected structural element based on similar sources. This book and others provide rules of thumb and tables that crudely, but directly predict approximate dimensions for various types of common structural systems. An early text entitled *Structure and Architectural Design* by Corkill, Puderbaugh, and Sawyers contained such tables. Unfortunately it is now out of print, but the tables have been revived in Fuller Moore's excellent current book entitled *Understanding Structures.*

System capability

The sources mentioned above, as well as the long respected *Structures* by Daniel Schodek contain tables that estimate the normal *span capability* (what distance the system will free span) as well as its *span/depth ratio* (a comparison of the typical depth of the structure and its span). As with load estimation, it is often wise to assume the worst case in direct preliminary structural sizing when using these rules of thumb and tables.

Codes provide fairly detailed guidance to assist the designer in developing final design loads for all of these. Unfortunately, this guidance usually requires preliminary design decisions that have already been made, rather than providing assist in making these critical decisions. For instance, the choice of building materials is a critical preliminary design decision. Code tables might be used once concrete or steel is chosen, but they are not intended to assist in initially choosing between them.

Weight of building materials

If a more accurate estimate of the dead load generated by selected building materials is required, detailed tables are available in such widely used sources such as *Architectural Graphic Standards* by Ramsey and Sleeper. They are usually based on either a cubic foot of selected material, or on the commonly available prefabricated thickness of that same material (i.e., $^1/_2$ inch gypsum board). Some building materials are so widely used that designers commit them to memory. Concrete weighs roughly 150 pounds per cubic foot (PCF), for example.

Superstructure/foundation relationship

If a designer has a crude estimate of the applied loads, the total weight of a superstructure, and a similar knowledge of the rough bearing capacity of the soil on the site; a relevant match in the superstructure and foundation may then be made. For such a vague preliminary need, typical summation rules of thumb might arbitrarily include such crude figures as total roof load as 75 PSF and crude floor loads as 140 PSF. Later these crude rules of thumb can also help the young designer to recognize when an error has been made during more exacting mathematical calculation of structures.

LOAD COMBINATIONS

Conceptually, it must be recognized that loads act in combinations, not in isolation. Therefore codes require that all potential load combinations be evaluated (i.e., dead load + live load + snow load, etc.)

Vocabulary Review		
Equivalent uniform load	Load interpolation	Span/depth ratios
Horizontally projected load	Lateral loads	Impact loads

REVIEW QUESTIONS

1. Briefly explain the impact of load estimates in the design of a building structure.
2. How does a preliminary load estimate differ from a final design estimate of structural loads?

3. List the most important types of loads that are addressed in building codes.
4. Briefly describe the means that designers commonly use to crudely estimate loads early in their design process.
5. List the load combinations that must be studied in complying with building codes.
6. Does wind act as a vertical or horizontal load on a building?
7. What is the difference between a static and an impact load?
8. Give an example of an internal load?
9. If a source gives a range of values for a load, why does the designer usually use the worst case?
10. Briefly describe a progressive failure.

Figure 5-1

Extreme bending failure in the Nuevo Leone Apartment Building in Mexico City, 1985 earthquake.

5 Lateral Support

LATERAL LOADS

Horizontal loads, such as wind, earthquake, soil, and hydrostatic loads, have been previously introduced: of these lateral loads, wind and seismic ones have traditionally preoccupied designers. Therefore this chapter initially provides a brief description of the effects of wind and earthquake on buildings, building sites, and urban infrastructure. Then alternative structural responses to these lateral loads will be identified. While some types of superstructure inherently resist these common lateral loads, most of this chapter focuses on shear walls, braced frames, and other systems specifically added to a superstructure for resistance to lateral loads. Blast loads are an increasing concern, but will only be given brief coverage in this chapter. Soil pressure and hydrostatic pressure will be presented in a later chapter dedicated to foundations.

DIFFERENCE BETWEEN WIND AND SEISMIC LOADS

To the extent that both wind and earthquakes cause horizontal forces to be applied to the side of a structure they are similar. Indeed, codes have traditionally required that both wind and seismic forces be quantified, and the structural design for a given project be based on the more severe of the two. However, there are many significant differences that contrast wind and earthquake loads. Light buildings are vulnerable to wind, while heavy buildings are vulnerable to earthquakes. The duration of a very long earthquake might be 60 seconds. A hurricane can last for hours. Therefore the reader is encouraged to take note of both similarities and differences in the following brief discussion of these two types of lateral loads. Since the loads differ, structural response to these loads may be different.

EARTHQUAKES

General earthquake behaviors

Plate tectonics (movement of the earth's crust), nuclear blast, and volcanic action are all sources of earthquakes. There are three general sources of earthquakes. *Plate tectonics* is of the greatest concern in this text. Plates formed by the cooled crust of the earth tear, slide against each other, and collide as they move about on the molten core of the earth below. At times these plates "stick" and build up energy until at some point a rupture takes place releasing seismic waves. The specific point of rupture under the earth's surface is known as the *hypocenter*. The point on the surface of the earth above the rupture is known as the *epicenter* (Fig. 5-2).

Figure 5-2
The "hypocenter" is below & the "epicenter" is above.

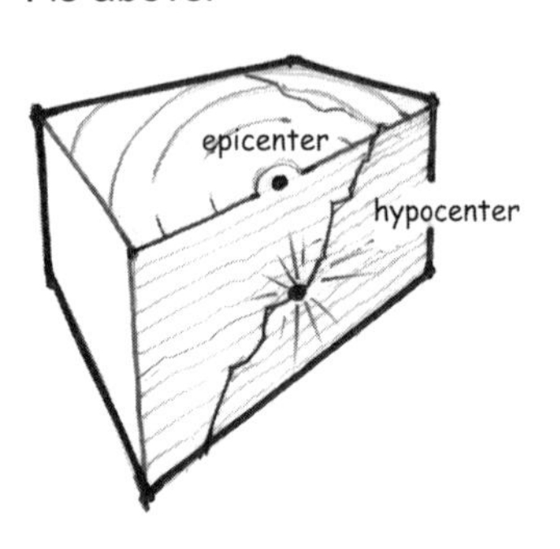

Seismic waves

Primary waves (known as *P-waves*) and shear waves (known as *s-waves*) travel through the ground below the surface. For this reason they are both known as *body waves*. Two types of *surface waves* are also released. These are known as *Rayleigh* and *Love* waves. P-waves are compressive waves like sound waves, and are the fastest seismic waves. S-waves produce a shearing action perpendicular to the line of the P-waves. Rayleigh waves are the surface equivalent of a P-wave, just as Love waves are the surface equivalent of S-waves.

MEASUREMENT

Instruments

Two types of instruments are widely used to measure seismic movements. A *seismograph* is very useful to geologists. However, they are far too sensitive to measure movements that are destructive to buildings. For this purpose, a *strong motion accelograph* is needed. It will produce graphs that show the acceleration, velocity, and displacement of a structure due to an earthquake (in each of the three directions). The duration of shaking can also be evaluated by a study of accelograms. The duration of shaking should not be neglected. The longer the shaking takes place, the more joints open up. The more joints open up, the more the building moves. The more it moves, the more it damages itself, and approaches failure.

Scales

Two scales are currently used to measure the intensity of earthquakes. The *Richter scale* measures the amount of energy released by the earthquake. It is the scale most used by geologists. Some other countries, such as Japan, have a similar scale. The *Modified Mercalli scale* is based on observable damage done by the earthquake rather than by measuring the energy released. It allows us to interpret the severity of historical earthquakes by reading the descriptions of damage recorded by witnesses.

INFRASTRUCTURE IMPACT

Earthquakes damage *transportation* such as railroads, airports, roads, and bridges. The destruction and blocking of transportation can prevent or delay rescuers. Loss and overloading of *communications* such as telephones, radio towers, and alarm systems can deepen the impact of data denial that is much needed to locate and assess damage. Control is profoundly inhibited by the loss of communication. Loss of television and public radio limits the spread of true information and instructions to the general population. A wide range of *life-lines* can be damaged. Normally waterlines rupture during a serious earthquake. This leads to the loss of firefighting means. The rupture of natural gas lines often leads to post-earthquake fires. While the rupture of sanitary sewers is not an immediate concern in an earthquake, it will soon become a serious health problem. Broken sewer and water lines mean that drinking water cannot be trusted until fully tested.

Figure 5-3
Quiescent fault.

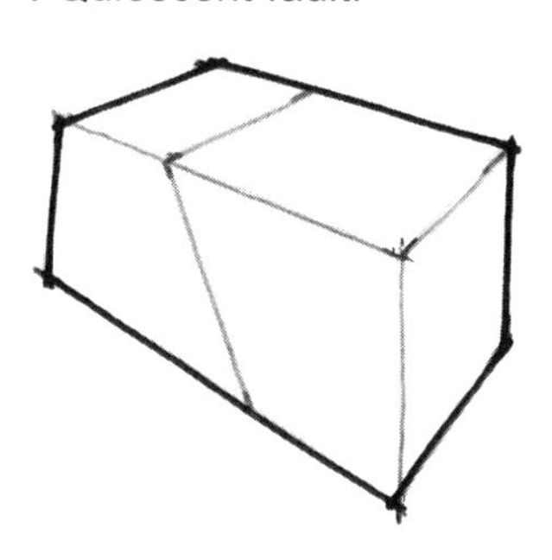

Figure 5-4
Normal fault.

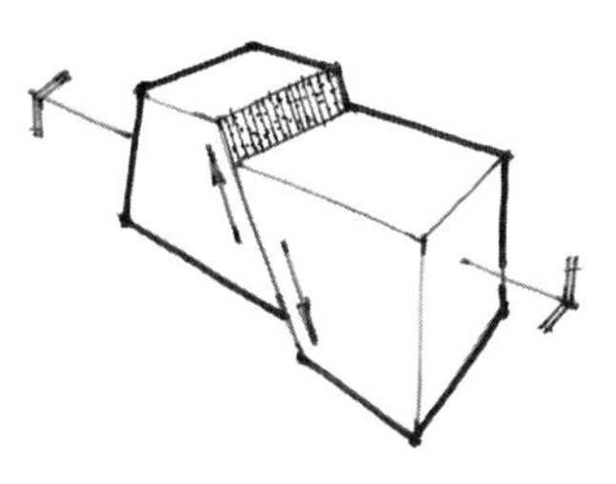

BUILDING SITE IMPACT

The widely accepted first reader "*Architects and Earthquakes*" describes the quiescent, normal, thrust, lateral slip, Horst, and Graben *ground faults* that occur during an earthquake. (NSF and AIA Research Corp., 1975) (Fig. 5-3 through 5-8).

Soil Amplification may result from the seismic shaking of alluvial soils. To visualize this phenomenon, imagine placing a block of "Jell-O" on a plate, and matchbox on top of the block of gelatin. Now shake the plate in a minor way. Notice that the matchbox is moving more than you are moving the plate. Seismic waves are similarly amplified when passing through alluvial soil during an earthquake.

Figure 5-5
Thrust fault.

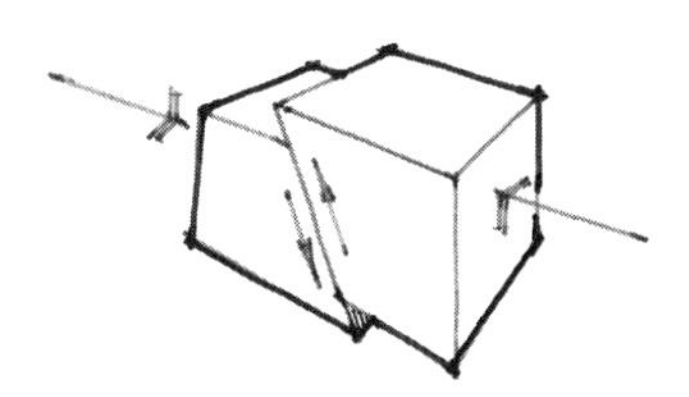

Figure 5-6
Lateral slip.

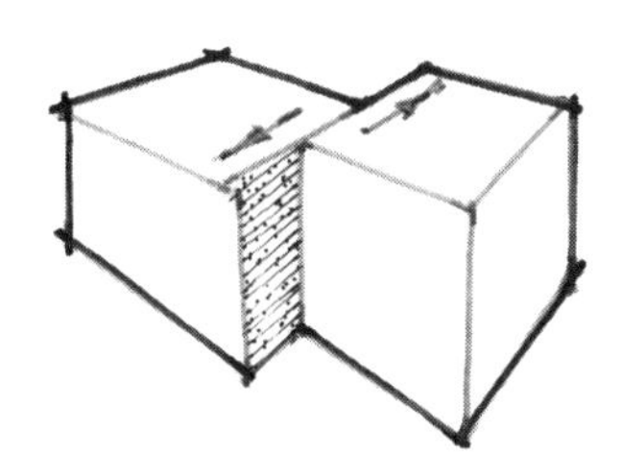

Figure 5-7
Horst fault.

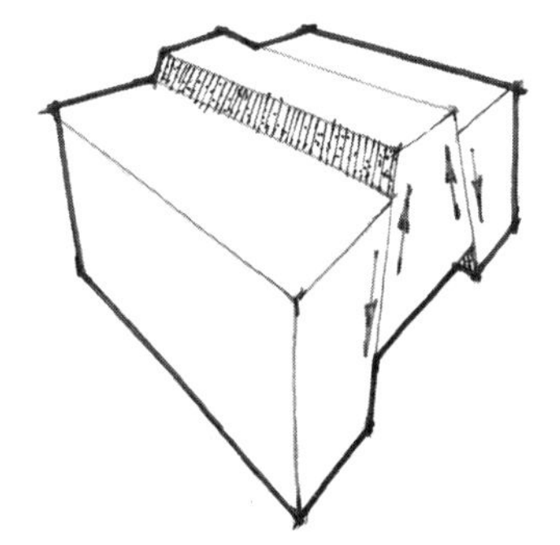

Figure 5-8
Graben fault.

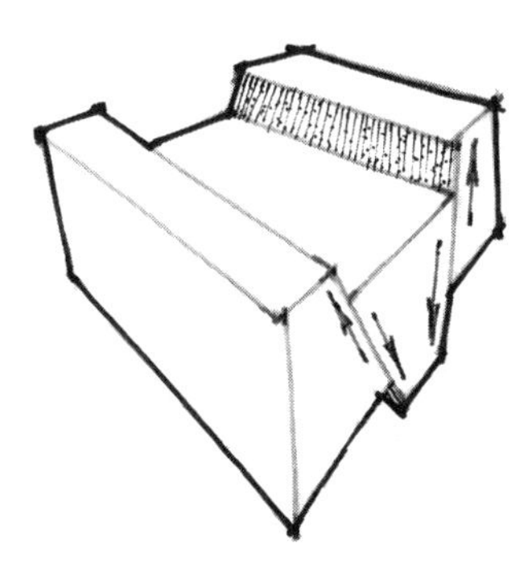

Rifts: These tears in the earth open up when the ground surface is placed in tension (Fig. 5-9).

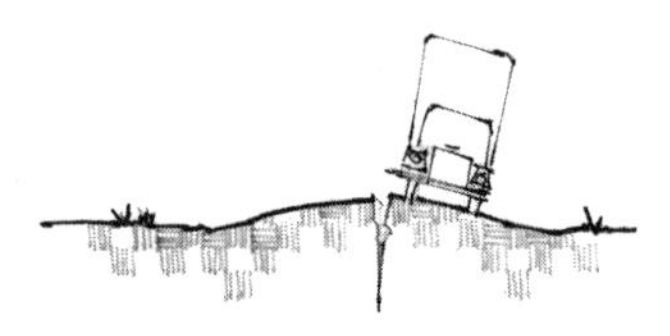

Figure 5-9
Surface rift.

BUILDING IMPACT

The building issues selected for a brief introduction here, are thoroughly explored in *Simplified Building Design for Wind and Earthquake* by Ambrose and Vergun.

Building use: Building codes demand greater protection for buildings that house such critical functions as hospitals, fire, and police stations.

Base shear: As the ground accelerates under the building due to the earthquake, the building will resist that acceleration due to inertia. The heavier the building, the greater its resistance to movement will be. Hence it is said that earthquakes don't cause deaths, heavy buildings cause deaths (Fig. 5-10).

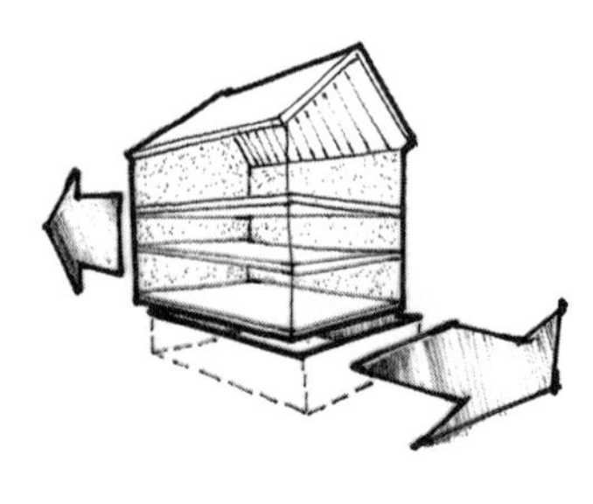

Figure 5-10
Base shear.

Horizontal shear: The shear developed at the base can be transmitted to the floors above if the base is adequately connected to the foundation (Fig. 5-11).

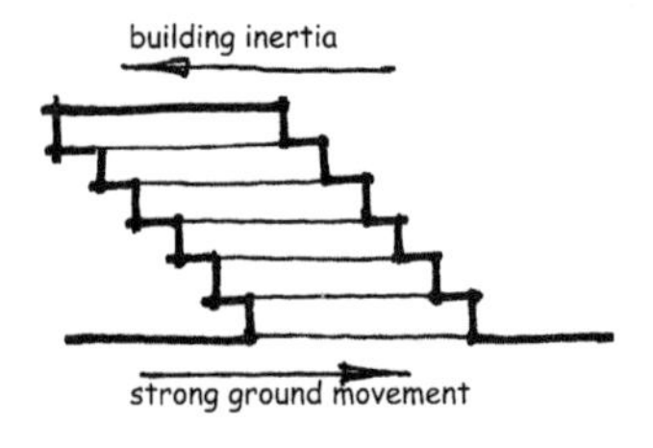

Figure 5-11
Horizontal shear.

Soft story: The first floor of many buildings may be higher from floor to ceiling and have fewer columns due to commercial reasons. This makes it particularly vulnerable to horizontal shear (Fig. 5-12).

Figure 5-12
Garages forming a soft story in the Marina District of San Francisco 1987.

Wracking: Inadequately braced frames distort in a characteristic manner known as wracking. Shear walls and diagonal bracing are normally used to prevent this distortion (Fig. 5-13).

Overturning: Stiff buildings have a tendency to overturn under seismic acceleration if they are adequately supported laterally. This overturning may take place about the toe, by uprooting the heel, or some combination of the two (Fig. 5-14).

Bending: Buildings bend in a manner similar to a cantilevered beam. This puts one side of the building in tension and the other side in compression (Fig. 5-15).

Drift: Tall and flexible building frames will displace more at the top than shorter stiffer structures. This lateral displacement is called drift. Some drift is unavoidable, but excessive drift can be a serious problem.

Pounding: One of the problems with drift occurs when tall and short buildings stand closely side-by-side. Building of different construction and height oscillate at a different rate. Since they don't "dance together" well they will hammer against each other if not separated by adequate distance (Fig. 5-16).

P-delta: The drift of the top of the building is due to "global" bending of the total frame, which is behaving like a cantilevered beam sticking vertically out of the ground. During the drifting of the top, one side of the frame goes into tension, while the opposite side goes into compression. This compression due to global bending must be added to the compression already present due to the building's dead load (Fig. 5-17).

Figure 5-13
Wracking of a book shelf during an earthquake. Building frames can behave similarly.

Figure 5-14
Partial overturning of building in earthquake in Kobe Japan.

Figure 5-15
Bending in the Pina Suarez, Mexico City, 1985. Loose joints yielded excessive bending and drift.

Figure 5-16
Pounding in San Salvador earthquake in 1986. Notice that one building was much shorter.

Oscillation: During an earthquake a building's frame will wave back and forth in an action called oscillation. Each building has an inherent rate of oscillation called its fundamental period. The fundamental period (natural frequency) of a tall building is longer than a short one. If the frequency of the shaking matches the fundamental period of the structure, a condition of resonance is reached. Each cycle of oscillation will be amplified more than the last even if the imparted seismic energy is no greater. Resonance will eventually lead to the collapse of the building. Conceptually a deliberate design effort is made to mismatch the frequency of the building, the soil of the site, and the probable frequency of the seismic shaking. The fundamental period of bedrock is very short, inviting a tall building that has a long period. Wet clay soil has a very long fundamental period, which invites a short building with a very rapid natural frequency. All children know a simple personal example of period matching. When pushing a sibling in a swing, it is not so much a matter of how hard you push, but rather the timing of your push.

Roof casting: The shaft of a building can oscillate in different modes. One mode is similar to "cracking a whip." This leads to a phenomenon known as roof casting in which the top floors collapse (Fig. 5-18).

Projection shedding: Both horizontal projections (i.e., balconies) and vertical projections (i.e., chimneys) break off of a building due to their vulnerability to stress reversals and inertia (Fig. 5-19).

Stress reversals: Stress reversals are very common during seismic oscillation. During a blast, loads often come from the opposite direction that is normally

Figure 5-17
P-Delta collapse of the Nuevo Leon in Mexico City.

expected due to gravity loads. Overhanging balconies bend up, not down. They are not usually designed for this stress reversal. This can lead directly to their failure even in the face of minor loads. It may not be that the load was so great; it may simply be that it came from an unexpected direction.

SITE/BUILDING INTERACTION

Along with the threatening condition known as period matching, other building/site interactions exist during earthquakes that deserve design understanding.

Shallow foundation interaction

Several types of foundation damage may take place during an earthquake. Shallow foundations may experience:

Ramming: The building may surge back and forth under seismic excitation, causing it to "ram" against the soil adjacent to the foundation (Fig. 5-20).

Rocking: Short stiff building may rock back and forth, causing soil to become more compacted at the outer edges than in the middle (Fig. 5-21).

Subsidence: To understand subsidence in a simple conceptual way, first fill a clear drinking glass with loose soil. Then use a grease pencil to mark the top

Figure 5-18
Roof casting of the Nacional Finaceria in Mexico City 1985.

Figure 5-19
Projection shedding of a heavy cantilevered entry cover.

of the soil on the outside of the glass. Start shaking the glass to mimic the shaking of an earthquake. Gradually the soil in the glass will "find a better fit" due to this shaking. Now compare the new height of the soil in the glass with the old line. The soil will have become more compact. This is soil subsidence (Fig. 5-22).

Liquefaction: If wet sand soils are shaken during an earthquake, they become "quick sand." Rigid buildings on wet sand may sink intact at an angle into this liquefied soil. The most famous failure of this type was at Nigata in Japan. The wet sand displaced by the sinking of buildings will erupt nearby in the form of sand geysers.

Slides: Rotational slides and *translational building* movement can be provoked by seismic shaking. This is due in part to the type of soil present, the amount of water in the soil, the steepness of slopes, and the character and duration of shaking. Landslides and mudslides are provoked during earthquakes. Slides are studied in a bit more detail in the next chapter entitled geology and soil (Fig. 5-23 and 5-24).

Figure 5-20
Ramming.

STRUCTURAL RESPONSE TO SEISMIC LOADS

In "*Earthquakes and Architects*" the following guidelines are recommended (NSF and AIA Research Corp., 1975). In seismic areas keep the building light

Figure 5-21
Rocking.

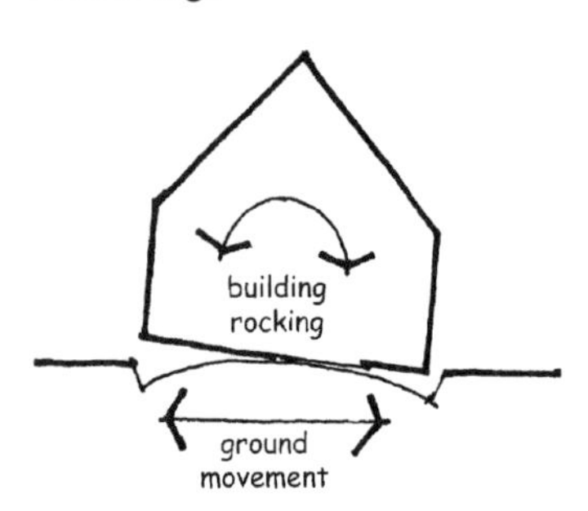

Figure 5-22
Subsidence.

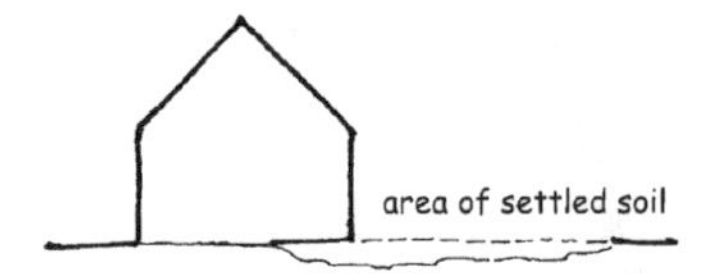

Figure 5-23
Translation slide.

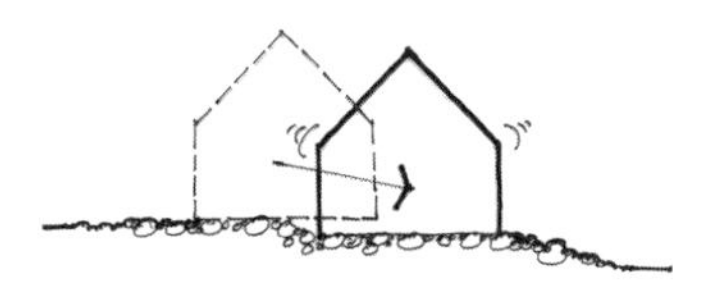

Figure 5-24
Rotational slide.

and symmetrical. Avoid exaggerated dimensions in the building massing. Keep the structural frame simple and provide redundancy. Maintain continuity of load propagation along smooth direct routes. Provide for, but limit, both torsion and movement in the structural frame. In part this is done by controlling flexibility. Often it is better to bend than to break. Keep all of your individual structural joints tight to avoid excessive "drift" at the top of taller buildings. Don't let the fundamental period (natural time of oscillation) of the building match that of the soil upon which it rests. Use ductile materials. They absorb a lot of punishment, give warning, and provide escape time. Remember that it is better to fail in a member than a joint, and a beam before a column. Failure in joints and columns often cause much more of a building to collapse (Fig. 5-25).

Figure 5-25
Vertical collapse of columns in San Salvador 1986. You are looking at the third floor at ground level.

SPECIFIC TYPES OF SEISMIC RESISTANT STRATEGIES

Base isolation: A number of current high tech connections have been developed to allow the building to remain at rest while the ground below it is accelerated by an earthquake. The intention is to isolate the building from the energy of the earthquake. However, various methods of base isolation have long been used on the Pacific Rim (Fig. 5-26).

Passive response: In the United States many designers have chosen to let the building wave about in flexible passive response to seismic shaking. In part this is due to the abundance of steel that is available for use. Steel is light, strong, and most importantly ductile. Ductile materials yield and bend, but do not break. This permanent bending (taking a *plastic set*) and the *resilient* waving "eat up" seismic energy, give warning to occupants, and provide escape time. The Japanese have widely explored a more rigid passive response to earthquakes since they are forced to use concrete as their dominant structural material.

Active and semi-active response: To understand this type of response in a simple conceptual way consider the way the human body actively responds to earthquake shaking. Humans use the muscles of their body to alter the position and balance of their body in order to avoid becoming imbalanced and thrown to the ground.

TSUNAMI

A *tsunami* is a series of very large tidal waves generated by a sub-aqueous (below water) earthquake. Such waves may be thirty feet tall (as in the Alaska earthquake), go as far ashore as one half mile (as it did in Nicaragua), and wipe out total towns (as it did in Hilo, Hawaii).

Figure 5-26
An ancient form of base isolation in a Buddhist temple in Kyoto Japan.

BLAST

Blast sources

Blast damage can result from the accidental explosion of natural gas lines. The most recent example of a major explosion of a gas line was in Guadalajara, Mexico, when more than one block of gas lines exploded. The more common concern is the deliberate bombing of a building as an act of terrorism, or as a direct result of conventional war. The blast effect related to nuclear detonation has been considered so massive that it exceeds the concerns that can normally occupy an architect's design consideration. War damage has two prominent features. Often projectiles penetrate outer walls, and explode inside the building causing the collapse of interior bearing walls. The loss of all the roofs in a town is also quiet noticeable. While this is largely the result of fires that are ignited by blasts, it may also be an evidence of deliberate scavenging for fire wood by desperate survivors and refugees (Fig. 5-27).

Blast location

One obvious response to the threat of blast load is to relocate any potential source of such explosion. In industrial projects, this may not be possible if the product being manufactured is inherently explosive. If terrorist explosions are feared, it is wise to move roads and parking away from occupied structures. In the case of war, specialized structures have long been designed as shelters against bombing and shelling, but adequate hardening of standard civilian buildings have seldom recognized this concern, even in settings where war is all but inevitable.

Figure 5-27
Typical roof destruction in the recent Balkans war.

Blast direction

In cases where the direction of any potential explosion is largely predictable, the blast waves may be shielded, directed, or dampened so that the structure does not have to resist the total impact load.

Figure 5-28
Murrah bombing site. These floors initially failed from reverse bending.

Target hardening

Where blast elimination or direction is not possible, target hardening must be done. Part of this activity will include strengthening the building structure, and possibly making it a bit more resilient. *Resilience* is the ability to "spring back" or resume the original shape. Common rubber bands are resilient. Certain important government structures are said to be mounted on large springs for this reason.

Stress reversals

As in seismic shaking, *stress reversals* are not uncommon due to blast loads. During a blast, loads often come from the opposite direction than is normally expected due to gravity loads. Overhanging balconies may bend up, not down (Fig. 5-28).

WIND

General issues

Comparison to earthquakes

Many of the effects of winds on buildings are very similar to those caused by earthquakes. Base shear, wracking, overturning, global torsion, drift, and P-delta all take place during strong winds just as they do during earthquakes, but for different reasons.

Measurement

Strong winds are currently measured on the *Fujita scale* (F0 to F5) based on the damage caused. For example, in an F3 wind the roof and some walls are torn from well constructed houses, trains are overturned, and most trees are uprooted.

Building effects

There are some important differences between wind and seismic loading. Heavy buildings are bad in an earthquake due to inertia, but are good during strong winds. Light buildings such as tents and pneumatics blow away during strong winds. Winds also have some unique types of loads and responses. *Simplified Building Design for Wind and Earthquakes* by Ambrose and Vergun provides an excellent deeper study of the effects that are briefly summarized below.

Figure 5-29
Windward stagnation.

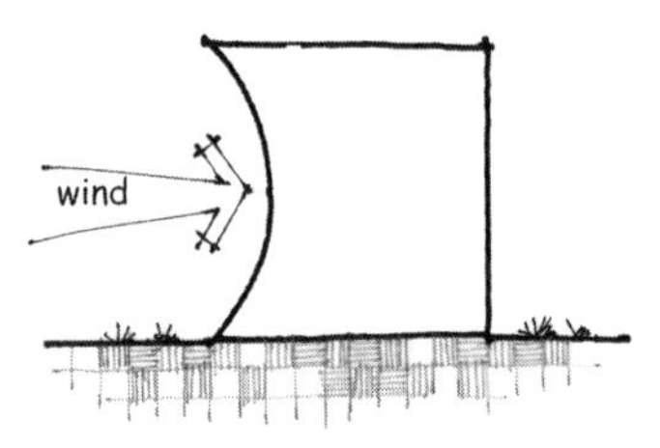

Windward pressure: Pressure on the windward side of a building varies with wind velocity, and is also known as *windward stagnation* (Fig. 5-29).

Leeward suction: Turbulence and suction on the "down wind" side of buildings is a considerable force if high velocity winds are present. Streamlined shapes like airplanes reduce both windward pressure and leeward suction; unfortunately, most buildings are bluff bodies (not streamlined) (Fig. 5-30).

Roof uplift: Just as the wings of an airplane are lifted by the flow of air across them, so are many buildings.

Drag: Wind friction pulls on a building as the wind passes over it (Fig. 5-31).

Rocking: Because wind load has gusts and causes turbulence, buildings oscillate (Fig. 5-32).

Vibration: Many structures (such as tents) have surfaces that "flutter" due to the wind passing over them (Fig. 5-33).

Clean off: Roofing materials, roof-mounted equipment, chimneys, and roof mounted antennae are often stripped off by strong winds. These items become dangerous projectiles (Fig. 5-34).

Drift: Bending and drift occur with wind in much the same way as it does during earthquakes, but for different reasons. The P-delta effect is also present (Fig. 5-34).

Cupping: Large open doors and the openings left by large broken windows open a building to further damage due to cupping (Fig. 5-35).

Pressure increases: Wind pressure is exceedingly difficult and complex to study. It is safe to say that wind concentrations take place, particularly under overhangs, and at roof projections such as parapets (Fig. 5-36).

Figure 5-30
Leeward suction.

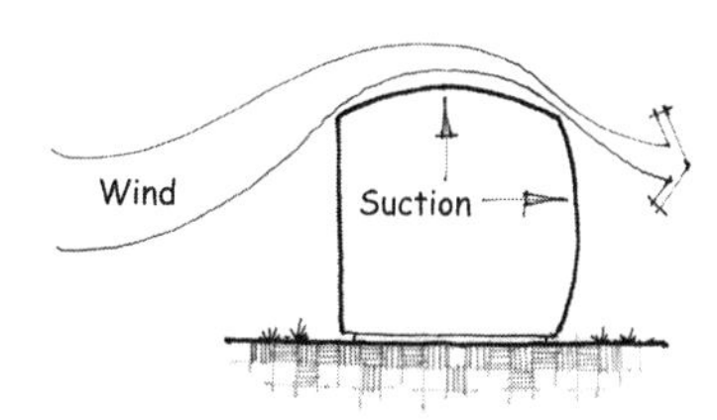

Figure 5-31
Wind drag.

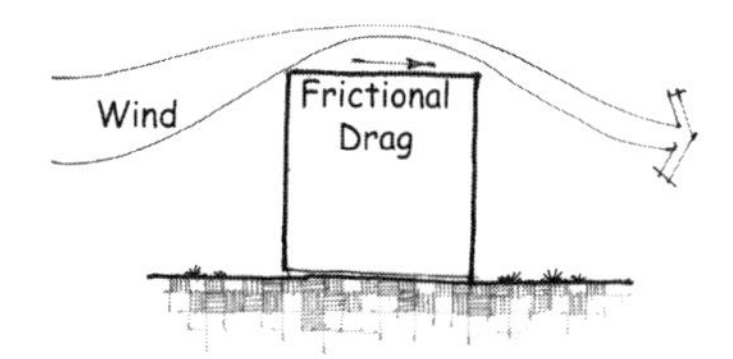

Figure 5-32
Building oscillation.

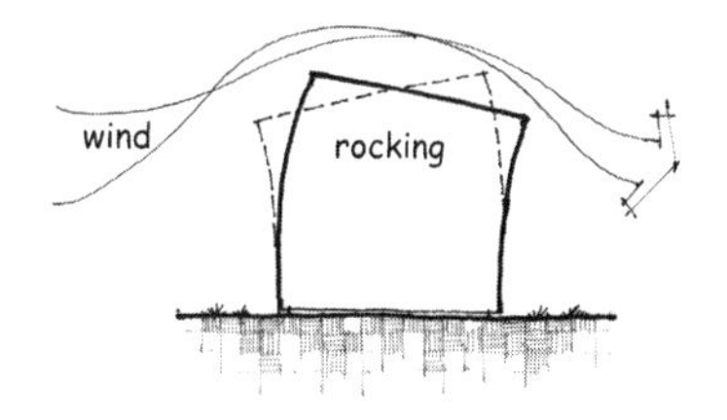

Figure 5-33
Wind vibration or flutter.

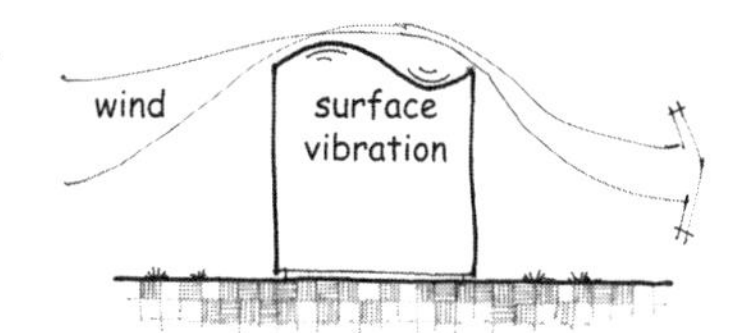

Site issues

The surrounding topography, adjacent building heights, and ground surface texture can modify the velocity of any winds that may be present. Trees may overturn in strong winds causing considerable damage to adjacent buildings. Branches, gravel, and other site debris can become damaging projectiles when driven by strong winds. Even the asphalt surface of roads has been lifted and transported during tornadoes. In an urban context even fairly mild breezes may be concentrated into higher velocity winds when squeezed between tall buildings (Fig. 5-37).

Wind design guidelines

In strong wind areas it is best to *streamline* the shape of the building, and to limit any projections from the building surface. Unfortunately, most buildings are bluff bodies (Fig. 5-38). Minimize the height of the building, and consider subterranean or semi-subterranean architecture. If the direction of the most threatening winds is predictable, present a narrow facade to it. Since this is not normally possible, avoid long unsupported exterior walls.

Figure 5-34
Roof debris "cleaned off" by strong straight line winds in Paul's Valley Oklahoma.

Figure 5-35
Cupping damage due to a tornado in Ft. Smith Arkansas.

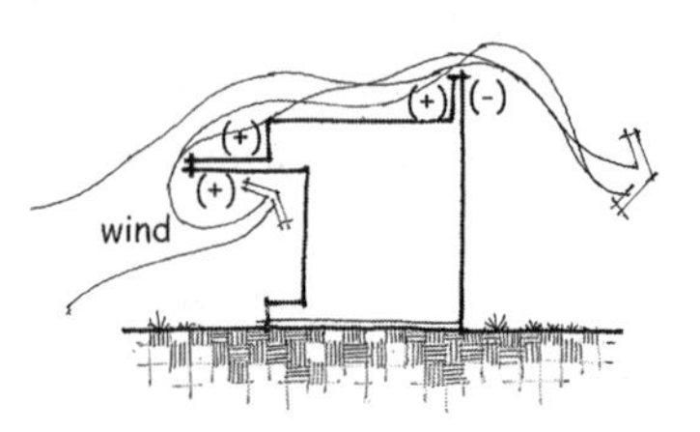

Figure 5-36
Pressure concentrations.

Structural response to wind and seismic loads

Lateral bracing in all directions

To resist lateral loads, building structures must have some form of lateral bracing. Remember that stability happens within six degrees of freedom. A frame that is laterally braced in one axis may still fail in another (Fig. 5-39).

Alternative lateral support systems

Five general types of lateral support are widely used:

1. *Form stabilization:* Some structural systems will be inherently resistant to lateral loads. Domes, vaults, and most other forms of shells are form stabilized. Form stabilization against earthquakes and wind usually begins with a wide base to resist overturning. The Transamerica Title Building in San Francisco is a commonly cited example (Fig. 5-40).
2. *Stabilizing cores:* The fireproofing of stair towers and elevator shafts and/or deliberate additional bracing of these towers leads to great stiffness. These towers can be then used as stabilizing cores to support a more flexible frame that surrounds them. Many types of cores have been developed

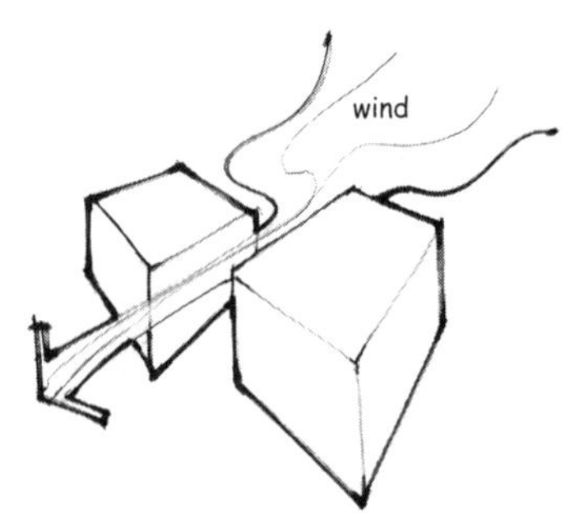

Figure 5-37
Locally increased wind velocity.

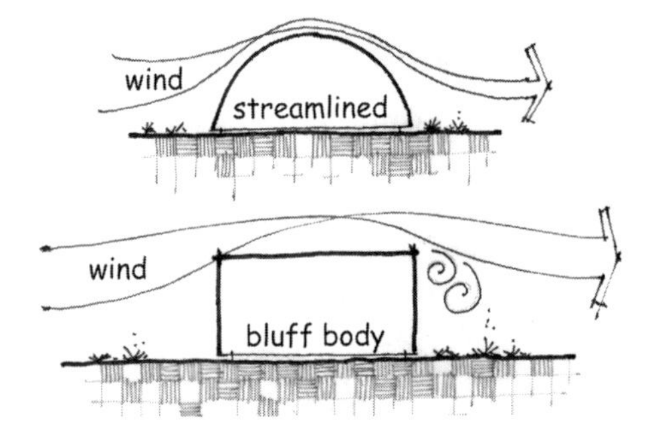

Figure 5-38
Streamlined mass vs. bluff body.

(Fig. 5-41). Remember that the *center of stiffness* will rest at the center of the core. The *center of mass* for the surrounding frame may, or may not match. When the center of stiffness and the center of mass do not match, global torsion develops in the structural frame (Fig. 5-42). A ratio can be made between the building's height, and its least dimension at its base. This is known as the *slenderness ratio*. There is a difference between the mass slenderness ratio generated from the building mass, and the effective slenderness ratio generated from the structurally effective lateral support mechanism. Modern high-rise buildings push the limits of this slenderness ratio, making them very vulnerable to overturning in the face of wind loads. In such tall buildings lateral loads become a dominant concern over gravity loads.

3. *Moment connections:* Post and beam frames, (which will be discussed in greater detail later in this text) may have pinned or rigid connections. Rigid connections are also known as *moment* connections. If they have pinned connections (meaning the members connected to the joint may rotate freely like scissors or pliers), then some type of lateral support must be added; however, if they are rigidly welded, the joints themselves may be sufficient to resist lateral loads.
4. *Shear walls:* Like rigid connections, shear walls are intended to resist wracking in the structural frame. Vertical load bearing walls often simultaneously serve as shear walls to resist lateral loads. However, shear walls of a stiff material such as concrete may be "in-filled" into the pinned frame of a post and beam structure.

Figure 5-39
Must laterally brace in all directions.

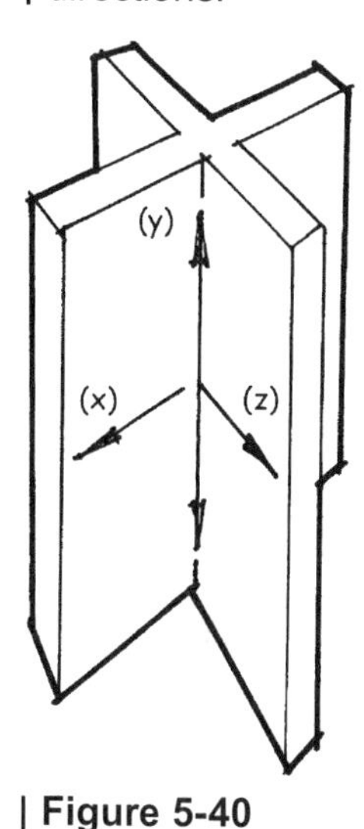

Figure 5-40
The Transamerica Building in San Francisco is a form stabilized high-rise.

Diaphragms (stiff floor plates) collect lateral loads, and transfer these loads to shear walls. If that shear wall is located so that symmetrical loads are collected about the shear wall, then no torsion is generated. However, if the floor areas are unequal, then torsion is the inevitable result (Fig. 5-43).

There are appropriate ratios between shear wall height, width and length; however, it is primarily the length of shear walls that allow them to resist lateral loads. Short shear walls have little effect. Three short shear walls are not as effective as one long shear wall (Fig. 5-44).

Figure 5-41
A few selected alternative core configurations in plan view.

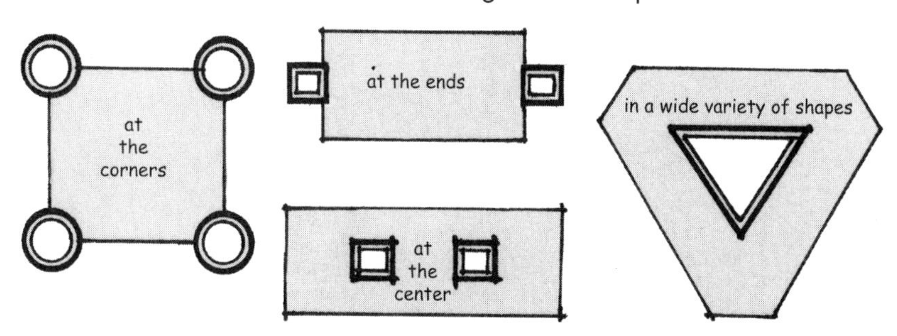

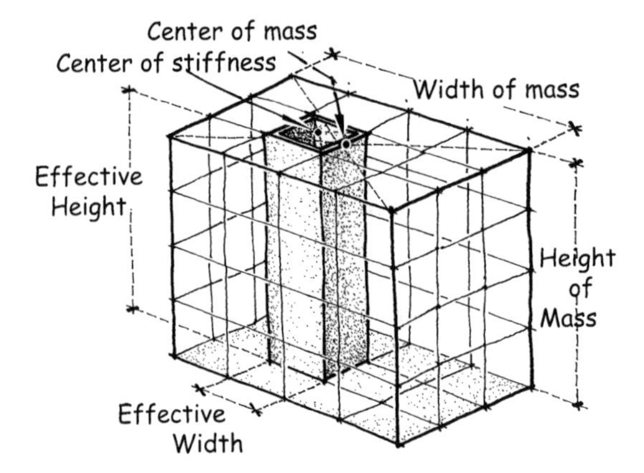

Figure 5-42
Center of mass vs. center of stiffness.

5. *Braced frames:* A triangle is a rigid geometric form. Unlike a rectangle it cannot change shape without changing the length of one of its sides. This characteristic has long been exploited to gain rigidity in resisting loads. Trusses, space frames, and a wide variety of lateral bracing systems use this principle of triangulation. Many alternative types of lateral bracing are available to a designer. Some of the more commonly used ones are cross bracing, diagonal bracing, K-bracing, knee bracing, internal and external struts (Fig. 5-45).

Continuity of lateral bracing is necessary for lateral load propagation all the way to the underlying soil and geology. Also, lateral bracing should be broader at the base (Fig. 5-46).

Other lateral support mechanisms

External guying

A frame that is not inherently capable of resisting lateral loads can be externally guyed by attaching cables to the outside of the frame, then securing the cables to the ground. Many radio towers are externally guyed.

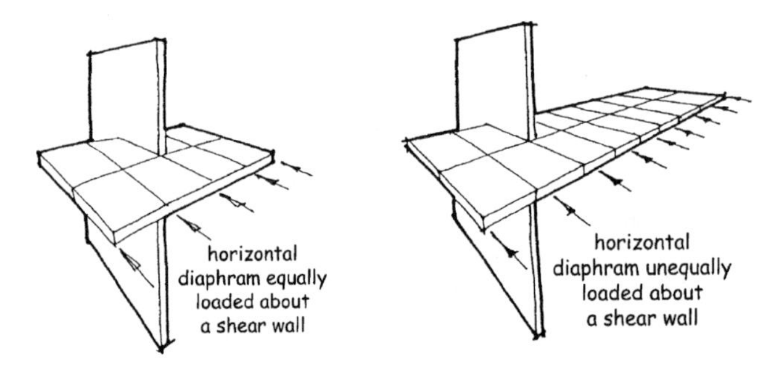

Figure 5-43
Keep horizontal floor diaphragms symmetrical if possible.

Figure 5-44
Shear wall length matters.

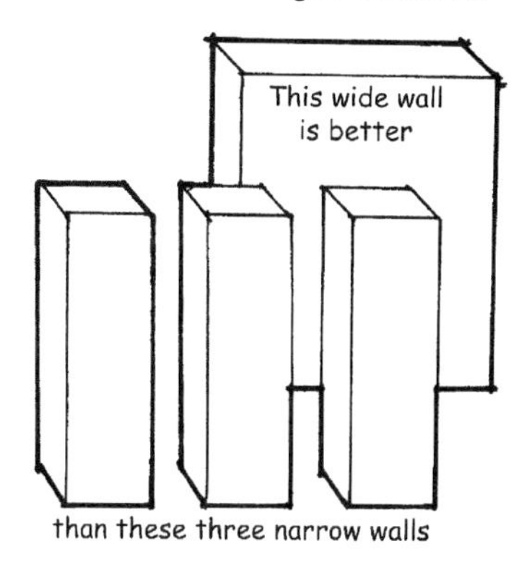

Figure 5-45
Alternative bracing configurations.

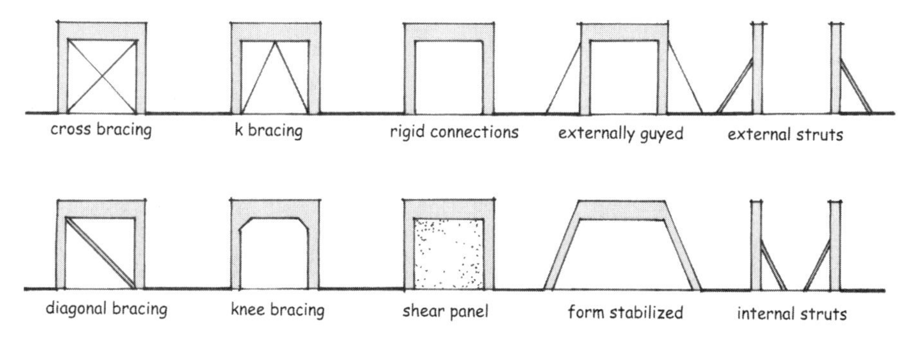

Figure 5-46
Bracing continuity is like a human spine.

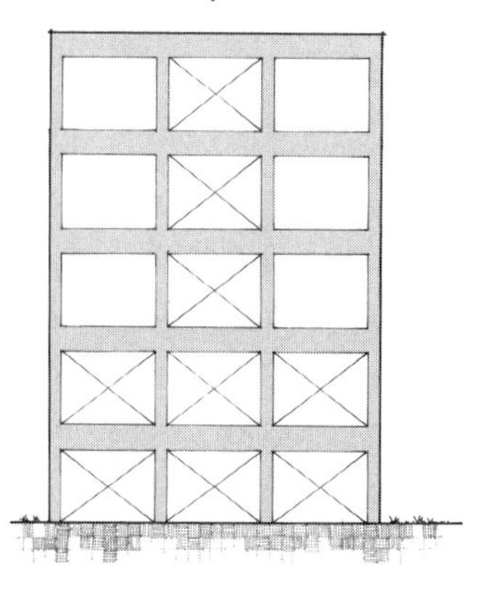

Figure 5-47

External struts at the Viking Ship Stadium in Hamar Norway by Nils Torp.

Struts

A compressive member that is positioned at some angle other than vertical is known as a strut. Struts may be placed either internally or externally to support a completed structure; however, they are even more commonly used for temporary support during the construction process. Tilt-up concrete walls, and partially framed stud walls, are usually temporarily braced by either internal or external struts until they can be permanently attached to other walls (Fig. 5-47).

Migration of the lateral support mechanism

No matter what lateral support type is selected (shear wall, cross-bracing, etc.) it will tend to migrate from the center of the floor plan toward the outside building envelope in order to give the structural system a "wider stance" as lateral loads increase. This is quite visible in the Hancock Building in Chicago (Fig. 5-48).

Figure 5-48

Notice the lateral bracing on the outside wall of the Hancock Building in Chicago.

Vocabulary		
Lateral load	Plate tectonics	Hypocenter
Epicenter	P-wave	S-wave
Rayleigh wave	Love wave	Soil amplification
Liquefaction	Seismograph	Accelograph
Richter scale	Tsunami	Modified Mercalli scale
Fault	Rift	Base shear
Wracking	Pounding	P-delta effect
Base isolation	Resilient	Plastic set
Drag	Bluff body	Windward stagnation
Clean off	Form stabilized	Center of stiffness
Center of mass	Diaphragm	Mass slenderness ratio
Strut	Ductile	Effective slenderness ratio

REVIEW QUESTIONS

1. Briefly describe three general sources of seismic waves.
2. List and describe four types of seismic waves.
3. What is the importance of resonance in seismic resistant design?
4. What is the basic concept behind base isolation?
5. Quickly draw 15 different ways to resist lateral loads.
6. Graphically and verbally explain diaphragm action and the significance of tributary area imbalance.

7. Graphically and verbally describe the common effects that wind has on a building.
8. Graphically and verbally describe the common effects that an earthquake has on a building structure and its site.
9. What are ductile materials, and why are they important in seismic resistant design?
10. Why should the center of stiffness coincide with the center of mass if possible?

Figure 6-1

House on a rock in Eureka Springs Arkansas.

6 Geology and Soil

GENERAL ISSUES

For most clients, geology and soil are only minor indirect issues in the purchase of a building site. However, for architects and structural engineers, subsurface soils and geology may be so significant that they may even be forced to recommend sale of the current site, and purchase of another. Loads applied to, and resulting from, a building must ultimately be dispersed in the subsurface materials upon which the building stands. The heavier the building, and the worse the soil conditions, the more likely it is that a change of site may be advised.

GEOLOGY

Rock classification

Rock may be classified in a number of ways. The following discussion addresses means of classification that give a conceptual understanding of the issues that normally influence the structural performance of subsurface rock.

Type

Rocks are broadly categorized depending on the method by which they were formed.

Igneous: These types of rocks are solidified from a molten state such as the lava that flows from a volcano. Examples are granite and basalt.

Sedimentary: These have been formed under water where pressure and cementation take place over time. Examples include sandstone, limestone, and shale.

Metamorphic: This type of rock is reformed from igneous and sedimentary materials that are recombined under conditions of heat, compression, and/or moisture. Examples are gneiss, schist, and slate (Faber and Johnson 1979).

Weathering

Exposed rock is gradually modified by surface forces. It becomes fractured by the freeze/thaw cycle. Weathering, movement, bedding pattern of deposits, slope of strata, the extent of cracking, and direction of cracking all affect the final bearing strength of rock. Rock and soil may be classified by the nature and extent of such alterations: *Residual* soil is an unmoved material resting directly over the parent rock from which it was weathered. *Glacial material* is moved and deposited by glacial action. *Colluvial rock and soil* are the result of down slope movement by gravity, while *marine rock and soil* are the result of wave, tidal, or other oceanic movement. *Alluvial soil* is moved and deposited by water such as rivers, and *Aeolian* is a soil that has been moved and deposited by wind.

Strata and faults

Not only the rock type, but also the slope of rock strata and the presence of faults can affect foundation design. For instance, if clay soil overlays sloped subsurface bedrock, it will likely be necessary to "socket" the foundation piers into the rock just to keep them from sliding on the sloped surface of the rock (even if the ground surface is level).

Continuity

Fairly homogeneous subsurface conditions are generally more predictable, and normally require less diverse foundation configurations. They are, therefore, generally less open to human error in construction, and tend to be less costly to build.

Bearing capacity

The structural property of subsurface rock that most interests us in foundation design is its bearing capacity. This capacity largely results from the shear strength of the rock, but other issues influence it. *Hard sound rock* might have a bearing capacity around 120 kips per square foot (KSF), while *soft rock* might be closer to 16 kips per square foot (KSF) (Seelye 1960). For comparison, it may be useful to know that concrete has a bearing capacity of about 140 KSF. In building codes such numbers are known as the *presumptive bearing capacity* of different rock. While useful in preliminary design, final design must be based on actual sampling at the proposed building site, and testing in a soil lab. *Bearing capacity* in subsurface rock is related to, but not the same as, its *compressive strength* when the stone is used in the superstructure as a building material.

SOILS

General

Soil is composed of air, water, and solid matter. The ratio of these parts profoundly affects its structural potential. Soils are the result of decomposed rock material due to weathering, combined with constituents of decomposing organic matter. Soil, therefore, has both horticultural and engineering potential. Topsoil, which is very extensively weathered rock combined with a great deal of decomposed organic material, is found at the ground surface. It has the greatest horticultural potential, but the least structural potential. For this reason, it is usually stripped and carefully stockpiled for later landscape use. This bares the more useful bearing material. These superimposed layers of soil are called "horizons".

Horizons

When core samples are taken at the building site, these horizons are normally visually distinct in color, texture, and compaction (Fig. 6-2).

A Horizon: As previously noted, topsoil is a mix of both mineral and decaying organic matter that makes a suitable growing medium, but has poor engineering properties. It is usually 0 to 24 inches deep.

B Horizon: Subsoil varies greatly in depth. It is clearly weathered and differs in color from the topsoil.

C Horizon: This is the partially weathered parent material that rests below the subsoil in a residual setting. It normally differs in color and compaction from both the A and B horizons.

D Horizon: Bedrock below the partially weathered parent material may be relatively deep.

Soil classifications

Soil is made up of grains of varying sizes. These sizes are established by passing the soil through sieves (screens) of different sizes, then measuring the

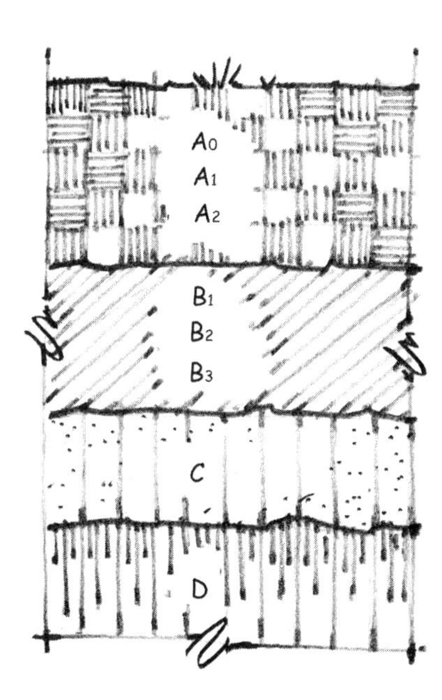

Figure 6-2
Soil horizons.

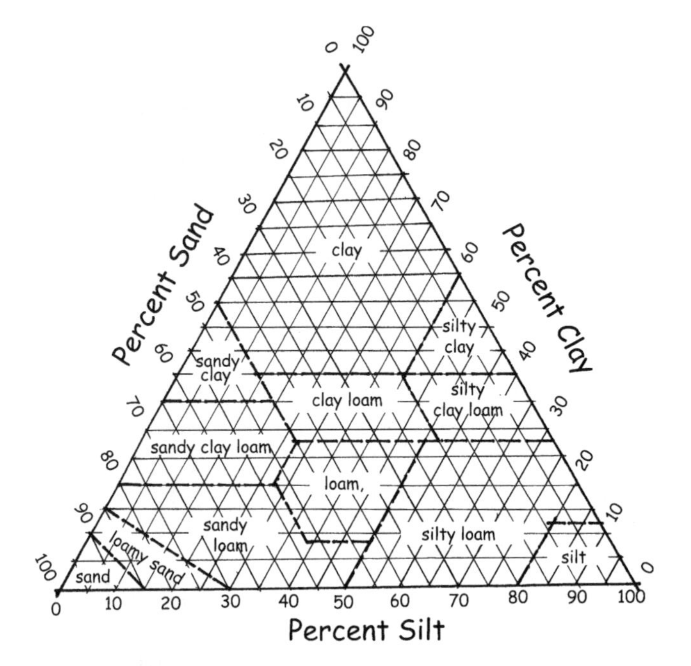

Figure 6-3
Soil textures.

percent content for each size of grain. The chart illustrates this classification method based on the percent of each grain size. Well-graded soils (those with many different size grains) are usually stronger than poorly graded ones (Fig. 6-3).

Soil Evaluation

Soil exploration

Several methods of soil exploration are possible. *Borings* are by far the most common soil sampling method in the United States. It is best to drill at the actual location where foundations will finally rest; however, this location is not usually known at the start of design when these samples are taken. The next best alternative is to sink several holes. *Pit tests* are simply digging a hole. It is probably the cheapest and the most reliable because the soil may be inspected directly in place, in the walls of the excavation. As a third option for very small buildings, a *sounding rod* can be driven into the soil, and its density evaluated by the number of blows required. Unfortunately, this method does not tell what type of soil is present. Finally *geophysical sounding* is used in petroleum exploration, but is only useful when very deep strata are of interest.

Testing

Once soil samples are taken, they are moved to the laboratory for testing. A wide range of methods is used in the lab to evaluate the engineering properties of the soil samples taken at the site. The detailed testing procedures are beyond the scope of this text; however, during these tests the following important soil properties are determined:

Figure 6-4
Monadnock building in Chicago immediately started sinking.

1. *Weight:* This is one of the factors that affect the lateral force that the soil will exert on the foundation wall.
2. *Constituent ratios:* These ratios are used to classify the soil.
3. *Grain size and shape:* The size and shape of the individual particles in a soil sample affect internal friction of the soil, and therefore the soil's bearing capacity.
4. *Soil texture:* If grains are individual particles in the soil, texture is the relationship or amount of variation in these particle sizes.
5. *Shear strength:* This is critical to the soil's capacity as a structural material.
6. *Compressibility:* It will affect the settlement that can be anticipated once the building is completed. Excessive settlement became visibly apparent once the very heavy Monodnock building was completed in Chicago. Some of its solid masonry walls were several feet thick (Fig. 6-4).
7. *Permeability:* This is a measure of the ease with which water will migrate through the soil under the force of gravity.

Documentation

The soil engineer will ultimately provide a soil report to the architect or engineer. It will have the *boring plan* or layout of the pattern of borings that were taken. It will have a *boring log* which shows a section of each boring that was taken. A *general discussion* will address each type of soil encountered. Many turn immediately to the *summary or conclusions*. Here, the engineer will give clear, direct design guidance based upon what she or he encountered in the soil investigation and analysis. Various types of soil properties will be addressed in the report. The *horticultural properties* of soils are not of direct interest in this text. It is useful to notice that soils that are good for growing plants are normally poor as an engineering material. The *engineering properties* of greatest interest are its bearing capacity, permeability, compressibility, and shrink-swell. These will occupy a designer's interest. Constructors will be interested in the wearability of the soil as a working surface during construction. Wet clays can limit the mobility of personnel, and some equipment. The opposite is also a concern. "Working" soft clay with heavy equipment can make it even weaker as a structural material. That is why potters "work" clay before throwing it on a potter's wheel.

Relative bearing capacity of soils

The following list crudely ranks the relative bearing capacity of soils from the best to the worst. The best of these soils might have a capacity around 38 KSF, while the worst might be closer to 0.5 KSF. You might wish to compare this to the range of bearing capacities previously mentioned for rock.

1. Compact gravel
2. Hardpan overlaying rock
3. Loose gravel
4. Hard dry clay
5. Course sand
6. Fine dry sand
7. Compact sand-clay
8. Loose fine sand
9. Firm or stiff clay
10. Soft wet clay
11. Silt and loess
12. Peat, loam, and other organic deposits
13. Mud, quicksand, and bentonite

As a designer, it is useful to keep the general hierarchy of bearing capacities for the different soils in mind when selecting an appropriate foundation. At the very least remember the lower third of the above table, because these represent real problems to which you should be immediately alert.

Some common subsurface concerns

Soil material

Seelye's long respected text entitled "*Design*" contains an excellent section called "Soil Red Lights" which describes a wide variety of undesirable subsurface conditions (Seelye 1960). Some of the more common indications of soil problems include:

1. *Significant deposit of peat* or other organic material. This is too compressible to be structurally useful.
2. *Soft clay which will be high "shrink-swell:"* That means that it will change size dramatically when it is wet or dry. This leads to differential settlement and the cracks that are associated with that problem.
3. *Water bearing sand:* This was previously discussed, and is commonly known as "quicksand."
4. *Shallow bedrock:* It presents excellent bearing, but will be about three times as expensive to excavate.
5. *Evidence of slides, or the potential for slides.*
6. *Presence of sand lenses:* These can collapse into the excavation during the pouring of drilled piers. This will lead to weakening of the pier.
7. *Inadequately compacted fill:* This will lead to excessive settlement.

Ground water

The presence of water on soils is also significant. Like shallow bedrock, a *high water table* can profoundly increase construction costs, and may require continuous dewatering for the life of the completed building. It is central to frost heave failures. Clays will settle excessively when they dry. Shear strength of most soils is reduced by the addition of water causing it to lose bearing capacity. It may require pumping during construction operations.

Water problems are often addressed by draining the foundation by the introduction of subsurface drainage pipes. Capillarity in the soil can be overcome by introduction of gravel as a backfill under slabs.

Water related vocabulary

The following vocabulary will be helpful in understanding the soil report provided by the soil and foundations engineer (Fig. 6-5). An *aquifer* is a subsurface strata that holds or transports water (i.e., gravel). An *aquaclude* is a subsurface stratum that resists the passage of water. *Aquifer recharge areas* are permeable surface areas that allow water to enter a subsurface aquifer. *Springs* are just the exposed edge of an aquifer. *Artesian wells* are an opening into an aquifer that allows water to come forth under pressure due to hydrostatic head.

Seasonal ground water: The ground water table may rise and fall in response to seasonal variation of available subsurface water.

Capillarity: Subsurface water may be drawn up in the narrow air spaces in a soil known as *pores*. Capillary action can lift water up to 20 feet above its normal water table in clay soils.

Lateral foundation load: Soil presses laterally against foundation walls. This pressure varies with soil type, and the presence of water in the soil. It is addressed in most building codes.

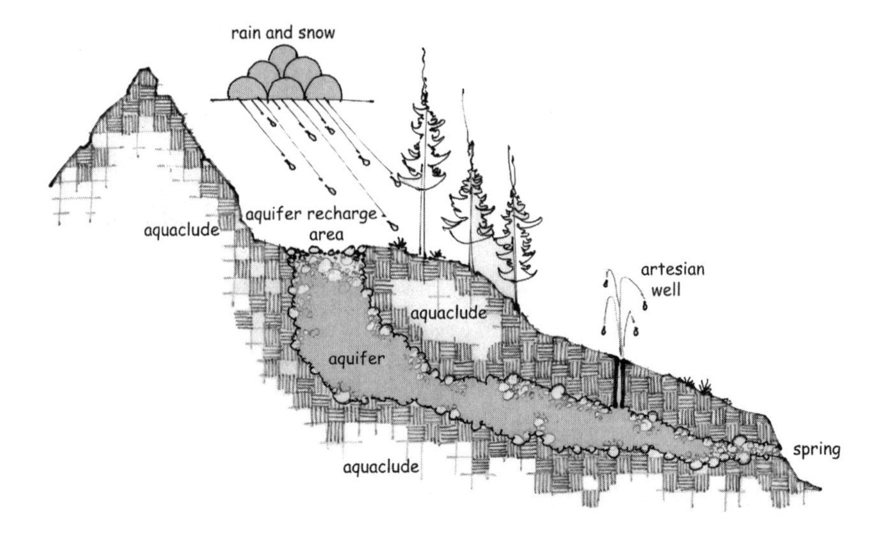

Figure 6-5
Nomenclature of subsurface water.

Foundation uplift: High subsurface water table can lift a building much as a boat is supported by displacing water. Foundations can also be lifted by frost heave if the footing is too shallow.

Dissolved rock: Some bedrock can be dissolved by water. In places like Florida, limestone erodes into caves and sinkholes into which whole buildings occasionally drop.

Undermining and scouring: Floods and tidal surge can scour the supporting soil out from under building foundations.

Soil color: During visual inspection of the walls of building excavations, seasonal presence of subsurface water may be implied by soil color. For example, beware of bluish soils that overlay an aquaclude.

Topography

Slope becomes a structural issue in several ways. There is, of course, a stability problem if the structure is sited on very steep slope. *Slope instability* has physical evidence such as rifts at the top of a slope or bulges at the base of a slope. *Erosion* on slopes is usually immediately visible. The design of the site will cause many slopes to be re-contoured. To avoid slumps and slides on such slopes the natural *angle of repose* for the soil must not be exceeded. Otherwise retaining structures must be used. Approximate angles of repose for common soil types may be adequate during conceptual design, but the engineer's soil report should guide final design development. Tables with approximate angles of repose for common soil types can be found in sources such as civil engineering handbooks.

Vocabulary

Residual soil	Colluvial soil	Alluvial soil
Aeolien soil	Presumptive bearing capacity	Well-graded soil
Soil horizon	Permeability	Shrink-swell
Angle of repose	Capillarity	Aquifer

REVIEW QUESTIONS

1. Identify three general types of rock encountered in soil borings, and give examples for each of these general rock types.
2. List in order of bearing desirability the types of soil commonly encountered in soil tests.
3. List and briefly describe the impact of subsurface water on soil as a structural material.
4. Give a brief list of soil types that immediately suggest soil problems on a site.
5. What type of damage does high shrink-swell soil do to a building?
6. What concerns does a highly compressive soil provoke in building design?
7. If either the existing site or the re-designed site design has significant slopes, what concerns are awakened?

Figure 7-1
Foundation under construction.

7 Foundations

STRUCTURAL ROLE OF THE FOUNDATION

The foundation gathers the loads from the superstructure above, conducts, and distributes these forces into the soil and geology upon which the building rests. In this, mitigation of topography and the forces of climate must also be addressed.

DESIGN CONSIDERATIONS

Three major issues confront the designer in conceptual design of a foundation (Ambrose 1981).

1. What is above the ground?

   Is it a large or small superstructure? Is the superstructure balanced or imbalanced (Fig. 7-2)? What forces are climate, occupancy, and the dead load of the building itself placing on the foundation? Will the forces transmitted to the foundation arrive at concentrated points (such as at the base of columns), along lines (such as at the base of bearing walls), or on planes such as an automobile parking lot on grade)?

2. What is below the ground?

   What type of rock and soil are under the foundation? Are subsurface conditions under the building homogeneous, or diverse (Fig. 7-3)? Where is the subsurface water table? How deep is it to appropriate bearing strata? Will shallow rock be an excavation problem? What additional loads (not yet studied) will be exerted below the surface of the soil?

3. What is happening inside the foundation itself?

   What internal failure modes will be encountered? Will the foundation fail in stability by sliding down slope, settle excessively, or rotate due to some angular load? Will the foundation need to resist bending, shear, torsion, or other types of stress (Fig. 7-4 and 7-5)?

Figure 7-2
Be alert to uneven building weight of the superstructure.

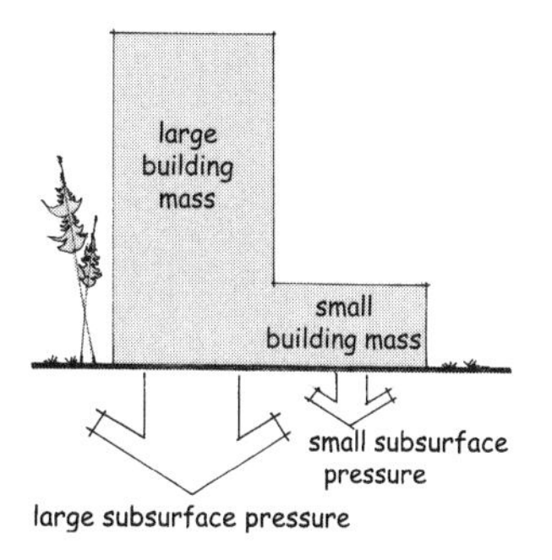

Figure 7-3
Beware of diverse subsurface conditions.

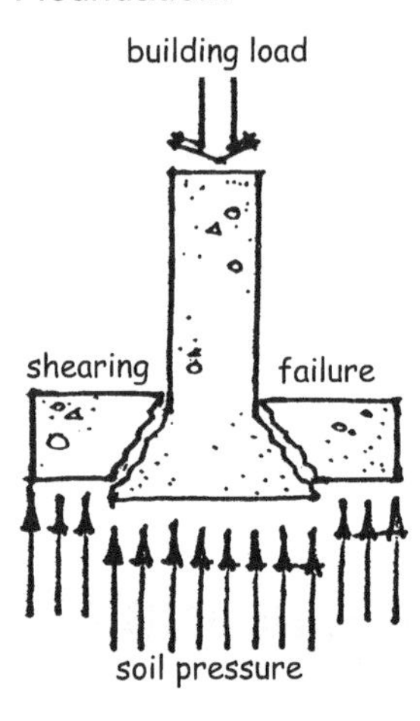

Figure 7-4
Shearing failure in a foundation.

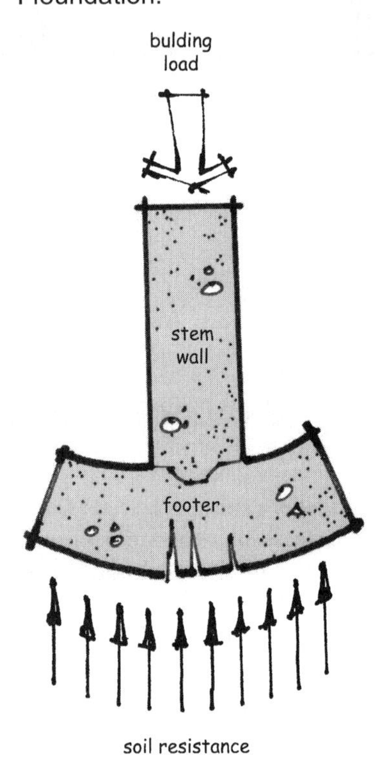

Figure 7-5
Bending stress in a foundation.

TYPES OF FOUNDATION

Foundations are traditionally grouped into two general families: shallow and deep. This division is made not only on the relative level of the subsurface horizon or strata selected for bearing, but also on the supporting mechanisms used to achieve that bearing. Pad, ribbon, and slab-on-grade are *shallow foundations*. They are used for small buildings, broadly distributed loads, and buildings that are located on soils with strong bearing capacity. Occasionally a *buoyant foundation* may be used to overcome a high water table. *Deep foundations* like piles and piers are used to reach through weak, expansive, or compressible shallow surface soils to a deeper bearing material that is stronger. Large buildings, buildings with highly concentrated loads, and buildings that rest on soil with poor bearing capacity usually use deep foundations.

Shallow foundations

Pad

Isolated columns that do not support large loads often rest on pad foundations (Fig. 7-6). The size of the pad is based on the size of the applied load compared to the bearing capacity of the soil upon which it rests. For example, if 4 kips (4000 pounds) of load falls on a soil that supports on 1000 pounds per square foot, then a pad footing will need to be at least 4 square feet in bearing surface area. Conceptually the load considered to propagate at about a 45-degree angle from the base of the column (Fig. 7-7). This will give a rough idea of the minimum thickness that the pad should be. If a small strong column carrying a big load rests on very weak soil this angle may imply a very thick pad. Pad on pad may be arranged to save a bit of concrete, or individual members may be assembled into a mat in a similar manner (Fig. 7-8). Pad foundations develop shearing stress in the pad that can result in *punching shear*. This is similar to shoving a pencil through a piece of paper (Fig. 7-9).

Figure 7-6
Pad foundation under an isolated column.

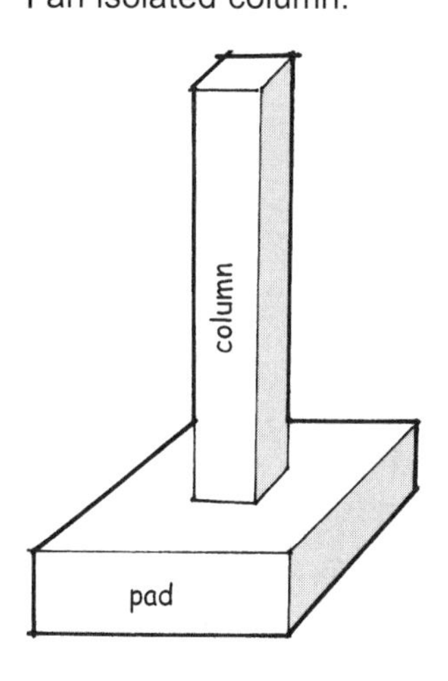

Strip or ribbon.

As bearing wall superstructures, light wood frame buildings often rest on a strip or ribbon foundation. The *stem wall* may rest directly on bedrock if that rock is shallow. This is known as a narrow strip foundation (Fig. 7-10). If rock is deep, then a *ribbon* (or wide strip) *footing* may be placed under the stem wall. The greater the applied load and the weaker the soil, the wider the ribbon must be. Again, the thickness is limited by the 45-degree angle study just discussed. If the ribbon is wider than that, bending and shear similar to that found in beams become a consideration. More will be said on bending and shear during the "beams" chapter later in this text. If *attached pilasters* are

Figure 7-7
Note the 45 degree load propagation.

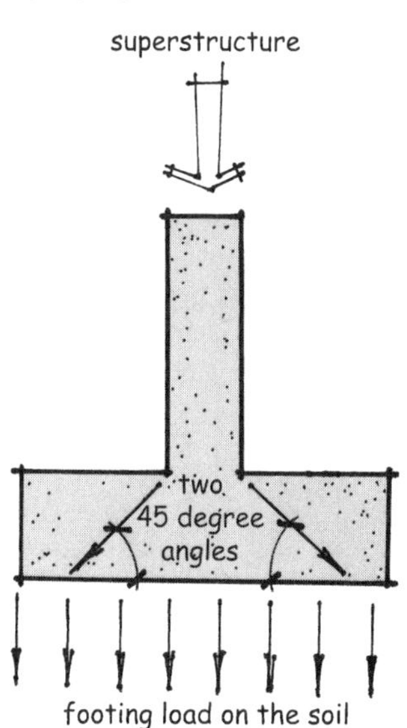

Figure 7-8
Mat type foundation.

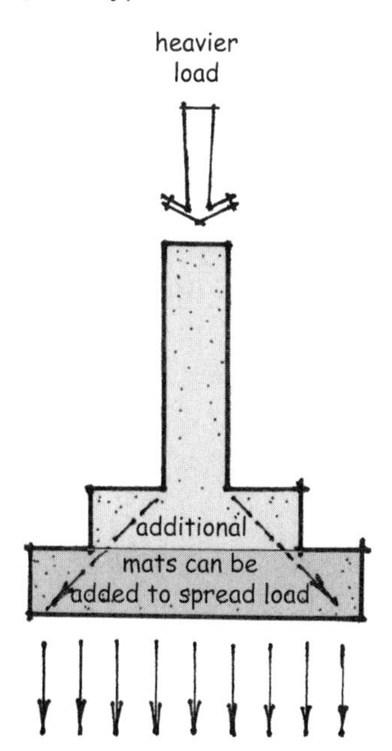

Figure 7-9
A column can "punch" through a foundation.

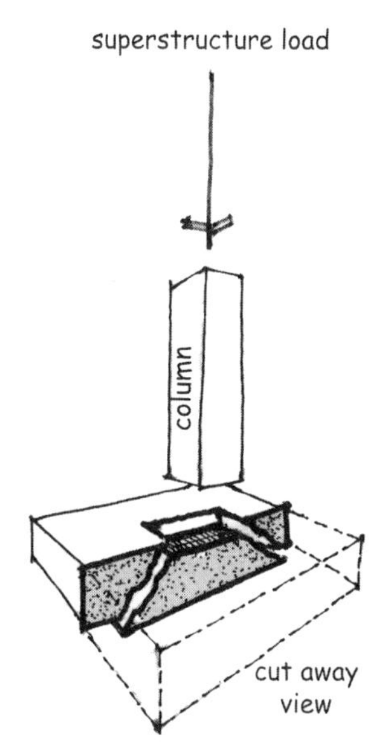

Figure 7-10
Stem wall resting on a ribbon foundation.

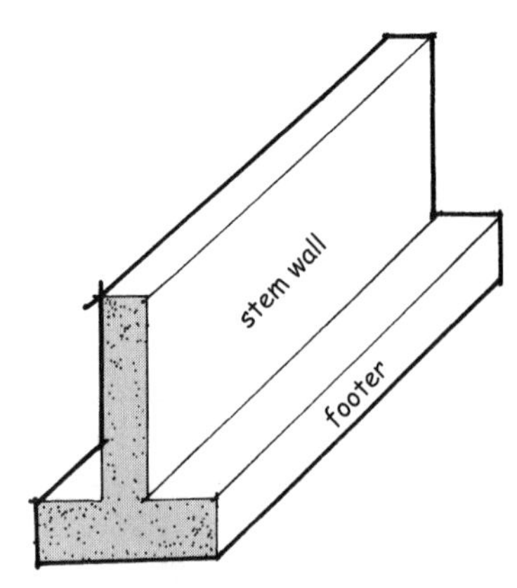

attached to masonry bearing walls of a superstructure, a thickened wide strip foundation will probably be appropriate under the pilaster (Fig. 7-11). In urban settings where buildings are often built right to the property line the ribbon cannot be symmetrically located under a stem wall, so an *"L" shaped* arrangement may become necessary (Fig. 7-12). In situations where both bearing walls and columns are used, it is wise to tie the resulting pads and ribbons together in order to limit differential settlement and potential column rotation (Fig. 7-13).

Slab on grade (raft)

If the building load is distributed across a wide area (i.e., a single story warehouse) a slab-on-grade foundation may well be appropriate (Fig. 7-14). At the edges of the slab, and under any bearing walls, these slabs are normally thickened. It is common to place "engineered fill" (crushed rock) under such slabs. In addition to the other structural roles that this fill plays, it may also break capillary action of water in the soil if that is a local problem.

Buoyant or floating foundation

Just as a boat floats because it displaces water, so a building may also be floated on soil with a high water table. Such sites are common next to rivers. A ratio between the weight of the upper stories of the building, and the displacement by a single story below ground is conceptually significant. Roughly three to five stories above ground might be balanced by one displacing story below grade (Fig. 7-15) (H.Q. Golder within Winterkorn and Fang 1975).

Figure 7-11
Thickened wide strip foundation.

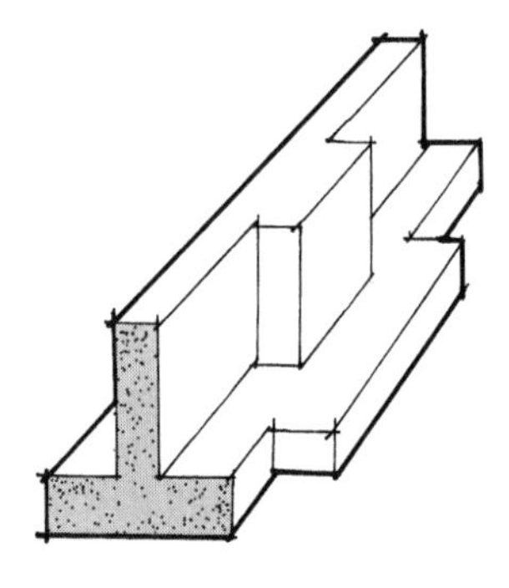

Figure 7-12
An "L" type foundation.

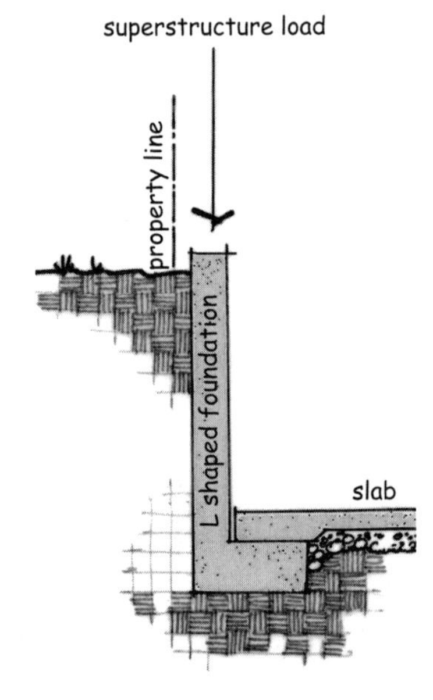

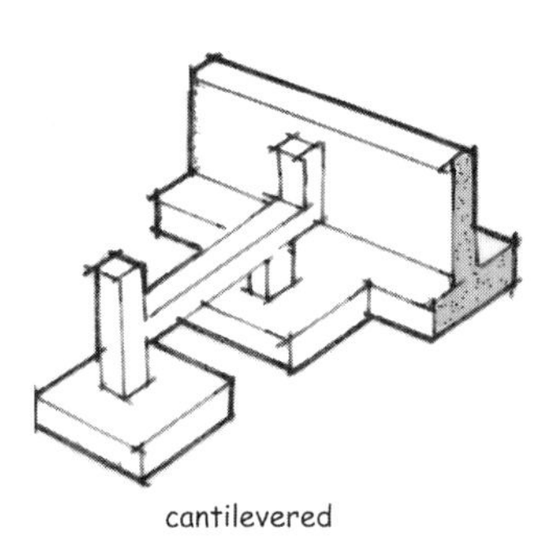

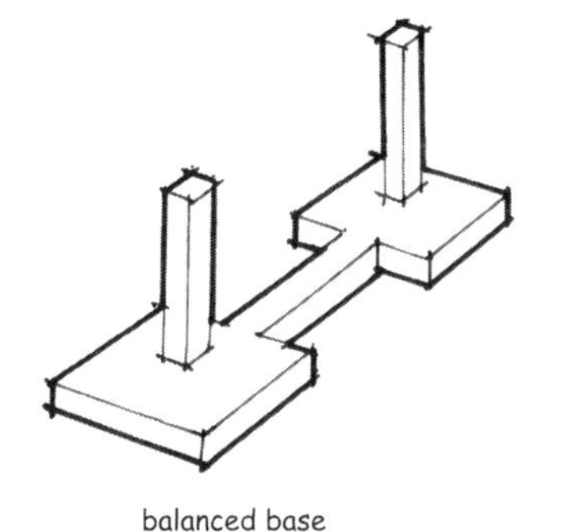

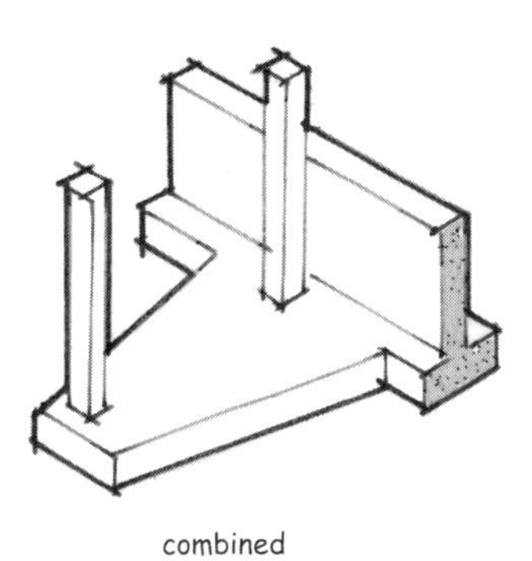

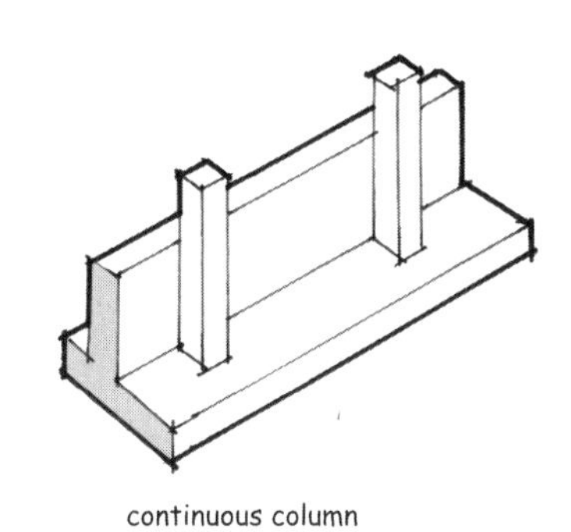

Figure 7-13
Four types of tied foundations (cantilevered, balanced base, combined, & continuous column).

Deep foundations

Piles

Piles are long slender members driven into soil very much as a tent peg. They are used when larger loads must be placed on weak soils such as the mud in port towns like Singapore, the swamps of Louisiana, and the reclaimed land of Holland. Two general types of bearing may be obtained by driving piles. *End bearing piles* are driven through weak overlaying soil (overburden) until they strike, and bear on, bedrock (Fig. 7-16). When the *overburden* is very deep, *skin friction piles* will be used instead of end bearing. Use of a *pile cluster and cap* is likely under heavier applied loads and weaker soils. A cap will be cast on top of the cluster in order to distribute the concentrated load of the superstructure column to all of the piles in the cluster (Fig. 7-17). Vertical piles, even in clusters, have a limited capacity to resist lateral loads. In these situations, *battered piles* may be driven at an angle to increase this capacity (Fig. 7-18).

Figure 7-14
Slab-on-grade (abbreviated SOG).

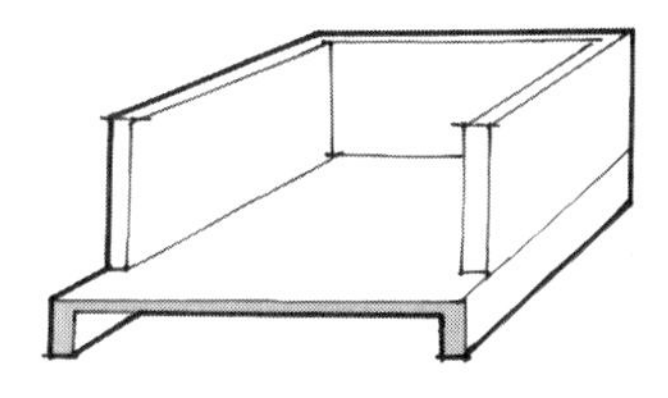

Figure 7-15
Buoyant foundation.

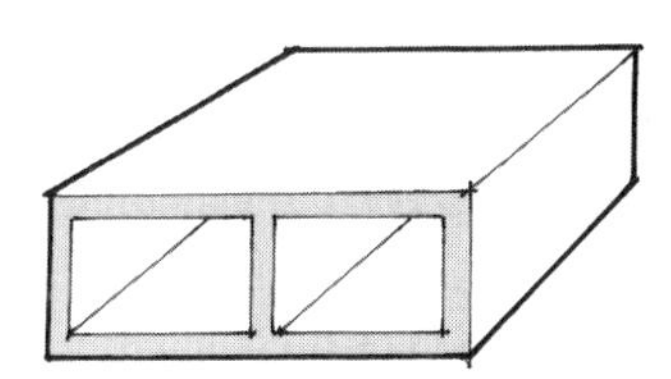

Types of piles A wide range of pile shapes and materials are commercially available. Rolled steel sections such as wide flanges may be used. Metal capped reinforced concrete is also used in conditions such as the volcanic pumice found near the beaches of Hawaii. Pole buildings use round timber that not only acts as foundation, but also as column in the superstructure above ground. Piles may be straight-sided or tapered. They may be smooth or

Figure 7-16
End bearing piles.

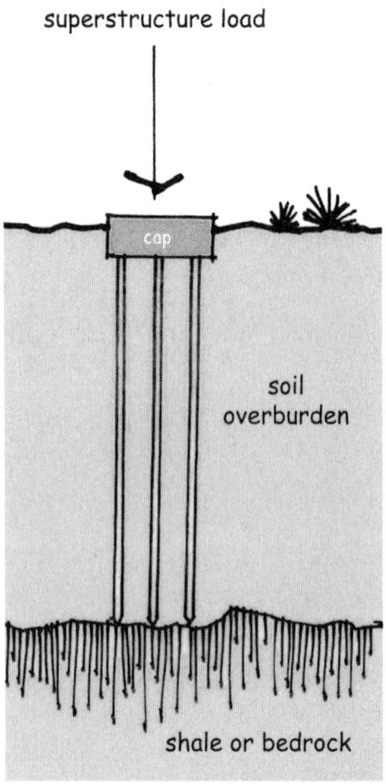

Figure 7-17
Skin friction pile cluster with a pile cap.

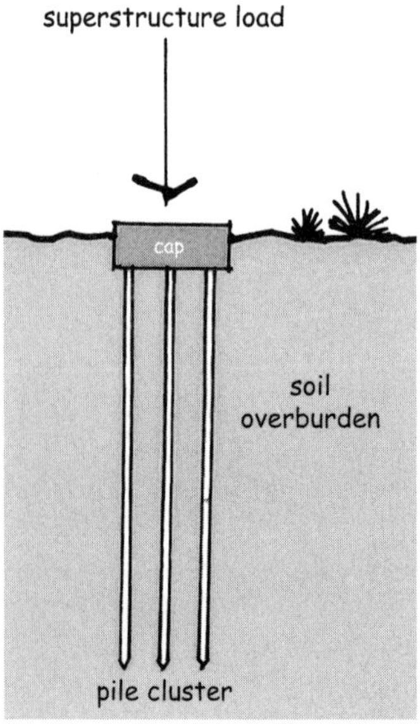

Figure 7-18
Battered piles.

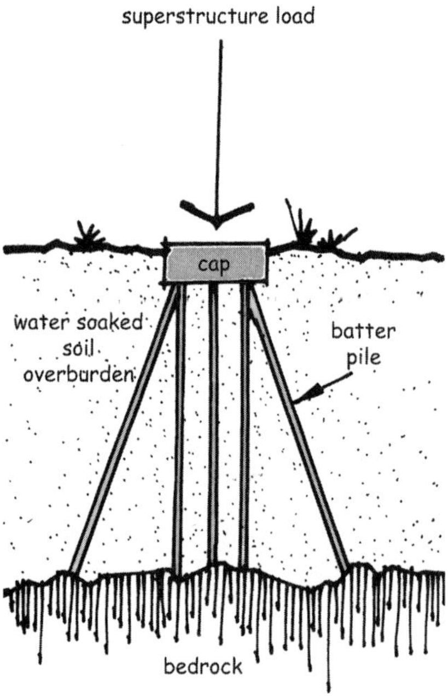

"shouldered" to increase bearing capacity. Usually solid, they may also be hollow sections (Fig. 7-19).

Piers

While piles are driven, piers are *drilled* or *excavated*. Truly large modern buildings will inevitably rest on drilled piers. As early as ancient Rome, piers for bridges and buildings were hand-excavated to receive masonry piers.

Drilled piers Like piles, drilled piers may pass completely through the overburden into a socket in the bedrock below. In some cases the inherent skin friction on the shaft of the pier may be significantly supplemented by broadening the base into a "bell" shape. Like the shallow pad, this *belled pier* gives more bearing area to the end of the pier (Fig. 7-20). This bell can also offer withdrawal resistance that might uproot a pier due to unanticipated overturning forces placed on a very tall building. When a drilled pier is necessary, but high water table will fill the bored hole, a hollow tube called a *caisson* is usually used. The Franki displacement caisson is also an alternative (Fig. 7-21).

Excavated piers Traditionally piers have been excavated by hand or machine. Bridge piers have required a waterproof chamber, access tower, and air lock for workers to enter and exit from their work.

Figure 7-19
Shoulderered pile.

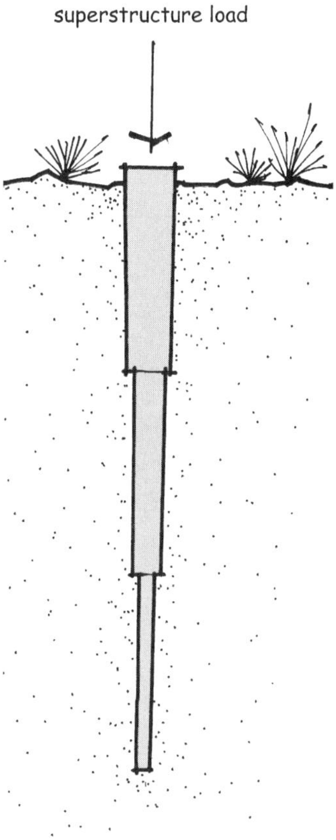

Figure 7-20
Belled pier.

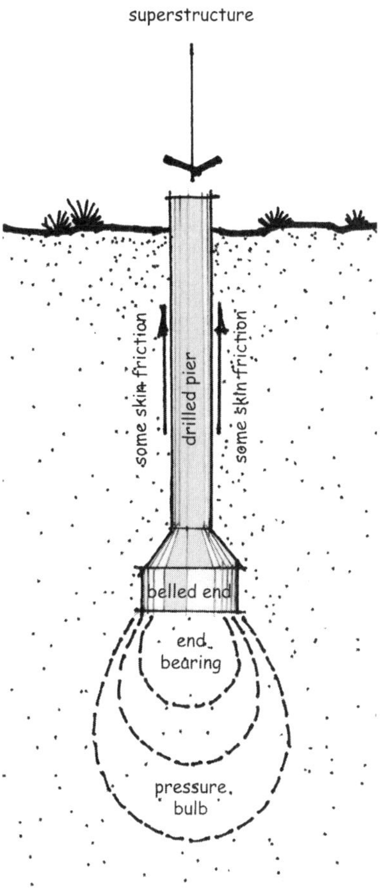

Grade beams Even in post and beam superstructures, walls between columns will also require foundation support. To provide this support a *grade beam* is used to bridge between drilled piers. Due to concern for shrink/swell in clay soils a 4-inch void is usually cast under a grade beam. If the soil swells because of increased ground water, it will not expand enough to fill the void and lift the grade beam (Fig. 7-22).

Moment foundations

In addition to vertical loads, many types of superstructures impart rotational loads to their foundations. This rotational force is known as "moment." Therefore, special *moment-resisting foundations* are needed. Retaining walls are structures whose main role is to resist overturning or sliding due to the

Figure 7-21
Several types of piers.

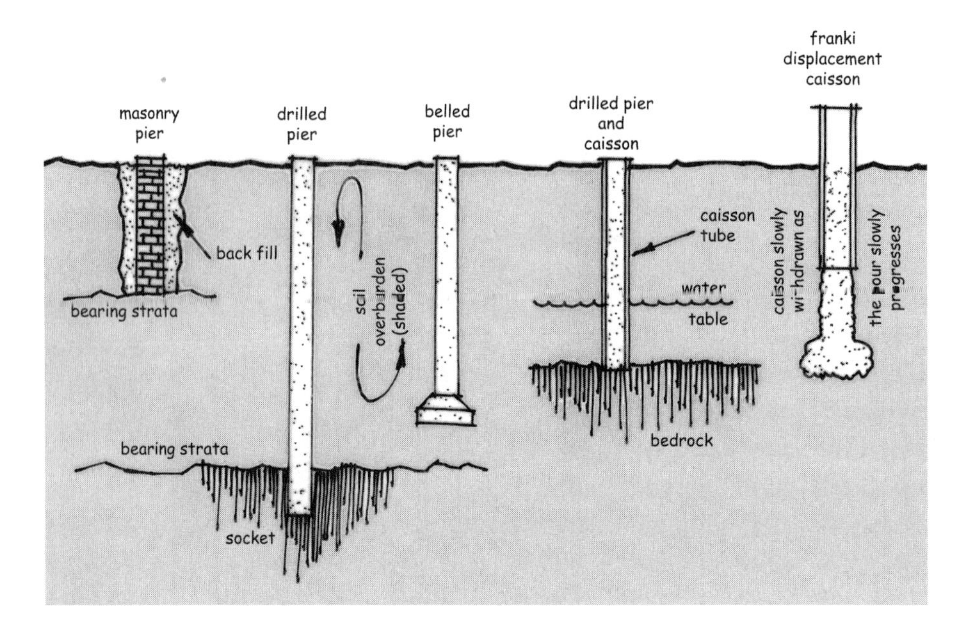

Figure 7-22
Grade beam resting on drilled piers.

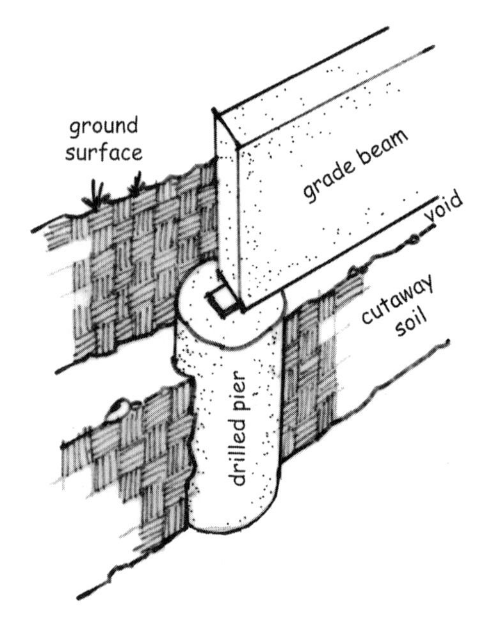

weight of the soil held behind it. Freestanding walls receiving lateral loads from vaults, wind, or earthquakes must also consider this issue. The inherent imbalance of a rigid frame and the lateral thrust of an arch also usually demand moment resistive foundations (Fig. 7-23).

Figure 7-23

Moment foundations are needed where lateral thrust is present.

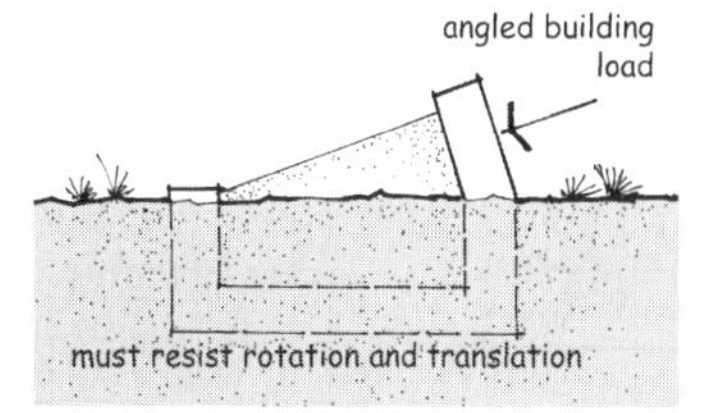

Foundations on slopes

Buildings sited on steep slopes are vulnerable to sliding (translational) instability failures (Fig. 7-24). Just because the surface of the ground is level, does not guarantee that the underlying strata is not sloped. Deep foundations will slide along the top of such sloped bedrock if not *socketed* into bedrock. A common solution for shallow foundations on steep slopes is to *step* them. In general it is best to keep the length (L) of these steps as long as possible, and the height (H) as small as possible. Ambrose offers the following guiding limits in his text "Simplified Design of Building Foundations": Length (L) should be equal to, or less than, three times the height (H) of each step; while the height (H) should be equal to or less than 1.5 times the width (W) of the foundation (Fig. 7-25) (Ambrose 1981).

Figure 7-24

Deep foundation sliding on sloped subsurface strata.

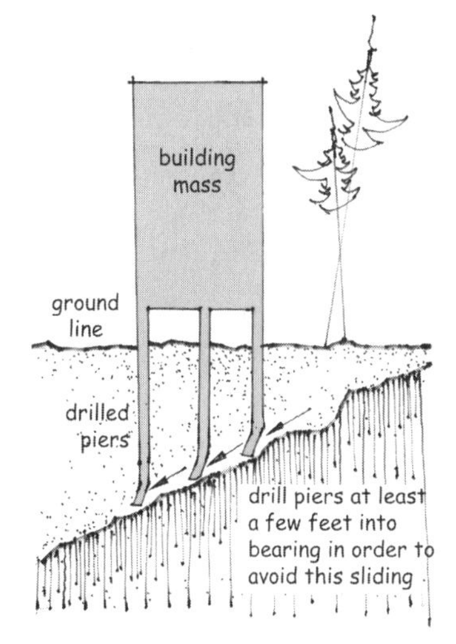

LATERAL LOADS BELOW THE GROUND SURFACE

Beyond the vertical dead weight of the foundation itself, several important loads exist below the surface of the ground.

Frost heave

Statistically the maximum anticipated depth of frost has been developed, and is included in building codes. As water in liquid state freezes into a solid due to frost, it grows in size. This places a powerful lateral thrust on the wall of the foundation, which produces a horizontal crack. In addition, if the footing does not extend at least 6 inches below the frost line, ice may form under the footing. This unfortunate condition will allow the building foundation to be thrust vertically up out of the ground. (Fig. 7-26)

Figure 7-25

Stepped foundation proportions.

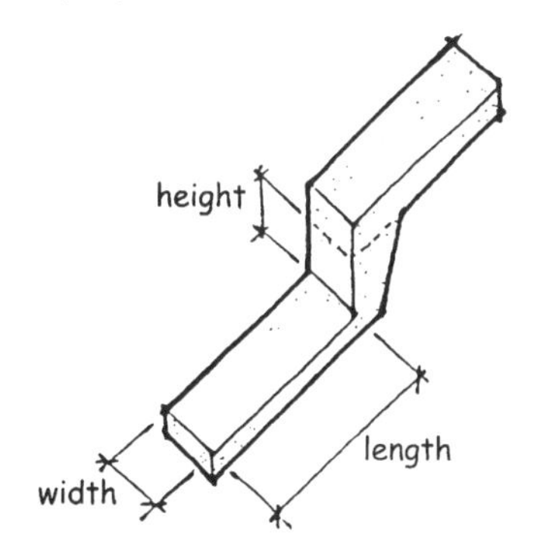

Soil pressure

Much as water behind a dam presses horizontally on the dam, so does soil press laterally against the foundation. This horizontal force tends to force the foundation wall inward. The lateral bracing provided by a basement floor resists the lateral load of the soil pressure, but the upper portion of the wall is not necessarily similarly supported (Fig. 7-27). Just as the pressure against a dam becomes greater with depth, so does soil pressure.

Water pressure

Soil pressure will become worse with the presence of a high water table. This water will lower the internal *angle of friction* in the soil, (causing it to press more against the foundation), and the water itself will cause additional pressure on the foundation wall. So soil pressure and *hydrostatic pressure* are additive. Hydrostatic pressure also increases with depth. The subsurface pressure of soil and water can be shown graphically, and it is essential to note that they are additive (Jensen and Chenowith 1983) (Fig. 7-27).

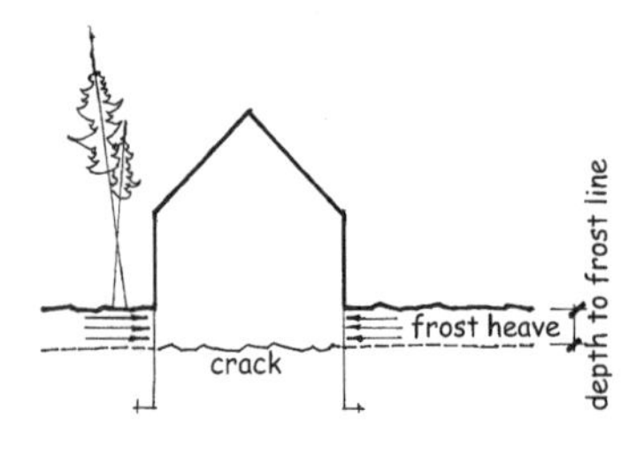

Figure 7-26
Foundation crack resulting from frost heave.

VERTICAL UPLIFT

As previously introduced, a high water table can make the building foundation behave like a boat. Even when not anticipated or desired, subsurface water that is displaced will uplift the foundation of the building (Fig. 7-28). As indicated in the previous chapter on geology and soil, presence of aquifers and springs are largely predictable if adequate soil investigation precedes conceptual design. Their presence should alert a designer to heightened concern for hydrostatic pressure and uplift. Location near rivers and other large bodies of water implies a shallow water table, since a river is actually just the exposed subsurface water table (Fig. 7-29).

Figure 7-27
Soil pressure is like water against a dam.

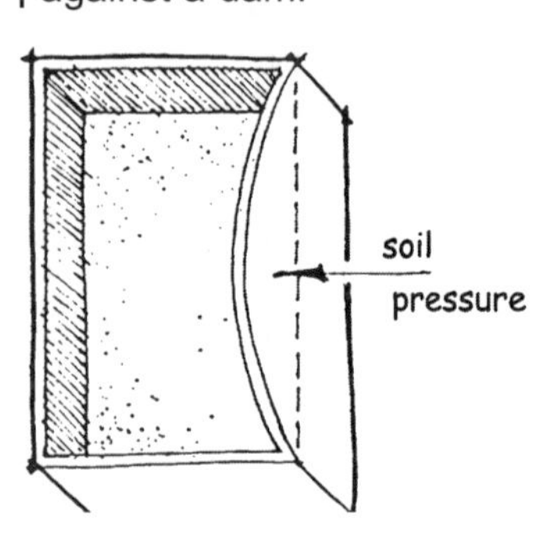

VERTICAL LOAD DISTRIBUTION BELOW FOOTINGS

Whether on shallow or deep foundations, the vertical load imposed on the foundation from the superstructure above must be distributed to the soil around and below the foundation. For example, a *pressure bulb* develops under a foundation pad (Fig. 7-30). The shape of the pressure bulb varies in different soil types. The force that it distributes to the soil varies with the depth below the pad. The pressure radiates from this bulb downward below the bulb, laterally

Figure 7-28
Hydrostatic pressure can uplift a foundation.

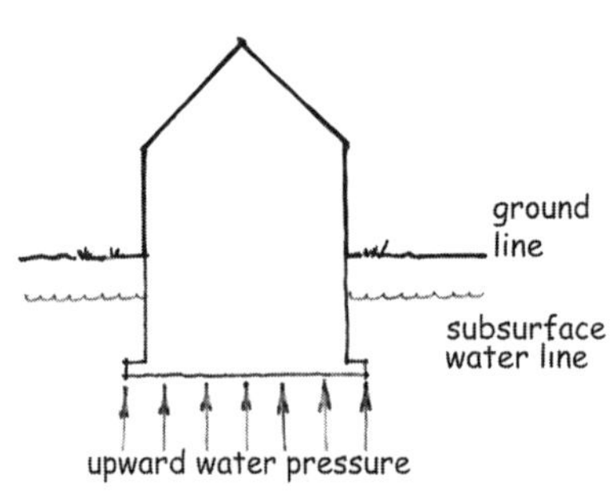

Figure 7-29
Expect high water table near rivers.

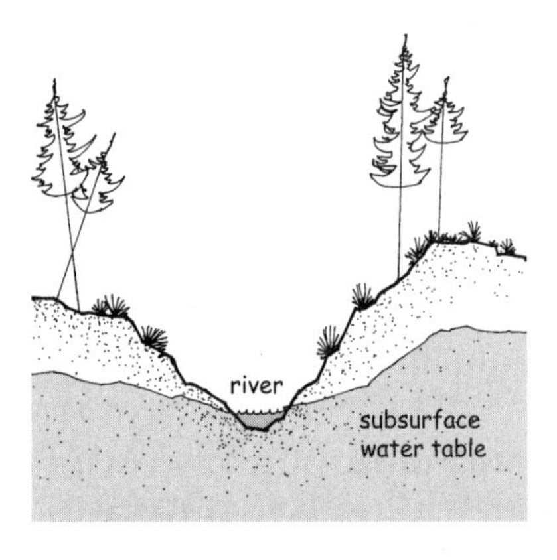

Figure 7-30
Pressure bulb under a pad foundation.

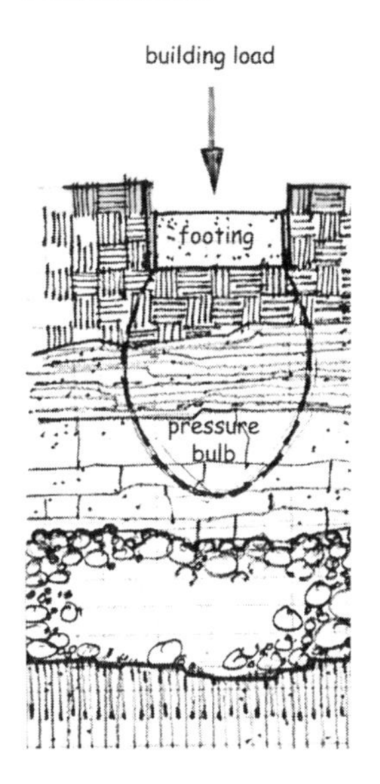

Figure 7-31
Soil shear and displacement.

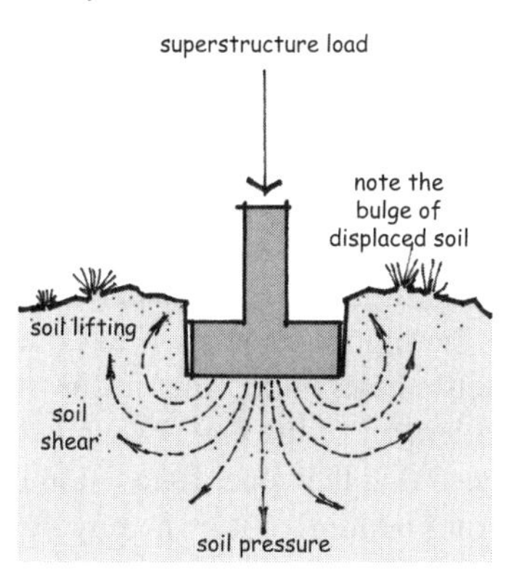

Figure 7-32
Pressure varies with depth under the pad.

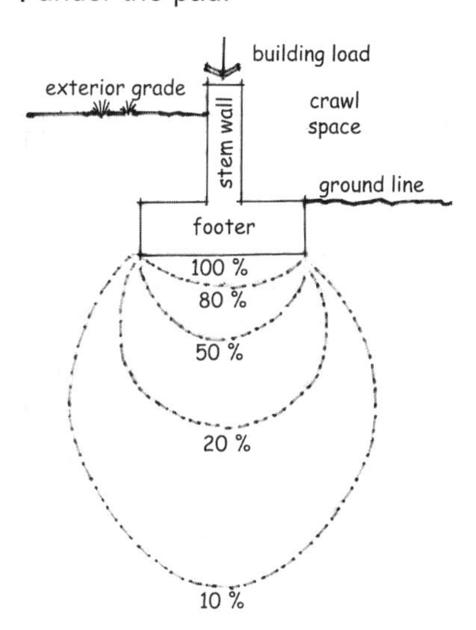

next to the bulb, and even upward adjacent to the footing. As the foundation is pressed downward, soil is displaced, bearing and shear develops in the soil, as the weight of adjacent soil actually resists movement of the footing (Fig. 7-31). Displacement of soil under the footing causes soil to bulge up adjacent to the foundation. This pressure bulb reaches down through various underlying types of bearing materials. The percentage of load distributed varies with depth (Fig. 7-32). The wider the pad, the deeper the forces reach into the soil (Faber and Johnson) (Fig. 7-33).

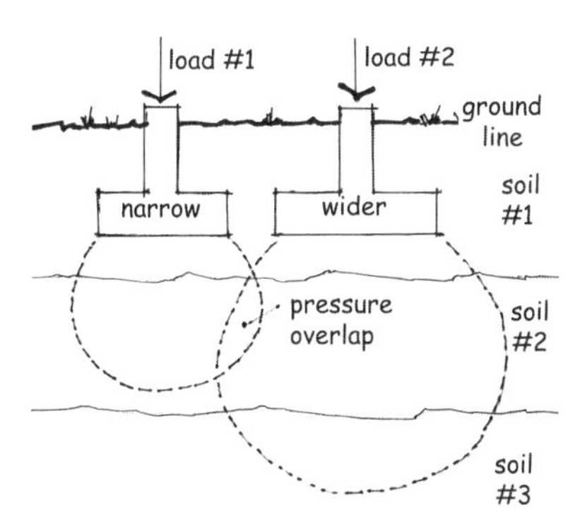

Figure 7-33
Depth of the bulb varies with the area of the pad.

Figure 7-34
Lateral thrust from a higher foundation.

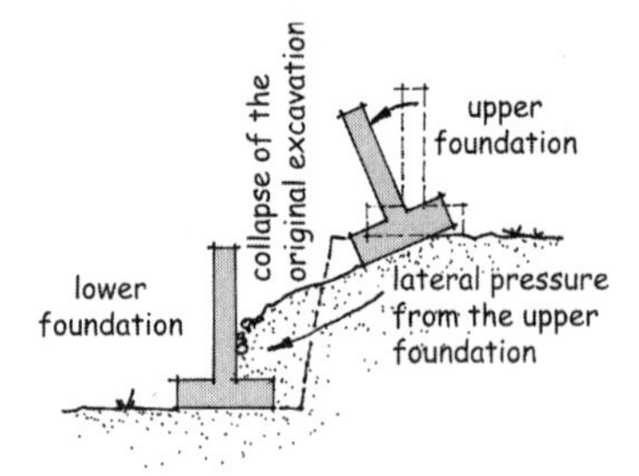

ADJACENT FOUNDATIONS

Care needs to be exercised in locating footings close together. Aside from the construction inconvenience that may result, the pressure bulbs may overlap generating stress concentrations. When adjacent footings bear at different levels, a number of difficulties must be understood conceptually. The pressure bulb from the higher footing may exert lateral thrust on the lower foundation (Fig. 7-34). The excavation for the lower footing may undermine the upper foundation (Fig. 7-35). The soil under the upper footing may fail causing both the soil and the higher foundation to collapse against the lower foundation. Excessive settlement under the lower foundation may similarly lead to increased settlement of the higher foundation (Fig. 7-36). The reader is especially cautioned that the upper foundation in these failures often belongs to an already existing building not owned by your client. If even one of these failures occurs, it will probably be accompanied by particularly ugly litigation. For that reason, shoring and underpinning are normally necessary conceptual considerations (Ambrose 1981).

SHORING AND UNDERPINNING

Underpinning puts additional vertical support under an existing foundation, while *shoring* usually refers to additional lateral support. Both are usually temporary during construction, but they may be remedial if the original design was inadequate. The loss of soil support due to construction activities, overloaded soil, eccentric loading of a foundation, excessive or differential settlement, drop in the level of the water table, and foundation failure such as a sheared drilled pier are common reasons for such support (Edward E. White within Winterkorn and Fang 1975).

Figure 7-35
Undermining.

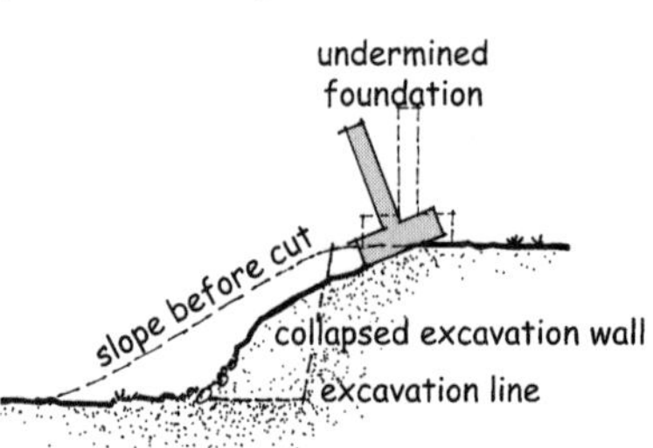

Figure 7-36
Excessive settlement may be contagious.

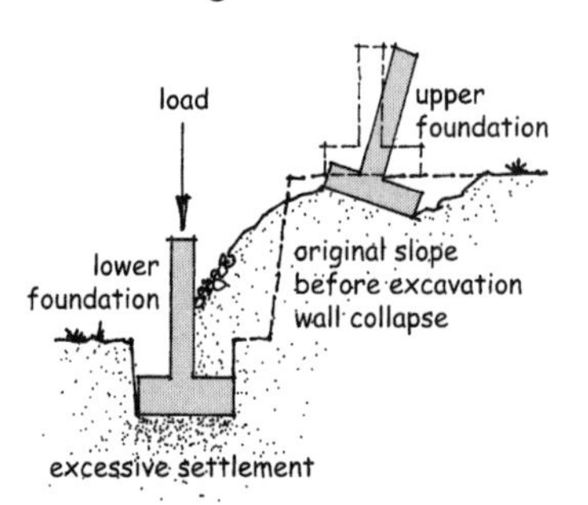

EXCAVATIONS

During excavation it is often necessary to shore up the adjacent property. If the excavated area is sufficiently narrow, one side may be braced against the opposite side. However, this type of bracing can obstruct movement in the bottom of the excavation (Fig. 7-37). When the walls of an excavation are successfully shored, the unsupported bare earth floor of the excavation may bulge upward (Fig.7-38). In wider excavations, diagonal bracing may be employed, or *tiebacks* may be drilled into the soil that lies behind the shoring. In more permanent installations *sheet piles* may also be assisted by the use of tiebacks (Fig. 7-39). With or without temporary shoring, the presence of heavy equipment at the rim of the excavation *surcharges* the soil in a way that must be anticipated. This behavior is similar to adjacent foundations at different levels discussed above. Surcharging will be further discussed in a subsequent paragraph addressing retaining walls. The collapse of trenches is a common danger during construction. Suffocation under the slumped soil in a trench takes place so rapidly that rescue is often unsuccessful even when conducted immediately, and with urgency. *Dewatering* of excavations by pumping may be needed in excavations after rainstorms, or may have to be continuous when springs appear in the walls or floor of an excavation (Fig. 7-40). While this is necessary for construction operations, it often reduces groundwater in properties adjacent to the excavation, which can lead to excessive settlement of existing buildings (Carson 1965).

Figure 7-37

Bracing was elevated so that it would not obstruct other operations in this Singapore construction site.

Figure 7-38

The floor of an excavation may be forced upward.

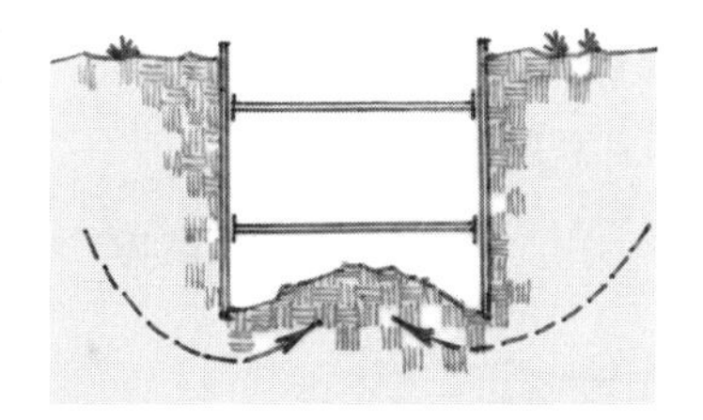

Figure 7-39

Tiebacks were used to support shoring in this Kuala Lumpur construction excavation.

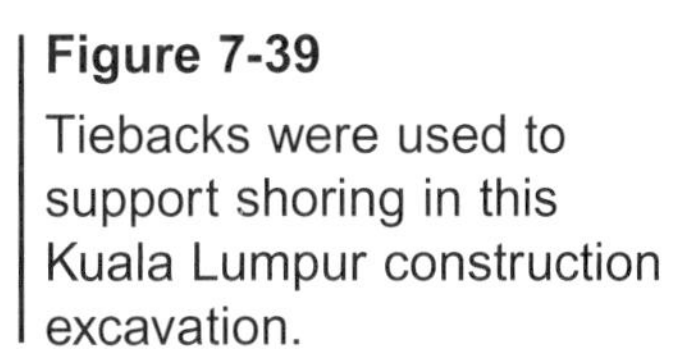

Figure 7-40

Strong continuous dewatering during excavation at a site on the Thames river in London.

SLOPES

Slope stability

When the *angle of repose* for a soil is exceeded, the threat of landslides is immediate. Bengt B. Broms (Winterkorn and Fang 1975) identifies four general types of slides. When the face of a slope peels away, it is known as a *fall* (Fig. 7-41). *Rotational slides* result from slumping of a slope in which the top of the slope collapses downward and the base is thrust up and outward (Fig. 7-42). *Multiple rotational slides* may also develop (Fig. 7-43). *Translational slides* result from weak planes in the soil nearly parallel to the surface of the soil on a slope (Fig. 7-44). *Flow slides* occur when the soil mass becomes liquid. This is also called a mudslide (Fig. 7-45).

Respect existing slopes

In conceptual design, don't change existing slopes if they are stable (Fig. 7-46). If you must increase an existing slope above the angle of repose (discussed in the last chapter) then some retaining method will be required. Lesser methods include terracing and the use of riprap. Riprap is fairly large (6-10 inch) broken rock. While it has some retaining potential, its primary purpose is to prevent erosion (Fig. 7-47).

Figure 7-41
Earth collapse known as a "fall".

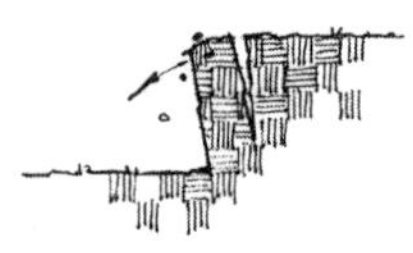

Figure 7-42
Rotational slides often occur with slopes are cut to too steep an angle.

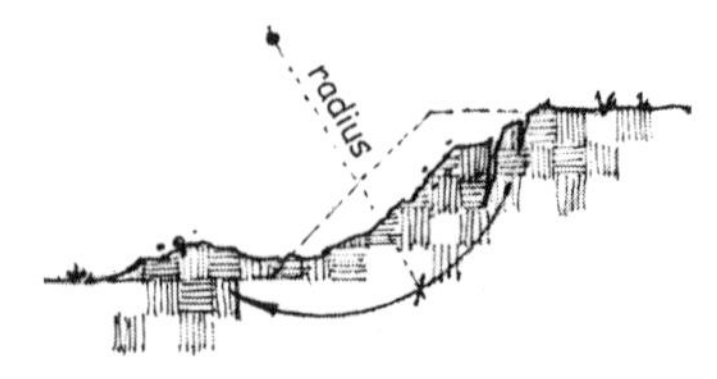

Figure 7-43
Multiple rotational slides are possible.

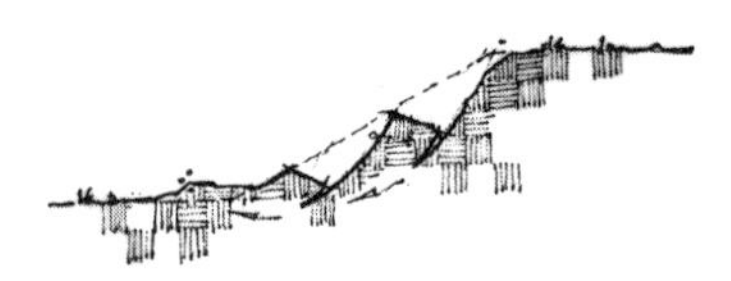

Figure 7-44
Subsurface strata can encourage translational slides.

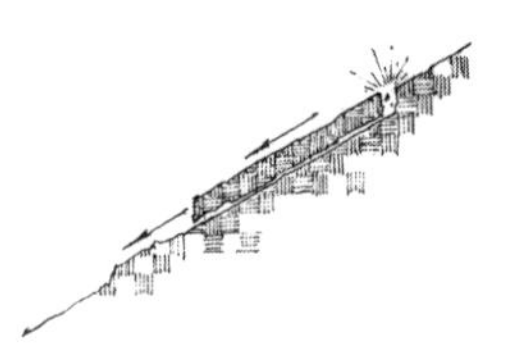

Figure 7-45
Flow slides are commonly called mudslides.

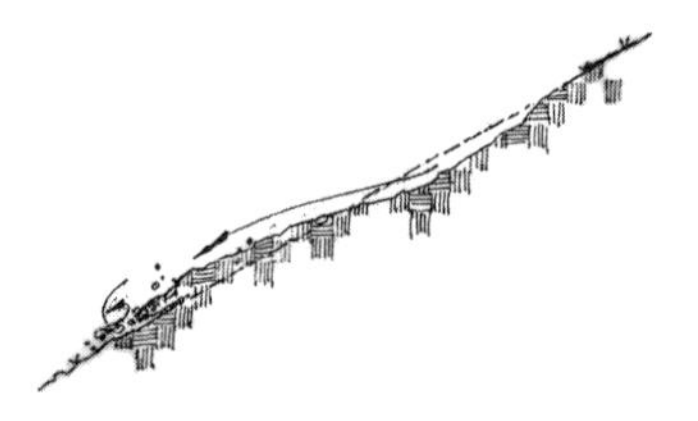

Figure 7-46
Earth slides are common on the coast highway in Santa Monica California.

notice the slide
area behind
& to the left
of the
building

Figure 7-47
A rip-rap covered slope used to resist wave erosion as well as to retain this slope in Rotterdam Holland.

Retaining walls

Given enough time, all retaining structures will fail eventually. For this reason, we avoid them when other options are available. If unavoidable, they are limited to two feet in height. If that is not possible, then higher walls will be used. The higher they are, the more they cost, and the more failure prone they become. Commonly used retaining structures include *cribbing, sheet pile bulkheads*, and various types of *retaining walls* (Fig. 7-48).

Retaining walls are divided into three general types:

1. *Gravity walls* rely on the raw mass of the wall material to resist the thrust of the soil (Fig. 7-49).
2. *Cantilever retaining walls* are more economical in material than gravity walls, and use the weight of the retained soil itself to resist the lateral thrust. They are constructed in two basic configurations: L-type and T-type (Fig. 7-50).
3. *Counterfort walls* are necessary for high retaining walls. They have vertical webs perpendicular to the face of the wall (Fig. 7-51).

Retaining walls usually have granulated fill (gravel) placed behind the wall. These enhance the drainage of the retained soil through regularly spaced weep holes. *Soil capping* and *interdiction trenches* may be used to eliminate entry of water into the soil behind the retaining wall (Fig. 7-52). If the retained soil is sloped upward behind the wall, this *surcharge* increases the pressure behind the wall (Fig. 7-53). Other heavy loads behind the wall such as buildings or construction equipment can have the same effect (Fig. 7-54).

Figure 7-48

An example of a sheet pile bulkhead.

note the interlocking nature of
sheet piles in the forground

Figure 7-49

Gravity walls use a lot of material.

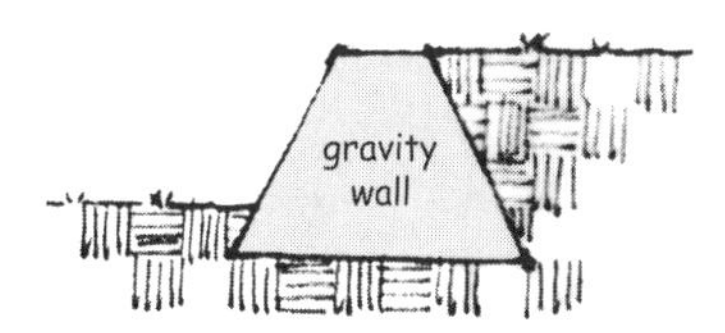

Figure 7-51

If you need a counterfort wall you may be making a significant conceptual error in your design thinking.

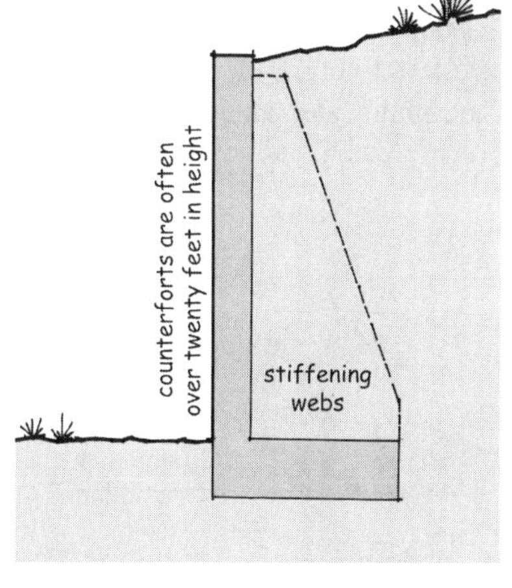

Figure 7-50

Cantilever walls are the most common type of retaining wall.

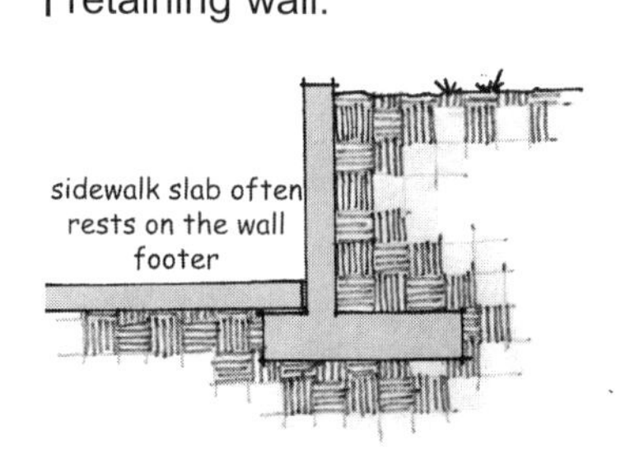

Figure 7-52

It is good to keep surface water out from behind a retaining wall.

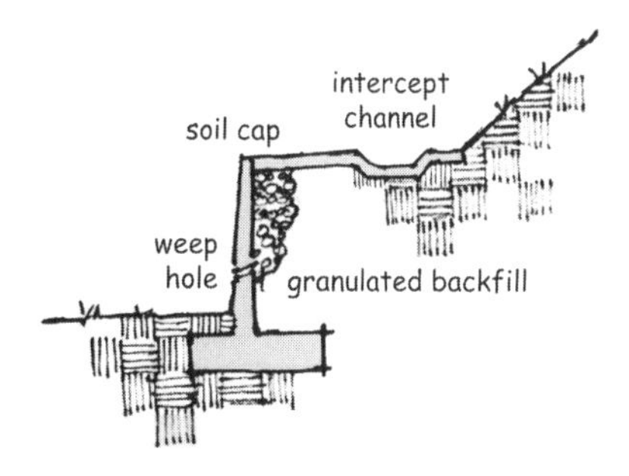

Figure 7-53
Surcharge should also be avoided if possible.

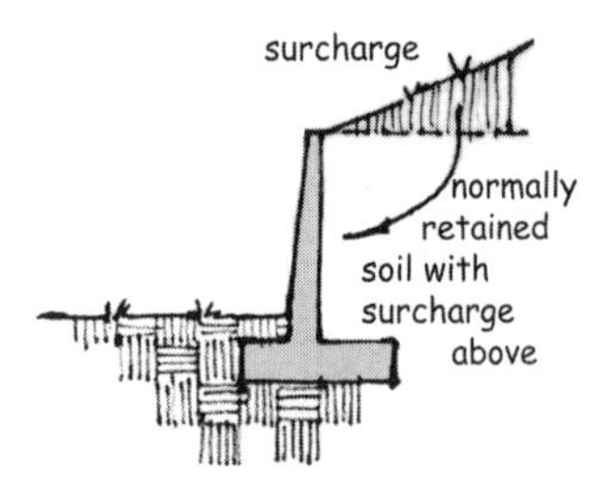

Figure 7-54
Buildings and equipment can also surcharge a retaining wall.

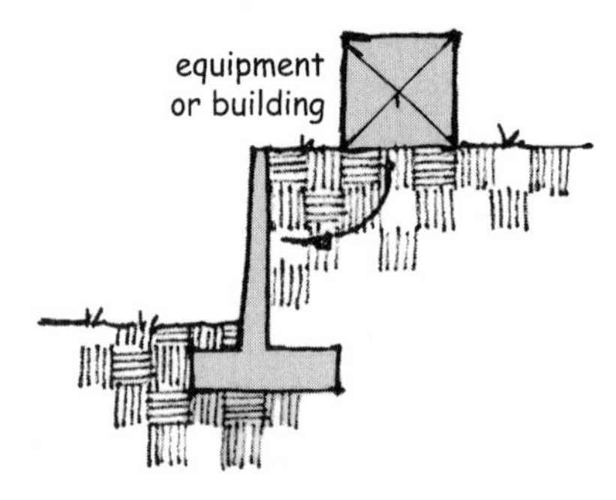

Figure 7-55
Retaining wall failing in translation.

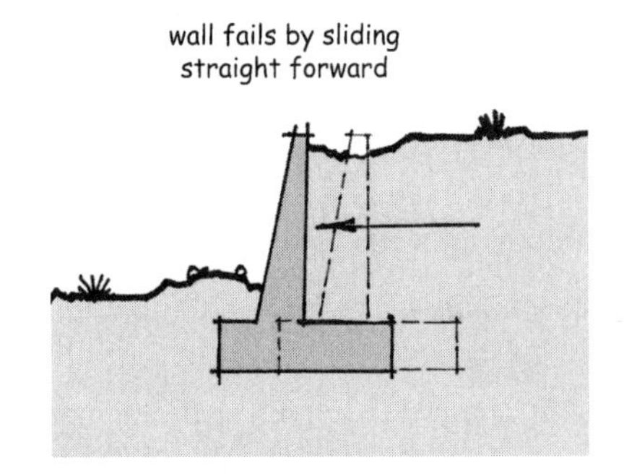

Figure 7-56
An overturning failure of a retaining wall.

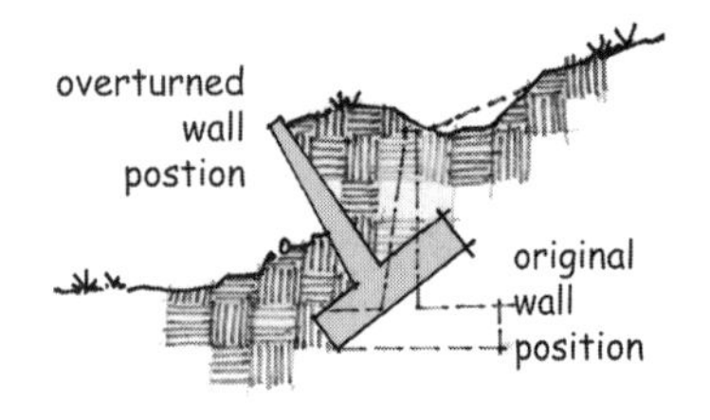

Retaining wall failures

While retaining walls may fail in both strength and stiffness, stability failures are by far the most common threat. These stability failures take many forms. In a *translation* failure the horizontal thrust of the retained soil simply pushes the wall outward in a straight line (Fig. 7-55). If the wall is too heavy, has adequate friction at the base, or is otherwise restrained at the base from sliding; the thrust of the retained soil may cause the wall to rotate in an *overturning* failure (Fig. 7-56). Another type of rotational failure involves a *rotational slide* of the soil under retaining wall (Fig. 7-57). Excessive pressure on the toe of the retaining wall may also cause an overturning failure of the wall (Teng 1962) (Fig. 7-58).

Bulkheads and cofferdams

In ports and harbors retaining structures may become necessary. *Bulkheads* consist of *steel sheet piling* being driven vertically into the soil (Fig. 7-59). *High bulkheads* use *tiebacks* and *deadman* arrangements to provide additional lateral restraint (Fig. 7-60). Knowing that soils next to large bodies of water often have high water tables, such sheet piling may also have to resist the lateral

Figure 7-57
Rotational slide under a retaining wall.

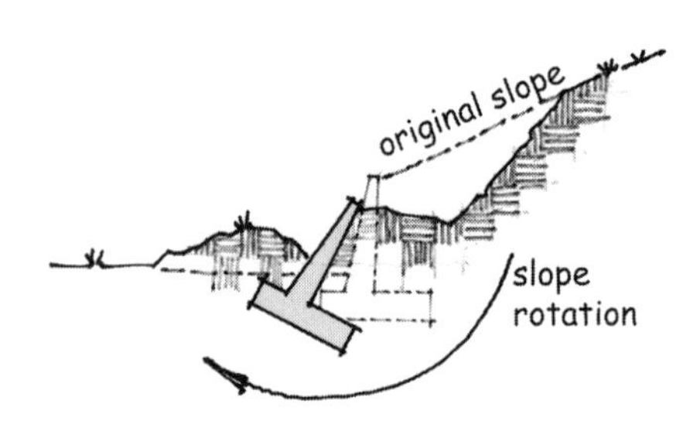

Figure 7-58
Bearing failure of the soil under the toe of a retaining wall will behave like the leaning tower of Pisa.

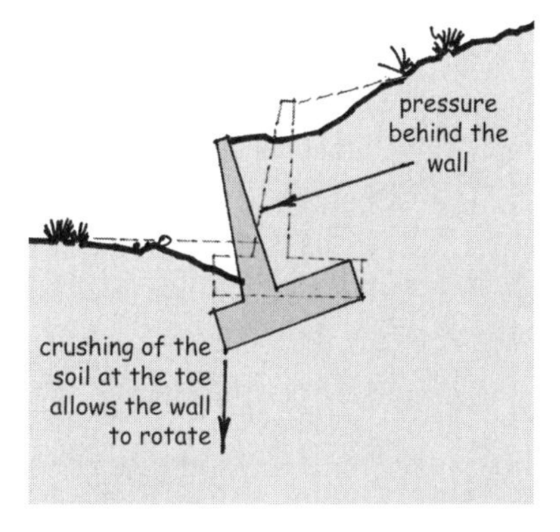

Figure 7-59
Bulkheads during excavation in Singapore.

hydrostatic pressure from behind the wall. When pressure behind the wall is sufficiently increased a *tie rod and anchor block* may need to be used (Fig. 7-61). Two retaining walls can sometimes provide mutual support to each other using either tie rods or braces, it is known as a *cofferdam*. (G.M. Cornfield within Winterkorn and Fang 1975) (Fig. 7-62).

Figure 7-60
Bulkhead with a tieback.

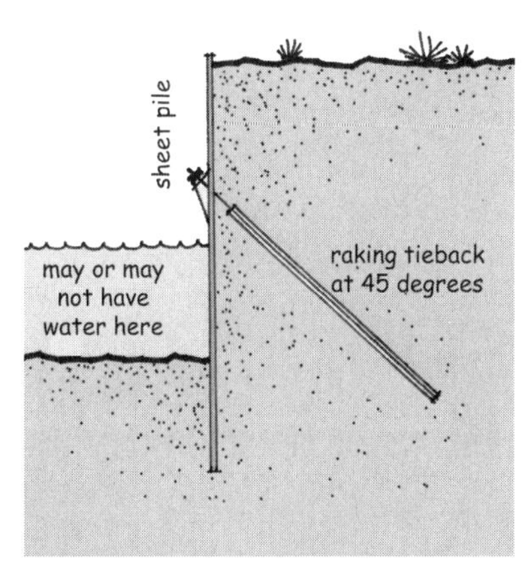

Figure 7-61
Bulkhead with an anchor block.

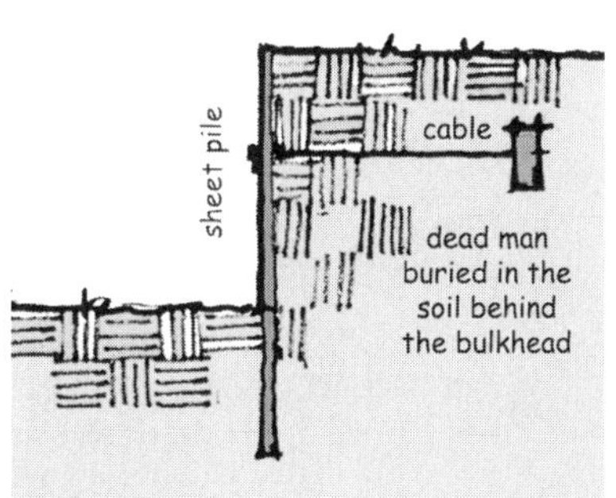

Figure 7-62
Two walls that are mutually supporting are called a cofferdam.

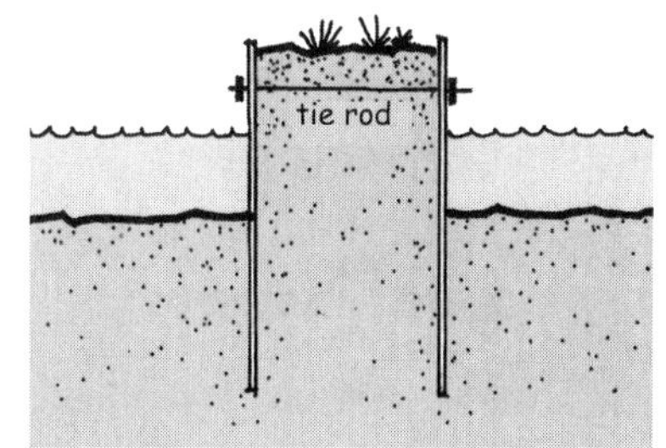

Vocabulary		
Caissons	Soil pressure	Moment foundation
Stepped footing	Stem wall	Frost heave
Hydrostatic uplift	Pressure bulb	Skin friction
Lacing	Braces	Lagging
Sheet piles	Cofferdam	Gravity wall
Cantilevered wall	Counterfort	Surcharge
Flow slide	Translational slide	Rotational slide
Wales	Grade beam	Sheet Piles

REVIEW QUESTIONS

1. What is the structural role of the foundation?
2. Draw the common alternative shallow foundations and verbally describe the circumstances in which each is appropriate.
3. Draw the common alternative deep foundations and verbally describe the circumstances when each is appropriate.
4. What is a buoyant foundation, and how does it work?
5. How does a pile cluster and cap transmit loads?
6. What are the differences between piers and piles?
7. What are some of the common problems caused by adjacent footing at different levels?
8. What are some common reasons for underpinning?
9. Draw a typical single wall cofferdam held back with braces within the excavation.
10. List three general types of landslides.
11. Verbally and graphically describe three types of instability failures common to retaining walls.
12. Why do retaining walls have weep holes?

Figure 8-1
Pedestrian bridge in Bilbao Spain by Santiago Calatrava.

8 Cable Structures

GENERAL

Cable systems are among the most efficient of structural systems available to a designer. As we begin to study the many alternative types of superstructures currently available to the designer, we must also begin to more fully explore the types of stress that are acting within them. (Remember that stresses were briefly introduced in an earlier chapter.) In this chapter the reader will not only explore cable type superstructures, but also members under tension (*tensile stress*). In many ways tension is the simplest of all stresses but perhaps the most important. Cable systems make the flow of forces within them directly visible. These reasons make cable systems a good starting point.

HISTORY AND SIGNIFICANT EXAMPLES

Examples in nature

The best examples of cable systems in nature are to be found in the garden. Spider webs respond directly and uniquely to the site in which they are spun. Although conceptually based on a single idealized pattern, the same spider will spin a unique web in every different setting (Fig. 8-2). That web will be stable in three dimensions, remarkably economical, light, and strong. Human exploitation of these great cable builders is still incomplete even with the advent of steel. This is particularly true in the relatively naïve erection procedures used by humans, when compared to spiders.

Figure 8-2
Every spider web is unique.

Non-building examples

At the small scale, musical instruments such as harps, and strung sports equipment such as tennis rackets offer potentially useful cable design lessons. Much of the nomenclature, operational theory, and early knowledge from which cable structures evolved were based on the rigging of early sailing vessels. Primitive bridges, ladders, and lifting mechanism were made of natural fiber ropes even during the primitive prehistoric period. Later in the industrial age, steel cable structures have been used for long span bridges such as the Hungerford Bridge in London by Lifschutz Davidson and the WSP Group (Fig. 8-3).

Figure 8-3
Hungerford Bridge in London.

Building examples

One of the most significant cable structures in the ancient world was the covering over the Coliseum in classical Rome. More modern examples of cable structures include the West Coast Office Building in Vancouver, the new Flower Market in Pescia, Italy, and the Federal Reserve Bank in Minneapolis (Fig. 8-4). Notice the sag of the cable expressed on the skin of the building.

Figure 8-4
The cable sag is expressed on the façade.

BEHAVIOR UNDER LOAD

Stresses

Under load, cables only experience simple tensile stress (tension). Bending, shear, and other stresses are not normally significant in them. Before introducing the great variety of cable systems that have already been evolved by designers, it is probably best to first study the action of a single cable under various loads. Loads in cable systems are concentrated into the narrow lines of, and made visible by, the cables. Cables *span* between supports in forming a roof or making a bridge. The amount that the cable hangs downward is called its *sag*. The supports at the ends of the cable are known as its *reactions*. These reactions act as *vectors* (discussed in an earlier chapter). That part of the reaction which is pulling upward is called its *vertical component,* while the part that is pulling horizontally is known as its *horizontal component.*

Response by changing shape

What is conceptually important at this time is to notice that as the sag decreases, the vertical component of the reaction decreases, and the horizontal component increases (Fig. 8-5). Also as the sag in a cable is increased, tension in the cable is relaxed. Pulling increasingly harder on both ends of the cable causes the sag to decrease and the cable to approach being a horizontal line. It will never quite reach that condition in the physical world, since the tension would have to reach infinity for the cable to do that. Instead, it will break first. Note that cable systems respond to changes in loads and changes in reactions by changing shape. Therefore, cable systems are inherently unstable. Factors that influence the shape of a cable system under load are the number, location, and magnitude of the loads; the sag, and tension in the cable; and the elevation of the reactions (Fig. 8-6). These ideal cable configurations are called *funicular* curves (meaning "ropelike"). When uniformly loaded, a cable will assume a centenary or parabolic funicular curve (shown in figure 8-4 above). When

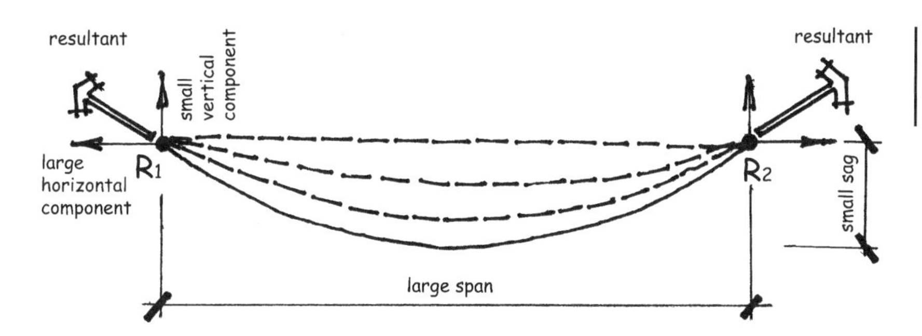

Figure 8-5
All of the sag can never be pulled from a cable.

loading a cable, an optimum curve is the one that will use the least material (and should therefore cost the least). The volume of material required is due to two dimensions: the cable length, and the cable thickness. As sag is reduced the length of the cable is also reduced; however, the tension in the cable increases. This means that while the cable gets shorter, the diameter of the cable gets thicker. At the optimum cable curve these two conditions find their most economical balance.

Figure 8-6
Cables respond to load by changing shape.

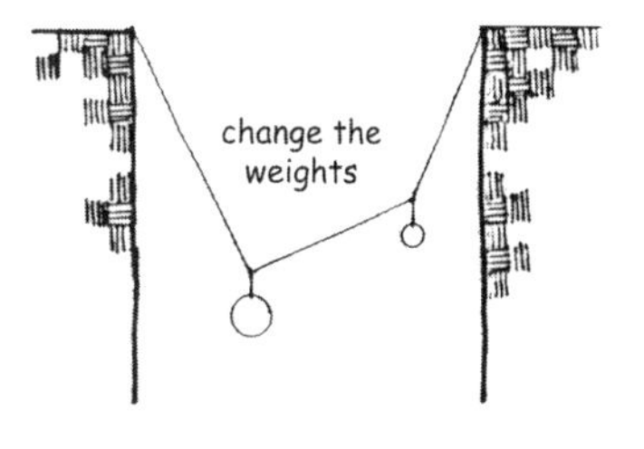

and

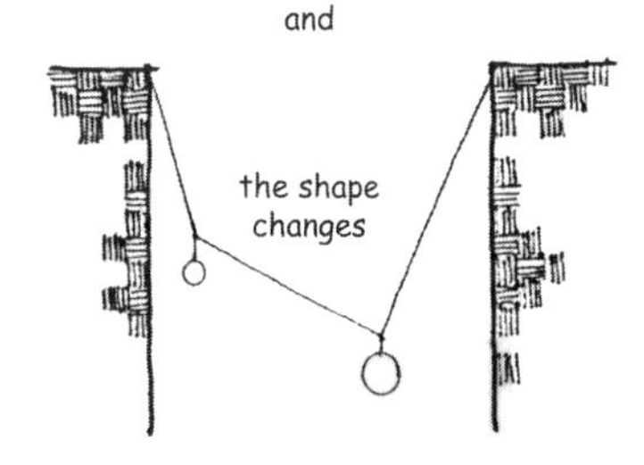

Resolving inherent instability

The inherent instability of cable systems causes them to be particularly vulnerable to wind. Being light, thin, and flexible, they are subject to *uplift*, *vibration*, and *lateral movement.* In order to stabilize cable systems, some form of *prestressing* (initial tensioning) is used. If the load on the cable is sufficient, the placement of this mass may be sufficient in itself to provide at least some stability (Fig. 8-7). Bridges often attach the suspending cables (called *suspenders*) to girders, trusses, or box sections that form the roadway (Fig. 8-8). Note that box sections (Fig. 8-9) can also resist torsion. This stress played a significant role in the famous collapse of the Tacoma Bridge. Stabilization or counter-cables can also be introduced. Such *stabilization cables* may be either perpendicular (Fig. 8-10), parallel (Fig. 8-11), or parallel planar (Fig. 8-12).

Figure 8-7
Cables can be stiffened by loading.

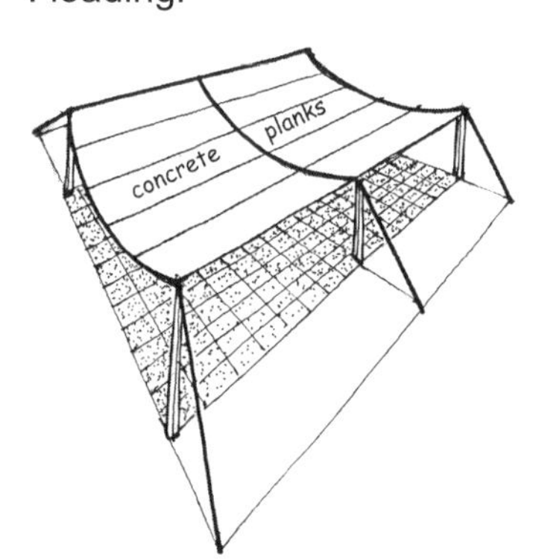

Figure 8-8
The road bed is suspended from the cable system.

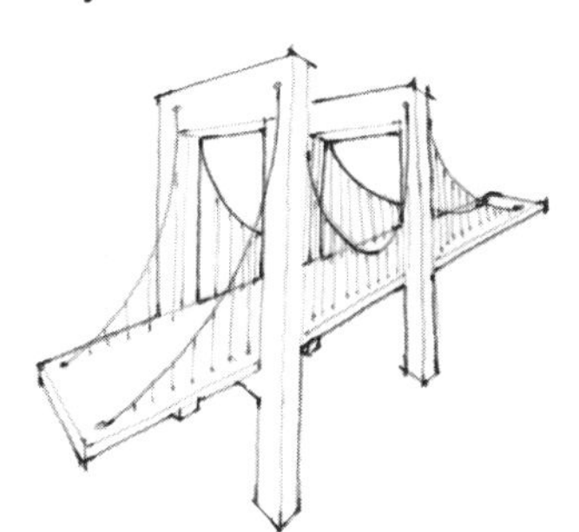

Figure 8-9
The suspended box section gives lateral stiffness.

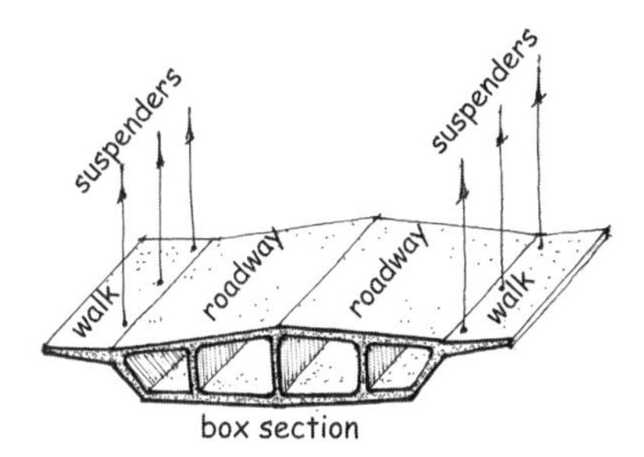

Figure 8-10
Perpendicular cables.

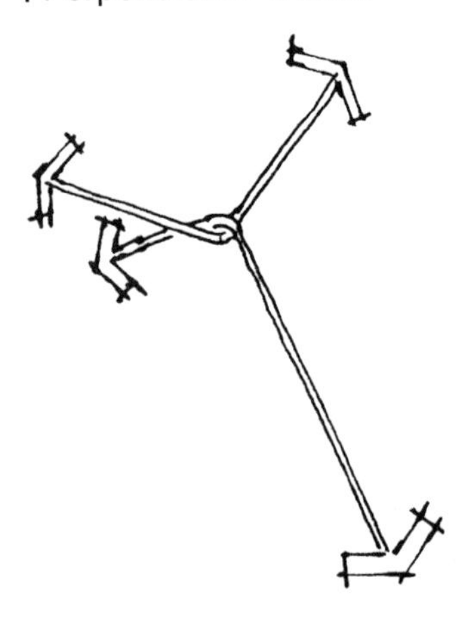

Figure 8-11
Parallel cables.

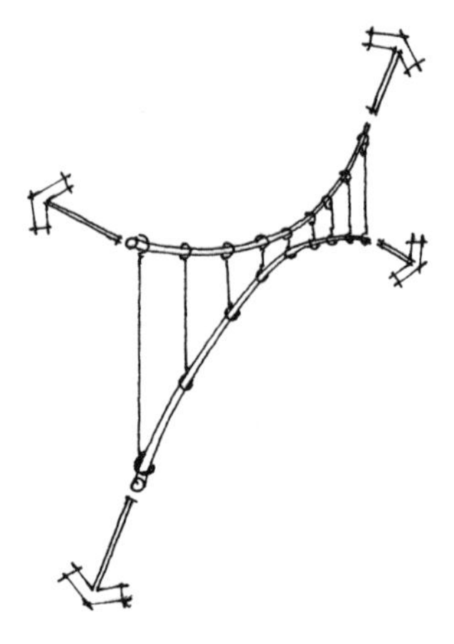

Figure 8-12
Parallel planar cables.

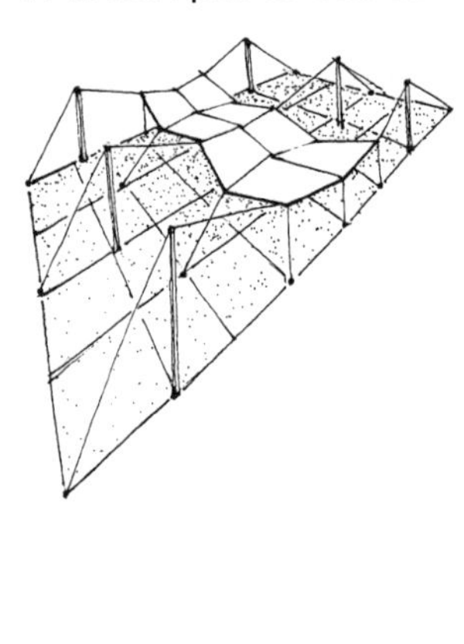

Figure 8-13
Masts are often made of several columns to accommodate other members.

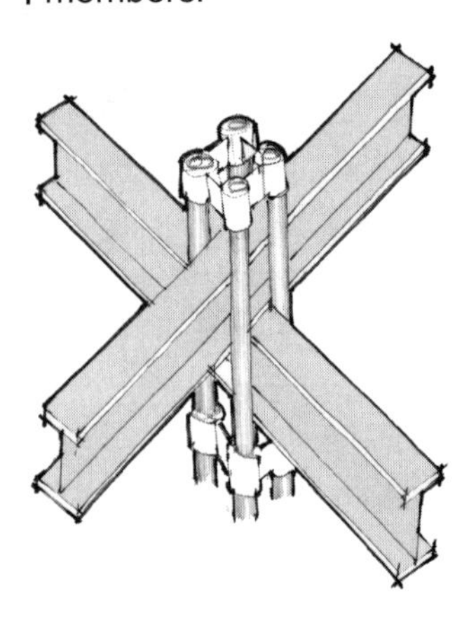

METHOD OF SUPPORT

Cables and cable networks can be supported in a variety of ways.

1. Support by *mast* (Fig. 8-13).
2. Support by *edge beam* (Fig. 8-14).
3. Support by *edge buttresses* (Fig. 8-15).
4. Support by *edge cable* (Fig. 8-16).
5. Support at the center by *pylon*. Note that pylons can provide some lateral support to cable systems (Fig. 8-17).
6. Various forms of *rigid edges* such as arches can simultaneously provide both support for the cable net, and stability (Fig. 8-18).

Figure 8-14
Edge beams are insufficient in themselves to provide stability.

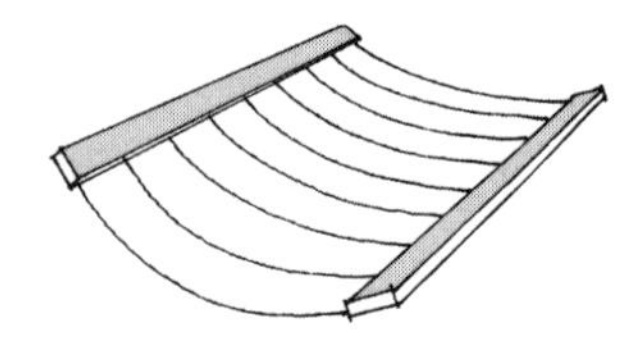

Figure 8-15
This type of support was used at the Dulles Airport in Washington DC.

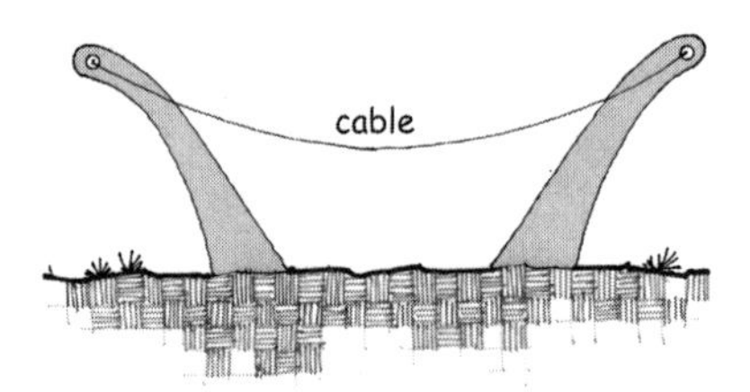

Figure 8-16
Use of edge cables usually implies a warped membrane.

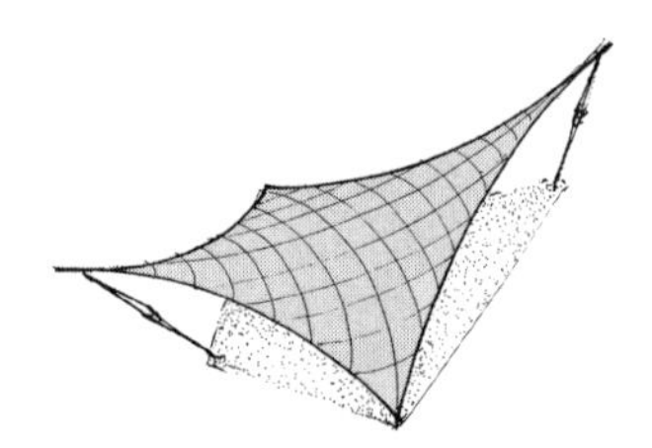

Figure 8-17
A variety of pylons are used to support suspension bridges.

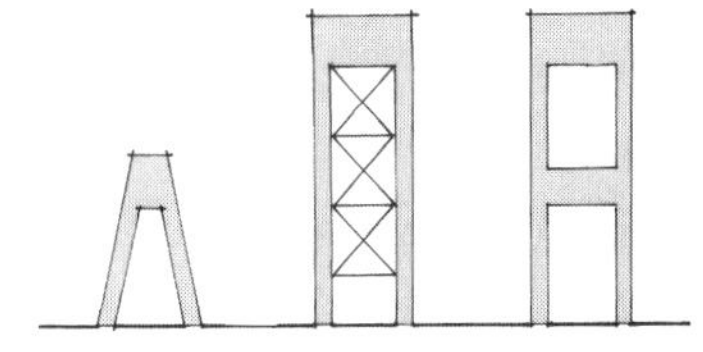

Figure 8-18
Rigid edges have been used at the Yale Hockey arena and in other configurations.

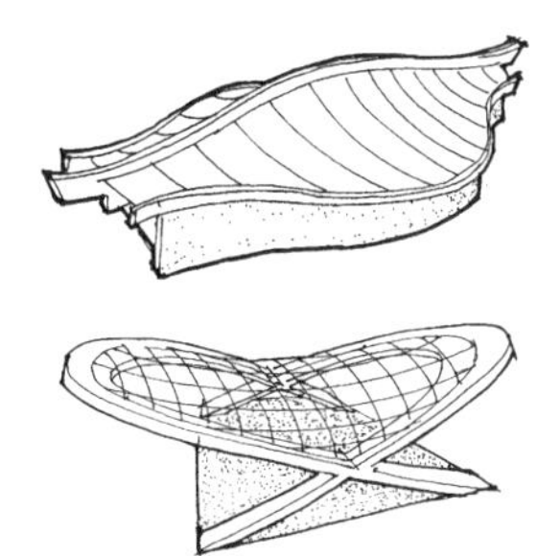

CABLE ARRANGEMENTS

Figure 8-19
Growth by translation (notice the counter-cable stabilization).

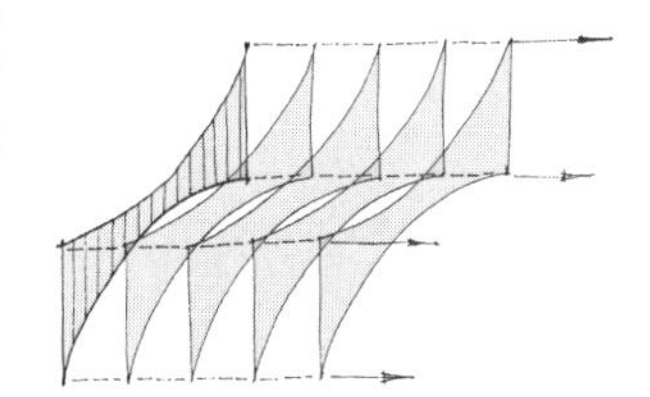

Stabilized cable systems may grow in either linear (translational) arrangements, or circular (rotational) arrangements. Cable systems in *translational* arrangements may have stabilization by planar counter cables, or parallel plane counter cables, but both must be stabilized in the perpendicular axis by some other means (Fig. 8-19). Pre-stressing beams is one such method that will be subsequently discussed (Fig. 8-20).

Planar stabilized cables may also grow in *rotation*. Several types are available, but the sag type (Fig. 8-21), and the bicycle wheel type (Fig. 8-22), are among the most common. Rotational cable systems are inherently more stable in three dimensions than translational cable systems.

Figure 8-20
Use of prestressing beams for growth in translation.

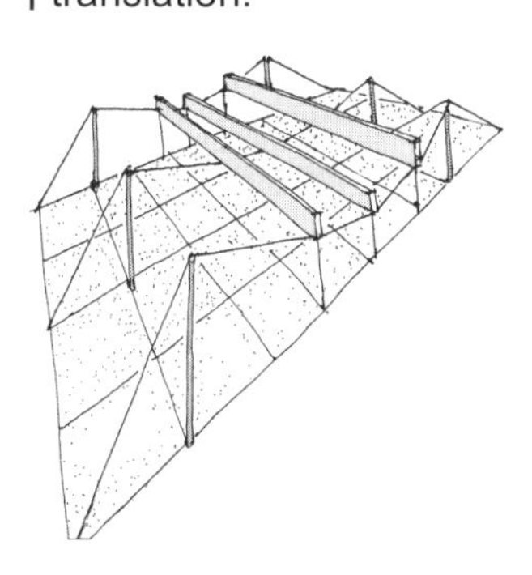

FAILURES

Although cable systems may fail by uprooting anchors, the most common concern is for uplift and harmonic oscillation. The failure of the Tacoma Bridge is

Figure 8-21
Rotational growth of a sag type system.

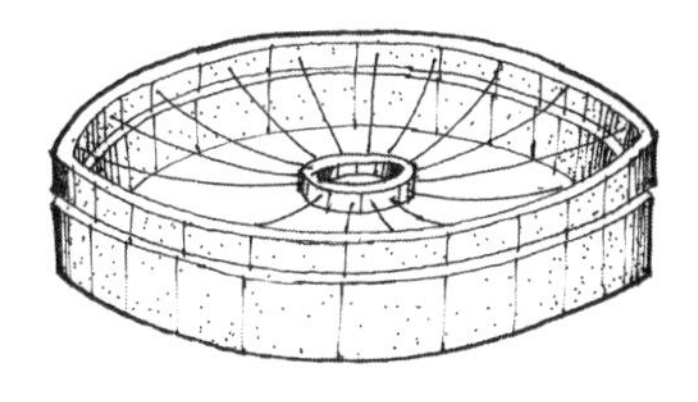

Figure 8-22
Bicycle system.

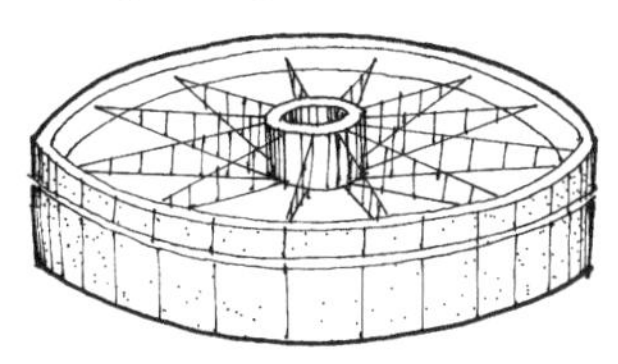

Figure 8-23
Tacoma bridge failure.

the most famous example of this type of failure. Adequate weight and stiffening are common responses to this threat (Fig. 8-23).

OPTIMUM CONFIGURATION

Types or categories

Since it has been necessary to describe alternative forms of support, stabilization, and form growth for cable systems, it will come as no surprise to the reader to find that these also form the basis for categorizing cable systems. Selection of an appropriate system is based in part on the functional footprint inherently implied by each system.

Functional footprint

Translational cable nets grow into rectangles. Rotational cable systems shelter a circular functional area below. Cable nets can be made to cover very irregular footprints as well. As cable nets become a very dense web, they grow into tent type structures (which will be covered in a later chapter). The Munich Olympic stadium will be covered at that time, but it could have equally been considered to be a cable structure. Cable structure footprints are big.

Span range

Spans from 150 feet up to about 2500 feet are possible with cable systems. Optimum sag to span ratios are in the range of 1:3 or 3:10; however, these are usually impractical. Therefore, a sag to span ratio of about 1:15 is more commonly used. For example, a cable structure stadium roof spanning approximately 500 feet would require a practical sag of about 34 feet. Notice that sight lines and roof drainage are an issue with such sag roofs (Schodek 1980).

NOMENCLATURE

Cable supported frames

Cables can be used to support a system of girders and beams, or slabs. Such slabs may become a wide range of shapes given an adequate number of cables, and appropriately located supports. If mast support is provided at the center, it is best to locate such masts at the *centroid* (center of mass) of the slab shape that the cables will be required to support (Fig. 8-24). Lateral support cables may also be extended on outriggers from the masts (Fig. 8-25). Wherever cable stayed girders are found, the supporting cables may have several alternative arrangements (Fig. 8-26). Similarly, several alternative forms can be used for pre-stressed stabilizing cables (Fig. 8-26). In these arrangements, the *top cable* is known as the primary cable, the lower is called the *stabilizing cable*, or

Figure 8-24
Mast carrying a cable supported frame with external guying.

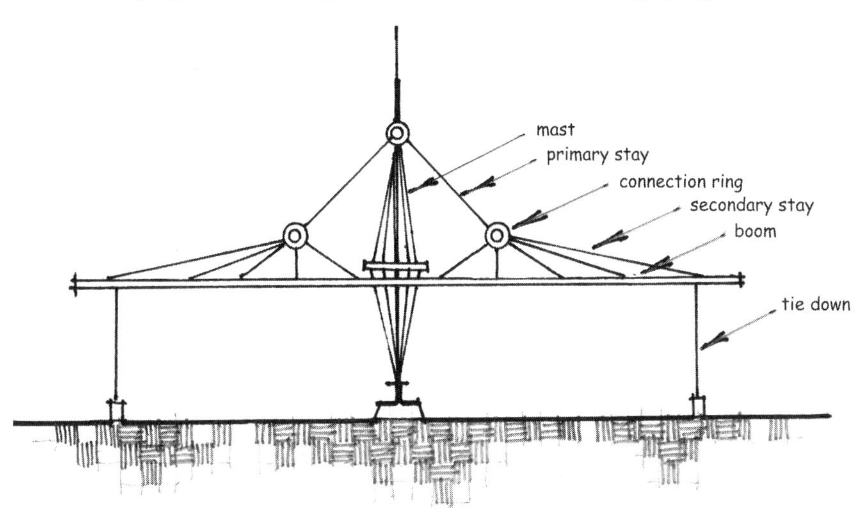

Figure 8-25
Cables used to stabilize outriggers.

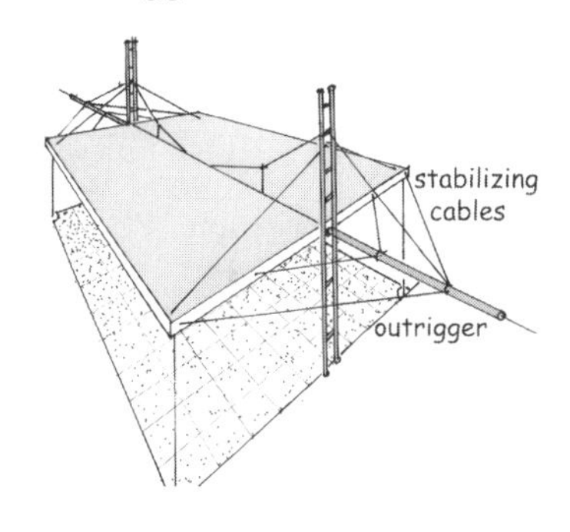

Figure 8-26
Alternative stabilizing cable arrangements.

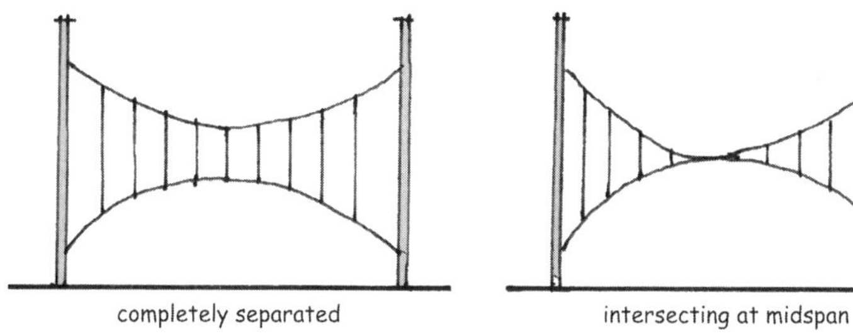

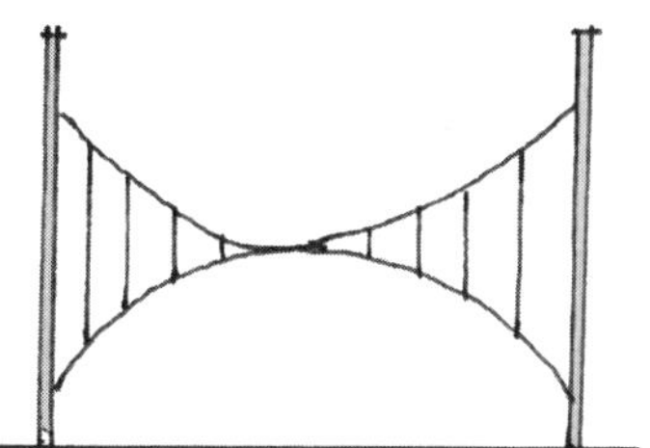

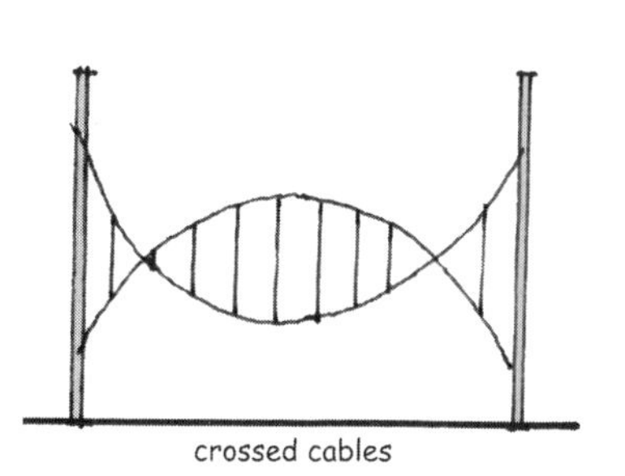

intersecting at supports

counter cable. If the members between these two cables are in compression, they are known as *spreaders*. If they are in tension they are sometimes known as *suspenders*. It is possible to use diagonal cables between. These configurations are known as *cable trusses*. The stability offered by cable trusses is not significantly more than planar systems with parallel suspenders. Therefore, they are fairly rare.

PATTERN OF GROWTH

Figure 8-27
An overlapping method of growth.

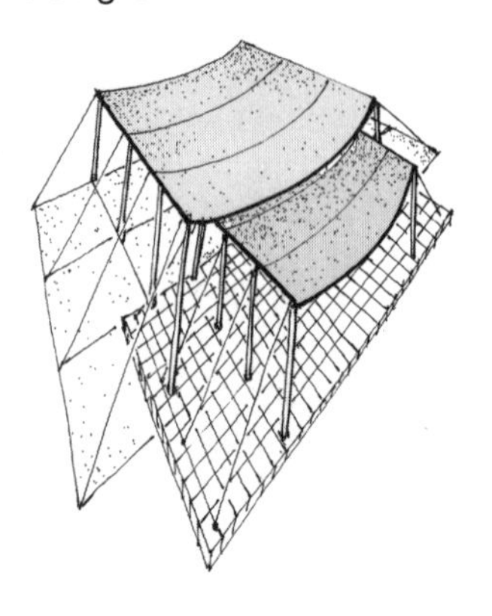

When a building project succeeds, the building is often forced to "grow". Some structural systems do this with greater ease than others. Even if the system can grow, the particular manner in which it accomplishes this growth is unique to each system. If a cable system is asked to grow, simply attaching additional cables to an existing mast or cable net will inevitably cause the existing structure to change shape. (Remember that cable systems change shape when loads are changed.) Additional three-dimensional counterbalancing cable would have to be added to counterbalance the forces of any new cables attached to an existing system. For this reason a new separate system may be located directly adjacent to the old. If necessary the new system may be developed in a different, but overlapping plane (Fig. 8-27).

CABLE SYSTEM DESIGN

Advantages

Cable superstructures are exceedingly economical in their use of material. Their joints generally require relatively little training or skill. The extreme spans, of which cable systems are capable, often make them the only structural option. Almost any cable system will leave a vast functional area completely free of structural obstructions.

Disadvantages

In addition to the inherent instability of cable structures, they cannot normally be used to directly achieve a flat floor surface in a building, and are usually used only for a roof. Cable supported slabs, girders, trusses, and beams can be used to overcome this problem. Cables are very vulnerable to fire and are difficult to fireproof. The large sag that is optimal structurally is usually unjustifiable functionally, as it requires extortionate heating, ventilating, and air conditioning if enclosed. If walking on the weatherproofing envelope is necessary to regular maintenance, cable structures may prove more difficult than some other types of superstructure.

Design methods

The major early design decisions for this system concern sag, stabilization, and anchorage. Cable systems are often best studied conceptually in scale study models. Such models make use of thread, rubber bands, chipboard, push pins, foam core board, and light weight dowels. This method is usually fast, and allows direct three-dimensional evaluation of loads and architectural space. Such models are relatively easy to construct, and can alert the designer to potential construction problems and instabilities. When detailed dimensions and math calculations are needed during later design development, the computer can be introduced as a design tool. A great many structural lies and impossibilities can be told with graphite pencil drawings on two-dimensional paper, and computer drawing programs. Frei Otto in his book *"Tensile Structures"* advocated the use of "freely suspended" (funicular) models. These powerful models are predicted by a sailor's hammock, but will evolve into optimum cable nets, tents, and even shell structures in the later chapters. Once conceptual design has been completed, a more carefully constructed model may need to be tested in a wind tunnel, and the structural engineer may wish to subject the design to math modeling using a computer.

Aesthetic potential

It is necessary to give direct consideration to aesthetics of cable systems beyond the normal calculated structural necessities. Part of the beauty of cable structures comes from the direct visualization of lines of force inherent in the system. The energy directly embodied within cables becomes more apparent to untutored viewers when cables converge and diverge. This phenomenon can also be seen in stringed musical instruments such as a violin.

Figure 8-28

Notice the relationship of the cables to the undulating topography.

The convergence of these lines into "bundles" and the "fanning" distribution of energy in these cables into implied planes provide both drama and interest in this type of superstructure. Cable systems inherently minimize the importance of surface qualities such as hue, value, intensity, and texture. It is the line scheme that assumes exaggerated importance in cable structures. Special attention should be given to the beginnings and endings of the lines formed by cables in the system. While structurally the anchors at the ends of cables must resist unusually large forces, they also carry the aesthetic necessity of an appropriate visual termination. Generally it is best to consider the scheme of lines in the structure, compared to the scheme of lines in the site to which it must be attached (Fig. 8-28). Because the cables are so thin, objects such as a roof may appear to "float" on them much as a magician's assistant might appear to be suspended in mid-air.

Architects can learn much of the visual appeal of cables from a garden spider. The direct spontaneous response of a spider to each individual garden context leads to an inexhaustible number of creative ideal forms. Human designers too often disregard the site context in configuring cable structures, and lose this opportunity.

The sweep of primary cables in a suspension bridge has a visual role similar to "melody" in music composition. The evenly spaced suspenders or spreaders act somewhat like "rhythm" in music. Stabilizing cables perform the role of "countermelody" in this analogy. Fussy and fretful melody seldom has the impact of a more sweeping one. This is also true in cable systems.

DETAILS

Innovative details may be required when cable systems are used. A clear example of such a need can be seen on the Hungerford Bridge in London by Lifschutz Davidson and the WSP Group (Fig. 8-29).

Figure 8-29
Complex cable detail on the Hungerford Bridge in London.

Structural details

There is no shortage of evolved details for structural joints in cable structures. Normal design precedent research will easily unearth them. What is important in this text is to underscore the issue of thermal expansion and contraction with temperature, and the need for adjustability in cable tightness. Because steel changes size significantly with temperature, and because this condition is made more profound in long members such as cables, this is an important issue. Similarly, not only is adjustment in cable tension necessary, but it should be placed at a location where it can be done with ease. Many choose to accomplish this at ground level where the cable connects to the anchoring foundation. For small adjustments, a turnbuckle is often used (Fig. 8-30).

Figure 8-30
Cable tightness is conveniently adjusted at ground level on this suspension bridge in Grenoble France.

Redundant cables

Structurally it may be better to hang multiple small cables (in even numbers) than one massive one. This redundancy not only provides greater safety against structural failure, but will also allow replacement of cables during maintenance. Remember that if one cable fails, its load is transferred to those adjacent to it. If the cable lost is small, its load is small, and there are many adjacent cables available to share the additional load. However, for maintenance reasons, fewer larger cables will have less surface area to maintain.

Related envelope

While the cable structure is relatively easy to accomplish structurally, it is a significant challenge to attach a weatherproofing envelope to that completed structure. Certainly it has no inherent weatherproofing potential, as do such alternative superstructure systems as shells and tents. If a rigid roof is suspended under a cable system, an untidy detail known as a "pitch pot" is used to seal the openings where cables penetrate the roof. While product suppliers are normally quite willing to show you how their product may be attached, it is wise to leave considerable design time to the study of this problem.

CONSTRUCTION

Factory fabrication

Cable may easily be cut at the site, but not with the same accuracy as at the factory. Also the labor at the site will probably cost more than that found in the factory. Certainly all cable joints will come completely prefabricated to the site. Assembly of the structural frame can be remarkably rapid. Attachment of the envelope to the frame is a more difficult proposition.

Related lateral support

Three-dimensional stability during the erection of the structure is a special concern. Normally connections are made one at a time. As each new connection is made, the net will often want to change shape, and move. A carefully thought out and calculated erection procedure is therefore required. In small structures it may be possible to completely connect the net on the ground (even to the final foundation anchors), and then erect the masts, something like the erection of a circus tent. In larger cable structures, it may be better to weave the net in place in the air, one cable at a time. In early suspension bridge construction, a single cable was passed over the span, upon which all other cables would be fed.

There are some major challenges in erecting a cable building. For example consider the procedures used for a sag type roof (also known as a single layer cable roof) (Fig. 8-21). In addition to the stability questions previously voiced, there is also the issue of cable *trajectory* and tension. The cables were designed to ultimately have a carefully specified curvature (trajectory) and tension, but during construction as loads change, so does the curve and tension in the cables. Without the weatherproofing roof panels, the cable trajectory and tension is different than when the roof is finally in place. Therefore some adjustment method will be needed. To limit the extent of this problem, prestretched bridge cable will probably be used. First, the outside compression ring of a sag cable system is placed. Then the central tension ring is placed near its correct final position (elevated on scaffolding). The cables are then hooked between the outside compression ring and the central tension ring in a sequence that limits temporary imbalances. The scaffolding is removed. The cables sag a bit more, and gain a bit of tension. Roof panels are then placed. The sag and tension increase once again. Then the roof is loaded with brick or other material that stretches the cables leaving a bit of gap between panels. When the sag and tension are right, the gaps are grouted, the roof is prestressed at the correct trajectory and tension, and the brick is removed (Huntington and Mickadeit 1975). A bicycle wheel type roof (Fig. 8-22) is done similarly, but may also use jacks until all is right. Then the jacks are gradually displaced, and are replaced with permanent pipe type spreaders. All finished rotational cable roofs will change a bit in response to temperature changes, so such roofs often have a skylight near the outer compression ring to allow a bit of movement. What ever the erection procedure is to be, it is an important concern in an architect's office during conceptual design. Having identified some alternative construction approaches, one still has to admire the skill of the common garden spider.

Vocabulary		
Pylon	Sag	Pre-stressed
Edge cable	Span	Turnbuckle
Edge beam	Sag/span ratio	Cable bundle
Suspender	Vector component	Box section
Spreader	Funicular	Optimum curve
Cable truss	Bundles	Pre-stretched

REVIEW QUESTIONS

1. What span range is appropriate for a cable superstructure?
2. What is a typical sag/span ratio?
3. What are the advantages and disadvantages of this type of superstructure?
4. Draw a cable supported frame and name the parts.
5. Draw at least four types of stabilizing cable arrangements for a planar cable system.
6. Name and draw the common support types for a cable structure.
7. What construction concerns does this text raise concerning cable structures?
8. What detailing issues does a cable structure carry?
9. Describe the behavior of cable structures under load.
10. Graphically and verbally describe the alternative methods used to stabilize cable structures.
11. What types of loading produce a cantenary curve and a parabolic curve?
12. What controls the configuration of a cable under load?
13. Briefly explain why a "freely suspended" cable study model is also called a "funicular" model.

Figure 9-1
Canary Wharf underground station in London by Foster and Partners.

9 Arches

CONTINUITY

In the previous chapter, the study of cable systems introduced the designer to the first of many alternative superstructures. It also provided an opportunity to study structural members in tension. The next logical system to study is closely related to cable systems. Arches present a second alternative superstructure for potential use by a designer, and also provide the opportunity to study structural members in compression. In many ways, arches are cable systems turned upside down. Like cable systems, arches are normally shaped by funicular curves. Therefore, we can build on much of the knowledge gained in the last chapter.

While masonry is not used as extensively for arches as it once was, much of this chapter will focus on stone and brick arches. The reason is that the behavior of arches under load is made visible in masonry, while many internal stresses remain invisible inside of steel, concrete, and laminated timber.

HISTORY AND EXAMPLES

History

Stone was one of the first materials to be used for building. It has considerable strength in compression, and very little strength in tension. Since a properly designed arch is only in simple compression, the arch became the ideal superstructure for use with stone. One of the earliest arches to become significant in architectural history is at Ctephion in ancient Mesopotamia. It was built of sun-dried brick, and assumed the optimum (funicular) parabolic shape suitable for equally loaded arches. Arches continued to be used extensively in classical Rome. Two of the most important surviving examples are the aqueduct at

Nimes, France and the arch of Titus in Rome, Italy. During the Middle Ages, the arch continued to be used because large distances could be spanned even when small local stones were used. Long experience led to considerable mastery of this type of construction that lives on in the title "*Architect*." Some of the most important examples that survived from the Gothic period are the Notre Dame cathedral in Paris, and Salisbury Cathedral in England. In more modern times impressive bridges using iron, steel, and reinforced concrete arches have been used to support both road and rail. The largest arch in today's world is found in St. Louis Missouri.

Figure 9-2
Notice the funicular curve of the arch and the logical thickening at the base.

Selected building examples

Arches are one of the most widely used structural systems in history. Certainly the St. Louis arch in Saint Louis, Missouri by Eero Saarinen is the largest, and perhaps the best example (Fig. 9-2). But the historically preserved entry arch to the Chicago Stock Exchange by Louis Sullivan in Chicago captures more of the traditional character of arches (Fig. 9-3). To gain an appreciation for how long arches have been used perhaps the Arch of Titus or the arches on the perimeter of the Coliseum in Rome should be shown (Fig. 9-4). Even a modest hotel in Cuzco, Peru shows how widespread the use of arches continues to be (Fig. 9-5).

Examples in nature

Erosion of sandstone and limestone has left a few examples of arches spontaneously occurring in nature. One of the best known in the United States is to be found within Arches National Monument.

Figure 9-3
Sullivan demonstrates appropriate ornamentation of an arch.

Some selected non-building examples

Any significant Roman bridge from the Classical Period will be an arch. Stone bridges have continued into more recent periods as seen in the Wallace Bridge in Sterling, Scotland (Fig. 9-6).

NOMENCLATURE

The diagram below identifies the components of a traditional masonry arch. More contemporary arches retain this nomenclature even though materials and configurations have changed (Fig. 9-7).

BEHAVIOR UNDER LOAD

Funicular curves

If the funicular curve for a cable is established, the appropriate curve for an arch similarly loaded is that same cable curve turned upside down (Fig. 9-8).

Figure 9-4
In addition to the arches also notice the fittings for tent masts at the top of the wall.

Figure 9-5
Arcades in a small hotel in Peru.

Figure 9-6
Variations on this stone bridge in Scotland have been built around the world for over 2000 years.

Figure 9-7
Arch nomenclature.

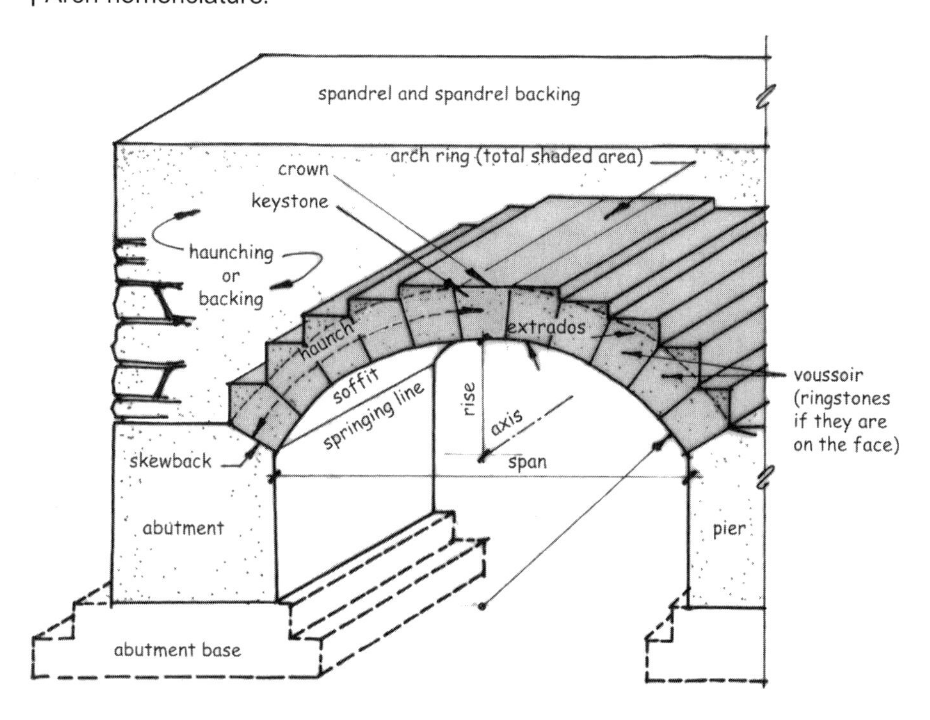

Figure 9-8
The inverted arch curve is in compression while the matching cable curve is in tension.

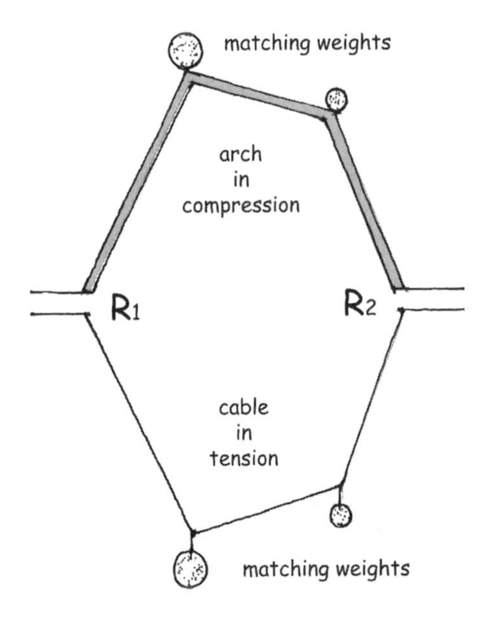

This being so, the cantenary and parabolic curves reassert themselves given uniform loading. However, unlike the cable system once the initial funicular form is established for an arch, it cannot change shape if the loading changes, without fear of collapse. Also, since the arch is ideally in simple compression, it is vulnerable to buckling, unlike the cable system (Fig. 9-9).

Figure 9-9
Buckling must always be considered in all compressive members.

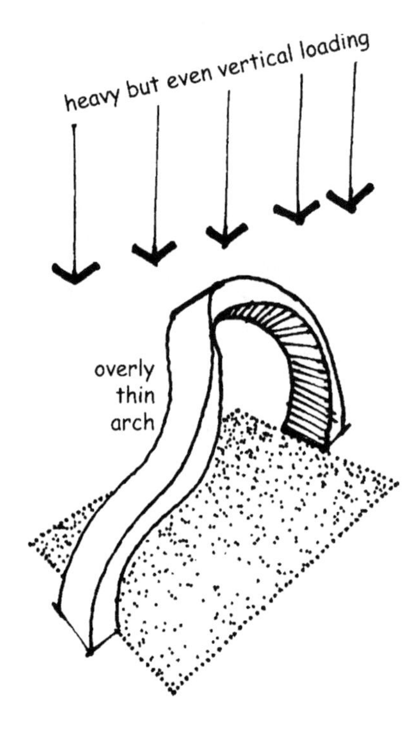

Resultants by parallelogram method

To understand arch action we must once again borrow a concept that properly belongs to the study of "statics." Vectors, which were introduced in Chapter 2, can be graphically added using a method known as the *parallelogram method*. A vertical force (shown graphically as a vertical arrow) can be graphically added to a horizontal force (shown as a horizontal arrow) (Fig. 9-10). If both of these arrows (or vectors) begin at the same point (origin) (Fig. 9-11), then a parallelogram can be constructed by drawing two additional parallel sides (Fig. 9-12). This is important because the diagonal of this parallelogram is the *resultant* of this simple two-force system (Fig. 9-13). This simply means that the two original vertical and horizontal vectors (known as *components*) can be taken away and replaced by the single resultant that has been graphically determined. Even better, the parallelogram method can be used to graphically add any two vectors, not just those that are horizontal and vertical (Fig. 9-14). But how is this important in arches?

Resultants and arches

If an arch is cut in half, the reader can intuitively see that without the support of the missing half the remaining half will collapse in the direction of the removed half (Fig. 9-15). This is called its *overturning force*. That means that the missing half must have been pushing against the keystone of the remaining half with a considerable horizontal force (known as its *restoring force*). Remember that the length of the arrow represents the magnitude of a vector (Fig. 9-16).

Ignore the rest of the arch, and look only at that first voussoir at the crown of the arch. The weight of that single stone (a vertical vector) would be relatively small when compared to the horizontal thrust of the restoring force from the now missing right half of the arch. Both of these forces can be converted graphically into vectors. Where the two intersect continuing along their axes of action becomes the origin discussed above, and a parallelogram of the forces acting on that single stone may now be drawn. The resultant from this first parallelogram is the beginning of the *pressure line* for this arch (Fig. 9-17).

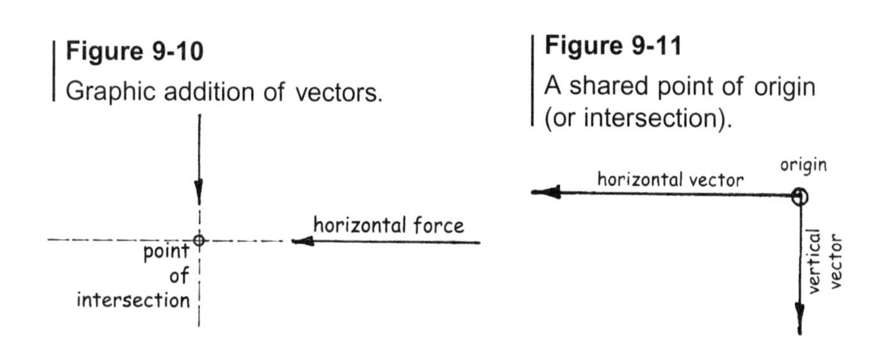

Figure 9-10
Graphic addition of vectors.

Figure 9-11
A shared point of origin (or intersection).

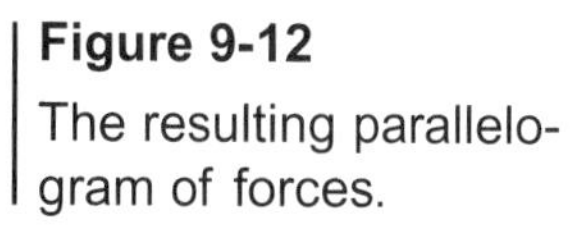

Figure 9-12
The resulting parallelogram of forces.

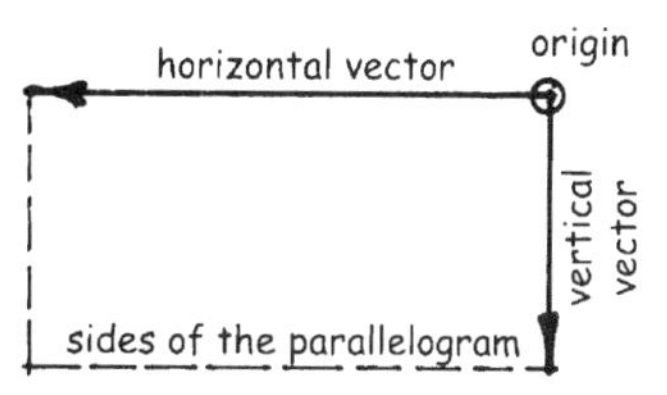

Figure 9-13
The resultant diagonal.

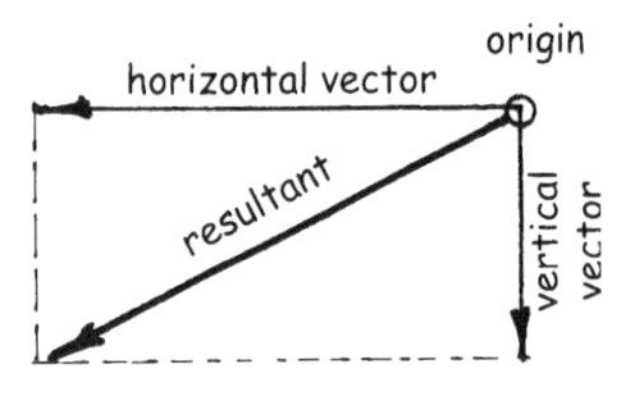

Figure 9-14
It is possible with any two intersecting forces or vectors.

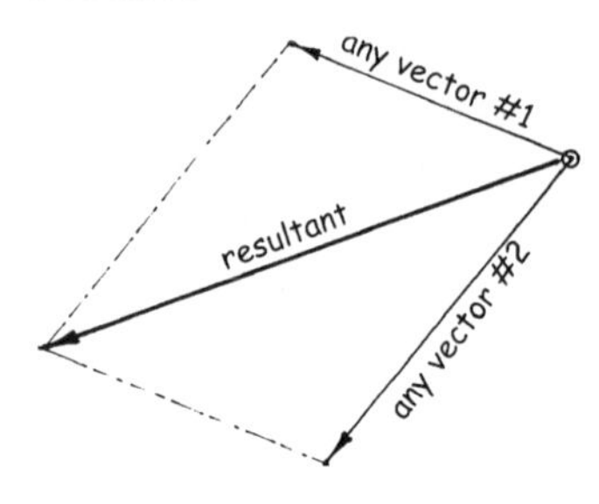

Figure 9-15
Without a supporting force it rotates.

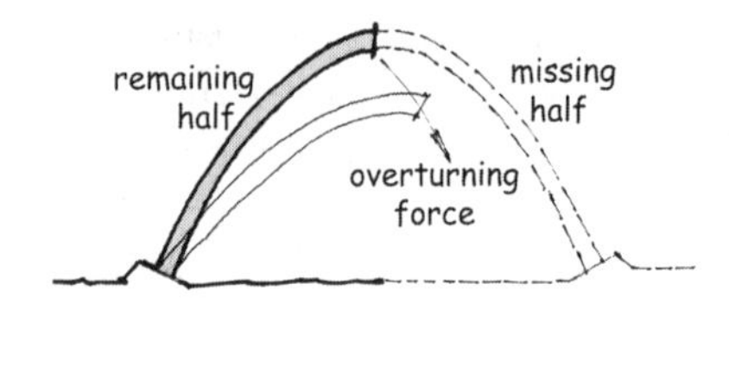

Figure 9-16
The restoring force holding the keystone against rotation.

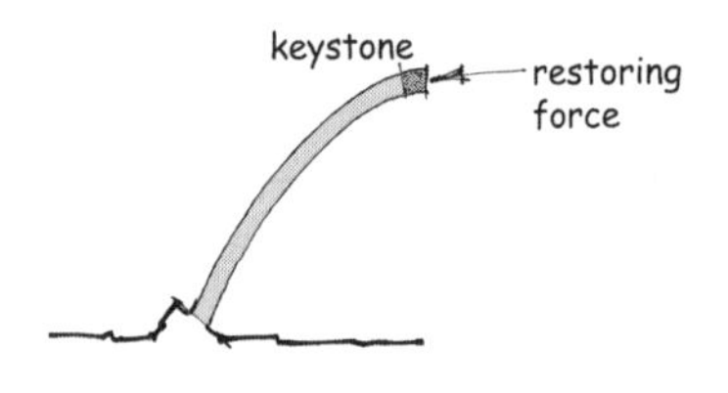

Pressure line

A similar parallelogram can be drawn for the next, and every subsequent voussoir progressing down the arch until the spring line is reached. At each stone the resultant from the previous voussoir is graphically added to the weight of the next stone. In this process the point of the last vector is connected to the tail of the next resultant. The continuous line generated by this series of connected resultants is known as the pressure line of the arch. To keep the voussoirs in simple compression this pressure line should stay in the middle third of each stone. The reader will notice that given uniform loading, the pressure line will become the funicular centenary curve previously discussed in cable systems (Fig. 9-18).

Figure 9-17
A parallelogram of vectors can be drawn at the keystone.

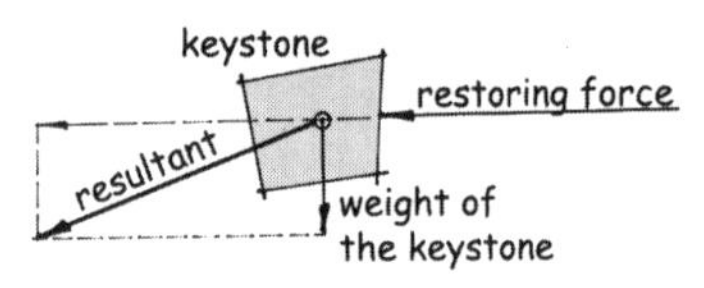

Lateral thrust

Notice that at the bottom of the arch, the last resultant in the pressure line is not vertical, that means that there is still some horizontal force left in it. That force is known as *lateral thrust*. Recall the sag/span ratio for cable systems in the last chapter. That concept can be directly reapplied in the rise/span ratio for arches. A large rise to span ratio will have little lateral thrust, while low rise/span ratios mean very large lateral thrust at the spring line. That thrust must be resisted. This has been done by a moment resisting foundation, buttressing, or a tie rod. *Moment foundations* for this purpose were introduced in Chapter 7. Such a foundation pushes back with an opposite and equal force against both the vertical weight and lateral thrust left in the arch at the spring line. A very heavy *buttress* will add a huge vertical weight (vertical vector) to the last resultant of the pressure line in the arch, "driving" the pressure line down into the soil. A *tie rod* can be introduced at the spring line. The tension in the tie rod directly opposes the lateral thrust of the arch at the spring line (Fig. 9-19). If a parabolic pressure line is graphically superimposed over a classical Roman semicircular arch, the reason for the wide arch ring can readily be seen (Fig. 9-20).

Figure 9-18

The parallelogram at each vousssoir leads to the next. Notice the similarity in shape to the St. Louis arch.

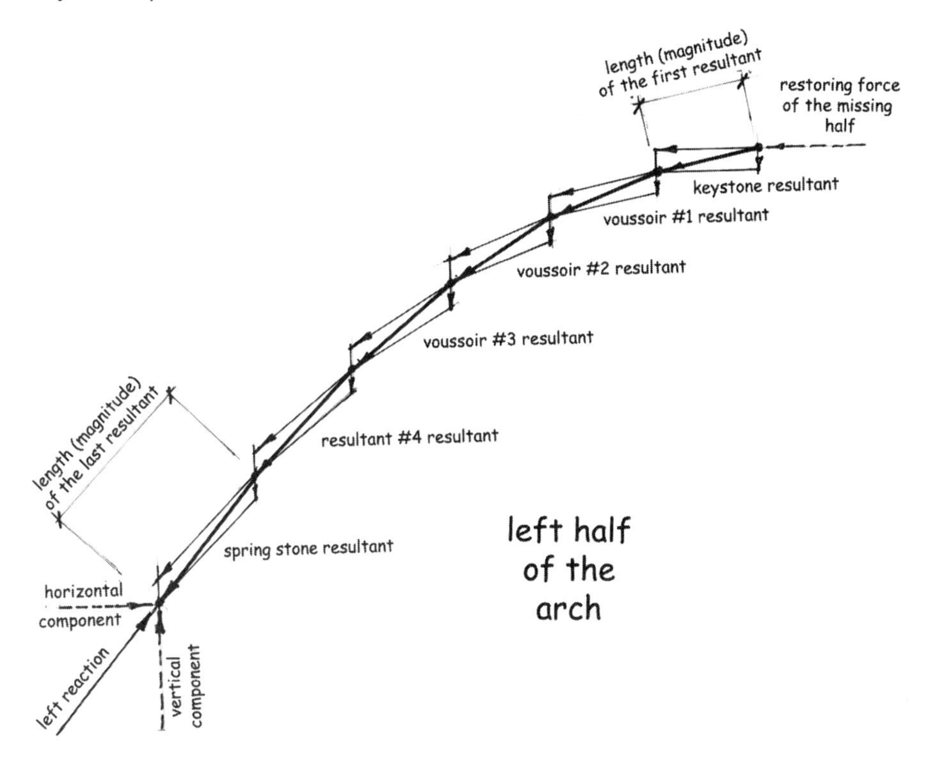

Structural logic in arches

Take a moment to look at the last resultant where the spring line and the pressure line intersect. Notice that this last resultant is a much longer arrow than the first resultant in the pressure line back up at the keystone. Every voussoir in the remaining arch must carry the same lateral thrust initially applied by the missing half arch at the keystone. But while the keystone must only carry its own weight, the last voussoir at the spring line must carry the vertical gravity

Figure 9-20

Roman arches are thick in order to contain the hidden funicular pressure line.

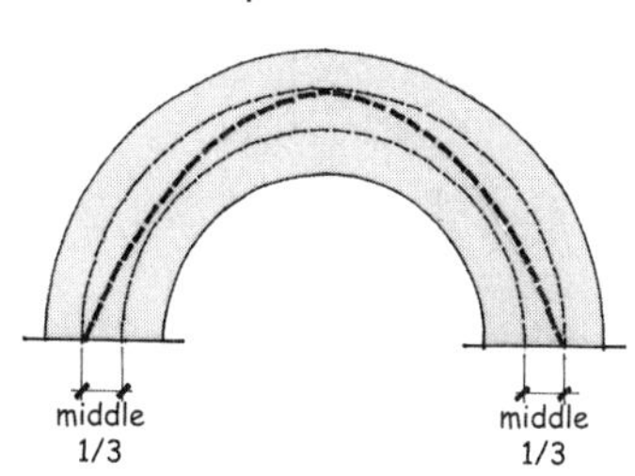

Figure 9-19

Lateral thrust at the base may be restrained in three ways.

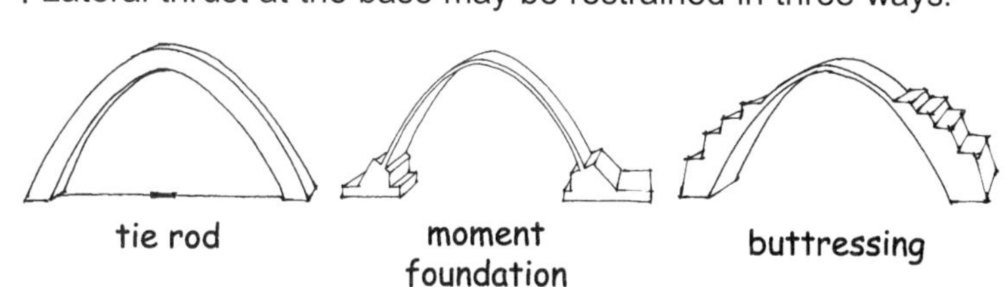

load of the total remaining 1/2 arch. Remember now that the principle of structural logic states that "big members should carry big loads, and little members should carry little loads." Therefore, it is logical that the bottom of the arch should be bigger than the top. This logic is quite pronounced in the St. Louis arch (Fig. 9-2).

TYPES OF ARCHES

By configuration

A wide variety of arch configurations have evolved over the course of history. The late Sir Banister Fletcher catalogs no less than thirty five in his authoritative and comprehensive *A History of Architecture on the Comparative Method.* They range from corbelled arches (Fig. 9-21), to Venetian, Florentine, and cinquefoil arches of Italy. Most arch variations such as the "pointed trefoil" are geometrically developed by varying the number and placement of "centers" (Fig. 9-22). The *corbelled arch* was commonly used in early ancient Aegean cultures. Basically the corbel relies on having each stone rest 2/3 on the stone below, and projecting 1/3 beyond the edge of the stone below. In spanning small openings (such as a window) with an arch, all of the stone above the arch does not rest upon the arch. Because of corbel action, only the 60 degree triangle of stone above the arch must be supported.

Figure 9-21
Corbelled arch at Borobudur in Indonesia. Most corbelled arches roughly mirror two 60 degree angles.

Out of plane rotation (i.e., falling over) by an arch may be opposed by joining two perpendicular arches at the keystone. Such intersecting arches are known as *crossed* arches. It can also be prevented if several arches are placed side by side, and securely attached, a *vault* system is developed. A complete chapter has been given to vaults later in this text. Similarly a series of intersecting arches can also be arranged into a skewed grid along a single axis (known as a *lamella* system) but it also properly belongs in a later chapter on vaults (Fig. 9-23).

Figure 9-22
These are "centers" used with a drawing compass, not centers for temporary construction support.

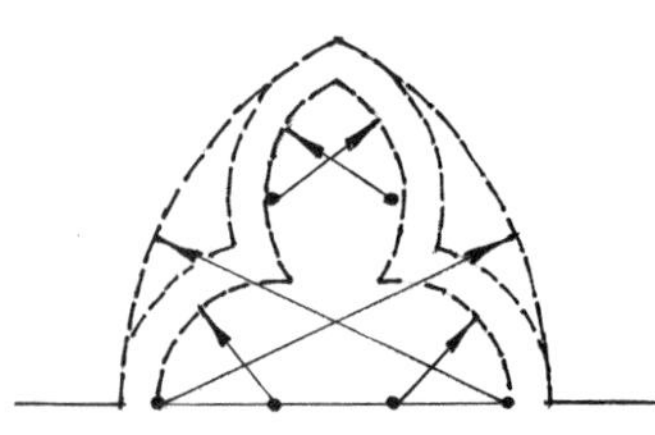

Due to the need for abundant natural day light in northern Europe, Gothic cathedrals reduced structure to the absolute minimum. This allowed very large openings into relatively open interior space. The *flying buttress* used in these gothic cathedrals was really just a series of half arches used to buttress the lateral thrust of cathedral naves. The Stone vaults had replaced wood trusses because of the regular burning of churches during the many wars in the medieval period. As you may guess, since vaults are just a series of attached arches, so most vaults have considerable lateral thrust at their spring line. Flying buttresses were used to receive this lateral thrust and conduct it down to the ground using arch action. Notice that once again the pressure line may be graphically determined by using the successive application of parallelogram method. Once again the pressure line must pass through the base of the flying buttress. To make this easier, the buttress is made progressively wide as the pressure line approaches the base. The buttress also rises high above the pressure line, and is further crowned by heavy spires and ornaments. Here is the key. This additional weight above the pressure line greatly increases the vertical vectors that get added into the pressure line resultants, forcing it rapidly more vertically downward toward the middle third (Fig. 9-24).

By material

Now that the forces that are at work in the arch have been visualized in masonry arches, it must be said that few modern arches are made of masonry. Certainly the longer span arches are usually made of steel (Fig. 9-25), reinforced concrete (Fig. 9-26), or laminated timber. Concrete and masonry usually require more time and labor than steel and laminated timber. This savings in time and labor normally makes them more economical, and their curvature more predictable. The major difference structurally is that reinforced concrete, timber, and steel will resist bending, but unreinforced masonry will not. As the pressure line begins to move about under dynamic loading, bending may begin to occur in arches. More will be learned about bending in subsequent chapters on beams and rigid frames.

Figure 9-23
Intersecting and lamella systems of arches can resist arch overturning in the direction of the arches narrow axis.

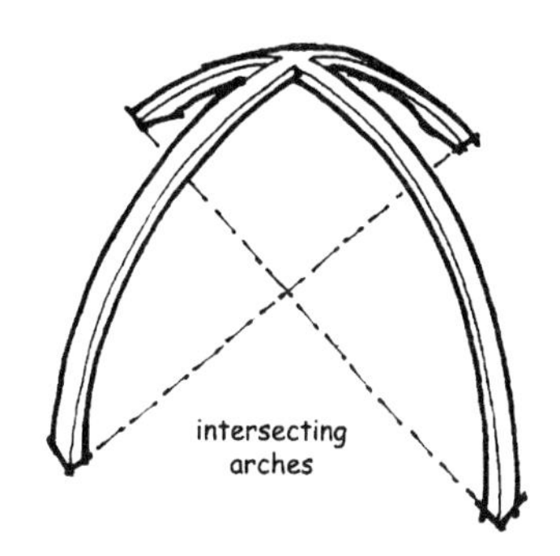

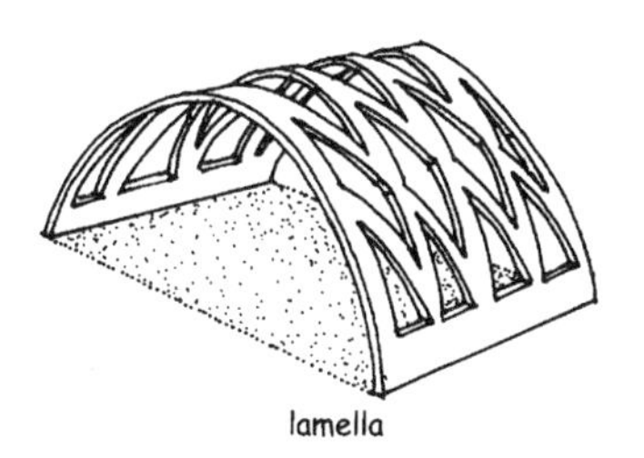

ARCH FAILURES

Common failure modes

Stability failures (in only two dimensions) can be predicted by passage of the pressure line outside of the middle third of the arch. However, remember that there are six degrees of freedom for stability failures, and that there are also strength and stiffness failures. Therefore there are many types of failure common to arches (Merriman and Wiggins 1942).

1. Crushing of the masonry
2. Sliding of one voussoir upon another
3. Voussoir overturning
4. Shearing in a horizontal or vertical plane in concrete arches
5. Failure as a column when the unsupported slenderness ratio exceeds 1/12
6. Premature striking of centers
7. Settlement of foundations
8. By sliding upon the foundation
9. By overturning (out of plane) (Fig. 9-27)

Of the various common failure modes listed above, the most common failures of arches are related to foundation movements.

Need for hinges

Now notice that arches grow in size when they are heated, and decrease in size when they become cold. Small span arches (particularly in stone) can be

Figure 9-24
A flying buttress in just a half arch.

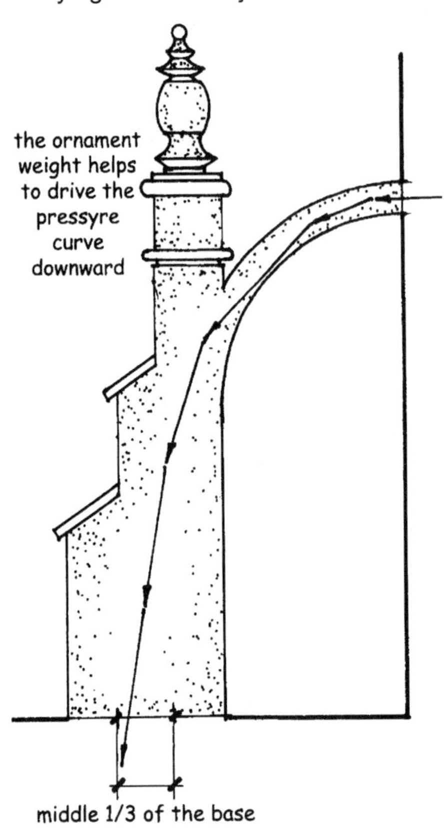

Figure 9-25
Underground entry in Bilbao Spain by Norman Foster.

Figure 9-26
Typical concrete bridge arch.

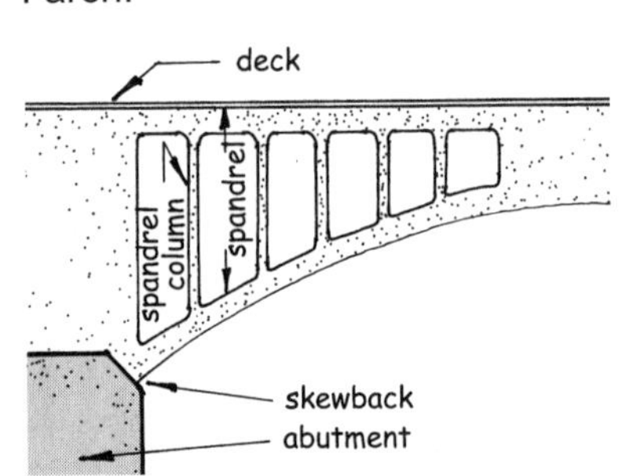

Figure 9-27
Out-of-plane means rotation against the narrow axis of an arch.

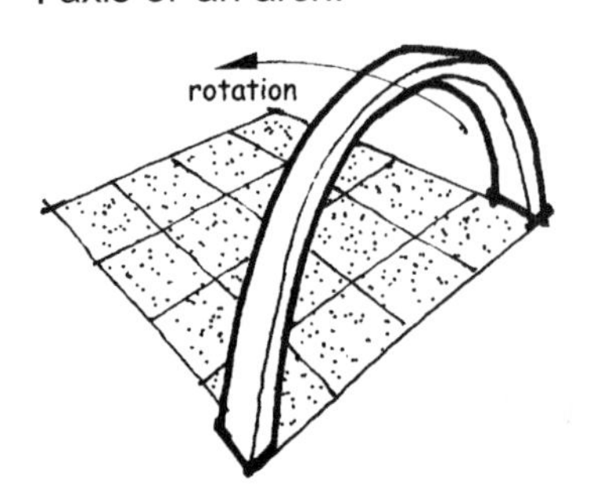

considered rigid arches. But long span steel and concrete arches will build up considerable internal bending stresses as they try to change length and shape due to temperature changes. Unfortunately, they are rigid against change. For this reason (and to make them easier to calculate) modern arches are usually *hinged*. They may be two or three hinged. However, if more than three hinges are developed, the arch becomes unstable in its shape, and will fail (Fig. 9-28).

Inadequate buttressing

The radius of an arch above a small window is roughly equal to the span of the opening. Therefore the minor arches above windows are usually relatively low rise, but have considerable lateral thrust against the adjacent masonry. If the mass of that masonry and the friction in its joints are insufficient, it will push a block of masonry out the side of the wall. This happens when an arched opening is placed too close to the end of a wall (Fig. 9-29).

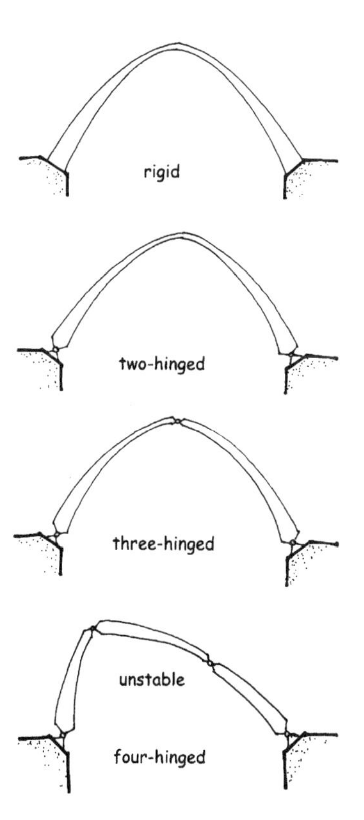

Figure 9-28
Effect of hinges on arch action.

Figure 9-29
Keep lateral thrust away from the edges of walls.

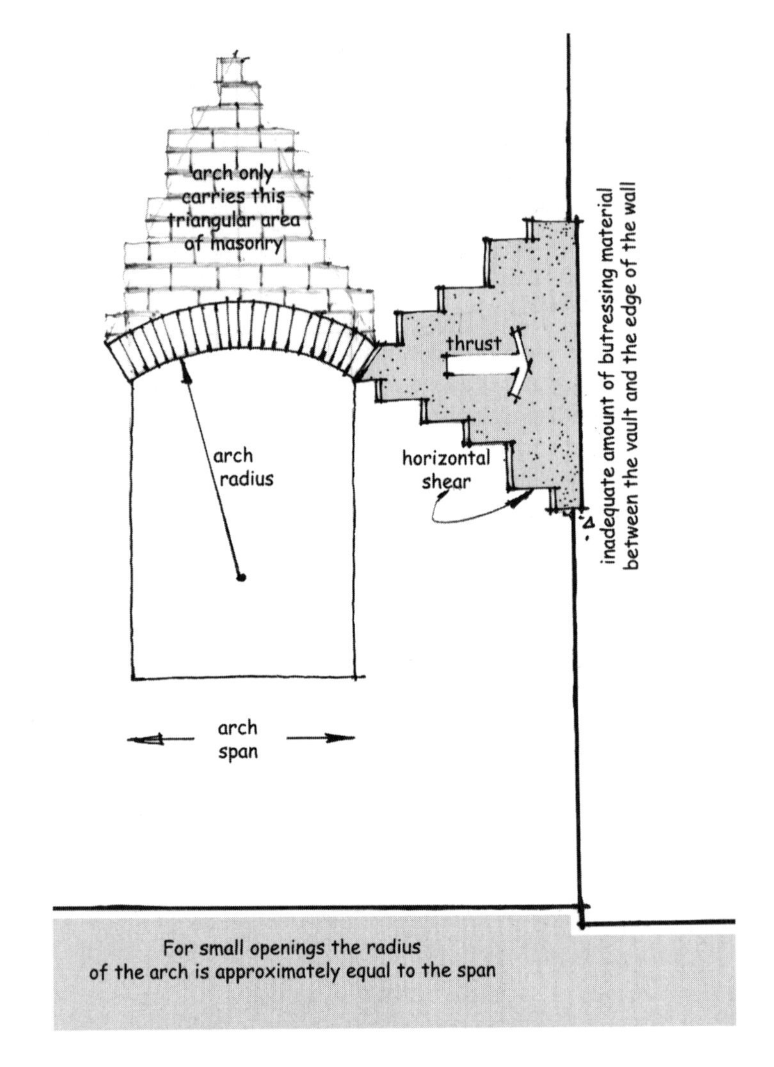

Changes in loading

As previously discussed when loads are altered on a cable system, the cable is free to respond by changing shape. The cable can continue its funicular behavior. However, the arch (which began in a funicular shape) is made of rigid material i.e. stone, brick, concrete, or steel. It is unable to change its shape when loading is altered. The initial funicular pressure line begins to move about (Fig. 9-30). If the pressure line moves outside the middle third of the voussoirs, the compressive stresses between stones will quickly double on one edge, leading to crushing. If the pressure line continues to shift further, tension will develop on the other edge of the voussoir. Sags and humps will develop (Fig. 9-31). Bending stresses will develop in concrete and steel arches, but masonry joints have no strength in tension. In masonry, one or more joints may

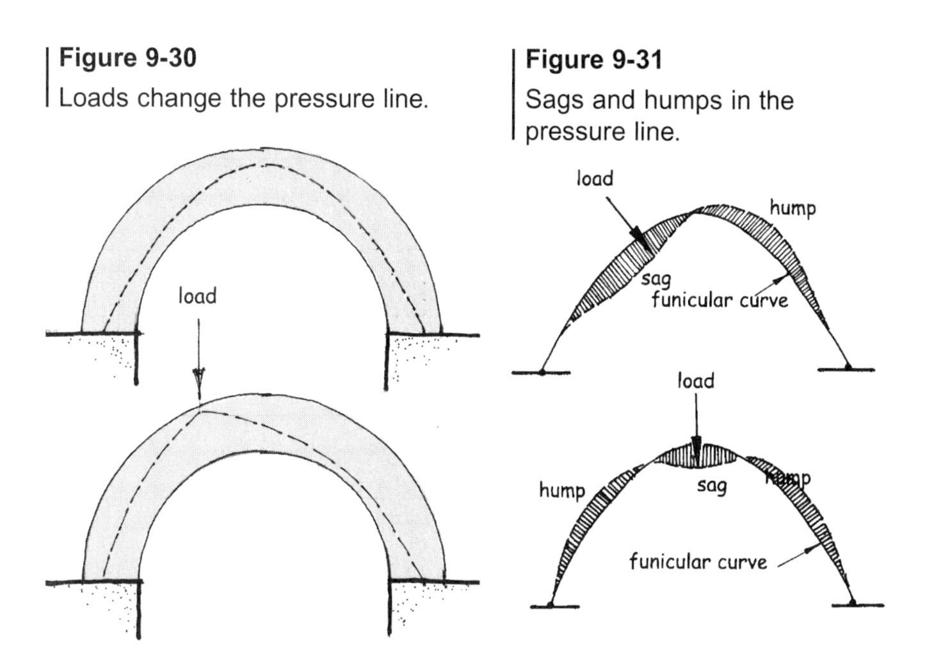

Figure 9-30
Loads change the pressure line.

Figure 9-31
Sags and humps in the pressure line.

start to open up (Fig. 9-32). Insufficient loading can also lead to a hinge opening at the crown (Fig. 9-33). When a hinge is formed, a voussoir fails by rotating. But voussoirs may also fail by sliding in shear against one another (Kidder and Parker 1949) (Fig. 9-34).

DESIGN OF ARCHES

Typical approximate span ranges

Like cables, arches are a long span structure. *Long span* structures are those that are used to span more than 60 feet. The span range for arches varies with the material from which it is made. For wood the span range from 60 feet to

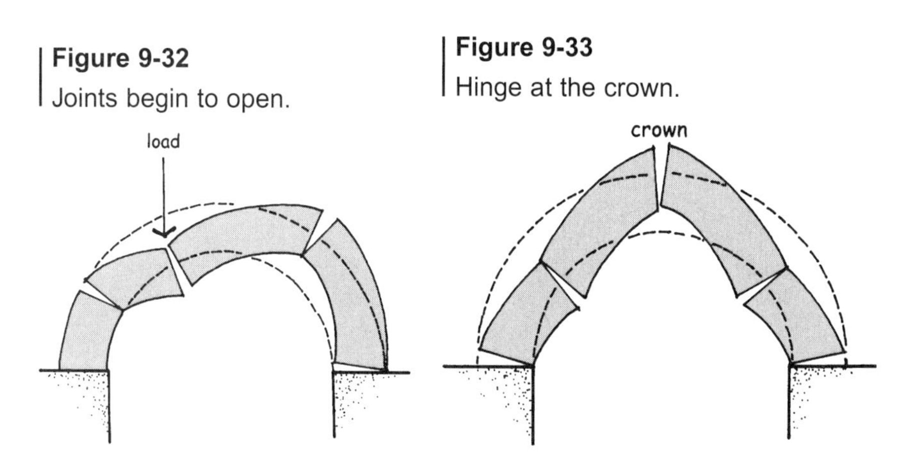

Figure 9-32
Joints begin to open.

Figure 9-33
Hinge at the crown.

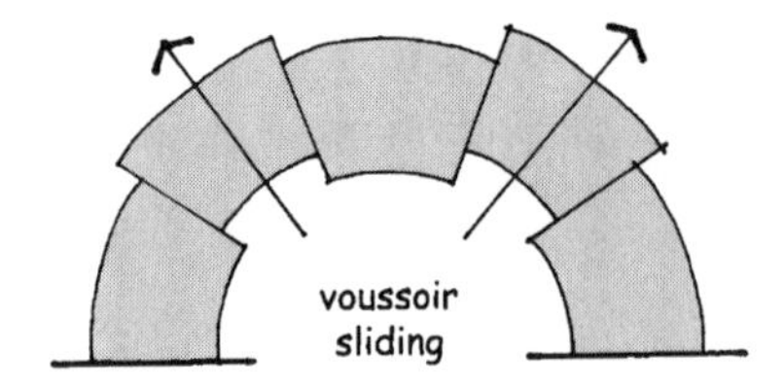

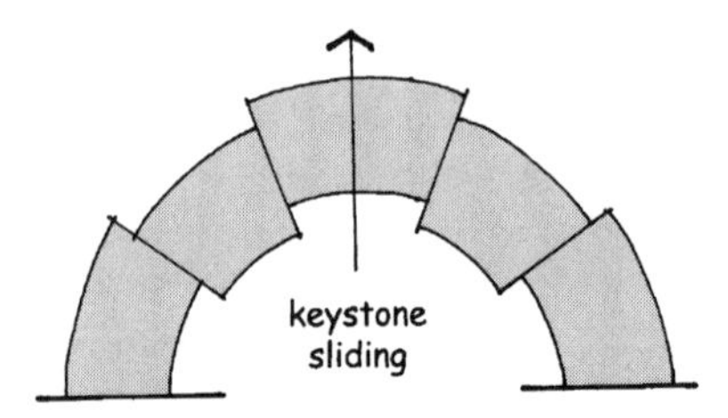

Figure 9-34
Voussoirs sliding against each other.

200 feet is typical, for masonry 4 feet to 220 feet, for reinforced concrete 60 feet to 300 feet, and for steel 60 feet to 500 feet is representative (Fig. 9-35). Similarly the approximate ratio of rise of an arch to its span varies with material. The rise to span ratio for wood varies from 1:3 to 1:6, for masonry 1:1 to 1:5, for reinforced concrete 1:3 to 1:7, and for steel 1:4 to 1:8. These rules of thumb are intended to give a crude starting point for the preliminary design of arches from various common materials (Fuller Moore 1999).

COMMON APPLICATIONS

Long span buildings such as churches, auditoria, airports, and rail terminals have made extensive use of this system. At the extreme limits of the span range, use of steel, (sometimes trussed or triangulated,) has often been used.

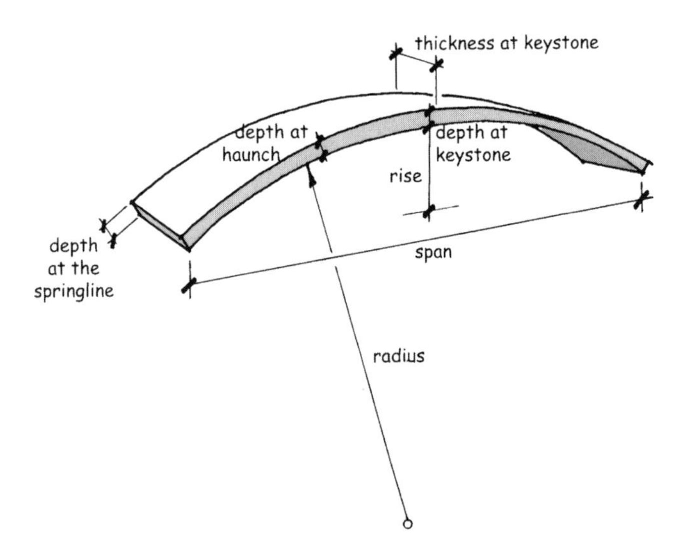

Figure 9-35
Dimensions of an arch.

Advantages of the system

The arch can be constructed in almost any common construction material. As a general rule, simple compression makes more efficient use of that material than bending; therefore, arches are relatively efficient. Structural materials such as steel, which are strong in both tension and compression, can be used in a wide variety of structural systems. Additional weight of a heavy building material actually tends to strengthen an arch.

Disadvantages of the system

While arches may be well used as a roof form, and tend to naturally shed water due to their curved shape, they are difficult to use as a floor. A flat deck of some sort must normally be added. There are several options on the location of a flat deck when added to an arch (Fig. 9-36). Some form of transition must be made in order to achieve a flat floor above an arched structure. Unfortunately, the more optimum the arch configuration structurally, the more likely it is to leave excessive unused head space functionally. This same excessive headroom will also require more heating, ventilation, and cooling. As the rise of an arch increases, so does surface area that must be weatherproofed to contain the same functional footprint. Most arches require a second temporary structure (called *centering*) to be constructed, before the actual final arch can be erected using the centering for support. This is discussed in a subsequent paragraph. Since the arch is an essentially a two-dimensional form, some additional form of lateral support is required to prevent "out of plane" failures in arches.

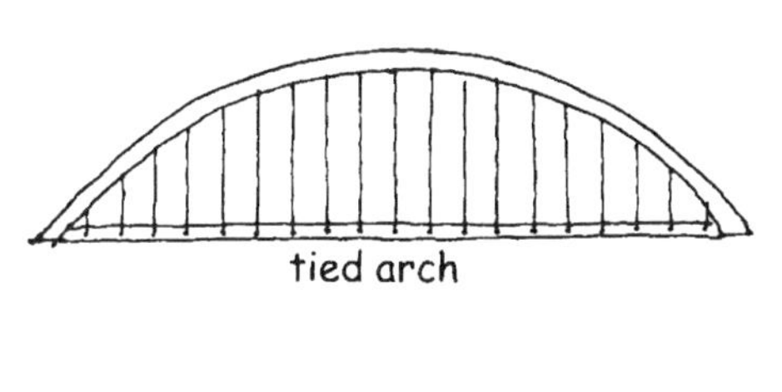

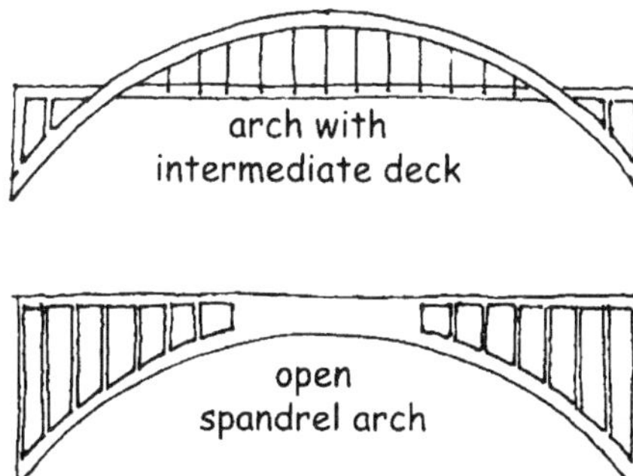

Figure 9-36
Alternatives for the location for a flat floor or deck.

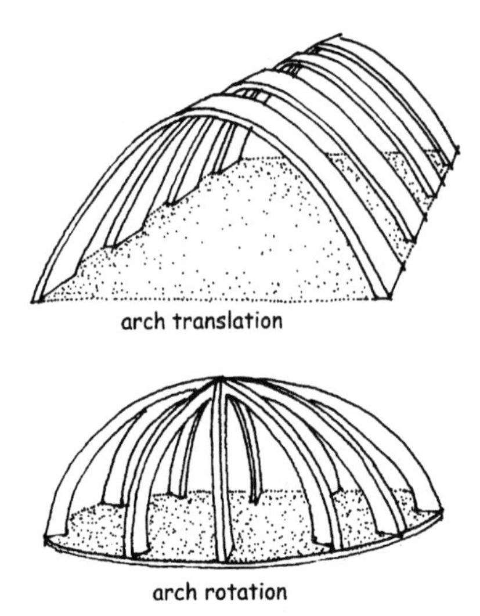

Figure 9-37
Two modes of growth.

PATTERN OF GROWTH

Just as with cable systems, single aches may grow by either translation or rotation (Fig. 9-37).

FUNCTIONAL FOOTPRINT

Arches in translation form rectangular functional foot prints, while rotational arches form circles. As arches grow axially they become vaults. As they grow radially they become domes. Both are discussed in later chapters.

DESIGN

Methods

As with cable systems, the *string polygon* graphic method can play an important role in the preliminary design of arches: however, it is beyond the scope of this text. Funicular scale models may be used just as they were with cable systems, but remember that the designer must be able to solidify the free hanging model and flip it over into the arch position. Obviously, in all structural systems, math and computer calculation will be required to proceed beyond early preliminary design (Zalewski and Allen 1998).

Aesthetic potential

Arches have a visual appeal similar to the graceful leaps of ballet dancers. When arranged into arcades, the designer is well served to think of the arches as choreographed series of leaps in a ballet sequence (Fig. 9-38). The rhythm patterns of these leaps have been considered since at least the time of gothic cathedrals. Technically the weight of ornamentation may be used to influence the pressure line if needed. It may also be used to express either the normal or actual path of the pressure line. The contrast of mass and void in arcades is particularly powerful when light and shade are contrasted strongly. The shadows cast by the arcade echo this interaction (Fig. 9-39). Be sure to consider paving patterns when the line of the arch shadow falls on it. Covered arcades form a type of "bonding space" between the interior rooms of a building, and the exterior urban space. Because circles are very assertive in the shape scheme of a composition, special attention should be given to the subjects that are framed by an arched opening.

Figure 9-38

The "leap" of arches at the Malmo rail station in Sweden.

ARCH DETAILS

Lateral stability

Steel cables can be used for cross bracing and external guying to stabilize arches. Short sections of vaults (fully discussed in a later chapter) may also be placed between arches (called *ribbed vaults*). As noted above, both intersecting and radial arches have historically been used to gain lateral stability.

Figure 9-39

The shadows repeat and emphasize the arches.

Connections

Pinned connections are common in modern arches. These hinges prevent the buildup of bending stresses in the arch. What is conceptually important at this time is that lateral thrust at the spring line and hinge movement make difficult companions in detailing. Movement of the arch due to pins also makes weatherproofing a moving building structure a bit of a challenge. If tension rods are used at the spring line, and that line is at ground level, then such tie rods are often located under a slab on grade floor.

Relating the weatherproofing envelope to the arch

With thermal movement, final exact location of the crown of the arch, and a consistent final arch curvature can be difficult to predict and realize. In such cases, windows under the arch will require significant amounts of movement tolerance and adjustability.

CONSTRUCTION

Centering

Arches must normally rest on a curved temporary surface (known as centering) during construction. Centering (also known as falsework in Europe) is usually some form of temporary timber truss. Several types of bowstring centering are used, depending upon the span, and height of the spring line (Fig. 9-40).

Figure 9-40
Wood trusses are often used for temporary construction support.

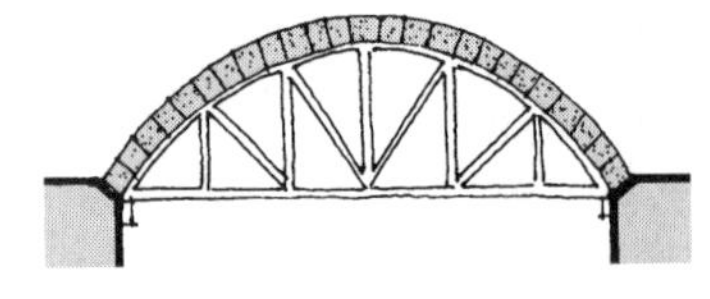

Types of centering

Most centering is a temporary wooden truss erected below the arch ring. Today scaffolding, steel beams, and steel trusses may be used for longer and higher arches. Centering can get in the way of other construction operations. If that becomes an issue worker access under or through the truss may be designed into its configuration (Fig. 9-41). Otherwise, centering can also be located above the arch ring, leaving the space under the arch open for movement (Fig. 9-42). Openings with arches with less than eight foot spans can easily be centered with the use of dimension lumber and plywood (Fig. 9-43). For aches longer than about eight feet some form of bowstring truss have often been used. Arches of over sixty feet are not unusual. The centering for these is often executed in laminated timber or steel. For really long span arches (over 150 feet) trussed steel arches may be fabricated on the ground in sections, and then lifted by crane into place. If concrete or masonry is to be used, the initial curvature must anticipate the changes of curvature that occur after the centering is removed (Merriman and Wiggin 1942).

Figure 9-41
Centering can get in the way of other construction work so it may be designed to allow passage underneath.

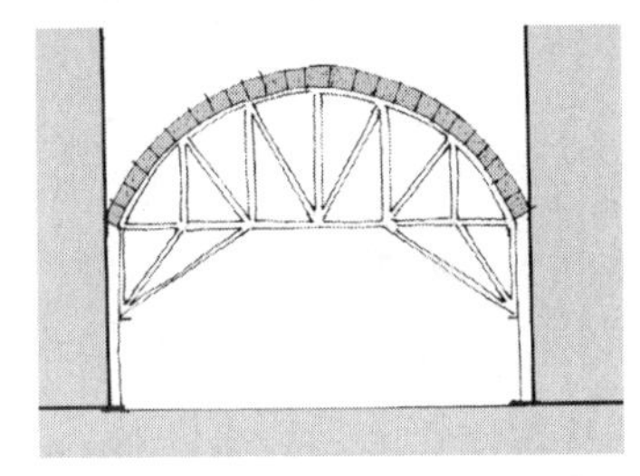

Changes in curvature

Centering must be struck gradually, usually beginning at the crown. This is normally accomplished by easing wedges or jacks under the centering. It is normally spoken of as "lowing" or "striking" the centering. As the support of the centering is lost, the arch will settle. Compression increases along the curve of the pressure line, and some change of trajectory (curvature) occurs. Concrete arches shrink as they cure. This will also cause a change of curvature in the arch. These changes may be anticipated, and the centering slightly enlarged. In this way the final arch settles down into its designed curvature. After the centering is fully struck, loads may continue to change as roofing material is added. Centering must be very stiff. As the load of the arch grows from the spring line toward the crown, the centering will begin to change shape. As the arch ring reaches a 30 degree angle, sags at the haunch and a hump at the crown tend to develop. Later as the arch ring reaches the crown the tendency reverses, with sag at the crown and humps at the haunches (Fig. 9-44). Similar problems may develop as the centering is lowered.

Figure 9-42
It is even possible to provide temporary support from above if necessary.

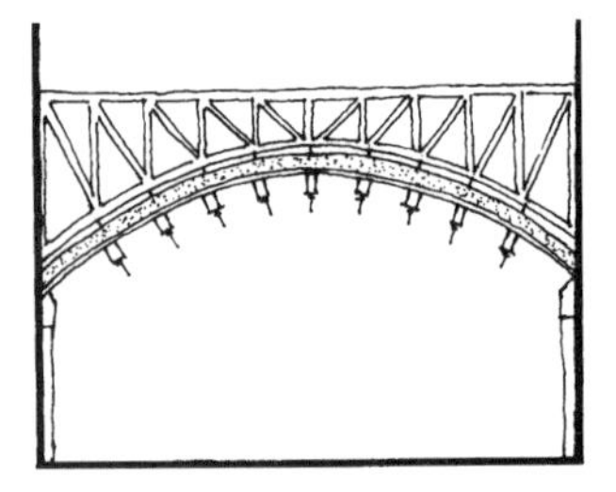

Striking the centering

Centering under an arch must be lowered very slowly, and uniformly. With laminated timber and steel arches this is not an issue, since no centering is required, but with concrete and masonry rapid striking of centering may not only cause unacceptable curve deformation, but may also represent a genuine safety hazard. For example, stone arches with a span less than 50 feet might be lowered about 1/2 inch per day. Some system for coordination (and tuning)

Figure 9-43
Short span arches don't require complex centering.

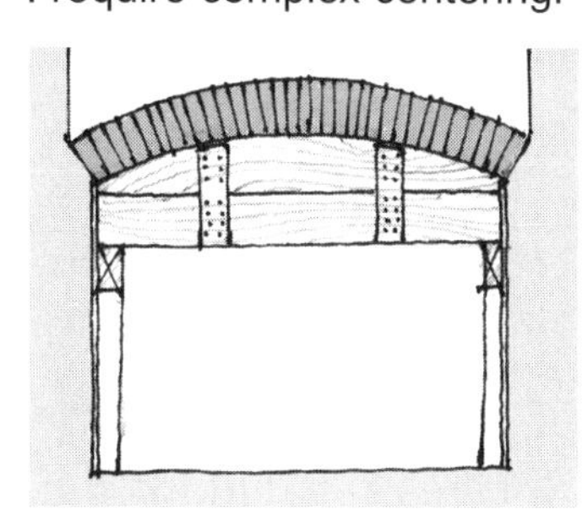

Figure 9-44
Humps and sags in the pressure line as the arch grows past 30 degrees.

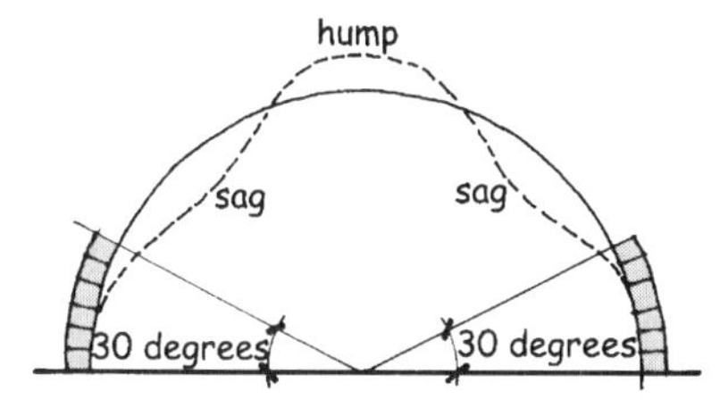

this lowering is needed. Because of the great weight involved, increased inertia due to rapid movement (even for a couple of inches) assumes terrifying proportions (Trautwine 1937).

Vocabulary		
Voussoir	Keystone	Intrados
Extrados	Haunch	Spring line
Crown	Centering	Arch Axis
Spandrel	Skewback	Arch Ring
Abutment	Spandrel Backing	Arch Radius

REVIEW QUESTIONS

1. What is a "normal" span for an arch in timber, steel, concrete, and masonry?
2. Briefly graphically and verbally describe the behavior of arch structures under both vertical and horizontal loads.
3. Name and locate the elements of an arch.
4. List and describe the most common modes of failure for masonry arches.
5. Briefly discuss the structural similarities and differences between arches and cables.
6. What are the problems associated with striking the centering?

Figure 10-1

Nederlands Architectural Institute in Rotterdam Holland with a large sculpture in the foreground.

10 Post and Beam

GENERAL

In the last two chapters the reader has explored cable structures and arches. Post and beam structures logically follow, since a beam is sometimes said to be just an inefficient arch combined with an inefficient cable system. This statement will be explained as you read on. The previous chapters on cables and arches also introduced members in simple *tension* and simple *compression* respectively. In this chapter we will have the opportunity to begin to explore all of the other "complex" stresses. *Complex stresses* combine tension and compression in some way. Specifically this chapter will introduce *bending*, *shear*, *bearing*, and *torsion* during the discussion on beams. Then *bearing* and *buckling* stresses will be discussed during the portion of this chapter given to columns. Post and beam systems (Fig. 10-2) are very common in use, but are uncommonly important in the structural lessons that they have to offer. Because of the wide use of post and beam superstructures, but more because it gives us an opportunity to understand a wide variety of new types of stresses and failures, this will be a long and important chapter.

Figure 10-2
Typical post and beam structure.

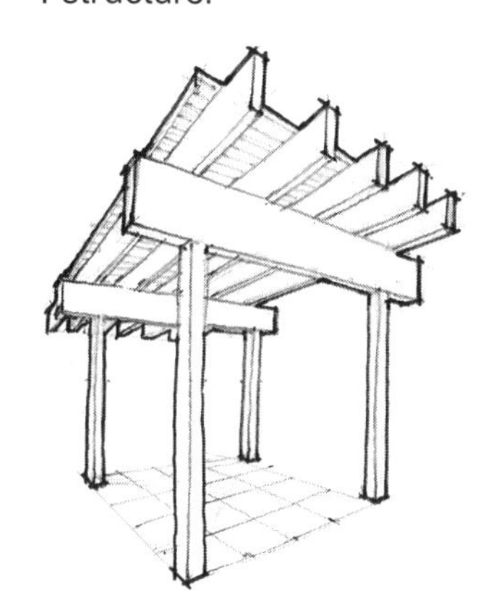

History and significant examples

History

Post and beam systems have been used from earliest written history, and before. Since they are simple to fabricate and inherently provide a flat functional floor for occupants, their long use is not surprising. Post and beam systems may be fabricated from almost any structural material. The simplest hut to grand palace, small factory to small temple; almost all building types have been attempted in this most common of superstructures. Many types of long span superstructures, such as trusses, mimic "beam action" in ways that will be explained in later chapters.

Figure 10-3
Traditional high quality timber post and beam in Japan.

Figure 10-4
Centraal Beheer in Apeldoorn Holland by Hermann Hertzberger. Notice that the beams are deeper at midspan.

Examples in nature

The trunk of a tree is a column structurally. Its branches are "cantilevered" beams. A tree that has fallen across a small stream can form what is known as a "simple" beam.

Non-building examples

Short span bridges used this system even during prehistory. Most tables and chairs use this structural system in some form.

Some building examples

The traditional Japanese houses (Fig. 10-3), and the Rotterdam Centraal Beheer (Fig. 10-4) illustrate the long historical use of post and beam structures. Even classical Greek and Roman temples used this type of structure (Fig. 10-5).

BEAMS

Beam types or categories

Types of beam connections

Beams are classified in different ways. One of the most common is by the number and type of supports that a specific beam is given. Before beginning this type of categorization, it is necessary to identify different types of connections that may exist at each vertical support. A horizontal beam may be connected in such a way that it may rotate like the *pinned connection* in a pair of scissors. While such a beam connection is free to rotate about the pin, it is restrained from sliding (translating) in any direction. A *knife edge* support would allow the beam to both slide (translate) and to rotate at the support. If a *fixed connection* is used, the beam is seized so tightly at the support that it may neither translate nor rotate. Symbols may be used to identify each of these types of connections (Fig. 10-6).

Types of beams by support

Now that we have this background concerning connection types, it is possible to briefly classify beams by the number and type of support that a specific beam is given. These include *simple*, *overhung*, *fixed*, *propped*, and *cantilevered* (Fig. 10-7). The reader is asked to take special notice of the fixed beam. Once post and beam superstructures have been fully discussed in this chapter, the next chapter will turn the reader's attention to rigid frame superstructures. Rigid frames often look like post and beam superstructures, but rely predominantly on fixed or rigid connections between their major structural members.

Now look at the *continuous* beam (Fig. 10-8). When this type of beam sags under load in one span, it tends to uplift the beam in any adjacent spans. This significant asset causes continuous beams to be widely used when economy is sought. A smaller beam can be used due to this "uplift" between adjacent spans.

Figure 10-5
Temple at Paestum, Italy.

Figure 10-6
Conventional graphic symbols for different types of standard connections.

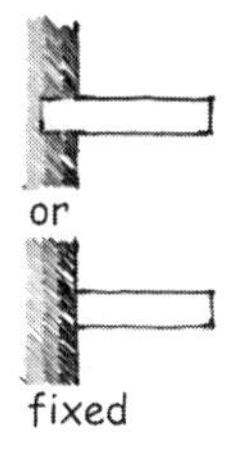

Figure 10-7
Graphic symbols used to show conventional types of beam support.

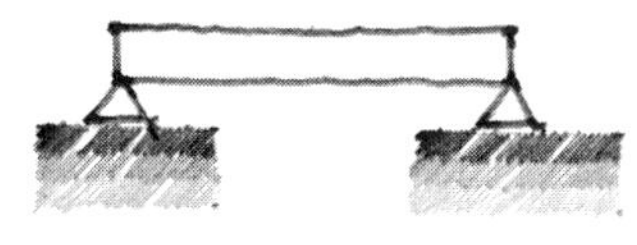

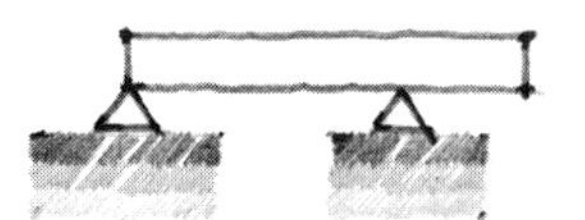

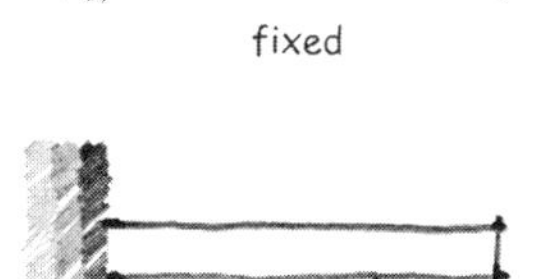

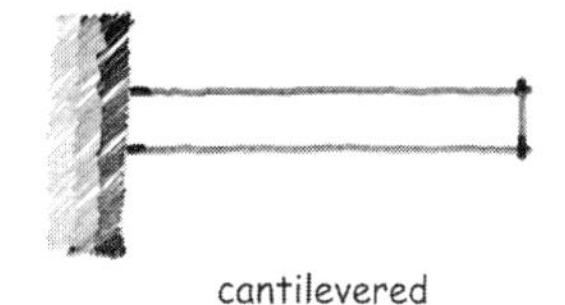

The *drop-in* beam is essentially two opposing overhung beams into which a simple beam is "dropped" (Fig. 10-9).

Classification of beams by structural material

The most common structural materials used to make beams are timber (Fig. 10-10), steel (Fig. 10-11), and concrete (Fig. 10-12). Several different beam configurations are available in each of these materials.

Classification of beams by structural use

Beams of varying size and span are given different roles in different parts of a building. In light wood frames such as *balloon* frames and platform frames, *headers* and *lintels* are used over and under the openings for windows and doors. *Joists* are small beams that are closely spaced at a regular interval to form the support for ceilings and floors (Fig. 10-13). These joists will rest on larger, more widely spaced *beams*. If large spaces are involved, these beams may rest on even larger and more widely spaced *girders*. Although they may be sloped, there are many members in a framed roof that behave like beams.

Figure 10-8
Continuous beam action.

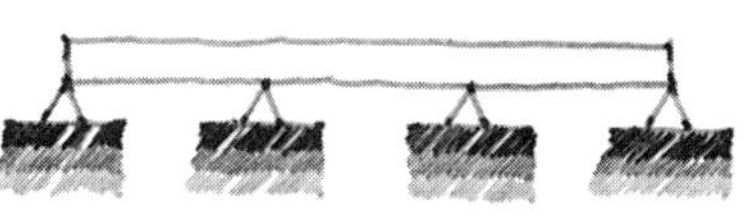

Figure 10-9
Drop in beam.

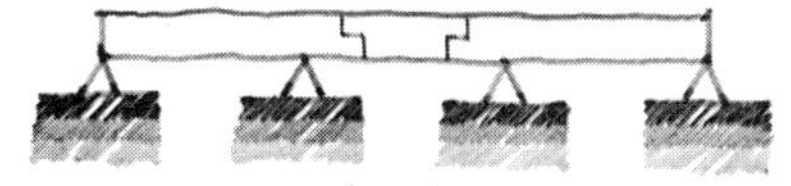

Figure 10-10
Some common types of wood beams.

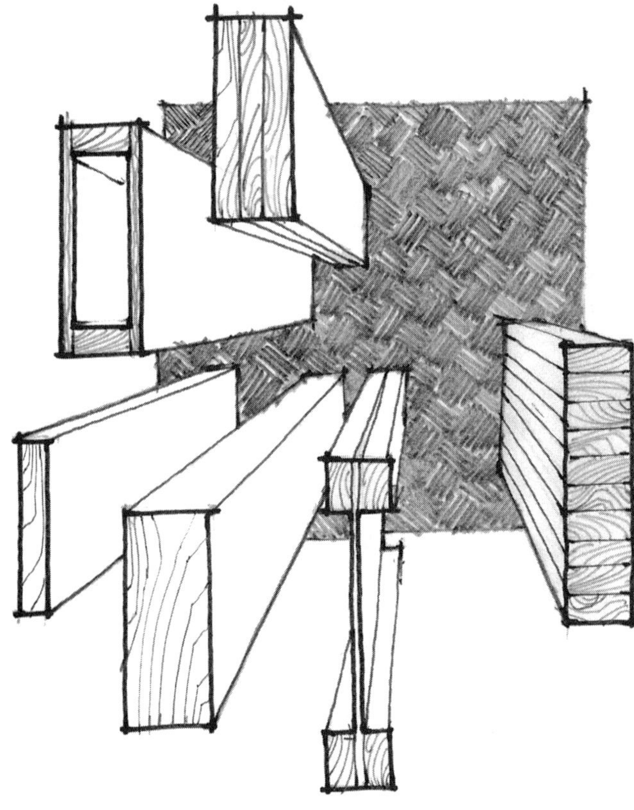

Figure 10-11
Some common types of steel beams.

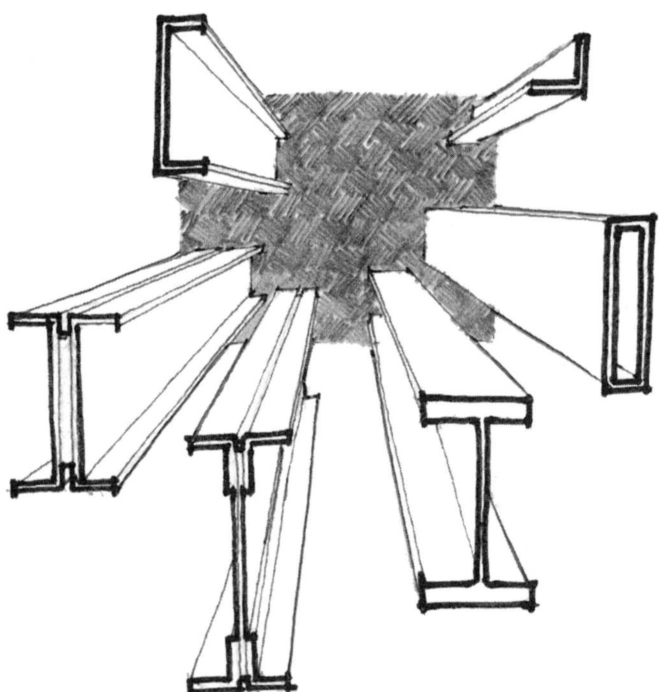

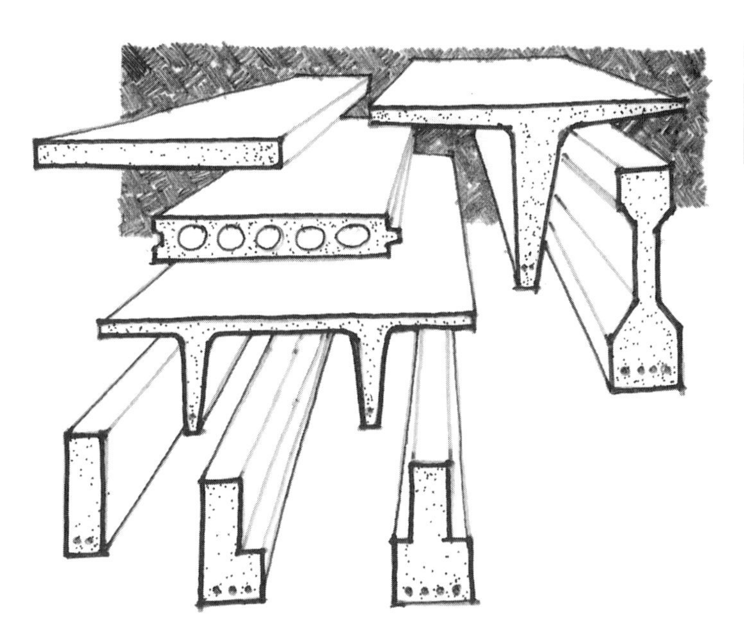

Figure 10-12
Some common types of reinforced concrete beams.

These are called *rafters* (Fig. 10-14). There are many types of rafters such as *common*, *jack*, and *valley* rafters. Their behavior is not purely that of a beam, but it is convenient to introduce them to the reader at this time. Most beams are horizontal; however, in heavy timber construction it is occasionally useful to use a sloped beam. These are known as *raker* beams. In a subsequent chapter we will introduce two other structural members that behave as beams. They are *purlins* and *girts*. We will discuss those when we cover trusses as a type of superstructure.

Figure 10-13
Notice the ceiling joists in this light wood frame.

Figure 10-14
Rafters in a partially completed frame.

Beam nomenclature

If the names commonly given to the various parts of a beam are introduced now, it will facilitate a subsequent discussion directed at how a beam works as a structural member under load. The *span* of the beam is the distance from one support to another. If we vertically cut across the beam, the face exposed by that cut is known as a *beam section*. If we look at the face of that section it has a *depth* and *width*. The top and bottom surface of a beam are known as its *extreme fibers*. Therefore there are two types of extreme fiber: the *top fiber* and the *bottom fiber*. Remember that these extreme fibers extend the full length of the beam on both the top and bottom surface. This is important because they are also the fibers that must usually resist the greatest bending stress in the beam (for reasons that will soon be revealed). Somewhere near the middle of the beam and running its full length, is the neutral fiber, also known as the beam's *neutral axis*. It is given this name because it is experiencing no stress due to bending. It will be interesting to see why this is so. Long beams require *cross bracing* or *blocking* of some type to support the beam against buckling and torsion. This requirement will be made clearer in the next few paragraphs.

Figure 10-15
Different types of built up wood beams.

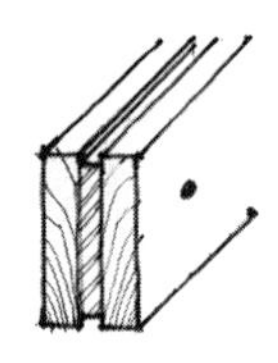

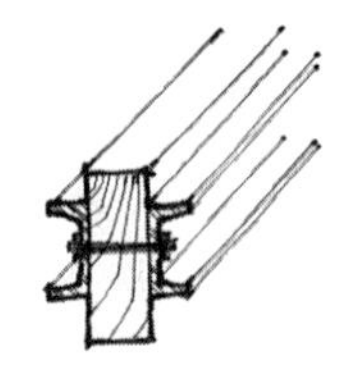

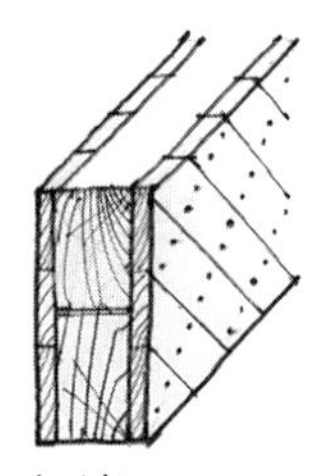

Common applications

Short spans

For short spans of (22 feet or less) light weight wood frame post and beam systems are most commonly used. Heavy timber post and beam construction has been historically used for longer spans such as those found in agricultural barns. It is possible to build up wood beams into configurations that will support somewhat increased spans (Fig. 10-15). Steel frame post and beam buildings are widely used in commercial construction such as offices when rooms do not require a span greater than about 30 feet. Reinforced concrete post and beam systems are widely used in commercial constructions with spans of 30 feet or less. It is possible to achieve much greater spans; however, the depth of such beams often obstructs heating and cooling ducts, and significantly reduces headspace in the rooms below such deep beams.

Longer spans

When wood members are glued together into *glulam* beams, spans up to about 60 feet can be achieved (Fig. 10-16). While longer spans are possible in this manner, it is likely that a different system such as a truss will be used. Similarly, steel plates can be welded into deep girders in a steel post and beam system (Fig. 10-17). The use of such girders can greatly extend the allowable span for steel post and beam buildings. At spans of 2 through 60 feet a steel wide flange can often be used, but at the long end of this span range it may be necessary to weld a steel plate to the top and bottom flange (Fig. 10-18). The reason that these built up sections add additional load bearing capacity to beams will be revealed in the next few paragraphs. Again, at spans of 60 feet and more, it is common to abandon the post and beam systems for a steel truss system of some type. As previously noted, simple reinforced concrete beams can become excessively deep when spans significantly exceed about 30 feet. With *post-tensioning* or *pre-stressing* greater beam spans are possible without resorting to excessive beam depth (Fig. 10-19). If a steel cable is placed as shown in a concrete beam, it can add considerable load carrying capacity to the beam when nuts are tightened on the threads found at both ends. If this tightening takes place before the concrete cures it is called *pre-stressing*. If the tightening takes place after the concrete has set up, it is known as *post-tensioning*. The additional tension in this cable tends to pull up the center of the beam, which will allow it to carry greater loads. When conventional steel wide flange sections are encased in concrete, they can be made to act jointly. This is known as *composite construction*. With this type of construction, not only are somewhat longer beam spans possible, but also it is self-fire proofing (Fig. 10-20).

Figure 10-16
Glulam beams.

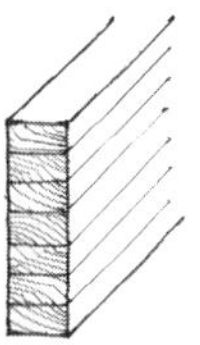

Figure 10-17
Built up steel beam.

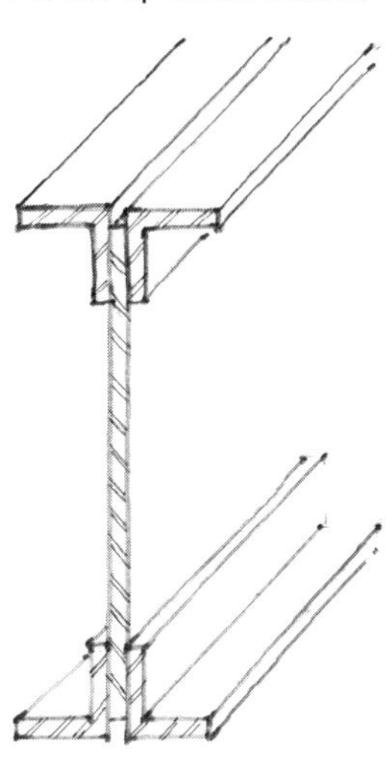

Beam behavior under load

Now it is time to begin to understand why these various beam configurations are widely used. The first issue is to understand how loads flow down through the members of a post and beam structure until they are transmitted to the foundation.

Load propagation

Some sort of floor *plate* collects superimposed loads, such as people and furniture, and transfers them to *joists*. The surface area of the plate that collects loads for a single joist is known as its *tributary area*. The joists then carry the aggregated load of their tributary area to the *beams* upon which the joists rest. In longer span post and beam systems, these beams may then transfer the aggregated loads from the joists to *girders*. In shorter span buildings such girders may not be required. Ultimately either the beams or the girders must horizontally transmit their aggregated loads to vertical *columns*, which then transmit the loads down to the foundation (Fig. 10-21). While upper floor columns may rest on strong beams in a lower story, that is a violation of the principle of structural continuity discussed in an earlier chapter. It is a better design for upper columns to directly rest on the columns of lower floors allowing simple direct flow of loads directly to the foundation.

Figure 10-18
Strengthened top and bottom flanges.

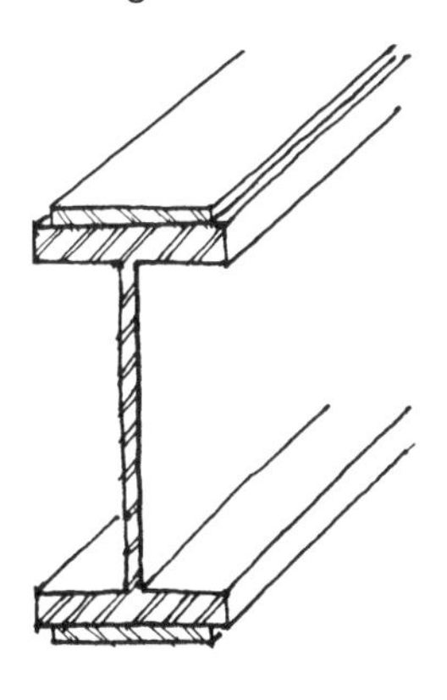

Figure 10-19
Prestressed and post tensioning cables in a concrete beam.

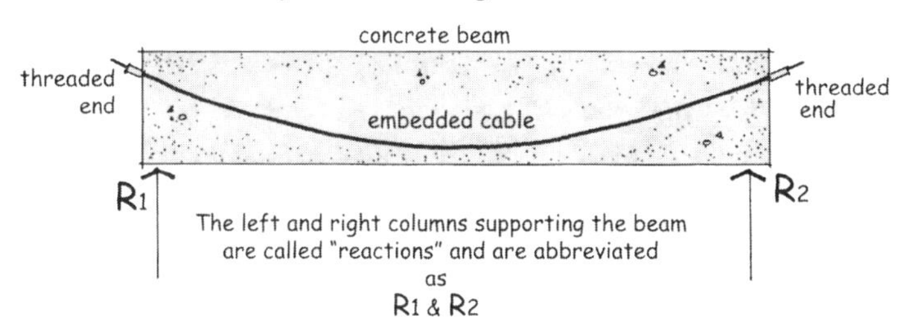
concrete beam
threaded end
embedded cable
threaded end
R1
R2
The left and right columns supporting the beam are called "reactions" and are abbreviated as
R1 & R2

Figure 10-20
A composite beam.

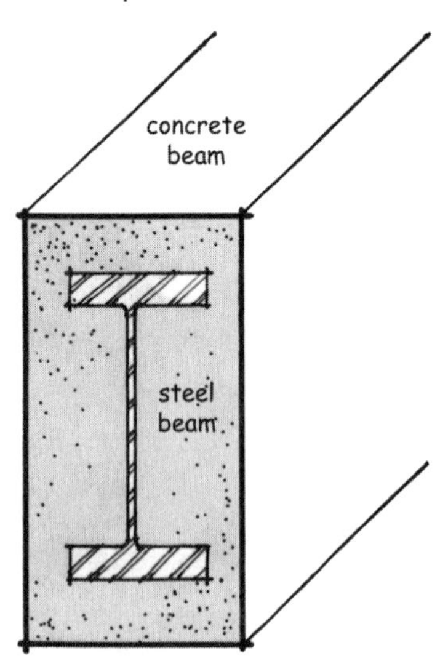

Figure 10-21
Load propagation in a post and beam superstructure.

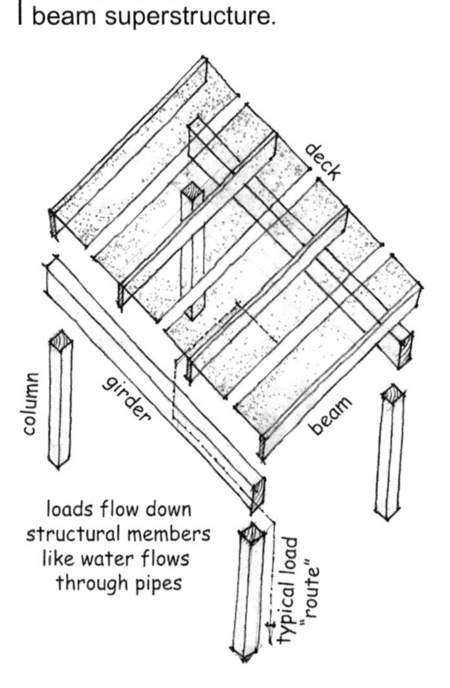

Stresses in beams

Bending stress A beam is simultaneously trying to be a bad arch, and a bad cable system. As you will recall from the last two chapters, both of these have a fairly deep parabolic "funicular" shape as their optimum uniformly loaded configuration. However, neither the cable nor arch inherently provides the flat walking surface sought in the usual building floor. The beam artificially flattens these two systems to provide the flat floor and ceiling often desired in a building (Fig. 10-22). Unfortunately, this flattening yields a beam of unacceptable depth. So in addition to flattening, we must also profoundly reduce the depth of both the hidden cable and hidden arch system within the beam in order to produce a beam of acceptably shallow depth (Fig. 10-23).

This significantly reduces the "floor-to-floor" distance of a building, which yields considerable cost economy. For instance, if the floor-to-floor distance can be reduced from 12 to 10 feet, then 2 feet less of exterior building wall material is needed for the full circumference of the outside of the building. In a 50-story building, these savings will be multiplied fifty times. Therefore, in such cases "shallow" beams are sought.

It is worth noting that where the optimum (funicular) curve of both the hidden arch and cable most deviate from the actual shape of the beam that imprisons them, is the location that is most likely to fail in *bending* (Fig. 10-24). Therefore it is also the point at which bending stress can be most easily understood.

Figure 10-22
Deep beam with the hidden cable and arch systems shown.

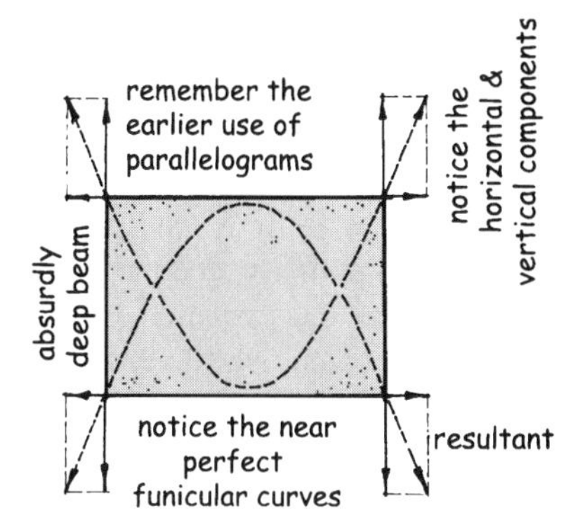

Figure 10-23
Shallow beam with the hidden cable and arch systems shown.

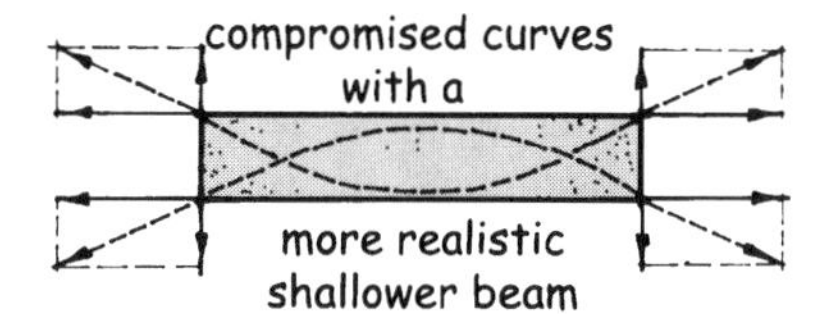

If we could feel the stresses at work at the beam's mid-span, we would feel compressive stress on the *top fibers* or *top chord* of the beam. This is because the beam is trying to be an arch, and arches are pressed together in compression (Fig. 10-25). If we could feel the *bottom fiber* or *bottom chord* at the same point at mid-span, we would feel great tension. This is because the beam is trying to be a cable system, and cables are tension. So in the bending failure of a simple beam, the top fiber will crush in compression, and the bottom chord or fiber will attempt to tear (Fig. 10-26). While tension and compression are "simple" stresses, bending is the first *combined stress* we will study. This is because bending simultaneously makes use of both compression and tension to resist loads. We can make diagrams that graphically show how much bending stress exists at any point along a beam. Such beam diagrams are important in the body of knowledge known as *strength of materials*, but are beyond the scope of this book. It is interesting to recognize visually that for a uniformly loaded simply supported beam, the greatest bending stress is at mid-span for the reasons discussed above.

Figure 10-24
Point of greatest bending stress.

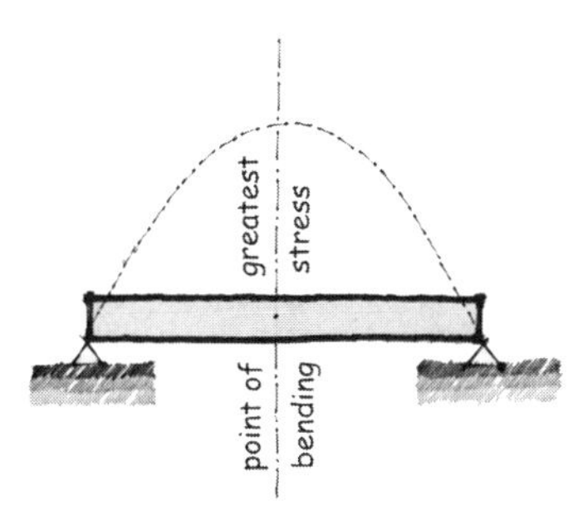

Figure 10-25
Notice the compression in the top chord of the beam.

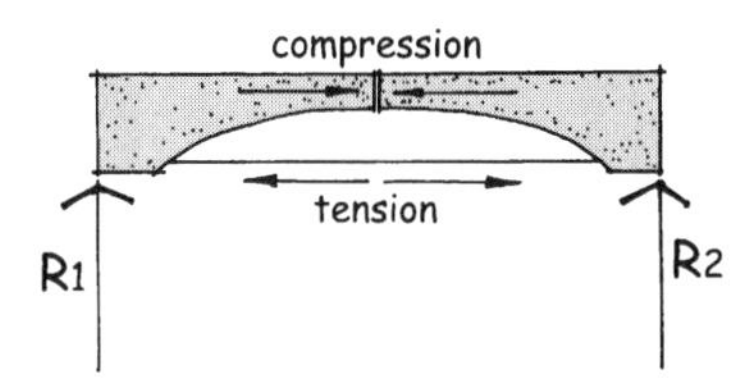

Figure 10-26
Tearing in tension in the bottom chord.

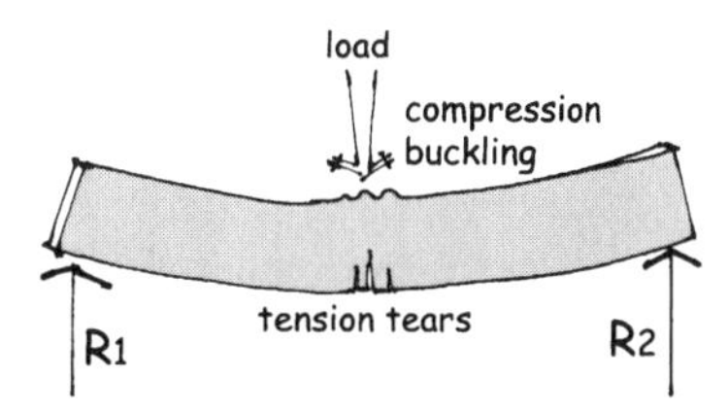

To understand how a beam resists externally applied loads, we have to cut the beam at some point (cut a beam section). Since we have been discussing the point at mid-span, let's continue to use it (Fig. 10-27). If the beam is cut at mid-span it will try to rotate in a clockwise direction. That rotational force (called *moment*) is due to both the external load on the beam, and the long length of the beam between the supports and where the beam was cut. Traditionally a clockwise direction of rotational force is known as *negative moment.* It can only be stopped by an equal and opposite counterclockwise rotation called a positive moment (Fig. 10-28).

Now let us return to the instant that we cut the beam at mid-span and the beam began to rotate in a clockwise direction. Obviously there was a rotational force (bending moment) hidden in the beam that did not become visible until the beam was cut. Since the original uncut beam wasn't moving (it was "static") the beam must be doing something that is keeping this rotation from happening. Notice that this rotation works something like a lever. It is like a wrench twisting on a bolt (Fig. 10-29). Please imagine pulling a nail with a claw hammer. The longer the handle and the harder we pull, the bigger the nail we can pull. The applied force of our hand multiplied by the length of the handle is known as "moment" in the study of structures. It is the tendency to rotate. The length of the handle is more technically known as the *moment arm.* If we are to stop the tendency of the beam to rotate due to the product of the applied load on floor beam times the length of beam (or moment arm) to where we cut, there must be a second opposite and equal rotation coming from somewhere else. That second opposite and equal moment is hidden inside the beam. Let's call these two moments the "external moment" and the "internal moment." But what causes this second internal moment?

It is the beam's *material resistance* to bending stress. Now notice that as we look at the fibers exposed by this cut, that the top fibers are enduring the greatest compressive stress, while the bottom fibers are resisting the greatest tensile

Figure 10-27
If a beam is cut, the remnant will rotate.

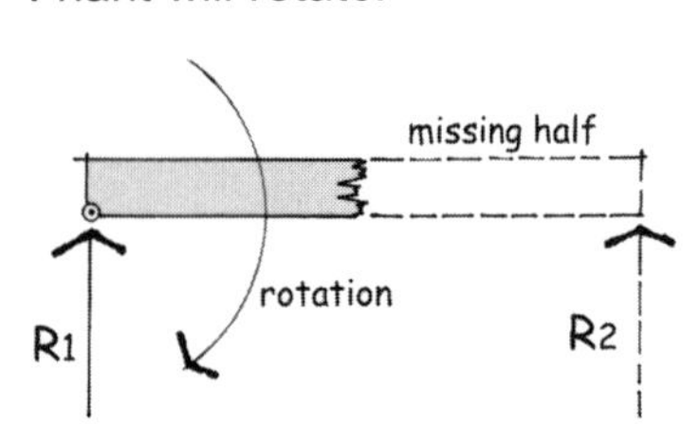

Figure 10-28
Rotation in one direction is stopped by equal rotation in the opposite direction.

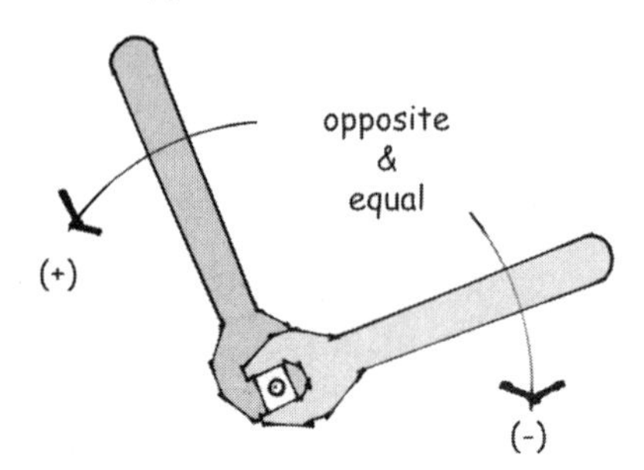

Figure 10-29
This leverage is known as a "moment" (a force times some length).

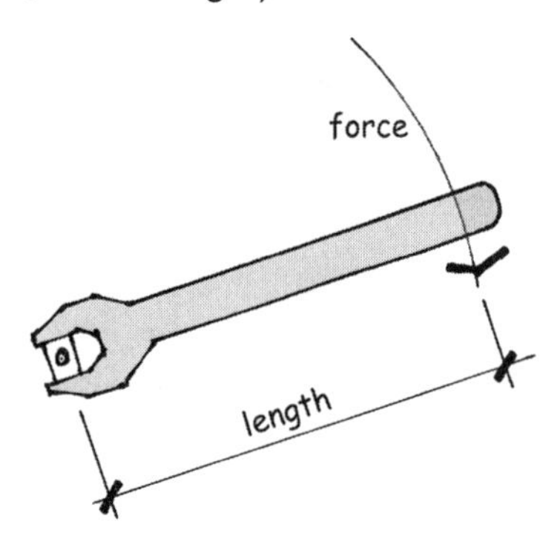

(tension) stress. If this is so there must be a gradual shift from compression to tension across the section of the beam. Therefore at the middle fiber of the beam both the compressive and tensile stress must be zero. We can draw a simple diagram next to the cut in the beam to show this (Fig. 10-30).

Since the middle of the beam isn't working as hard as the top and bottom fibers, we may have material cut out near the middle or *neutral axis* in order to make them lighter (Fig. 10-31). Also, if additional bending strength is sought, plates can be added to the top and bottom of a beam because that is where most of the serious resistance to load is taking place. Look at the beam section that we previously drew with maximum compression at the top fiber, maximum tension at the bottom fiber, and no stress at the middle or *neutral fiber*. The compression at the top fiber is a force, and the tension at the bottom is a force. The distance is the *internal moment arm*. This is that second opposite and equal moment we were searching for in order to resist the external moment previously discussed. Therefore, this *internal moment* must be equal to the external moment if the floor load on the beam is to be resisted. But compare the external and internal moment arms. The external beam length will be many feet long, but the beam will only be a few inches deep, so this resisting internal moment arm is astoundingly smaller than the external moment arm. Certainly we should keep the internal moment arm (beam depth) as great as possible. That is why beams are deeper than they are wide. But bending is not the only stress at work within a beam.

Shearing stress While bending stress is greatest at mid-span in the case shown above, shearing stress is greatest at the face of the supporting columns at both ends of the beam. To understand shearing stress, let us imagine a beam made of books that are pressed together between two hands. When a vertical load is placed on this "book beam," there is a tendency for one book to slide

Figure 10-31
The neutral fiber.

Figure 10-30
Stress diagram for a beam.

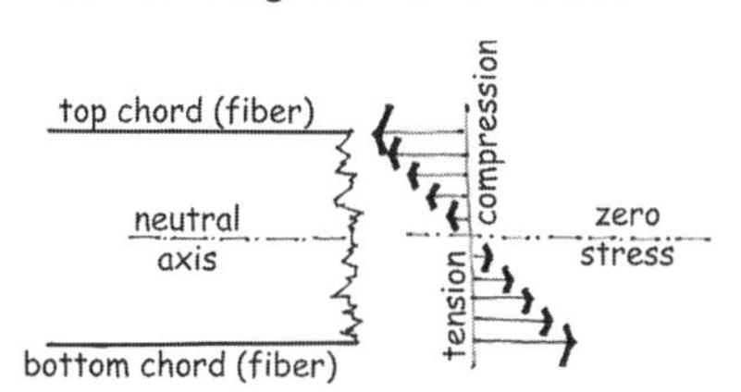

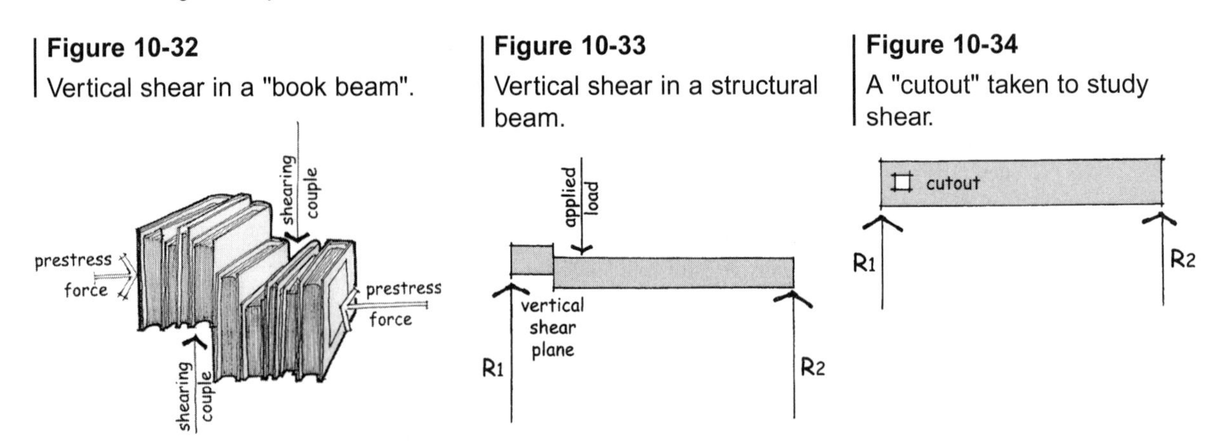

Figure 10-32
Vertical shear in a "book beam".

Figure 10-33
Vertical shear in a structural beam.

Figure 10-34
A "cutout" taken to study shear.

vertically past another (Fig. 10-32). This tendency is called *vertical shear* and it is hidden within the beam. This tendency is present whether the beam is made of books, wood, steel, or concrete (Fig. 10-33).

A second type of shear is simultaneously at work at the same point of the beam. Let's imagine that we cut a small square out of our beam, and study it separately (Fig. 10-34). The cutout would look similar to a block that children play with as a toy. If we place *vertical shearing stress* (parallel vertical forces-one up, one down) on two sides of the block, the block must either rotate or change shape (Fig. 10-35). These two opposite but parallel forces are known as a *vertical shearing couple*. As we look at both the individual point on the beam from which our block was cut and the total beam, we observe that both are sitting still (*static*), not rotating. Something must be resisting this rotation. If we wish to prevent this rotation, we would have to exert an opposite and equal rotation (or couple) on the block. But the two vertical side surfaces of the block already have a vertical shear couple applied to them. Therefore the top and bottom of our cutout block must have a *horizontal shearing couple* applied

Figure 10-35
The enlarged cutout.

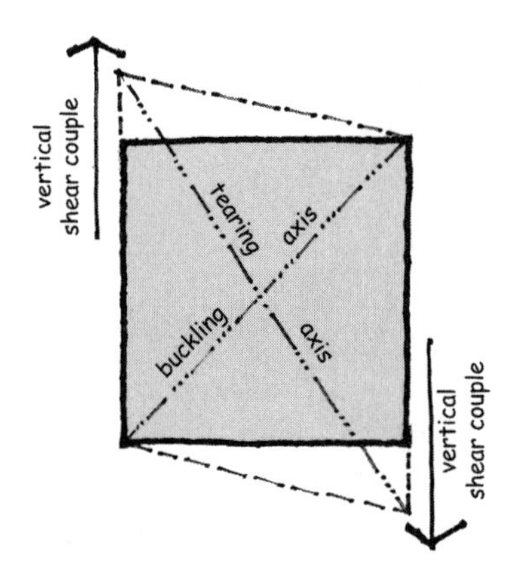

to them (Fig. 10-36). While this balances the vertical shearing stress caused by the vertical couple, it also tells us that horizontal shearing stress must be equal to the vertical shearing stress at the point in the beam where the block was cut. In simple terms this means that the material of the beam must resist an equal vertical and horizontal stress at this point. The effect of horizontal shearing stress can best be understood by stacking thin boards horizontally to form a simple beam (Fig. 10-37). Make a thick dark line vertically at mid-span on the side of this built-up board beam. Make a similar dark vertical line on both ends of the beam. Now load the beam and watch what happens to the lines. The line at mid-span experiences no change. No horizontal shear is present. However, the ends are profoundly shifted horizontally. This is horizontal shear. So, horizontal shear is greatest near the support and zero at mid-span. But remember that the horizontal shearing couple must equal the vertical shearing couple in our cutout. Therefore the greatest vertical shearing stress must also be at the supports, while the vertical shear at mid-span is zero. Now we can state an important conceptual insight about beams that is worth memorizing. "Where bending is the greatest, shear (both vertical and horizontal) are zero; and where shear (both vertical and horizontal) are greatest, bending is zero. We can also understand why shearing failures in beams usually happen at or near a column, and bending failures happen at mid-span. Before leaving the subject look once again at the cutout block in Fig. 10-34. Now notice that the force of the vertical shearing couples tended to distort the original square cutout into a parallelogram (Fig. 10-35). This distortion will tend to tear the beam material along the axis of one diagonal, and buckle the material along the other diagonal. However, both the buckling and the tearing due to shear happen at a 45 degree angle. Since wide flange steel beams have such a thin web, they will try to buckle at supports. Since concrete has essentially no strength in tension, concrete beams will try to tear at a 45 degree angle at supports.

Figure 10-36

The vertical shearing couple opposed by the horizontal shearing couple.

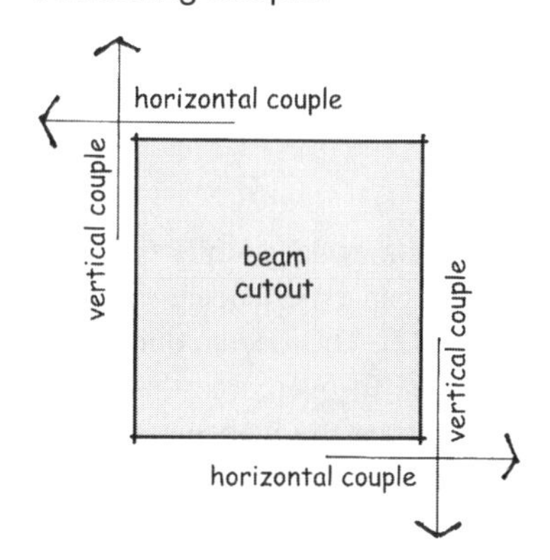

Figure 10-37

A way to visualize horizontal shear.

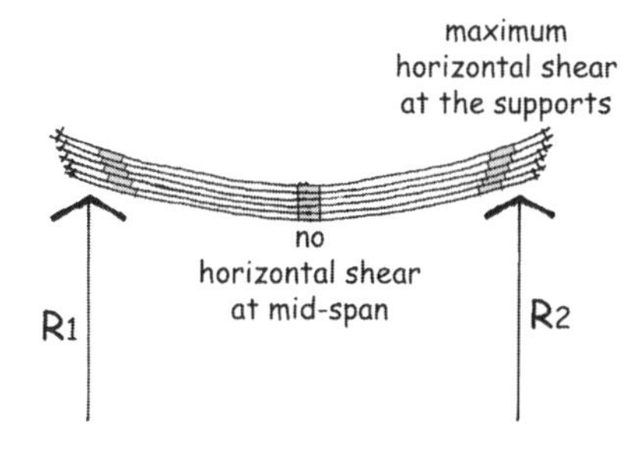

Figure 10-38
Bearing stress.

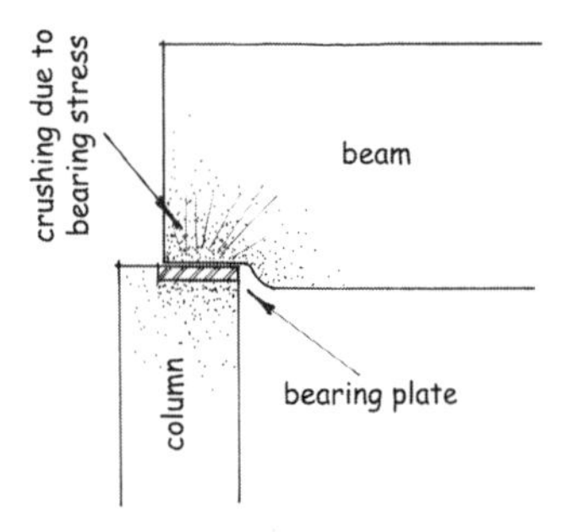

Bearing stress So beams must be designed not to fail in bending or in shear. But we are not done. The beam will rest on a column, a beam seat, or a girder. Where these two surfaces come into contact *bearing stress* is developed in both members. Both the beam surface and the column surface will tend to crush. This is known as bearing stress (Fig. 10-38).

Torsional stress A beam that is not laterally supported by blocking, cross bracing, or another device will have a tendency to rotate out from under the load (Fig. 10-39). The circumstances that require such lateral support are specified by the building code. If a beam is adequately restrained at its ends, there is still a tendency for the beam to twist (experience *torsion*) or for the top chord of the beam to buckle to the side (*lateral buckling*). This is also prevented or overcome with the use of well placed lateral beam supports such as blocking or cross bracing. Torsion stress is made worse by eccentric (off-center) loading on the beam.

Figure 10-39
Beam rotation.

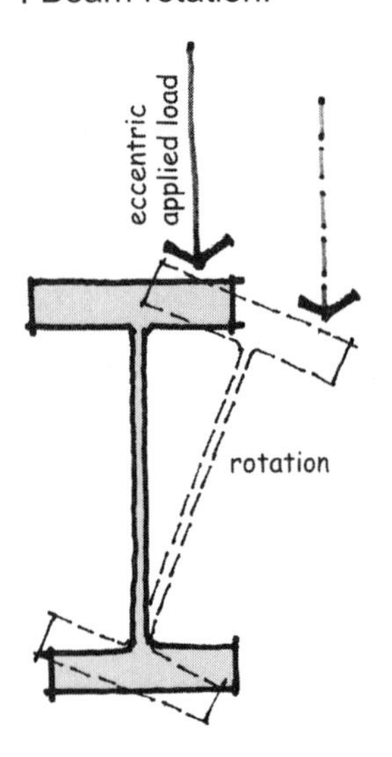

Torsion is the last type of complex stress that must be introduced in this chapter. Torsion can occur not only in beams, but also in bolts, and in total building frames. The most direct personal way to understand torsion is to wring the water out of a wet towel by twisting it. While connection failures are discussed at a later time, it is easier to address torsion using bolts since they are solid circular shafts (Fig. 10-40). Notice that the same type of "cutout" that was used in shear will once again be used to understand torsion. In wringing out the towel one hand twists opposite to the other producing shear, but in this case it is on a curved surface. One diagonal axis is placed under compression (tending to crush or buckle), and a second diagonal axis that is put in tension (tending to tear). However, in the case of torsion these two diagonals are wrapped around the circular solid shaft (Fig. 10-41). As we wring out our towel it is easy to observe that the outside surface of the towel is moving a lot more than the inside. One might guess that there is an axis at the center of the solid circular shaft that is not contributing much resistance to torsion, just as the neutral axis of a beam is not contributing resistance to bending. Therefore, just as it is wise to get as much material in a beam out at the extreme top and bottom fiber in order to resist bending, it is also more efficient to get as much material out at the outside edge of a shaft that must resist torsion. That is why the drive shaft in a car is made from a hollow pipe. Torsion failures in a brittle material (like cast iron) with little tensile strength will fail by tearing along the tensile diagonal shown above. Materials that are strong in tension, but that are thin-walled tubes (such as a soft drink can) will fail by buckling (Jensen and Chenowith 1983).

Figure 10-40
Beam torsion.

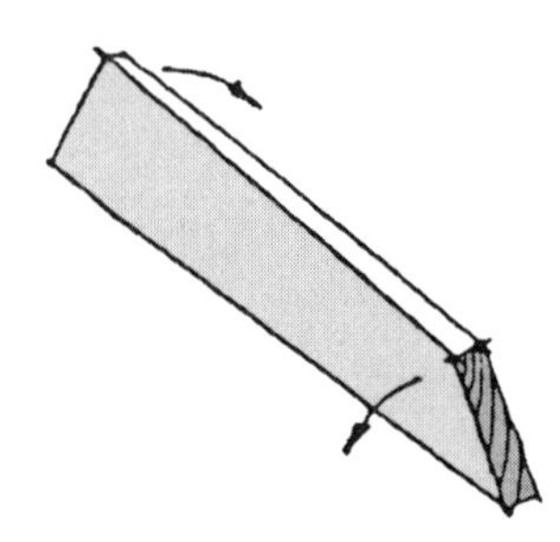

Web buckling

Different beam materials and configurations have somewhat unique types of beam failures. For instance, steel wide flange beams can experience *web buckling* under heavy concentrated point loads (Fig. 10-42). This occurs due to the extreme thinness of the web of a steel wide flange. To overcome this, steel angles (known as *web stiffeners*) are used to reinforce the web under such loads. They may also be used at other points on steel beams, but that is beyond the scope of this text.

Figure 10-41
Torsion is shear wrapped into a cylindrical movement.

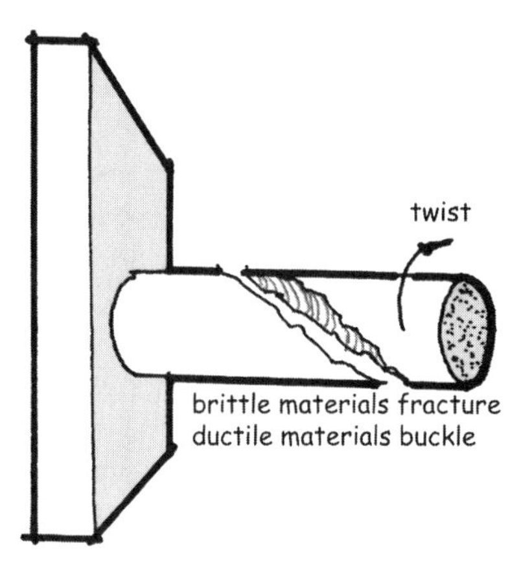

Figure 10-42
Web buckling is opposed by the use of web stiffeners.

Deflection

Most of the above stresses lead to "strength" failures in individual beams. In these the beam may have insufficient bending, bearing, or shearing strength. In such failures the beam will rupture, break, tear, or crush. A few of the above failures were really failures in stability. Beam rotation and top chord buckling are examples of inadequate beam "stability". However, we have not yet discussed inadequate beam stiffness. A beam may change shape downward (*deflect*) excessively. If it doesn't break, it isn't a strength failure. Indeed the beam may spring right back to its original shape as soon as the load is removed. However, if the ceiling under the beam was plastered, certainly the plaster would crack. Also, it can be disquieting to have a kitchen floor that is as "springy" as a diving board. That springiness is a physical symptom of *excessive deflection*, and excessive deflection is the final type of beam failure.

COLUMNS

Column nomenclature

The collection of loads above the column often leads to the presence of a *column capital or cap*. The most critical element of a column is its shaft. It is the *shaft* that conducts loads from above, vertically down to the foundation, and subsequently into the soil under the building. The top of the shaft may be broadened by ornamentation of various types. Beyond its ornamental value this broadening may also serve a legitimate structural role of increasing the bearing area at the top of the shaft, or collection of horizontal beam loads for concentration in the vertical shaft. The shaft may rest on some sort of column base. While it has had clear aesthetic uses, our interest here is that the *base* may disperse the loads collected within the column shaft over a larger bearing area.

Column types or categories

By period fashion

It is traditional among architects to classify columns by the period fashion in which it first appeared, such as Corinthian or Ionic. However, our interest here is in structural behavior, so that discussion is left to other texts. A brief discussion of post and beam aesthetics will close this chapter, but it will focus on aesthetic issues that are more universal to all column types.

Column types by material

Figure 10-43
Types of wood columns.

Wood columns come in varying cross sections from round to square and rectangular. It is also possible to aggregate two or more wood sections into several types of built-up timber columns. Since timber occurs in round trees, post type buildings make use of round sections, which produces less waste and an optimum column shape. Notice the spaced column at the extreme right of this set of column alternatives. The advantage of this gap will become more obvious as you read further (Fig. 10-43).

Steel columns also vary widely in cross-sectional shape. Steel pipe columns, tubes, and wide flanges are the most common. As with timber, two or more different types of steel sections may be combined into several different types of built-up steel columns. For reasons that will become better understood in this chapter, pipe columns and some built-up columns are the optimum shapes. For a little additional strength a pipe column can be filled with concrete to form a "lally" column. At the extreme right of this group of alternative column shapes is one of many built up steel column configurations (Fig. 10-44).

Figure 10-44
Types of steel columns.

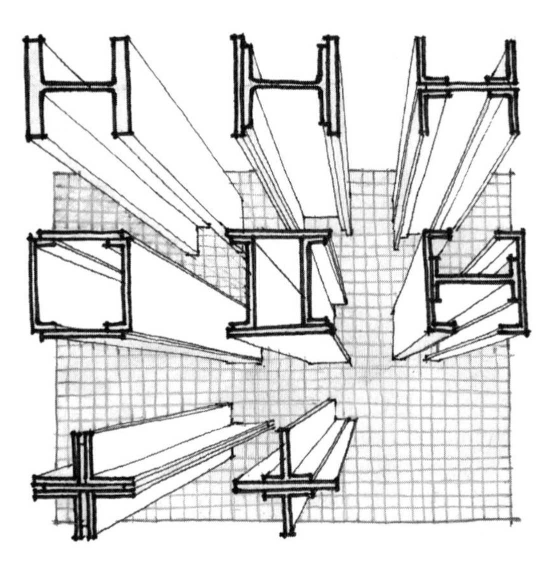

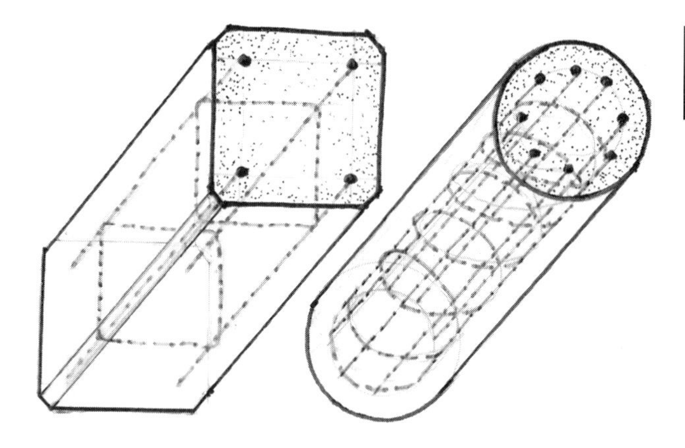

Figure 10-45
Steel reinforcing in a concrete column.

Reinforced concrete columns usually come in three general types of cross sections (round, square, and rectangular). Notice that in the square concrete column, both vertical and horizontal reinforcing is used. The purpose of the horizontal "hoop" is to restrain the vertical rebar from spreading when the column comes under heavy compression. In round concrete columns pre-formed spiral reinforcing is used instead of hoops (Fig. 10-45).

While single unit *masonry columns* are possible, it is currently more common to build up masonry columns, leaving a void in the center which can be reinforced with steel and filled with grout (Fig. 10-46).

Figure 10-46
Steel reinforcing in a masonry column.

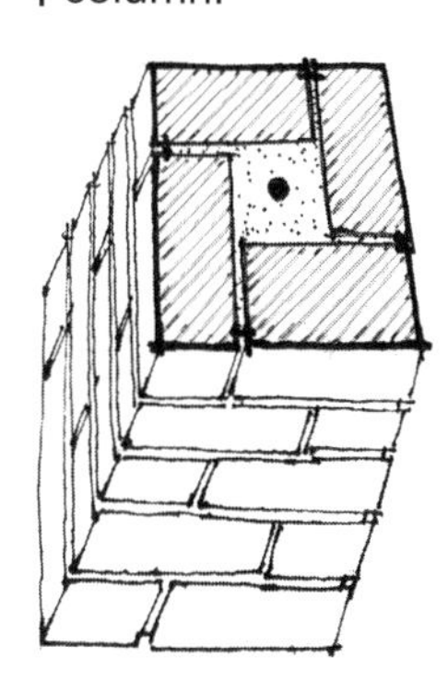

By structural role

Compressive members have several names depending upon their use. *Columns* are major vertical support under beams. *Posts* may either be columns that extend continuously down into the soil to form their own foundation, or they may be a vertical web member in a truss (more about that in a later chapter). *Struts* are usually any compressive member not in a vertical position. *Studs* are multiple small columns placed at close spacing in vertical walls of light wood construction. *Cripple studs* are the short studs that are placed above and under windows in light wood construction.

Column behavior under load

Stresses in columns

When a beam rests directly on a column, not only does the beam face in contact suffer *bearing stress*, but so also does the face of the end of the column in contact (Fig. 10-47). Extremely short thick columns (known as piers) are most likely to fail in simple *compressive crushing* (Fig. 10-48). This is a very rare failure in modern buildings. Columns that are a bit longer are more likely to *shear* than to crush due to simple axial compression. In order to understand shearing stresses in a column; recall that shear lines are usually at 45-degree angles in beams. The same can occur in columns (Fig. 10-49). It is most

Figure 10-47
Bearing stress in a column.

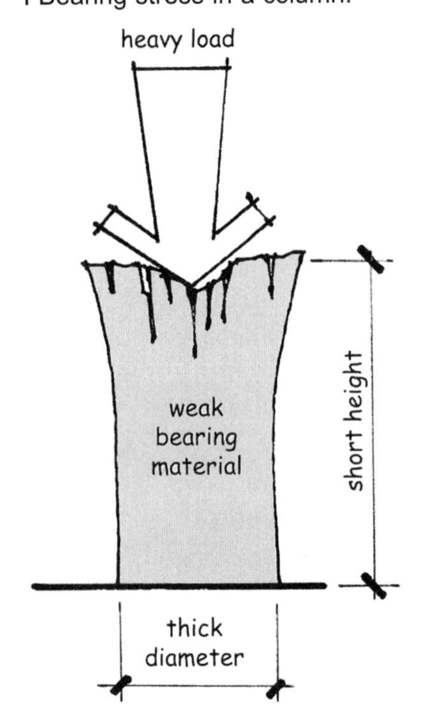

Figure 10-48
Column crushing.

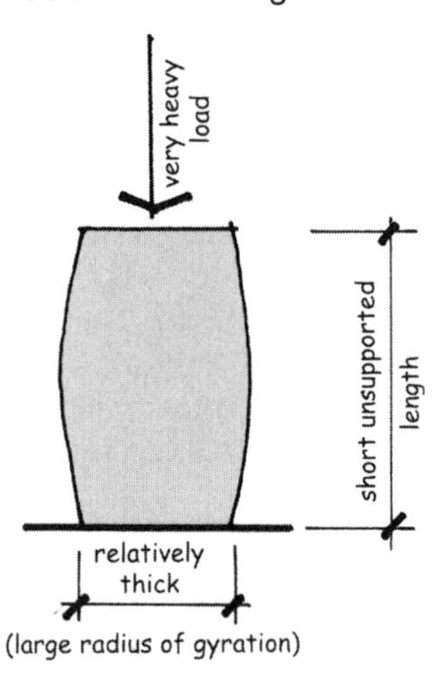

Figure 10-49
Column shear at the Oakland overpass collapse in the 1986 earthquake. Notice the 45 degree angle.

obvious in failures of reinforced concrete columns. This type of failure is known as a *dental failure* due to its similarity to the shape of two opposing canine teeth. Since the column is symmetrical and is made of a homogeneous material, it cannot decide along which diagonal axis to fail. Therefore it fails on all of them, spaulding out crushed material, exposing buckled vertical reinforcing bars, and breaking horizontal reinforcing rings known as "hoops." This leaves several failure planes all at about 45-degree angles (Fig. 10-50). Shear in wood columns is harder to see. The grain of the wood will compromise the clean 45-degree failure plane. The failure may tend to follow some weakness in the grain rather than conforming to the 45-degree failure plane found in a more homogeneous material such as concrete.

Figure 10-50
Dental type column failure in the 1985 Mexico City earthquake.

Very long columns will probably fail in *Euler buckling* (pronounced as "oiler"). It is also known as "long buckling." Long columns, even under axial loads, will splay out (*buckle*) to the side long before they have a chance to be crushed in simple compression, or even to fail in shear (Fig. 10-51). Stand a wooden yardstick on end, and press down on it with your hand as you would a cane. Increase the pressure very gradually, and keep the load as axial as you can. Feel for that moment that it suddenly buckles to the side. Feel how its load-resisting strength seems to suddenly disappear in that moment. Broadening the waist of a column can be used to resist long buckling (Fig. 10-52).

If thin-walled pipes or tubes are used as columns, yet another failure mechanism can be seen. Find an empty aluminum soft drink can. You have a thin-walled tubular column. Now set the empty can on the ground and very carefully stand on it. If the load is perfectly axial, very gradually applied, and not too great, the can will hold. However, if any of these conditions are violated, the can will buckle to the side. Now look at the buckled wall of the can. This type of buckling is known as *short buckling*. Again, we become concerned about short buckling with hollow columns with very thin walls (Fig. 10-53).

Optimum post and beam configuration

Column shapes

Optimum shapes for beams were previously discussed. While columns are available in a variety of cross sections (Fig. 10-54), it will not surprise the

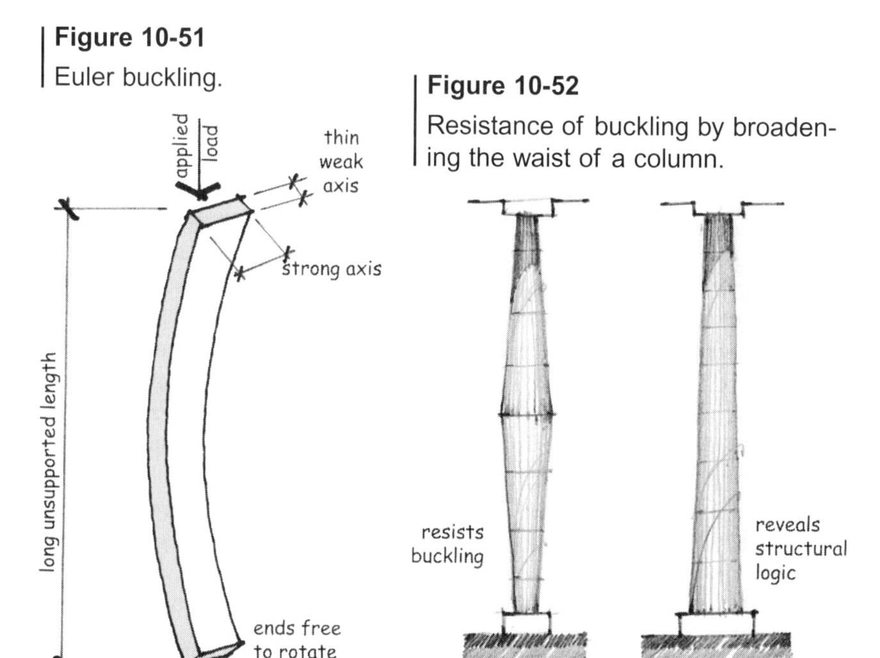

Figure 10-51
Euler buckling.

Figure 10-52
Resistance of buckling by broadening the waist of a column.

Figure 10-53
Short bucking.

thin
wall
eccentric
load
short height
large radius of gyration

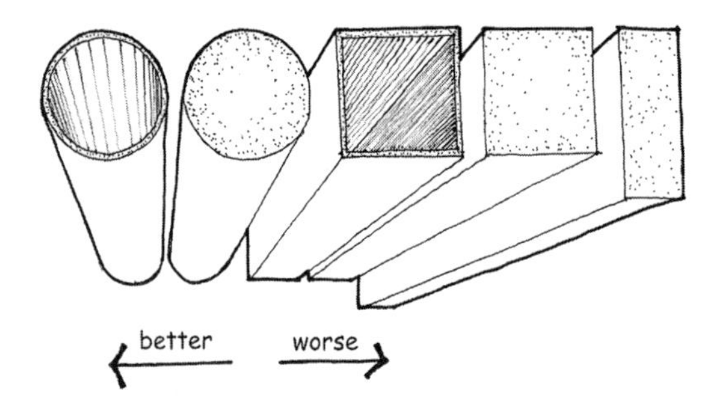

Figure 10-54
Optimum column configuration.

reader that some perform better than others. In cross section the optimum column shape is a round hollow pipe. It will take a moment to understand why this is so. Remember the way in which the yardstick buckled in the simple experiment we have just conducted. Notice that it always buckles in the direction of the shorter dimension (*weak axis*) at its base. Remember also that beams were harder to bend in their deep direction (*strong axis*) than in their narrow or weak axis. If we wish to avoid column buckling, we only need to eliminate this shorter weak axis. The only shape that doesn't have a short and long axis is a circle. Now, why should that circle be hollow? In resistance of simple compression, structural material at the center of the column does as much good as the material at the outside edge of a column. However, if buckling takes place, the material at the center of the column does almost nothing, while that at the outside edges is doing most of the work. For this reason the circle becomes hollow inside. So for optimum structural performance, a hollow pipe is best. A square tube is next best. Similarly a solid round column and then a solid square column follow. Columns that have a wide difference between their strong and weak axis, such as rectangles, may be used, but they are far from optimum structurally. Even when columns are built up from lesser members in steel or wood, the square shape is still sought.

End conditions

It is less obvious to a casual observer that the end conditions of a column greatly affect its *bearing capacity* (the amount of vertical load it will carry). What is meant by *end condition*? What is at issue is the degree to which each end of the column is restrained against sliding laterally or rotating. Look at a set of pliers. A pair of pliers is jointed by a pinned connection. The ends of a column can also effectively be "pinned", allowing easy rotation at that point. Now think of welding the joint of your pliers solidly. This would "fix" that joint against any such rotation. Columns may also be designed to fix one, or both, ends against rotation (Fig. 10-55). Why do we care if rotation is facilitated or restricted? For the column to buckle, the ends will try to rotate. Fixed ends will, therefore, make lateral buckling more difficult and the column will be able to carry a greater load.

Eccentric loading

Up until now we have always spoken of *axial loads* on the column (those that run right down the center of a column). Structurally this is most desirable;

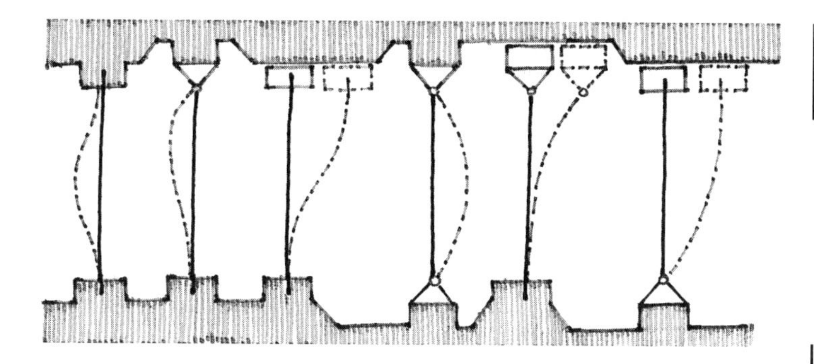

Figure 10-55
Alternative end connections for columns.

Figure 10-56
Eccentric loads on columns are common, but not preferred.

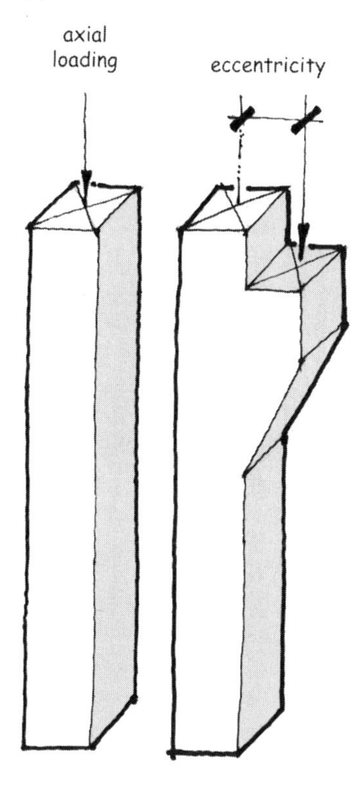

however, this is often not possible. When the connection between beam and column cause loads not to flow down the center of the column, *eccentric* loads are present (Fig. 10-56). The problem with eccentric loads is that they encourage buckling. Rotation in the actual joint produces an effect similar to the pinned end connections we have just discussed.

Column stability

If a column rests on uneven soil or is diagonally loaded, the full strength of the column may never be tested. Instead it may fail by simply rotating over. If the soil under a column is quite soft or the load quite heavy, the column may simply begin to sink into the ground. This is the second type of stability failure in columns (Fig. 10-57). Failure of a column is particularly dangerous. A failure in single column known as a *local failure* may lead to a total collapse of the larger structural frame known as a *global failure* (Fig. 10-58).

Figure 10-57
Column instability.

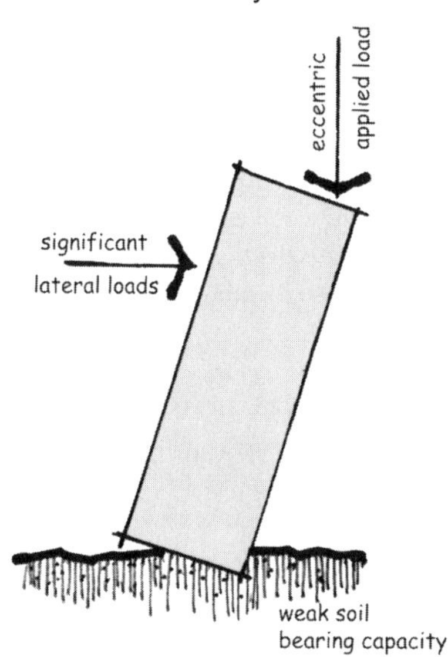

Figure 10-58
If one column fails, many floors will globally collapse.

Joints

Types of connectors Timber uses nailed or bolted connections. End, edge, and connector-to-connecter distance is a genuine concern in all of these types of connections. Steel plates, shear plates, and split rings are used to improve these timber connections where large loads are present. One of the best sources of information on timber details is *Design of Wood Structures*. Steel makes use of either welded or bolted connections. One of the best sources for information on steel post and beam connections is the *AISC Manual of Steel Construction*. Cast-in place (in-situ) concrete post and beams are often monolithic pours (continuously poured without stopping). The reinforcing bars inside the concrete for both the beams and the columns must usually continue clear through the joint. This is especially true where earthquakes are likely. Pre-cast concrete joints are a bit more complex. In reality it is usually the reinforcing steel that is joined by welding, and the grout is used to fill the void that was previously needed to have access to the weld.

Sizing and spacing of connectors Math calculations are necessary to establish the correct number, size, and spacing of connectors between a post and a beam. For example, if bolts are too close to an edge, end, or another bolt, a tear may develop. Specific types of failure in post and beam connections are beyond the scope of this text. However, conceptually it is worth mentioning that in some post and beam connections the eccentricity that was discussed in an earlier paragraph may cause the connection to try to rotate. This rotation is yet another type of failure that will require still more care and calculation.

Leverage and moment in beam-to-column joints The concept of a rotational force known as "moment" was introduced in an earlier paragraph concerning beams. Now we must reapply this concept to the total frame, not just a single beam. A beam forms a very long "moment arm." While the column is probably not as long as the beam, it is still a very long arm when compared to the handle of a wrench or a hammer. As a lever the length of a post or beam is impressive. This long lever arm is working against a very small joint between a post and a beam. Certainly it would be measured in feet. Joints in a post and beam superstructure are measured in inches. They are small. If the building begins to move, even very slightly, both the posts and the beams can become levers working against these small shared joints. They can easily tear the joint apart. Therefore, special attention must be paid to the selection and application of an appropriate lateral support system to prevent these members from moving.

Post and beam system.

When large loads or long spans demand large structural members, it is usually best to reveal them. When laying out joist and beams, always span the shortest direction. In his book *Structures* Daniel Schodek provides some useful rules of thumb. Timber beams are used for spans of about 8 to 20 feet with a beam depth that is about 1/16 of the span. Steel beams span about 10 to 70 feet, with a depth that is about 1/20 of the span. Reinforced concrete beams span with a depth that is about 1/12 of the span (Schodek 1980). The width of beams is usually about one third to one half of the beam depth. Rules of thumb for columns are much more rare. Instead sources such as the *Studio Desk Companion* by Edward Allen and the *AISC Steel Handbook* have tables which may be used directly for crude preliminary design dimensions.

Lateral support system

Post and beam superstructures are not laterally self-supporting. Some additional systems must be employed. The most common include diagonal bracing, cross bracing, and knee bracing. Shear walls are also used; as are rigid connections, but these begin to lead us to other types of superstructure that will be discussed in later chapters of this text.

Special issues in column to foundation joints

Care must be taken to assure that the superstructure is adequately secured to the foundation. This connection is the site of one of the most common structural failures in post and beam structures in both strong winds and earthquakes.

Figure 10-59

Typical joints between beam and column.

Failures in post and beam systems

Member failures in beams

Take a moment to summarize the types of failures to which individual beams are vulnerable. Beams fail in bending (top fiber crushing or bottom fiber tearing), horizontal and vertical shear, excessive deflection, rotation, torsion, top chord buckling, and end bearing.

Member failures in individual columns

Now let's summarize the types of failures which individual columns experience. Columns fail in bearing, crushing, shear, Euler buckling, short buckling, rotation, and excessive settlement.

Figure 10-60

Notice that reinforcing did not extend continuously through column joints.

Joint failures between columns and beams

Joints between beams and columns fail in bearing, joint rotation, end tears, edge tears, connector failures (i.e., bolt shear or weld failures), and excessive leverage at a joint where very long members connect to very small joints (Fig. 10-59).

Global failures

Post and beam structures are very vulnerable to wracking of the total frame, excessive drift at the top, torsion or twisting of the total frame, total frame torsion, joint continuity failure (Fig. 10-60), and separation of superstructure from the foundation (Fig. 10-61).

FUNCTIONAL FOOTPRINT

Post and beam superstructures are normally thought to produce rectangular footprints with modest spans. It is possible but unusual to attempt to achieve a circular footprint with a post and beam superstructure. If is the beam arrangement is rotated instead of translated, tapered beams are required for structural

Figure 10-61
Column uprooted from its foundation.

logic. This will produce a circular footprint surrounding a heavy central column. To omit such a central column either the beams must be sloped (rafters) and/or the beam column joints must be greatly strengthened. Both of these actions anticipate superstructures that belong more appropriately to a different type of superstructure.

PATTERN OF GROWTH

If a project succeeds there may be a future need for the building to grow. This growth may be to the left or right, forward and back, or up and down (Fig. 10-62). The rectangular footprint of post and beam buildings is best accomplished by "bay sized" increments. Even growth upward is possible by adding second story columns so that they rest on those of the first floor. It will be necessary to anticipate such upward growth, however, by over sizing the first floor columns during the initial construction of the first floor. Otherwise they will be insufficiently strong to also carry an upper floor. Growth downward is also possible by digging a basement under the original post and beam bay, but such excavation has very limited access for use of heavy equipment. For this reason it is unusual to see it done.

Figure 10-62
Expansion of post and beam structures is by bay sized modules in all three dimensions.

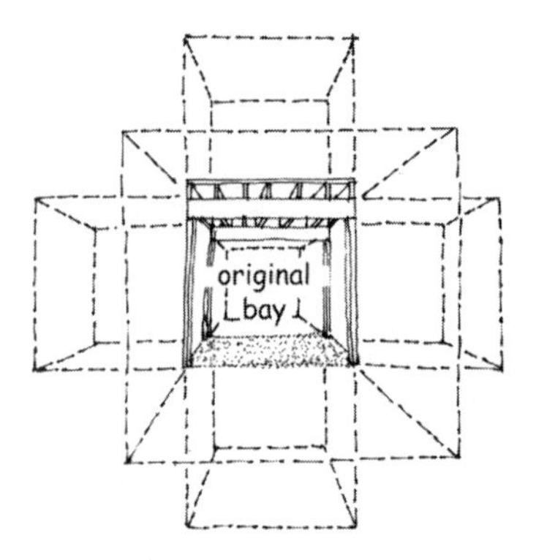

AESTHETIC POTENTIAL

Like the *rhythm* that we hear in music, the repetition of post and beams has its own rhythmic appeal. Look at a photograph of a post and beam building. Tap with your finger on the photo as you point at the first column on the left of a facade, then as you move your eyes to the right, tap your finger as it passes each column and listen for the rhythm (Fig. 10-63).

Recall that *structural logic* means that loads are directly opposed, and that big members carry big loads while little members are used to carry little loads. One expression of this principle is seen when the base of a column is made wider. While this adds additional lateral stability to the column it also recognizes that the top of the column is carrying the load above it. However, the bottom of the column is not only carrying that same load, but also the additional weight of the column itself. The bottom is therefore made thicker to express structural logic in carrying the additional load (Fig. 10-64).

The play of light on columns was emphasized in classical Greek and Roman buildings. Vertical grooves known as *volutes* were often carved into the shaft of column. As direct sun light fell on columns, strong shadows developed in the volutes that made the roundness of the column shaft more visually compelling (Fig. 10-65).

It is often particularly easy to fully expose a post and beam structure of a building. This adds considerable visual interest to the building without undue difficulty in design details (Fig. 10-66).

Figure 10-63

This Chicago hirise shows that the "rhythm" can occur both horizontally and vertically in a post and beam structure.

Figure 10-64

Column bases are thicker than the tops in the Hypostyle Hall of the Temple of Karnak in Luxor Egypt.

Figure 10-65

Column volutes.

CONSTRUCTION

One of the great advantages of post and beam construction is that a great many of the structural members are of the same size and shape. This makes manufacture both easy and less costly. Also, post and beam members are usually jointed at very simple joints. This type of frame springs up very quickly, and can usually be accomplished without the need for extensive training of construction crews. Much of the fabrication of individual members is often accomplished by the supplier at the factory. This greatly shortens the time of construction which leads to reduced construction costs. Extensive heavy equipment is usually not required for post and beam construction. Most post and beam structures have relatively small individual members. In wood construction, most members can be hoisted into place by workers without the use of heavy equipment. Even with steel and reinforced concrete the members are sufficiently small to limit the size of heavy equipment that is required. Since this type of superstructure has been used so widely, and for such an extended time in history, very well evolved construction details are available. However, care must be taken to match the module of windows and the building skin with the structural module. For example, if 2-feet-wide windows are to be used, it may be less expensive to use a structural bay of 12 feet, rather than 11 feet. Even though there will be an extra foot in each bay, the easy coordinated fit of the

Figure 10-66

Post and beam details at Horyuji Temple near Nara Japan.

Figure 10-67

Notice the cables being used to "plumb up" the columns and beams.

windows into the structural frame may provide significant savings. Such design coordination and potential economy must at least be considered.

In light wood and/or light steel construction, a floor surface is quickly put in place. Individual studs are usually assembled into walls while laid flat on that floor surface, and are then raised into vertical position. Joists are rested on the top of these walls in a group, and then spread at the appropriate spacing. Once the joists are "rolled" and cross braced, another floor deck is placed and the process begins again.

In heavier steel construction, particularly in tall buildings, two floors of columns and beams are assembled, then cross bracing or cables are used to plumb the columns and level the floors (Fig. 10-67). The joints are finally tightened up. The process of assembling beams and columns on the next two higher floors begins again.

Assembly of pre-cast concrete post and beam members is similar to heavier steel construction in its sequence; however, *insitu* (poured-in-place) concrete construction must first be formed. Columns, beams, and slabs are often poured separately. However, for reasons of strength they may have to be poured all at once (a *monolithic pour*). After the concrete for one floor has cured sufficiently, the forms must be "pulled" (disassembled), and the process begun again for the next floor above.

DESIGN METHODS

Preliminary design of smaller buildings makes use of span tables found in the building code, or rules of thumb. Ultimately standard beam calculations must be completed for final design. If standard post and beam configurations are used, most of these final calculations will be easily completed using standard computer software that has become widely available. Special attention to the spacing and integration of post and beam structure with mechanical and electrical systems, and the building envelope often leads many designers to begin their design on graph paper with a relevant grid size. Be aware that wall thickness makes this approach less than perfect. While this approach normally leads to design of great unity, they can become a bit boring and are sometimes criticized as being "son of graph paper".

Vocabulary		
Joist	Beam	Girder
Post	Strut	Moment
Shear	Bending	Deflection
Bearing	Euler buckling	Pinned connection
Fixed connection	Extreme fiber	Neutral Axis
Eccentric load	Short buckling	Torsion
Web buckling	Horizontal shear	Vertical shear
Local failure	Global failure	Tributary Area

REVIEW QUESTIONS

1. When is a post and beam system a good choice of superstructure?
2. What is the basis for selection of a material to use in a post and beam system?
3. What is a "normal" span for a beam in timber, steel, and concrete?
4. Briefly graphically and verbally describe the behavior of beams and columns under both vertical and horizontal loads.
5. Graphically produce the configuration of several of the most common alternative variations of the post and beam superstructures.
6. Name and locate the elements of a post and beam superstructure.
7. List and describe the most common modes of failure for post and beam structures.
8. Briefly discuss the ways in which your earlier understanding of cable systems and arches is needed to better understand the behavior of beams under load.
9. What is one major construction process advantage of post and beam over arches?
10. How does the aesthetic potential of a post and beam superstructure differ from that of arches or cable systems?
11. What is the single greatest functional advantage of a post and beam structure over an arch system?

Figure 11-1
TGV Station in Lyon France by Santiago Calatrava.

11 Rigid Frames

DESCRIPTION

In appearance a rigid frame can be quite similar to the post and beam system in the last chapter. However, instead of having connections that are free to pivot, they make use of *moment connections* (fixed joints). This single alteration causes the rigid frame to behave profoundly different from the post and beam structurally (Fig. 11-2).

HISTORY AND SIGNIFICANT EXAMPLES

History

Although rigid connections existed before the twentieth century, it was not until the development and wide use of steel and reinforced concrete that total structural frames with fixed joints began to evolve (Fig. 11-3). Bridges and train stations began to use rigid frames in the 1930s. One of the earliest was in 1937 at the University of Colorado at Boulder. Following World War II rigid frame structures rapidly evolved. Today a number of fabricators produce pre-engineered steel rigid frame storage buildings. Crabs and Spiders are examples of rigid frame structures that are found in nature, while rigid furniture such as conventional table and chairs are non-building examples.

Building examples

The advantages of rigid frame construction were quickly realized in the development of tall office buildings in New York and Chicago (Fig. 11-4). Today prefabricated steel gabled rigid frames are extensively used for a wide range of utility buildings because of the low cost, and rapid construction (Fig. 11-5).

Figure 11-2
Typical rigid frame.

Figure 11-3
Hamburg central rail station.

Figure 11-4
Carson, Pirie, and Scott building in Chicago by Louis Sullivan.

Figure 11-5
Prefabricated steel rigid frame building.

TYPES OR CATEGORIES

A rigid frame may be classified by configuration, number of pinned connections in the frame, or by the material from which it is made.

Classified by shape

1. The *portal frame* is characterized by a series of adjacent and superimposed rectilinear bays. A single bay is occasionally known as a *rectangular bent.* When several rectangular bents are placed together they are sometimes referred to as a *continuous frame*. As noted above, the portal frame looks a great deal like a post and beam system; however, all of the connections in a rigid portal frame are tightly fixed. This is accomplished by welding or extensively bolting in steel frame and is an easy and direct outcome of reinforced concrete. The structural advantage of such a frame is that both horizontal and vertical members can transmit stresses through the fixed joints, force adjacent members to deform, and therefore allow them to assist in carrying applied loads (Fig. 11-6).
2. A *Vierendeel truss* has rectilinear bays with fixed joints similar to the portal frame; however, it is used to span a significant gap in a beam-like way. It is capable of a long span similar to a truss, but it is not a true truss because it lacks the triangulation that is fundamental to true truss action. This will be further explained in a subsequent chapter. The Vierendeel has the advantage of providing functional space for occupants within the "truss". True trusses with triangulation have diagonal web members that intrude on occupied functional space (Fig. 11-7).
3. A *bent with sloped legs* is quite similar to the rectangular bent, but it is a bit more stable against lateral loads (Fig. 11-8).
4. The *gabled rigid frame* (such as the one shown in Fig. 11-5) is a compromise between an arch and a portal frame. The advantages of the compromise will be discussed in greater depth later in this chapter, but one of the advantages is that it provides a sloped roof that is well suited to shedding rain and snow.

Figure 11-6
The portal frame can transfer loads to other bays.

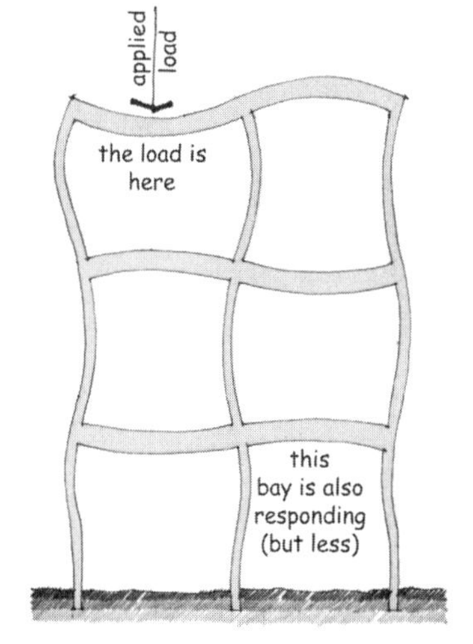

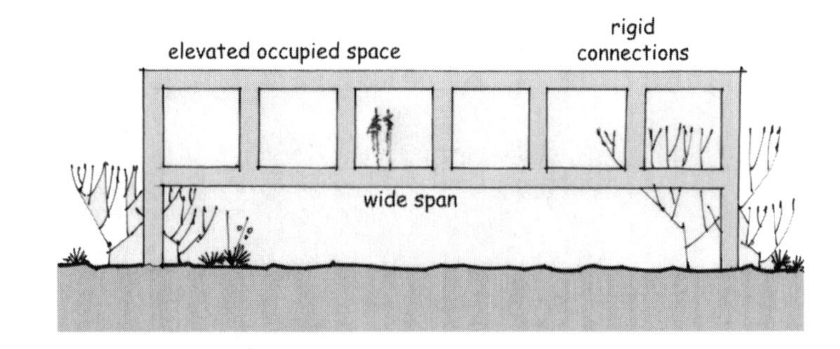

Figure 11-7
The Vierendeel truss is actually a rigid frame, not a true truss.

5. *A gabled frame with cantilevers* is quite similar to the gabled frame, but can also provide sheltered areas adjacent to the building. Such cantilevers are also useful in shading walls to lower unwanted heat gain in a building.

Figure 11-8
A rigid frame with sloped legs in Thailand.

By number and location of joints

Like arches, rigid frames change size and shape with temperature fluctuations due to thermal expansion (Fig. 11-9). Pragmatically the *three-hinged rigid frame* allows for expansion and contraction that takes place due to this temperature fluctuation. Although it exceeds the scope of this text, hinging a frame at three points also allows much easier mathematical calculation. The hinges also allow this type of rigid frame to adapt with ease to the spreading or settling of foundations (Fig. 11-10). The *two-hinged frame* eliminates one hinge making this frame less vulnerable to deflections than the three-hinged arch. It will also readily adapt to differential settlement of foundations, but it suffers unwanted bending in the frame if the foundations spread. A *fully fixed rigid frame* is vulnerable to thermal expansion, settlement, and spreading of foundations; while a four-hinged frame is inherently unstable (Fig. 11-11).

NOMENCLATURE

Rigid frames borrow heavily from arches in their nomenclature. *Span*, *intrados*, *extrados*, *springing line*, and *clear rise* are all examples of that borrowing.

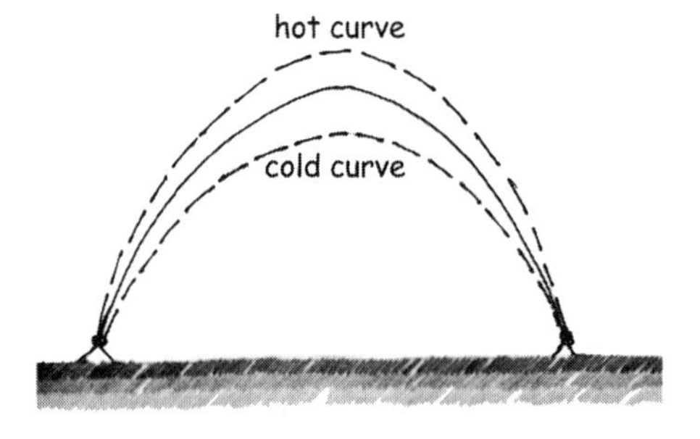

Figure 11-9
Remember from the arch chapter that when steel gets hot it gets bigger.

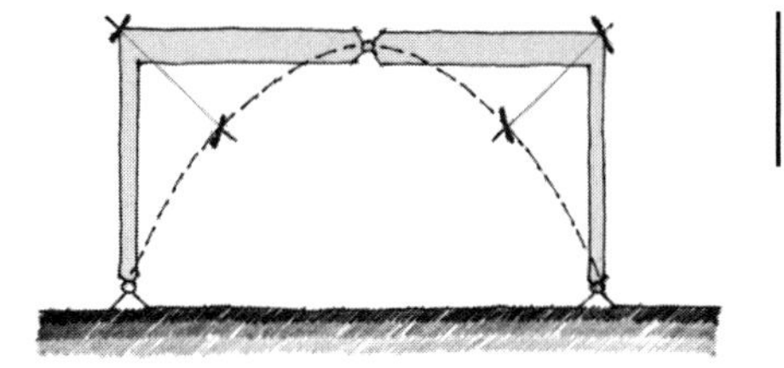

Figure 11-10
A three hinged rigid frame is the most common.

Footings can be found under a wide variety of superstructures, to include rigid frames. However, *legs*, *knees* or *haunch, stiffeners* and *transverse member bent ridge*, do not rely on arch structures as their origin. Notice that while the legs of the gabled rigid frame (Fig. 11-12) may look like columns and a rafter, the knee or haunch where they are joined is significantly thickened.

COMMON APPLICATIONS

Prefabricated steel rigid frames are manufactured, shipped to building sites and erected at a very reasonable cost. Since they enclose a large column free floor area they offer wide functional flexibility at this limited cost. For these reasons they are used for such occupancies as warehouses, small manufacturing plants, auto maintenance garages, barns, rural bars, and even small churches. They have the advantage of being reused in place by another type of occupancy, or if it is a bolted frame it may be disassembled and moved in smaller pieces for reuse at a different site. Such shipping is reasonable as the unbolted members and plates are relative light in shipping weight. *Wooden "glulam" frames* are normally exposed inside the building, provide very large column free floor area, and are inherently comparatively fire resistant. Typical uses for such frames are for medium to large size churches, small arenas, events centers, and small to medium exposition halls. *Built-up steel rigid frames* are usually considered aesthetically less pleasing and fire resistant than the shorter glulam frames, but are normally capable of significantly greater spans with less structural weight. They have been widely used for major exposition halls, arenas, factories, airplane maintenance facilities, and major warehouses. *Rigid bents or portal frames* are one of the most common frames for medium to large office buildings. Welding, bolting, or a combination of the two may be used to join their members. Such office buildings may assume the

Figure 11-11
A four hinged arch is unstable, but notice that the funicular arch curve acts through joints in a rigid frame.

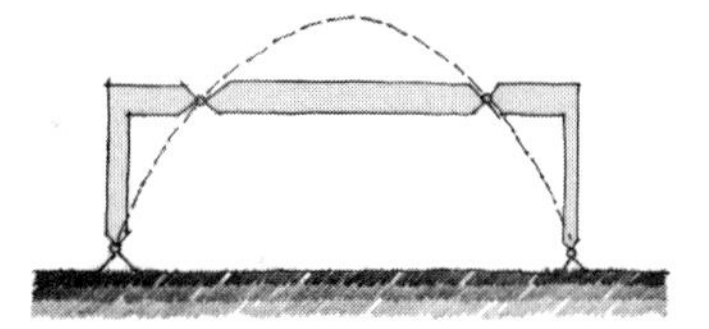

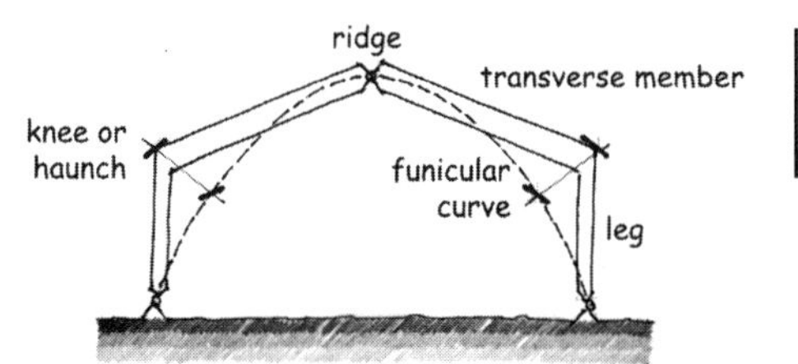

Figure 11-12
Nomenclature unique to the rigid frame.

form of skyscrapers, but at extreme heights such frames are excessively flexible and wave about (*drift*) excessively. While structurally less efficient than its near cousin, the arch, portal frame offers the advantage of a flat walking surface for the floor above. Steel bents also offer a minimal floor-to-floor distance. As previously discussed, this yields significant savings in multi-floor buildings. *Reinforced concrete rigid frames* are used in similar applications to the steel rigid frames, but are inherently more stiff, heavy, and less ductile, but inherently very fire resistant.

BEHAVIOR UNDER LOAD

The best way to understand the manner in which a rigid frame carries loads is by comparison and contrast with both the post and beam system and the arch system (covered in earlier chapters). The rigid frame resists loads by a simultaneous combination of several types of beam action and arch action with which the reader is already familiar. Salvadori and Heller were the first to systematically explain the complex behavior of rigid frames under load (Salvadori & Heller, 1963). Daniel Schodek also systematically unfolds an excellent detailed explanation of rigid frame behavior in his respected text entitled "*Structures*" (Schodek, 1980). We are indebted to them for allowing us to briefly parallel their work in the following short discussion.

Arch action behavior

The more the shape of the rigid frame approaches the parabolic shape of the "funicular" curve for an arch, the more it will behave as an arch structurally. As with arches the more the shape of a rigid frame deviates from this curve, the more material must be added to the frame in order to resist bending. Notice that joints in rigid frames are usually placed where the funicular curve intersects the frame in earlier illustrations in this chapter (Fig. 11-13).

Post and beam action

A post and beam superstructure uses "beam action" to gather and resist vertical loads. Beam action includes bending, horizontal shear, and vertical shear. Notice that since the ends of the beam are not fixed, they are free to rotate under load (Fig. 11-14). As mentioned in the last chapter a beam could be "fixed" at one end and cantilevered from that fixed joint. Here we see two opposing cantilevered beams with fixed joints. Notice that they could carry the same vertical load shown on the simple beam above, but they would do so in quite a different way (Fig. 11-15). The cantilevered beams would carry the load by resisting this rotation of the "fixed" joint (Fig. 11-16). If both ends of a beam are securely fixed to the top of the columns upon which they rest, a rigid "bent" is formed. When a rigid bent is vertically loaded it responds in a remarkably different way than a post and beam structure. If the bases of both legs rest on a roller connection, notice that they tend to splay outward under the vertical loading (Fig. 11-17).

Figure 11-13

Wide deviation from the funicular curve of the arch requires more material thickness in the frame.

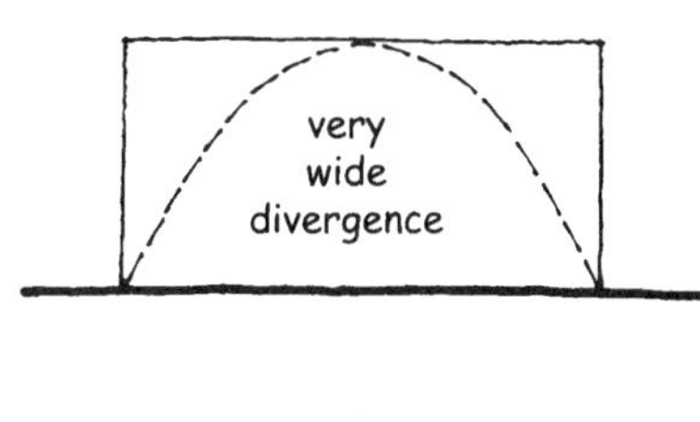

Figure 11-14

Simple beam action with unrestrained joints.

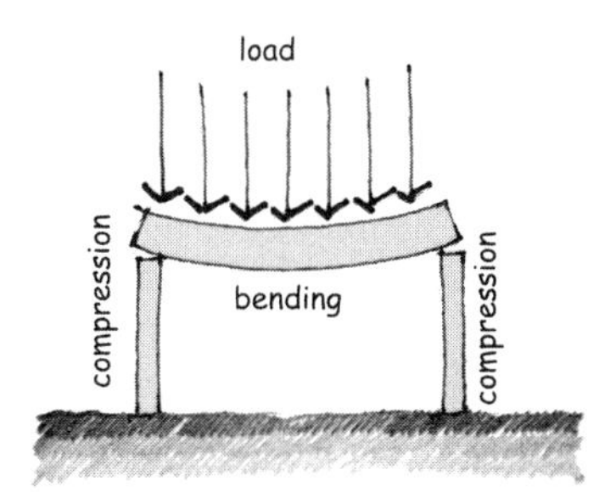

Figure 11-15

A fixed or moment connected frame can carry load similar to two mirrored cantilevered beams.

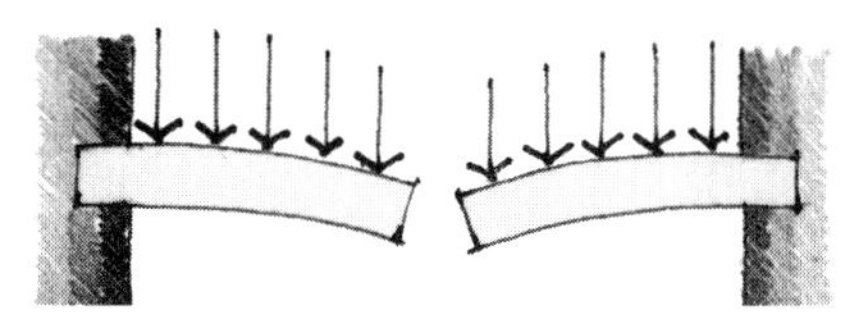

Figure 11-16

Rotation is opposed by a fixed joint.

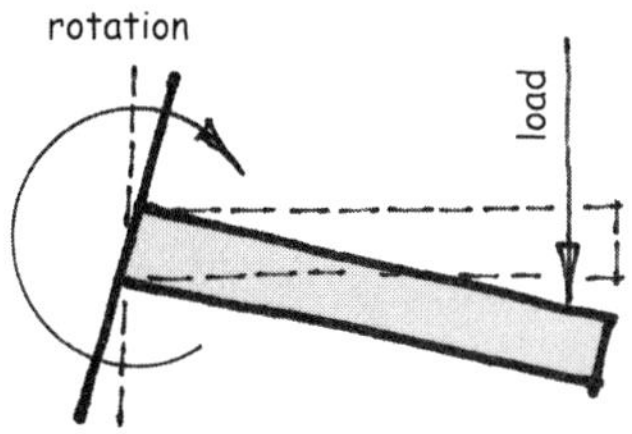
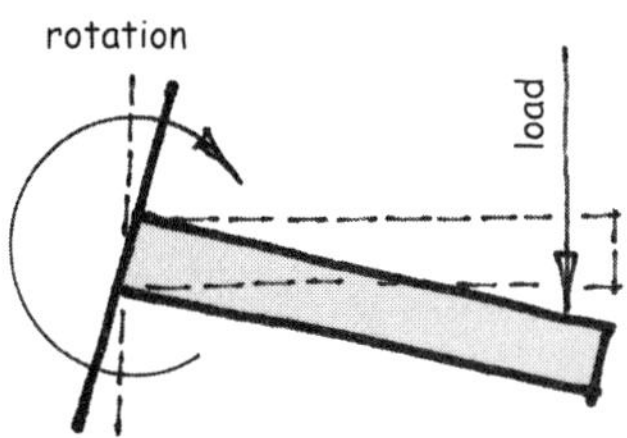

Figure 11-17

Rigid bent on roller connections.

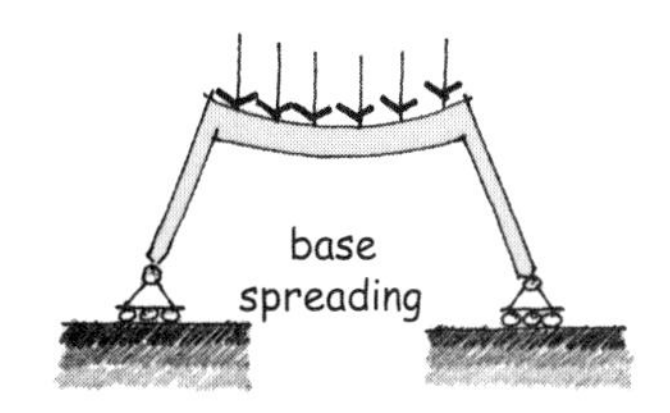

Therefore, the rigid frame has outward thrust at the base that must be restrained as in arches (Fig. 11-18). Like arches the necessary lateral restraint may be given to the base of the legs of a rigid frame in a number of ways, but tie rods are by far the most widely used method (Fig. 11-19). But what would happen if the base joints were also fixed in the same way that the beam-to-column joints have been fixed? How would the resulting rigid frame respond to vertical loading? To

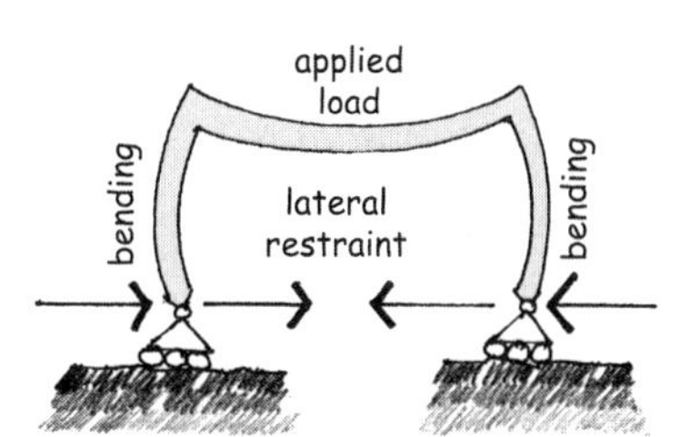

Figure 11-18

Rigid bent on roller connections, but with lateral restraint.

understand this we should first notice that such a connection at the base would result in a vertical member that would essentially be a beam vertically cantilevered out of the ground. For example, it is possible to drive a pole into the ground in order to gain the benefits of such a fixed end connection. It will resist bending by loads perpendicular to it (Fig. 11-20). Now once again apply the vertical loads to our initial rigid frame, this time with fixed base joints. In this configuration the restrained columns are forced to bend due the load. That means that the columns are now not only carrying the vertical loads axially, but are also assisting the beams in resisting the vertical loads by column bending. This is something new that did not occur in a post and beam system (Fig. 11-21).

Figure 11-19
Rigid frame with tie rod restraint.

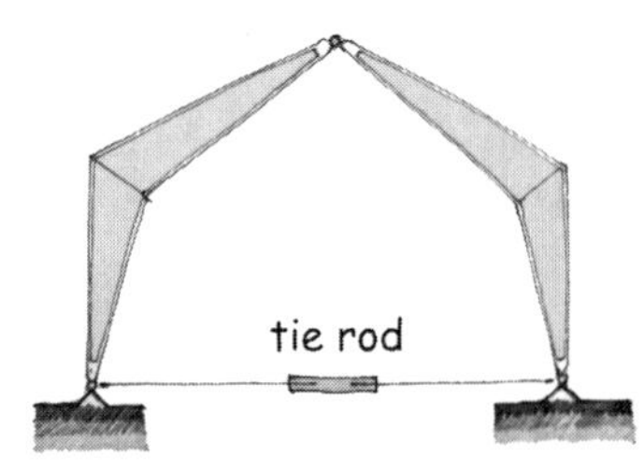

Figure 11-20
An embedded vertical post resisting lateral loading.

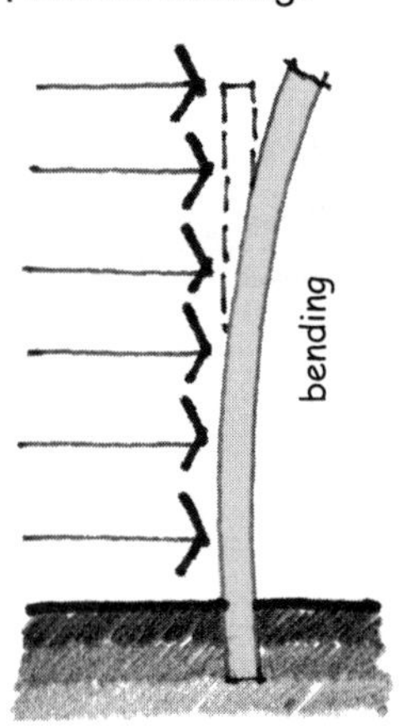

Horizontal loads

Observe that when laterally loaded, a post and beam structure can fall to the side like a house of dominos (Fig. 11-22). Now let's fix (or fuse) the beam-to-column connections and pin the base connections. This will allow us to compare the response of a rigid frame to the same lateral loading. Both fixed joints rotate very slightly, and in doing so distort both the columns and the beam (Fig. 11-23). This means that not only is the column resisting the lateral load by bending, but so is the beam. Therefore, the beam is assisting in resisting horizontal loads, and that is something new and different than we encountered with simple post and beam. But there are other forces at work. This time we will fix both base joints, pin the left column-to-beam connection, and place the other beam-to-column connection on a roller type joint (Fig. 11-24). When the horizontal force is once again applied, notice that this time the left column is solely responsible for resisting the load. It does so as a cantilevered vertical beam experiencing bending and shear. Notice that the horizontal force wants to shear the column at the ground. But yet another phenomenon must be emphasized. The beam experiences a horizontal force parallel to the long axis of the beam. It is obvious because the beam was visibly moved horizontally to the right. The roller joint at the right not only renders this visible, but also isolates the right column from accepting any of the horizontal load. Next we will fix both base connections as before, but pin both column-to-beam connections.

Figure 11-21
Resistance to vertical loads due to fixed base connections.

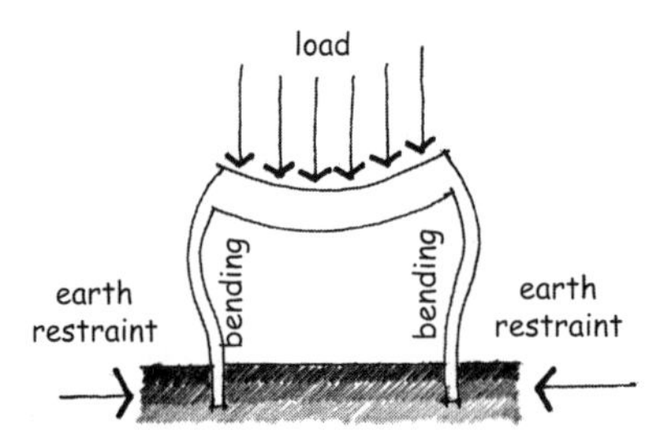

Figure 11-22
Instability without fixed connections.

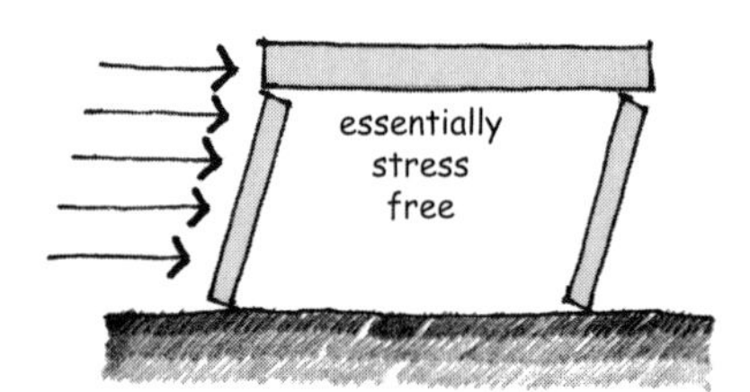

Figure 11-23
Rigid frame resistance to lateral loads with pinned base connections.

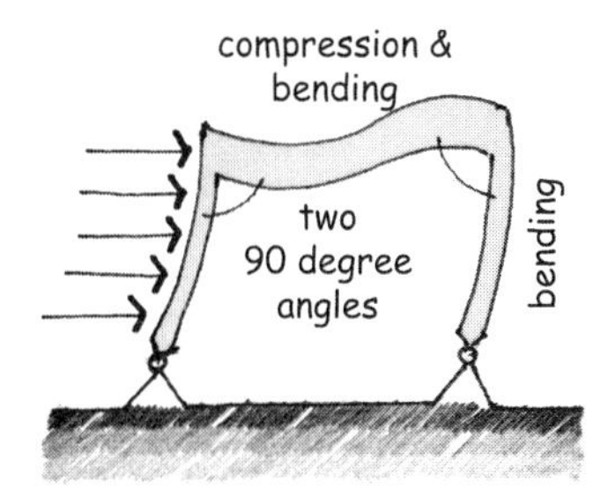

Figure 11-24
Resistance to lateral loads with only one pinned leg acting.

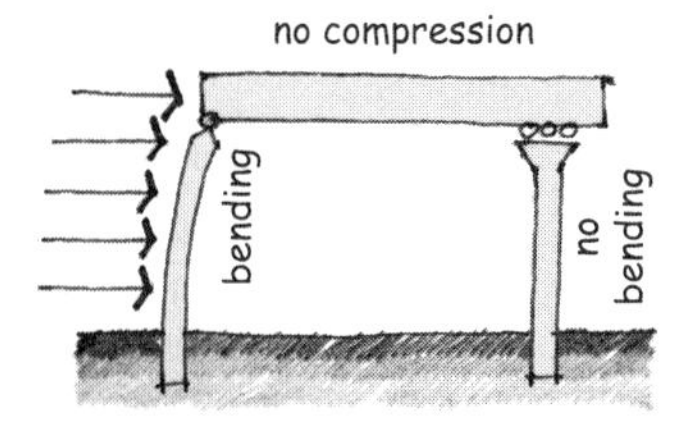

Figure 11-25
Shared resistance to lateral loading by two pinned legs.

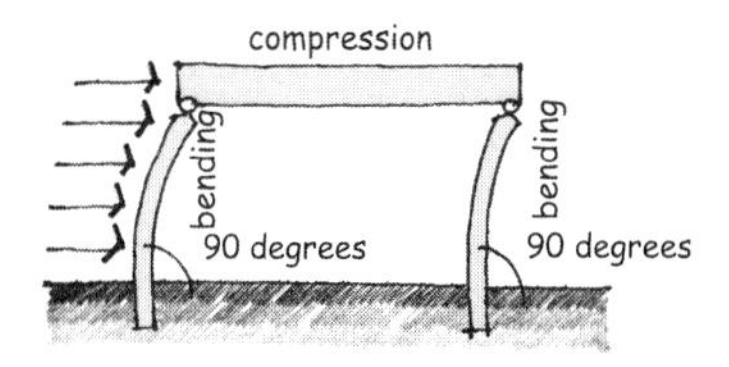

That will allow both columns to resist the same lateral loads by both bending and shear (Fig. 11-25). This is made possible because the beam carries an axial load along its long axis forcing the right column to also accept load. Finally we can fully understand the unique resistance to lateral load presented by a rigid frame in which all connections are fixed (Fig. 11-26). Just as the vertical load caused not only the vertical axial loads in the two columns (as in post and beam) but also bending and shear. Similarly, horizontal loads cause axial, bending, and shear stresses in the horizontal beam as well as the vertical columns. Summarizing this discussion it can be seen that all members (both horizontal and vertical) share axial, bending, and shear stresses in the face of either horizontal or vertical loads. This makes the rigid frame a very economical structure.

Figure 11-26
Resistance by the total rigid frame to lateral loading.

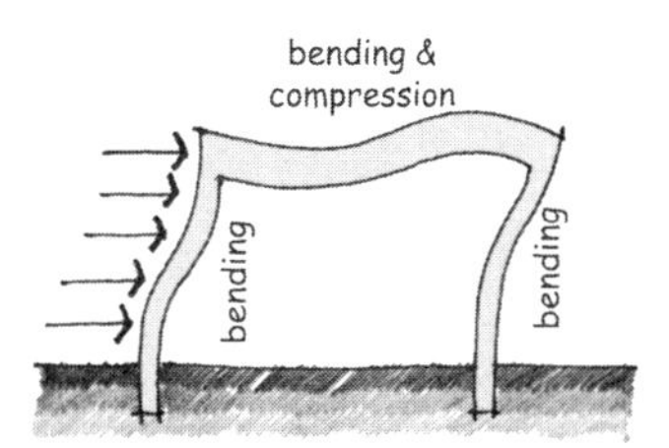

Implications on individual members

To fully appreciate the implications of these bending reversals it is easiest to see in reinforced concrete. Since concrete has little strength in tension, reinforcing steel must be used on the side of a structural member that experiences tension when the member bends. This may be the bottom chord of a horizontal beam when it bends downward, or the windward side of a column as it bends to the side in the face of a strong wind (Fig. 11-27). But if we look at the

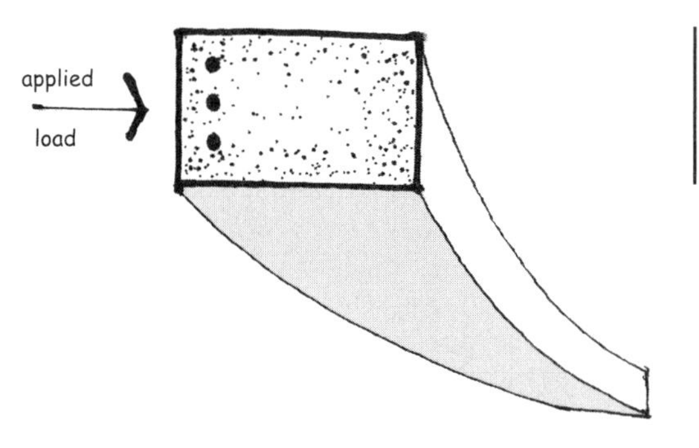

Figure 11-27
Reinforcing goes on the side that is placed in tension.

Figure 11-28
"S" bends will require reinforcing on two sides.

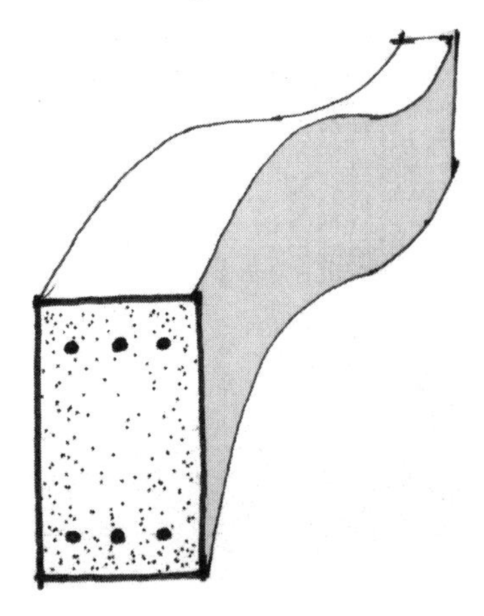

drawings used in the discussion above it is apparent that reverse or "s" type bends occur in both the columns and beams of rigid frames once their connections are fixed (Fig. 11-28). That means either side may go into tension, so both sides must have longitudinal reinforcing steel. Since a single free-standing column may receive wind loading from any direction, it follows that the column must be given longitudinal steel reinforcing on all four sides (Fig. 11-29).

Location of concentrated loads

Because of the reverse bending in both the beams and columns in portal frames, it matters where a concentrated load is focused (Fig. 11-30). If the load is concentrated at point "A", it is added to the bending that is already taking place at that point. However, if the same load is focused at point "B" it can be seen that the upward bending already present in the beam is "cancelled" or mitigated by the presence of the concentrated load. As a related issue, notice that the single concentrated load at "A" can cause a portal frame to move slightly to the right even in the absence of lateral loading.

Effect of adjacent bents or bays

If two or more bents are placed side-by-side, it can be seen that they will also participate in the resistance of a load (Fig. 11-31). For example, if a lateral load is applied to the original left bay, the beam will axially displace pushing on the second bay to the right. In fact the beam is *continuous*. It is the same beam in both bays. There is no break between the two bays. Further, rotation of the left side of the middle joint between the two bays provokes equal rotation on the right side of that same middle joint between the two bays. Rotation of that joint rotates not only the middle column as before, but also the continuous

Figure 11-29
In an actual column tension can occur on any of its sides.

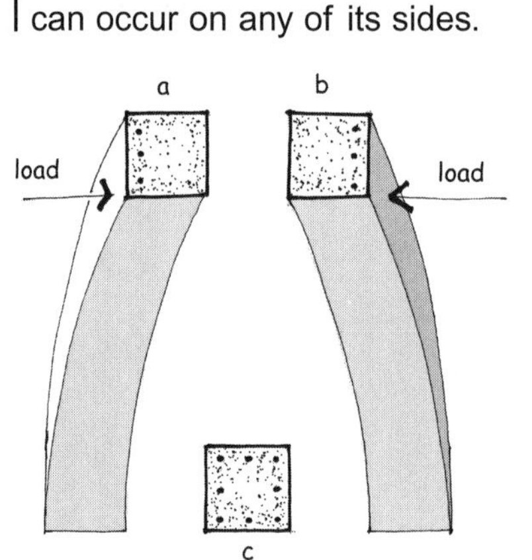

Figure 11-30
It matters where a point load is placed on a rigid frame.

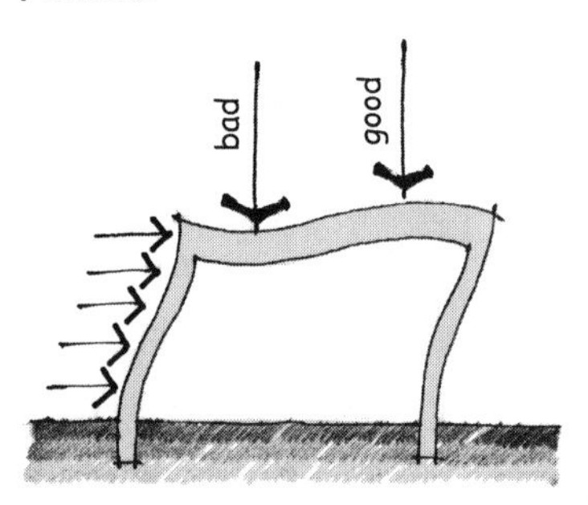

Figure 11-31
Two adjacent bays can share resistance to a lateral load by continuous action.

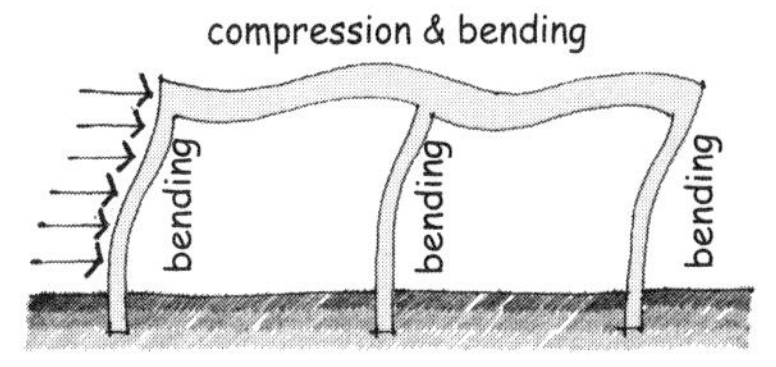

Figure 11-32
Two adjacent bays can share resistance to vertical loads in the same way.

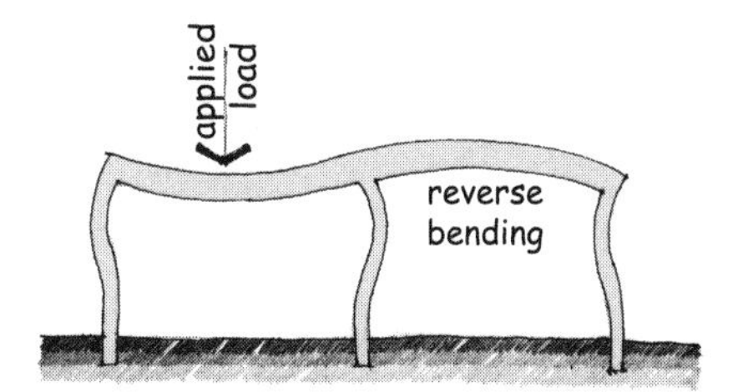

beam as it extends over the second bay to the right. That causes rotation of the beam-to-column joint at the extreme right, which of course forces response in bending by the column at the extreme right. Every part of the frame responds to a load applied at any point on the frame. True, the response becomes more muted or damped as the load moves more remote from the point of application, but it does respond. This will allow greater structural efficiency. Now apply a vertical point load in one bay, in order to observe the effect on the adjacent bay (Fig. 11-32). The point load causes the beam in the left bay to bend downward just as it would have in a simple post and beam structure. But while the beam bends downward in the left bay of a rigid frame, it bends upward in the adjacent bay to the right since the beam is continuous across both bays. Once again it is important to notice that not only is the continuous beam fully involved in both bays, but so are all of the columns. This is profoundly different than the response of a post and beam superstructure given the same loading, and it is all due simply to *moment connections* (fixed joints).

Effect of vertically stacked bents or bays

If one portal frame bay is stacked on top of another, it will be possible to examine the affect of their joint response to both horizontal and vertical loads (Fig. 11-33). One of the first advantages to be realized is that a tie rod is no longer needed to restrain the base connections of each superimposed portal frame against "splaying". The beam of the frame below acts as the necessary tie rod for the bay above. Now notice that the "drift" to the right of each bay above is added to the drift of the bay below. Finally, notice that one side of the combined (or *global*) frame presses down on the foundation in compression, while the other side pulls up on the foundation in tension. But there are other forces at work in the vertically stacked rigid frame that we must also study. The vertically stacked portal frame can be globally understood as a very large beam vertically cantilevered up out of the ground. Bending stress in such a "global cantilevered beam" would be very great at the point where it joins the ground, and essentially non-existent at the very top. Now remember the "P-Delta" effect introduced in the earlier chapter on lateral loads. This means that

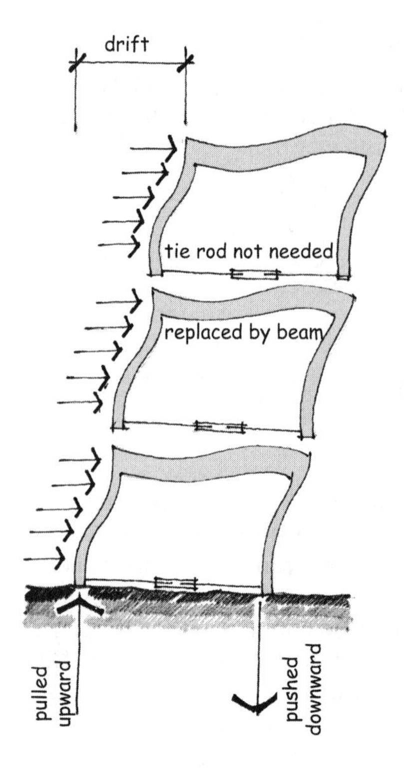

Figure 11-33
Notice that the beam in one bent becomes the tie rod for a second bent above it.

while all the members in a portal frame participate in carrying axial, bending, and shear stresses due to loads that are applied to the building, they are not equally stressed. Indeed even the dead loads increases from top to bottom as the loads above accumulate in their journey to the ground. The top floor must carry the dead load of the top floor, but the next floor down must carry itself and the top floor. The bottom bay must carry its own dead load, and that of the total building above. Therefore, even in a post and beam frame columns in the lowest floors must be thicker than columns in the top floors.

Behavior of gabled frames

Before leaving the discussion of the load propagation in rigid frames let us briefly look at some additional issues related to the gabled form of rigid frames. If a gabled frame has its legs fixed at the foundation, but hinged at the shoulders and apex of the gable, a single vertical load at the apex will force the vertical legs to splay outward at the shoulder (Fig. 11-34). The sloping roof members will receive an axial load similar to a column, and the legs will have to resist lateral loads like those related to wind loads previously discussed. However if all of the joints in the gabled frame are fixed, then all members are forced to flex. That means that they will all contribute resistance to the applied load (Fig. 11-35).

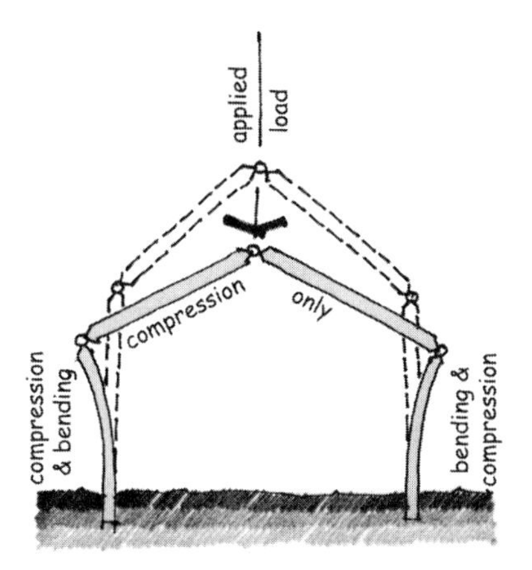

Figure 11-34

Pinned gabled frames "splay" outward at the top under vertical loading.

OPTIMUM CONFIGURATION

Rigid steel frames with a short (30–40 feet) span should be spaced at about 1/16 of their span, while frames with a longer span (50–100) have a preliminary design spacing of 1/20 of the span. For example, if a steel rigid frame has a 100-foot span, the frames will be spaced at about 20 feet for preliminary design. Also in preliminary design try a radius at the knee that is four to five times the thickness of the leg and transverse member. For steel frames with small spans it may be possible that no lateral bracing is required if purlins and a deep deck are used. For longer spans, rigid frames bracing at the haunch and ridgeline will be needed at least in the end bays (Fig. 11-36). For reinforced

Figure 11-35

The joints and members are forced to provide resistance to vertical loads if they are fixed.

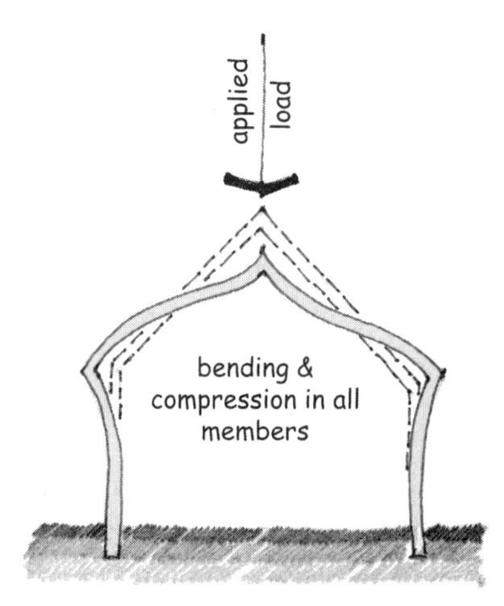

Figure 11-36

Cables are often used to laterally brace a rigid frame.

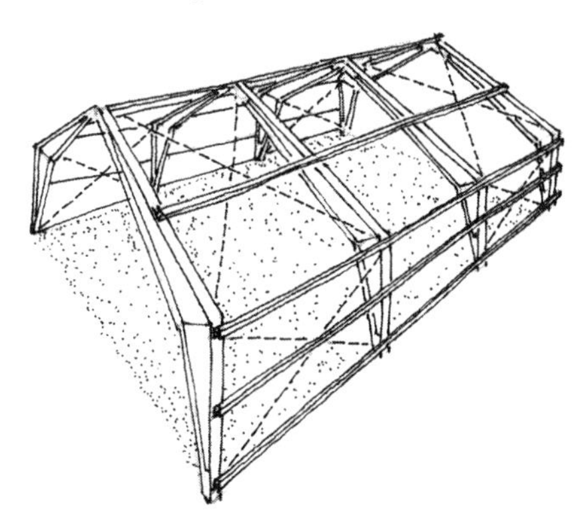

concrete the thickness of the transverse member at center span is about 1/35 of the span, while the base thickness of the legs ranges from about 1/20 of short span to about 1/25 of a long span. For preliminary design thickness at the haunch is about 1/15 of the span (Gaylord, Gaylord, and Stallmeyer 1997).

FUNCTIONAL FOOTPRINT

Normally rigid frames have a rectangular foot print and relatively long span. A round footprint is unusual, but is possible if the bents are rotated (Figs. 11-37 and 11-38).

PATTERN OF GROWTH

Like post and beam structures, the axial growth of rigid frames is easily accomplished by adding bays. Lateral growth in portal frames is also done by bay; however, be aware that if additional gabled bays are added, rain water tends to form in the valleys between. Vertical growth similar to post and beam structures is unusual, but possible, with prior planning. Be certain to maintain continuity of vertical loads down through superimposed legs (Fig. 11-39).

AESTHETIC POTENTIAL

For many utilitarian steel rigid frames, there is no significant emphasis on the aesthetics of the building. There is certainly potential rhythmic appeal possible

Figure 11-37
It is also possible for frames to grow in rotation.

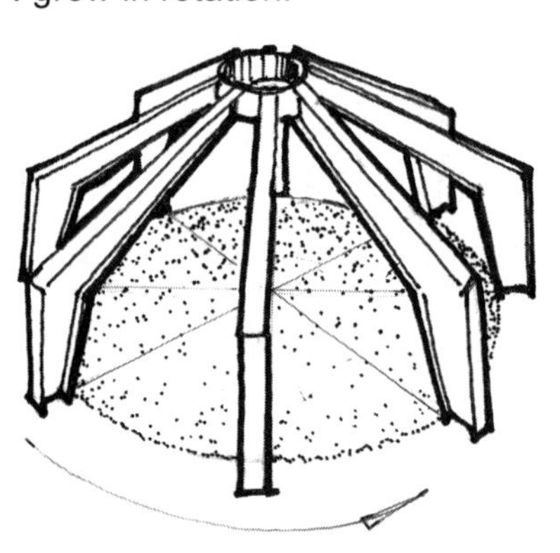

Figure 11-38
Notice that a rigid frame may also be rotated with the legs at the center of the circular footprint.

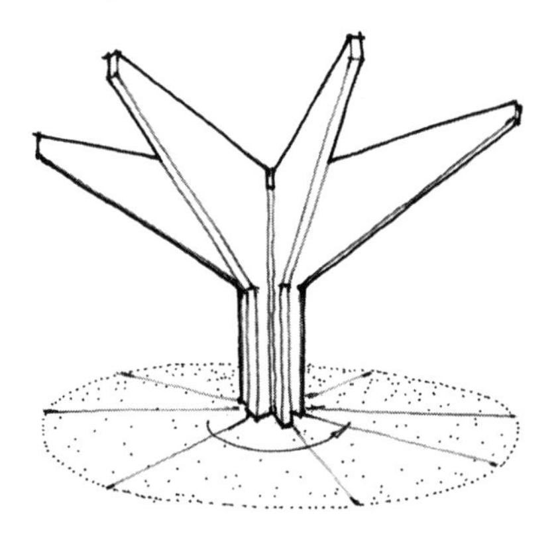

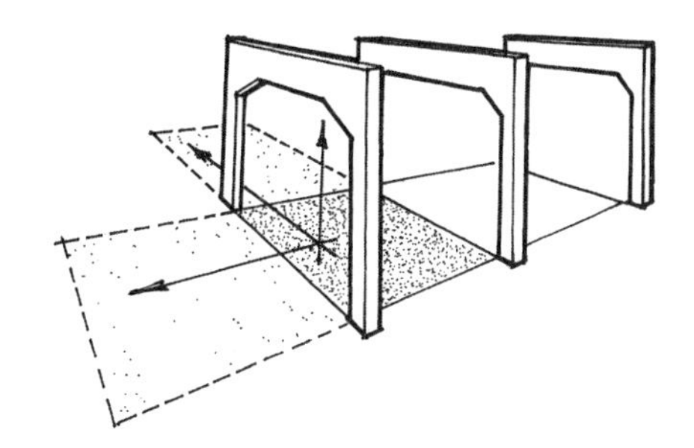

Figure 11-39
Like post and beam, rigid frames normally grow in all three axes by individual bays.

on either the inside or outside of the skin depending on the location of the frame. Gabled frames have diagonal lines, which can lend a bit of drama to the lines of the frame. Structural honesty is often stressed by brightly coloring the frame if it is to be exposed. Unfortunately, the need for fireproofing causes the frame to be concealed in many cases. Unfortunately termination of the utilitarian skin against the ground is often not adequately studied in pre-engineered gabled storage buildings. Glulam timber rigid frames are inherently attractive, and are normally varnished, not painted. While exposing them is the norm, it is important to get sufficient natural and artificial light on the wood.

CONSTRUCTION

Members for small gabled rigid frames are prefabricated at the factory and delivered by flat bed trucks to the site ready for assembly. Large multi-floor office buildings are erected in exactly the same manner as post and beams. Only the bolting and welding of the joints will be different. If in-situ concrete is used, monolithic pours of all members will be the norm.

DESIGN

During early preliminary design physical scale models are commonly used; however, their ultimate form of portal frames and gabled frames is so conventional that computer modeling may be introduced almost immediately as it is with post and beam structures.

Vocabulary		
Rectangular bent	Continuous frame	Leg
Haunch	Transverse member	Moment connection

REVIEW QUESTIONS

1. Although rigid frames often look like post and beam, what are the structural differences?
2. In what way does a rigid frame behave structurally like an arch?
3. Why is there often an increased thickness at the haunch of a rigid frame?
4. A gabled rigid frame is usually pinned. Why?
5. Briefly describe how multi-bay, multi-floor portal frames propagate loads?

Figure 12-1
Barcelona Museum of Contemporary Art by Richard Meier.

12 Bearing Wall and Slab

DESCRIPTION

Bearing wall

A solid building wall can be made to resist vertical loads. In addition to carrying vertical loads, bearing walls may also form part of the weatherproofing envelope, and provide lateral support for the building.

Slab

Structural slabs look similar to the slabs of concrete that rest upon the ground in a domestic driveway. However, if sufficiently reinforced and given adequate support by walls or columns below, a structural slab may be elevated to form the roof or an upper floor of a building. Structural slabs, also known as *plates* may be supported in many ways. While all of these common methods will be briefly addressed in this chapter, the continuous support of a bearing wall is the most direct and logical. For this reason they will form the focus of this chapter. In addition to providing a roof structure and weatherproofing, plates may also simultaneously play a significant role in the building's ability to resist lateral loads.

HISTORY AND SIGNIFICANT EXAMPLES

History

Bearing walls and slabs form one of the oldest structural systems in the world. They have been built by almost every society in history, and from almost all of the common building materials. Currently steel reinforced concrete is used worldwide to form most structural slabs, but in earliest history individual wood members have been placed immediately adjacent to each other to form a plate. Often subsequent "mats" of smaller wood members were superimposed at right angles to the mat below. A wooden slab formed in such a way was often topped with rammed earth to form a roof or upper floor.

Figure 12-2
Hovenweep National Monument in Utah.

Building examples

Native Americans were using bearing wall and slab structures in Hovenweep National Monument before the arrival of Europeans (Fig. 12-2). The Europeans also brought with them a bearing wall and slab tradition based on such buildings as the Palazzo Rucellai by Alberti, in Florence, Italy (Fig. 12-44). At the beginning of the modern era the Monodnock Building in Chicago by Burnham and Root continued to use bearing wall and slab construction (Fig. 6-4 in Chapter 6).

Examples in nature

It is quite possible that primitive man first learned to build bearing wall and slab systems by direct observation of natural "dolmens." A dolmen is a slab of flat stone that has fallen across supporting stones below. In fact, it is quite possible that primitive man may have initially occupied such dolmens, and later built them where they did not naturally develop.

Figure 12-3
Bearing wall and slab can be just as unstable as a house of cards.

Nonbuilding examples

One of the best non-building examples of bearing wall and slab systems is the house of cards that you may have constructed as a child. As an example the house of cards clearly shares many of the greatest strengths and weaknesses of the bearing wall and slab system. While both are quite economical in their use of material and ease of construction, they are both equally vulnerable to collapses due to instability (Fig. 12-3). Once taped for mailing, a cardboard box behaves very much like a bearing wall and slab structure.

TYPES OR CATEGORIES

Bearing walls by material

A bearing wall may be classified by the material from which it is made. These materials include brick, stone, concrete block, precast concrete, in-situ (poured-in-place) concrete, structural clay tile, glass block, logs, dimension lumber, and even corrugated steel.

Figure 12-4
Sloped or cambered walls on the Taos New Mexico mission.

Bearing walls by configuration

Bearing walls are also classified by their configuration. The simplest form of bearing wall is the solid wall. Such walls may have vertical sides, or may have a bit of *camber* for additional stability (Fig. 12-4). Sometimes, particularly in brick, a *cavity wall* may be formed by two *wythes* of brick with a space left between. This gap gives the wall more structural stability and also better thermal insulation. Concrete block walls are also capable of being *reinforced*. This is done by placing reinforcing steel vertically in the hollow cores of the block and occasionally in the mortar in the horizontal joints between blocks. *Reinforced brick walls* achieve extraordinary strength by placing steel reinforcing bars and grout between two wythes of brick. In addition to the added material strength of the steel and grout, this method places the grout in an ideal curing condition that allows it to be much stronger than would otherwise develop. In the current era of resurgent interest in environmental issues, vertically superimposed horizontal logs are again being employed to form traditional log buildings. Whether *precast* at the factory or *site cast* in horizontal beds at the building site, concrete *tilt-up* walls must be temporarily stabilized while final connections are being completed. This type of building springs up very rapidly, minimizing labor costs. As previously mentioned, both steel and wood studs are used to aggregate *framed bearing walls*. When studs are closely spaced they begin to behave as a bearing wall rather than a post and beam. Relative slenderness of bearing walls can lead to failures in instability before a wall is fully tested in vertical crushing. The increase in the performance of a bearing wall, *attached pilasters* may be periodically added to a bearing wall. Concrete block bearing walls are vulnerable to local bearing failures under the focused loads of such horizontal members as long-span trusses. These large point loads are therefore often supported on steel *bearing plates* resting on a reinforced grout filled *bond beam* at the top of the wall. Such bond beams also have lateral support benefits that are widely utilized in areas prone to very strong winds.

Structural slabs by material

As previously mentioned, mats of sticks overlain with adobe have long been used as a primitive roof or floor slab. By far the most common modern material used for fabrication of slabs is steel reinforced concrete. Concrete is also often placed over corrugated steel plate in *composite construction*. Short steel *studs,* which look a bit like bolts, are attached to corrugated steel deck to assure *composite* (joint) action between the steel deck and the concrete fill. Steel deck is sometimes welded into a floor slab and surfaced with plywood, particle board, and/or rigid insulation to form a structural roof slab. In such circumstances either the structural slab may be sloped, or the rigid insulation placed over the slab may be ground to a positive slope in order to assure rain runoff once a water proof membrane has been applied. Diagonal wood sheathing, plywood, and particle board are used in varying combinations to build up floor plates that behave like structural slabs. At the end of the nineteenth century concrete began to be used to overlay low, or flat, brick arches made of either brick or structural clay tiles. Slab-like structural behavior could be gained in this way.

Precast concrete is now used in several different types of interlocking configurations to aggregate a slab-like surface. These will be discussed in greater detail later in this chapter.

Figure 12-5
One way ribbed slab.

Figure 12-6
Waffle slab in Portland Oregon. Notice that some voids have been left open to allow penetration of natural light.

Structural slabs by configuration

The simplest type of slab is the *flat slab*. It is relatively easy to fabricate, and allows floor-to-floor vertical distances to be reduced to an absolute minimum. This produces savings in many ways. The flat slab and most of the following concrete configurations have the advantage of being self-fire "proofing". If flat slabs are supported by separate beams on two opposing sides, the internal steel reinforcing will only run one way. This type of flat slab is a *one-way slab*. If the supporting beams are poured integrally with the slab so that they act together, it is known as a flat slab with *turned-down edge beams*. If the flat slab is supported on all four edges, it will be steel reinforced internally in two directions, and known as a *two-way flat slab*. Poured in place (in-situ) slabs may be poured with *integral beams*. If such integrally attached supporting beams only run in one direction between larger beams, it is known as a *one-way ribbed slab* (Fig. 12-5). If the integrally attached supporting beams run two ways it is known as either a two-way ribbed slab or more commonly as a *waffle* slab (Fig. 12-6). An unusual ribbed slab is occasionally fabricated that directly exhibits the true lines of equal stress (called *isostatic* lines). It is therefore known as an *isostatic ribbed slab*.

NOMENCLATURE

Because the bearing walls and slabs vary so widely from one material and configuration to another, it is easier in this chapter to spread the necessary vocabulary throughout this chapter. It is hoped that this deviation from the normal chapter organization will not excessively inconvenience the reader.

COMMON APPLICATIONS

Bearing walls and slabs are used in a bewildering array of building types; however, they are particularly useful in apartment buildings, hotels, and small office buildings. This is because the spans can be kept short, fire resistant construction is important, and great economy is gained by minimizing floor-to-floor distances in multifloor construction. Further savings are possible since the bearing wall has the inherent potential to provide the weather proofing envelope for the building and lateral shear walls in addition to vertical support.

BEHAVIOR UNDER LOAD

Slabs and bearing walls

While post and beam systems concentrate load propagation along narrow lines, slabs and bearing wall systems both collect and disperse loads across broad surfaces. To more systematically introduce this behavior slabs and bearing walls will initially be addressed separately in the following explanation. *Structure in Architecture* (Salvadori and Heller 1963) was the first text to clearly describe *slab behavior* in a simplified and systematic way. We are fortunate to be allowed to parallel that thorough discussion in the following brief description.

Slabs

In order to understand the basics of plate (structural slab) action let us first look at a *two-way flat plate*. In such a configuration let's apply a single vertical point load at the center of a square plate with separate beam support under all four edges. Because all four beams are equally distant from the point of application, loads will be equally distributed toward all four sides by "two-way" action. Two-way action is much more efficient than one-way action (Fig. 12-7).

Figure 12-7
Two-way flat slab with a single point load.

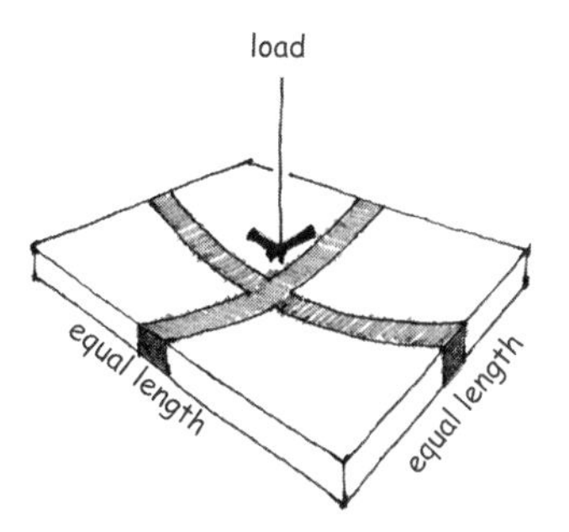

Let us similarly examine a *one-way flat slab*, again with a single point load applied at the center of the span. The one-way flat slab is usually rectilinear in shape, not square. It is reinforced in only one axis, not two, as in the two-way slab discussed immediately above. Only the two long sides of the rectangular plate are supported from below by beams. Notice that the long sides of the plate are closer to the point of application than the short edges which are much more distant. This means that more of the load will flow to nearby beams, and subsequently by columns to the ground. In engineering there is an axiom that "load is carried proportionally to stiffness". Here the short axis is stiffer than the long axis. One-way slabs must be considerably thicker and are significantly less efficient than the two-way slab (Fig. 12-8).

Two perpendicular shallow flat beams have been shaded in both the one-way and two-way slabs above. If we exaggerate the deflections in both, we will be able to more fully visualize the differing load propagation in the two. The "beams" running in the short direction might be referred to as *transverse*, while those running parallel to the long axis would be called *longitudinal*. If the number of flat beams is increased in the one-way slab, notice that the "beams"

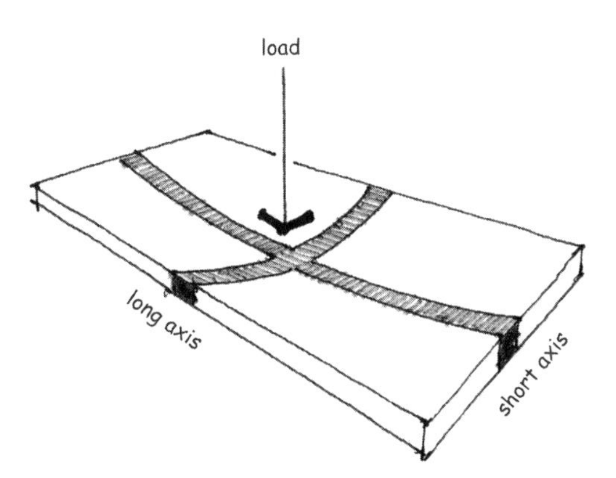

Figure 12-8
One-way flat slab with a single point load.

Figure 12-9

One-way flat slab with multiple flat "beam strips" (shaded).

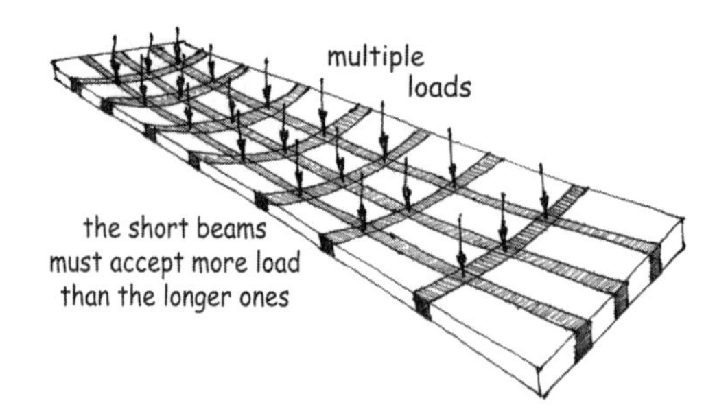

in the middle of the slab deflect more than the beams closer to the supported edges (Fig. 12-9).

If a single point load is applied closer to one end, notice that the *reverse bending* will take place in the slab. That means that uplift will occur toward the opposite end of the slab. This should remind the reader of the structural action of continuous beams discussed in an earlier chapter. Recall that deflections resulting from such bending reversals behave like a "diminishing sine wave". To restrain these bending reversals, the shaded flat beams would need to be "interwoven" (Fig. 12-10).

Plates resist loads by more than simple bending in two axes. A second supporting mechanism is known as *torsion* (or twist). To understand the nature of this second plate mechanism, look at the section cut from the center of the slab shown above. If this section is isolated from the rest of the slab, it forms a "transverse beam" with a single load at center span, and support at the outside ends. The three intersecting "longitudinal beams" have been shaded so that the reader may see that some of these "longitudinal beams" are subject to torsion (twist) as the transverse beam deflects (Fig. 12-11). There is no twist present in the longitudinal section or "beam" at the mid point of the transverse section, directly under the point load, but notice that some twist exists in the other two shaded "beams". Notice that the greatest twist exists at the supported ends. So the material in the slab must resist torsion when the point load at center span provokes twist.

Figure 12-10

Continuous action in a flat slab.

Figure 12-11

Twist or torsion in the slab.

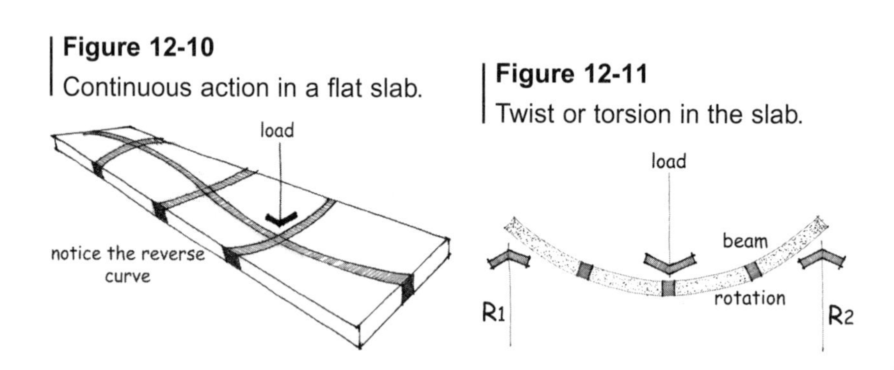

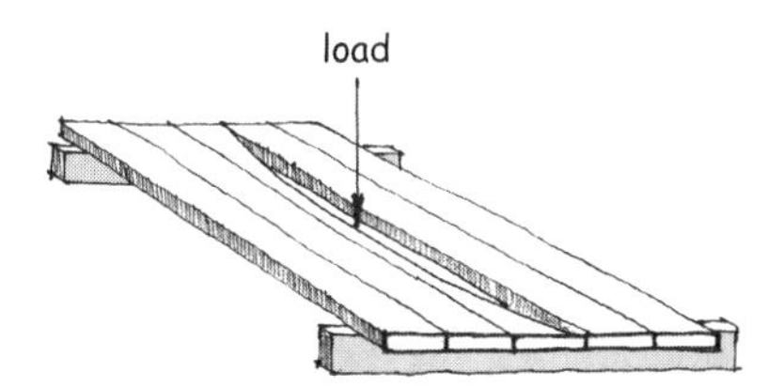

Figure 12-12
The plank under the point load moves, but the others do not.

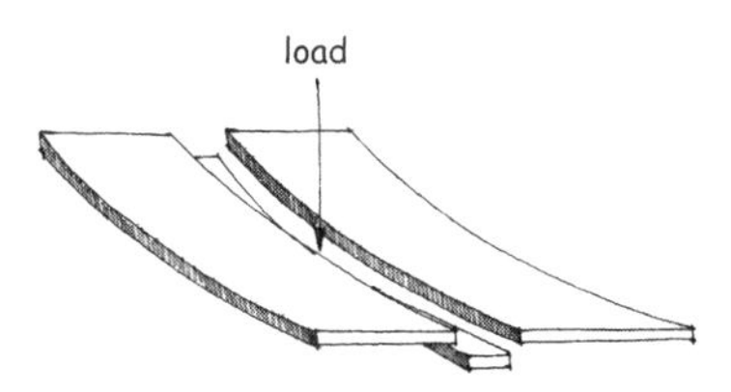

Figure 12-13
This makes the potential for shear in a flat slab visible.

A third resisting mechanism is at work in structural slabs. Let us view the plate as a series of parallel planks. When a point load is placed on one of the planks, it deflects downward, but those adjacent planks do not (Fig. 12-12). If all of the "planks" are now made continuous (except the single isolated plank under load) notice that "shearing action" takes place between the isolated loaded plank and the adjacent slab on both sides of it (Fig. 12-13). This shearing action also resists loads in a structural slab.

Finally we can draw a single illustration that shows how *bending*, *twist*, and *shearing* action work together to simultaneously resist loads that are applied to a structural slab (Fig. 12-14). Observe that twist takes place perpendicular to long axis of the planks in the illustration, and that such twist is continuous in solid plate. As previously identified the edge of the slab twists or rotates similar to the end of a simple beam. A beam's performance can be improved by fixing its ends against such rotation. Similarly the performance of a slab can be improved if the supporting beams are fixed to the slab. This resists rotation at the edges of the slab and at the corners (*corner turnup*). This configuration is sometimes referred to as a turned down edge.

Slab failures

Since a slab is in many ways like a series of beams fused directly side to side, it is not surprising that plates experience *beam-like failures*. Bending failures and excessive deflection are of concern near the mid-spans of slabs, and shearing failure in slabs is of concern near supporting beams or walls. However, remember that slabs have two-way bending, and two-way shear unlike beams. One unique type of failure becomes a concern when slabs are supported on

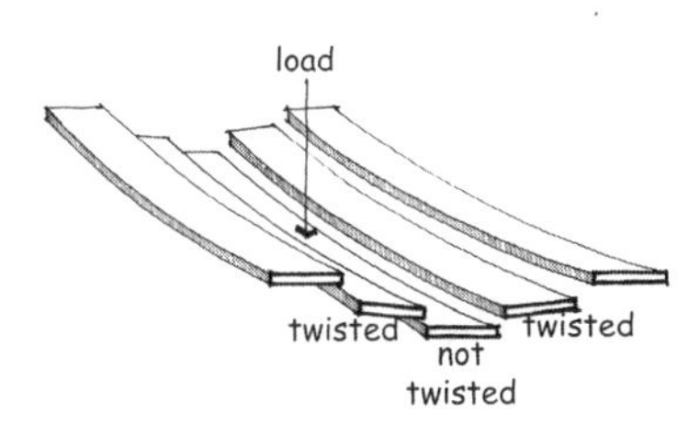

Figure 12-14
Composite of bending, twist, and shear all simultaneously at work.

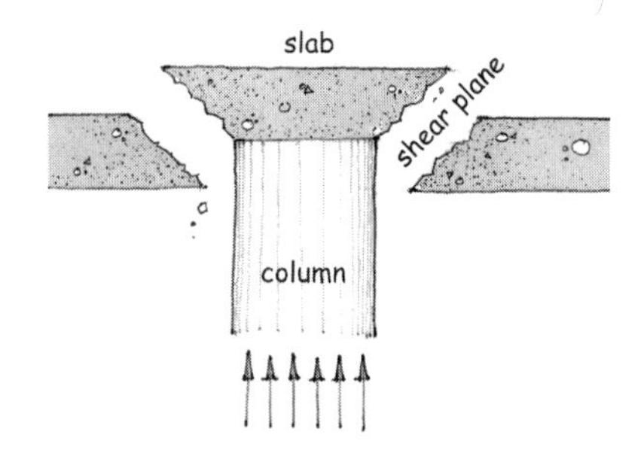

Figure 12-15
Punching shear happens roughly at a 45 degree angle.

columns. This type of failure is known as *punching shear*. The slab or plate is relatively thin, like a sheet of paper. The column exerts a considerable point load, like a sharpened pencil. It is easy to see that no great force would be required to force the point of the pencil through the surface of the sheet of paper. This is a simple example of punching shear. In slabs this shear happens roughly along a 45 degree angle (Fig. 12-15). A "collar" of ruptured concrete is left on the column in such failures. Prior to such a failure, *shear cracks* appear in the slab perpendicular to the isostatic lines of stress (principle lines of stress) discussed previously. Punching shear can be seen in the "pancake collapse" of a parking garage during the Mexico City earthquake in 1985 (Fig. 12-16). The earthquake energy did the "work" necessary to rupture the material. More energy and work would be necessary to produce a failure if more slab material had to be ruptured. This is why *drop panels* or *shear capitals* are sometimes used when columns are employed to support slabs (Fig. 12-17). If *waffle* slabs are used with columns, one or more of the voids in the slab are filled solid over the column for the same reason (Fig. 12-18).

Figure 12-16
Punching shear failure of a parking garage. Lots of gasoline made this rescue effort dangerous.

In normal vertical loading slabs deflect downward at mid-span; however, during earthquakes slabs flex both up and down. Stress cracks appear on both the top and bottom of plates exercised in this way along "yield" or "hinge" lines. From an earlier chapter, recall that when beams deflect excessively and form hinges, cable action can replace bending action in the failed beam. A similar change of mechanism can take place in a slab. Such a *reserve mechanism* for a plate must, however, rely on *membrane action*. Visualize a round slab supported by a continuous turned down edge. It looks a good deal like the head of a drum. When a single vertical point load is applied at the center of such a drum head, its flexible surface would go into dispersed tension toward all the edges. In structural

Figure 12-17
Thickening a slab to form drop panels can help overcome punching shear.

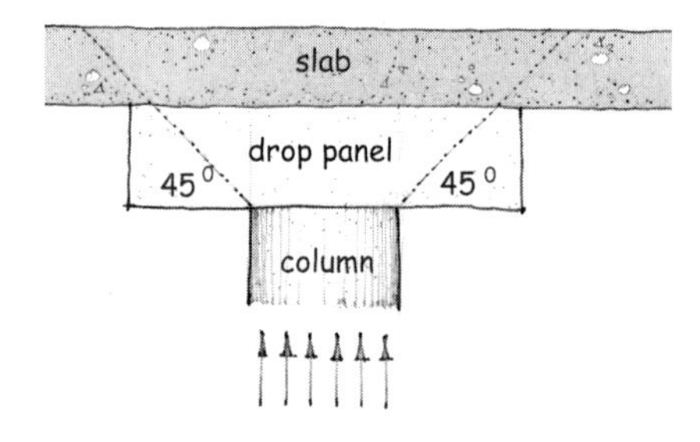

terms the slab can shift to a "sag cable" structure (assuming the shape of a shallow inverted dome), with the whole *membrane* in tension. The outside turned-down edge would become a sort of compression ring if this occurs. Such a reserve mechanism may form even in the absence of restrained edge conditions.

Figure 12-18
In waffle slabs, voids are often filled over columns.

BEHAVIOR OF BEARING WALLS UNDER LOAD

A bearing wall can be understood as a series of parallel columns, placed directly adjacent to each other, and structurally fused into a single vertical plane. This predicts the column-like structural behavior that a bearing wall will experience. Like columns, bearing walls can buckle if they become too thin for their height (*slenderness ratio*) (Fig. 12-19). Like columns, bearing walls are intended to carry loads down the vertical center of the wall, but eccentric loads can encourage buckling in walls. While most modern bearing walls have vertical sides for ease in construction, they may also taper from the base to the top. This slope or taper is known as *batter*. As the reader will recall, loads at the bottom of a column are greater than those at the top. This is true of bearing walls as well. For this reason the wall may need more resistive material and greater thickness at the base that at the top. This can also increase the stability of the wall. Finally bearing walls can act as a *shear wall* assisting a building against lateral loads such as winds. But be aware that several short sections of wall do not add up to the shearing resistance of a single long wall (Fig. 12-20).

Now let us turn our attention to the behavior of bearing walls under vertical load. Bearing walls optimally invite the continuous distributed load of slabs, but with bearing modifications (i.e., bearing plates, bond beams, etc.) will tolerate point loads such as joists, beams, and even trusses (Fig. 12-21). These

Figure 12-19
Walls may buckle like columns if the ratio of their height to their width is too great.

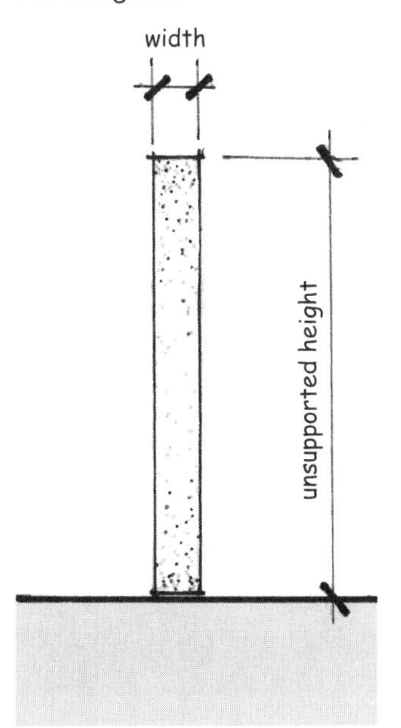

Figure 12-21
Load propagation in a bearing wall.

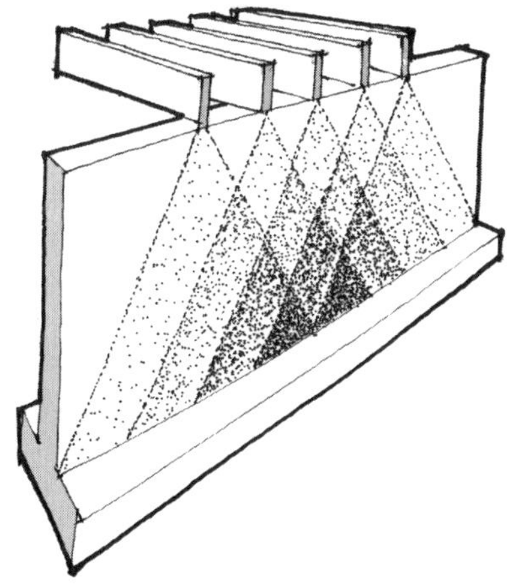

Figure 12-20
Several short sections of wall are not the same as one long section of wall.

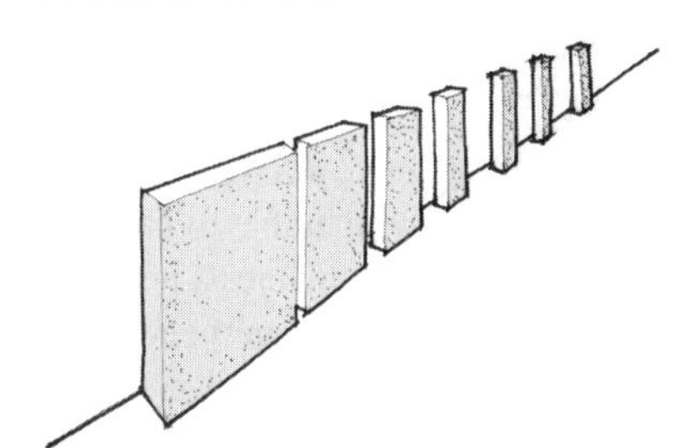

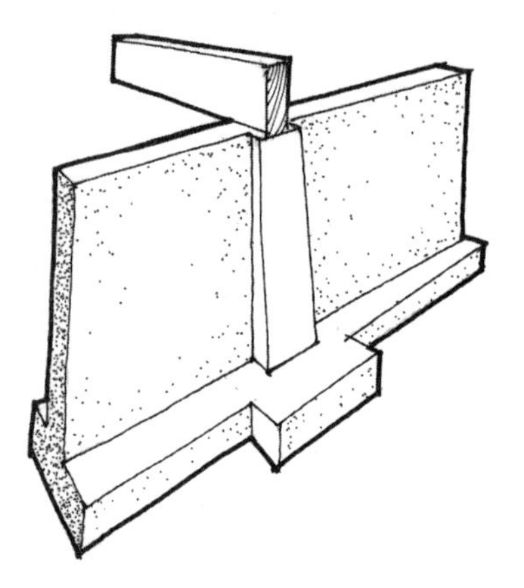

Figure 12-22
Bearing wall with attached pilaster.

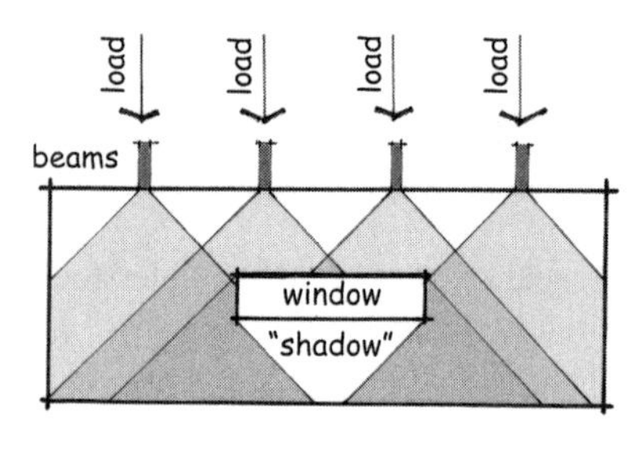

Figure 12-23
Notice the stress "shadow" under the window opening.

loads are dispersed downward across the wall to the foundation. In the case of extremely heavy point loads, an *attached pilaster* may be placed directly under the load. Such pilasters are also used for lateral support reasons, which will be discussed later (Fig. 12-22). As loads are dispersed downward across a bearing wall, holes such as windows interrupt the continuity of this dispersion, produce *load shadows*, and create undesirable *stress concentrations*. Small windows and round windows will be less intrusive; however, wide windows with sharp corners are more intrusive (Fig. 12-23 and 12-24). If the wall is burdened with point loads, an unusual triangular window can logically be placed in the "load shadows" formed at the top of the wall between beams (Fig. 12-25). A deeper understanding of the structural behavior of bearing walls may now be best pursued by reviewing the many failures to which these walls are vulnerable. (Corkill, Puderbaugh, and Sawyers 1974).

Figure 12-24
The brickwork of the building in Ghent Belgium directly expresses the load flowing downward around the window openings.

Bearing wall failures

The surface face of the top of the wall may fail directly under an applied vertical load such as a long truss. Weak brittle materials such as concrete blocks are particularly vulnerable to *bearing failures* (Fig. 12-26). Additional bearing plates or bond beams are used to overcome this problem. Once bearing stresses are overcome, the wall may simply be crushed in *compression failure* (Fig. 12-27). To overcome this all that is needed is to select a material with sufficient compressive strength. Like columns, bearing walls can suffer *vertical buckling* (Fig. 12-28). These failures are avoided by maintaining an adequate wall thickness with respect to the wall's unsupported height, referred to as the wall's slenderness ratio. Long walls that are too thin are vulnerable to *longitudinal buckling* (Fig. 12-29). In addition to increasing wall thickness, periodic placement of attached pilasters can overcome this threat. Given perpendicular lateral loads of sufficient intensity walls will fail by *rotating out of plane* (Fig. 12-30). To resist such overturning the wall may be "form-stabilized", or

Figure 12-25
Triangular window located in "load shadows".

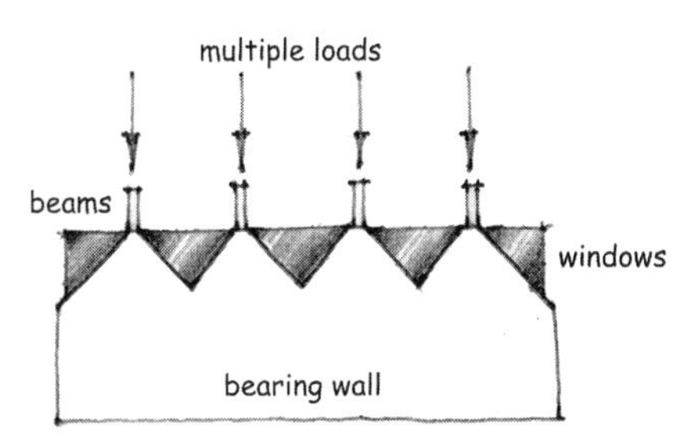

Figure 12-26
Bearing failure at the top of a bearing wall.

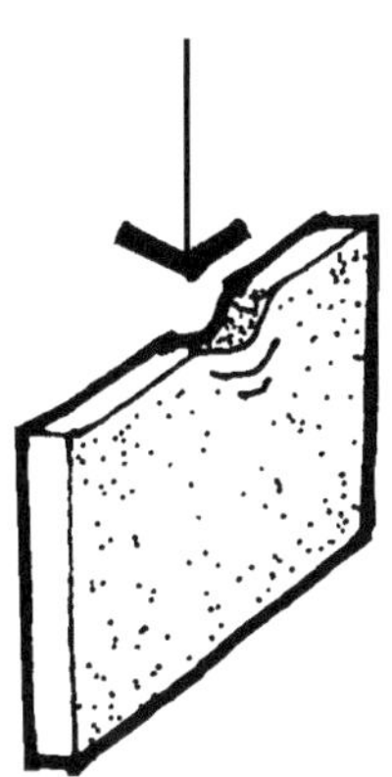

Figure 12-27
Crushing or compression failures can only occur in very short thick walls.

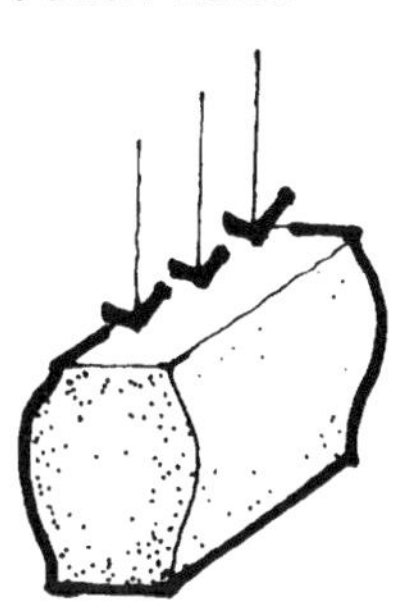

Figure 12-28
Wall failure by vertical buckling.

securely connected to both floor and ceiling slabs. Strong lateral ground surges parallel the wall due to earthquake can cause walls to slide at the base (*base shear*) (Fig. 12-31), or to slide at the top (*top shear*) (Fig. 12-32). This may be resisted by periodically pinning both the top and bottom of the wall to the floors both above and below it. When the bearing wall acts as a shear wall it becomes vulnerable to 45 degree *shear tears* if the wall material is weak in tensile strength (i.e., masonry) (Fig. 12-33). Diagonal (45 degree) *shear buckling* can occur if that same wall is made of a ductile material such as metal (Fig. 12-34). As a building sways during an earthquake, individual wall may experience the effects of *in-plane-bending*. This may take the form of crushing on one end, or tearing on the opposite end. These effects are overcome by thickened and reinforced vertical edges (Fig. 12-35). Differential settlement either due to poor soil compaction or settlement due to earthquake vibrations can yield in-plane bending tears and crushing at the head and base of the effected wall (Fig. 12-36). The same forces can also produce an in-plane *vertical shearing couple* (Fig. 12-37). These failures are overcome by proper soil preparation and foundation design.

Figure 12-29
Wall failure by longitudinal buckling.

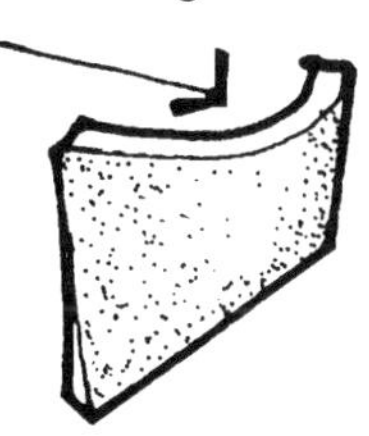

Figure 12-30
Out of plane rotation.

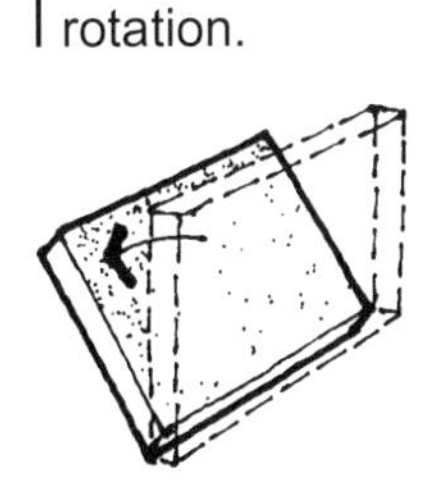

Figure 12-31
Base shear.

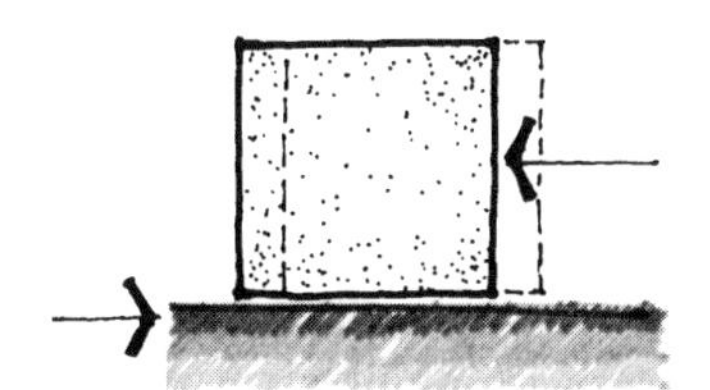

Figure 12-32
Top shear.

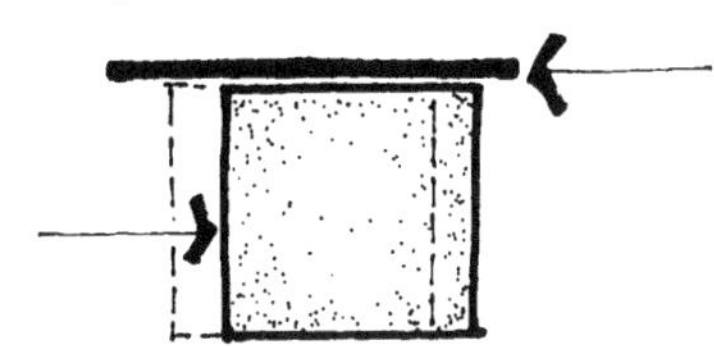

OPTIMUM CONFIGURATION

Figure 12-33
45 degree shear tears.

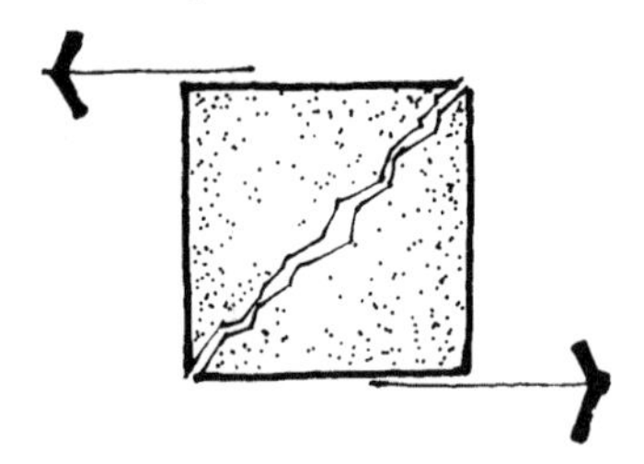

Foundation: Since the vertical loads imposed on a bearing wall are more or less evenly dispersed across the length of the wall, it is appropriate to use a continuous foundation under such a wall (i.e., a grade beam or stem wall).

Wall and slab proportions: Rules of thumb and tables are often used during early preliminary design to gain a reasonable estimate of an appropriate height, width, and length for a given wall or the depth of certain type of slab with a given span. Two of the best sources are *The Architect's Studio Companion* by Allen and *Structure and Architectural Design* by Corkill, Puderbaugh, and Sawyers. It is very important to underline the importance of clear conceptual understanding before attempting to use such tables. Design choices concerning spans, shape, thickness, and edge condition of all slabs must be based on that understanding. For example, even given support at all four edges of a slab, plates that exceed a 4:1 ratio of spans will still act as one-way slab. If the designer mistakenly thought that the four edge beams made it two-way, the slab didn't know it. Looking up preliminary proportions in the wrong tables would be the result of such a conceptual misunderstanding.

Figure 12-34
45 degree buckling due to shearing forces.

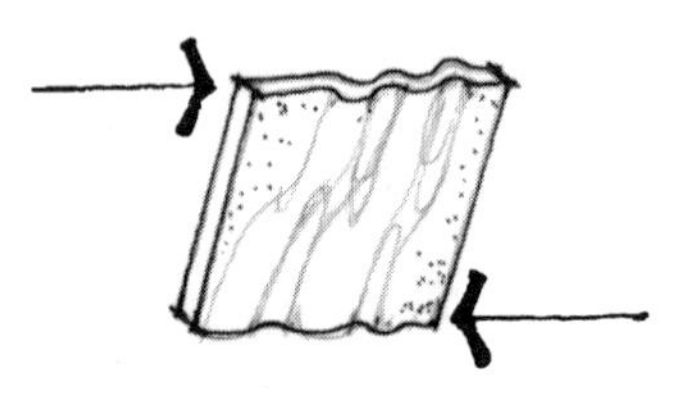

Continuous Action: Slabs gain benefits from continuous action over several bays similar to that of continuous beams discussed in an earlier chapter. Loads applied in one bay carry over in a "diminishing sine wave" pattern into adjacent bays.

Figure 12-35
In-plane bending.

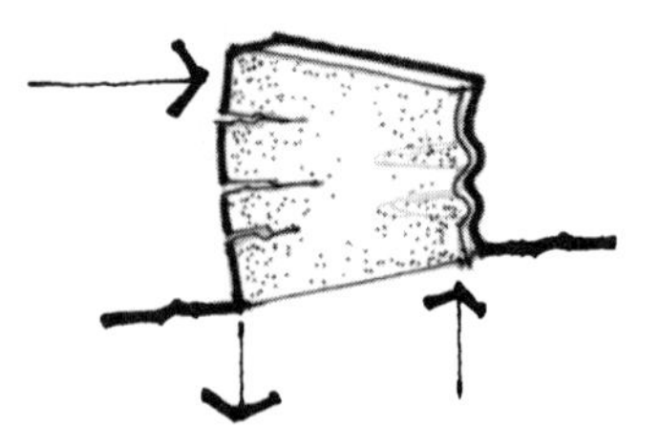

Space for systems: Sometimes systems are deliberately exposed. When flat slabs are used in multifloor buildings the maximum amount of overhead space for mechanical and electrical systems is provided. It is common to "drop" a ceiling down below such flat slabs to hide any unsightly systems (Fig. 12-38). If spans increase to the extent that ribbed or waffle slabs will be required, less overhead space will be available, and floor-to-floor heights will have to be increased. Where possible, two-way slab systems are normally preferred over one-way systems since reduced slab thicknesses are required.

Figure 12-36
Differential settlement.

Figure 12-37
Vertical shearing couple.

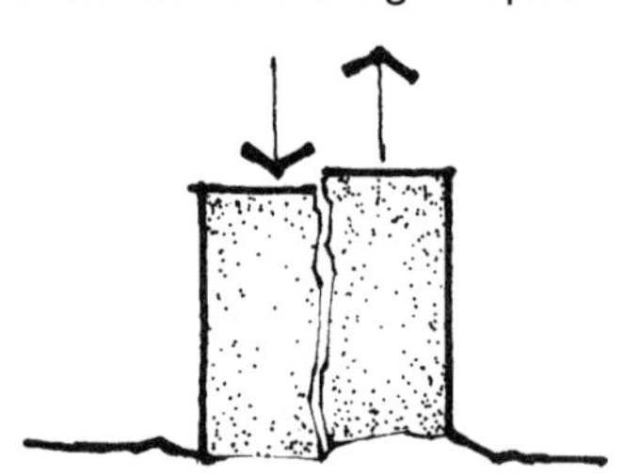

Figure 12-38
Drop ceiling grid and equipment behind, exposed at the San Francisco airport by the 1987 earthquake.

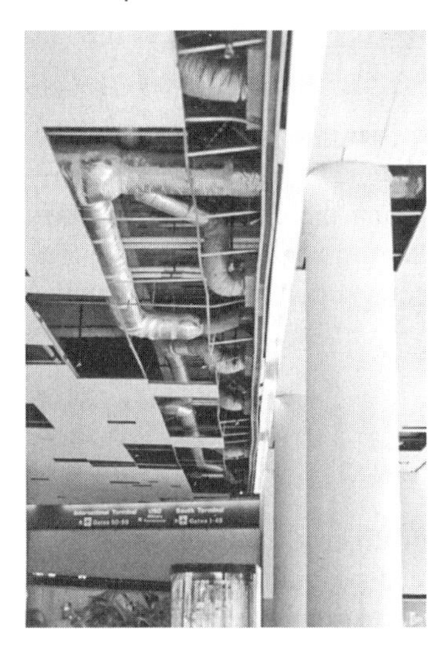

Figure 12-39
Reinforcing was not carried up through joints between walls, slabs, and columns for continuity.

Slab reinforcing: In flat slabs, it is common to use *welded wire steel mesh* near the bottom of the slab. Enough concrete cover must be left to assure fire resistance. In continuous slabs this mesh may change position vertically within the slab as it passes over beams. Ribbed slabs and precast tees are given reinforcing steel bars in positions consistent with the normal practice for beams previously discussed.

Joints: It is particularly important to carry all steel reinforcing continuously through joints in this type of structural system, particularly in seismically active areas (Fig. 12-39).

FUNCTIONAL FOOTPRINT

Bearing walls may be bent and warped to enclose a wide variety of volumes (Fig. 12-40). However, square and rectangular footprints with varying spans are typical to slab construction. This is due in part to ease in the construction process. Where precast concrete elements (planks, tees, etc.) are used, the footprint is inevitably rectangular.

Figure 12-40
Bearing walls don't have to be rectilinear.

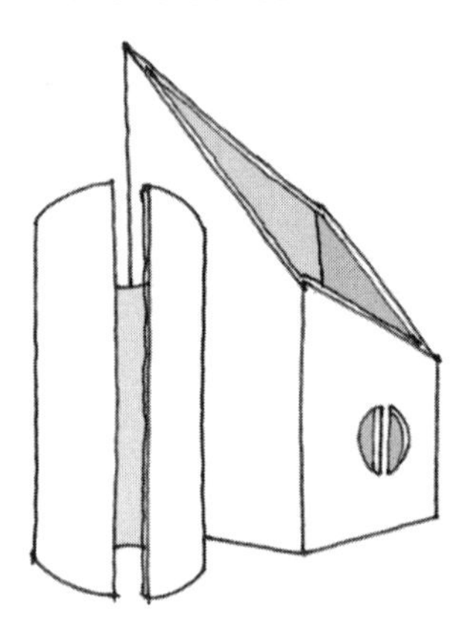

Figure 12-41
Modest overhangs are possible.

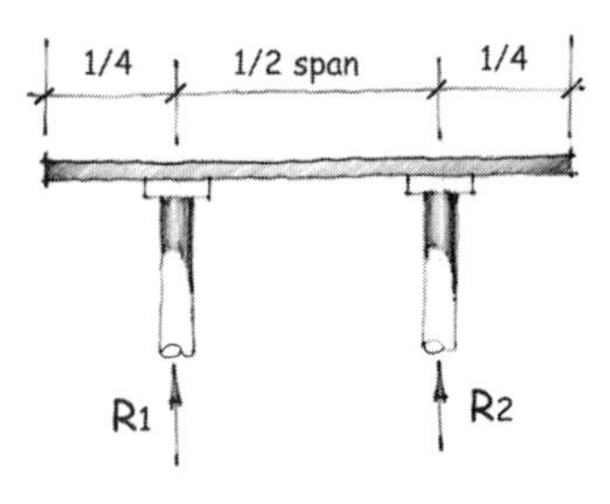

PATTERN OF GROWTH

While slabs may be given modest overhang, growth for bearing wall and slab structures is normally by full bay in both axis (Fig. 12-41).

DESIGN METHODS

Small scale models built from chip board are often the best way to conduct preliminary design of bearing wall and slab buildings. Pay attention to the preliminary thickness of walls and slabs when cutting the chipboard. You may have to glue multiple sheets of chipboard together to achieve the appropriate wall slenderness ratios outlined above, depending upon the scale that you choose for your study model.

AESTHETIC POTENTIAL

The broad surfaces inherent in bearing walls invite enrichment in both color and texture. Some materials such as stone need no additional enrichment. Brick, stone, and concrete block can be laid in an extremely varied number of patterns. Standard module sizes, such as those found in brick and block, must be respected pragmatically in laying out wall length and placement of openings; however, this same modularity adds an underlying order visually to bearing wall structures. The broad faces of adobe, concrete, or block walls offer excellent screens upon which shadows can be cast (Fig. 12-42). When bearing walls are left simple and plain, the openings for windows and doors will often receive considerable attention (Fig. 12-43). Even such minor elements as the necessary expansion, contraction, and construction joints may become important if a bearing wall building is sufficiently simple in other ways. Systems of proportion (i.e., the golden mean) are often studied closely in the placement of such elements (Fig. 12-44). The contrast of mass and void is particularly apparent and appealing in bearing wall buildings due to the significant thicknesses of many of the materials that have been widely used (Fig. 12-45).

CONSTRUCTION

Bearing wall buildings are usually self-stabilized against lateral loads. The bearing walls are usually strong enough, and long enough to perform as shear walls if they run at right angles. Bearing wall buildings are sensitive to differential settlement in soils, and invite continuous foundation support. For this reason, special care should be taken to be certain that soil is either left undisturbed or well compacted under their foundations. It is also quite common for the bearing wall to perform double duty as the weatherproofing envelope for a small building if heat transfer through the wall is not a critical issue.

Figure 12-42
Shadows on a concrete wall.

Figure 12-43
Window opening in Volterra, Italy.

Figure 12-44
Pallazzo Ruccellai in Florence Italy by Alberti.

Figure 12-45
Wall thicknesses can be considerable and varied in a bearing wall structure.

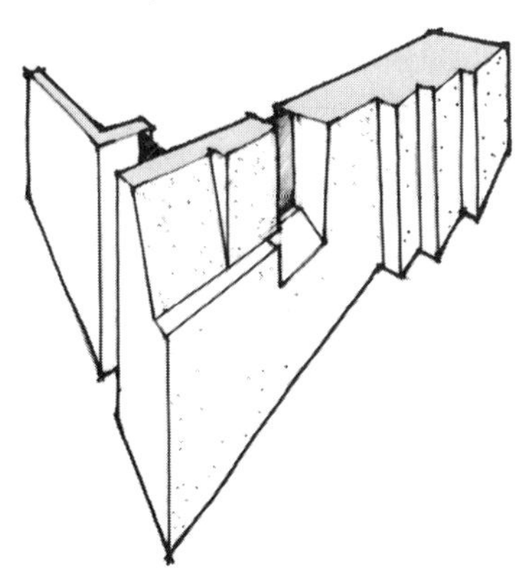

Sequence of construction

Masonry walls: Brick, stone, and block is laid unit by unit. Extensive scaffolding must be erected even for fairly low buildings. Particular care is taken to maintain level mortar beds and precisely vertical faces using strings and levels. Care must be taken with the mortar mix to be certain of its final strength. Freezing temperatures are a threat to mortar strength. If the voids in the wall or blocks are to be reinforced (and/or grouted) this must be done in relatively low "lifts" in order to assure complete fill, and appropriate vibration of the fill. Metal flashing and small holes, called "weeps" are made near the bottom of cavity walls to allow condensation to escape from inside the wall cavity to the outside. If this is not done, the condensation will freeze and push the lower units out from the wall.

In-situ concrete walls: Poured in place concrete walls require wood forms, in which reinforcing steel is placed, and then concrete is pumped or poured. Only about four feet of a form (a "shallow lift") may be filled and vibrated at a time. If the carefully controlled concrete mix is dropped for a greater distance, the large aggregate (gravel) will tend to separate from the rest of the mix. This produces horizontal lines of "honey combing" and weakness in the wall. Excessive vibration can also lead to this unwanted mix separation. In very large pours with very thick walls, the heat of the concrete curing can hurry the curing process excessively. In these cases it will be necessary to add retardants to the mix. If the pour is done all in one pour, "cold joints" are not a threat; however, if the pour is stopped at the end of the day and resumed on the next, the cold joint that results must be well cleaned, dry, and occasionally roughened prior to resuming the pour. After the concrete cures to the extent that it has adequate strength, the wood forms will be stripped. Steel reinforcing bars will often be left exposed at the top of the wall to allow the concrete of the structural slab to fully bond with the wall when it is poured at a later time.

Site cast concrete walls: Like in-situ concrete, site cast concrete is formed and poured at the final building site; however, site cast walls are usually poured in low panels laid directly on the ground, then "tilted up" to form wall panels. These panels must be temporarily stabilized by "struts" until all the panels are in place and the joints can be welded. This method of construction obviously requires that considerable space is available on all sides of the building foundation. Not only must the panel be laid flat outside the wall, but concrete trucks will have to move outside of the pouring beds. In essence plans must be made to establish a temporary "factory" all around the full circumference of the final building wall.

Precast concrete walls: Instead of site casting wall panels, it is possible to cast the wall panels at a remote factory, and then transport them to the site. Quality control is much better in precast concrete, than either in-situ or site cast work. Heavy equipment will be required to move the panels, but the procedure is otherwise quite similar to site cast during the "tilt-up" process. Precast tilt-up construction greatly minimizes on site labor time and costs.

Adobe walls: Adobe construction will normally only be attempted when the building is to be sited on heavy clay soil. First small adobe brick forms are made from wood, then filled with clay soil, water, and straw. Once they are sun dried the adobe units are removed from the forms and placed in the bearing wall similar to fired brick or concrete block. Once the wall is erected a coat of clay slurry, stucco, or bitumen is spread over the wall to resist moisture penetration. While this is sufficient in a desert climate, wide roof overhangs must be used if significant rain is anticipated. This is a low-tech construction process that may be successfully executed by an untrained labor force.

Flat slabs: Normally horizontal plywood forms are first set upon adjustable jacks. Reinforcing steel will be placed on small metal "stools" to control its position within the slab. Concrete is then poured and vibrated. Once adequately cured, the jacks are lowered and the plywood forms are stripped from below.

Ribbed and Waffle slabs: Ribbed and waffle slabs construction begins in a process quite similar to a flat slab; however, once the jacks and horizontal plywood forms are in place, an additional layer of "pans" are set on top of the plywood forms. These fiberglass or metal pans will form the concrete ribs. Steel reinforcing will then be placed in the voids left by the pans, and concrete will be poured and vibrated. In this way the slab, and the ribs, will be cast integrally during the same pour. Once the concrete is adequately cured, the jacks are lowered, the plywood forms and pans are stripped downward, and the ribbed slab remains behind.

Composite slabs: Corrugated steel plates may be rested on steel beams, and welded into a unit. Concrete may be subsequently poured onto the corrugated deck and vibrated. Once cured, the steel and concrete will perform jointly to form a very strong flat slab. This joint action is called "composite" action. Coordination of skilled trades will be required to assure no loss of construction time. One additional advantage is that no stripping of forms will be required.

Lift slabs: This is a form of site cast. A bond breaker such as Mylar plastic is laid on top of the finished ground floor of the building. A set of low wood forms are placed on the bond breaker. A flat floor plate is reinforced and cast in the low form. Lifting points must be cast into each of these site cast floor plates during this process. Once that floor panel is adequately cured, a second bond breaker is placed over the completed plate, the forms moved upward and reset, and another plate is poured directly on top of the first. This process continues until a series of floor plates are poured like a stack of pancakes resting on the ground floor. Jacks are placed on top of each of the building columns, cables are hooked to the lifting points of the top most slab, and the slab is raised upward by the jacks until it is positioned properly to form an upper floor. The slab is then welded off against each column. In this way, each slab is subsequently lifted and secured forming all of the floors of the building. While skill and special equipment is required, forming and pouring time is reduced to a minimum.

Precast concrete tees are widely used as a both tilt-up bearing wall, and as a ribbed floor/roof slab. As a tilt-up wall the tees must be temporarily stabilized until they can be sufficiently welded together. Once placed as a ribbed slab, an additional light weight concrete topping or rigid insulation will be placed over this rough surface. A final mopped or membrane waterproofing surface must be placed over the total construction.

Precast concrete planks are normally smaller, lighter, and easier to manage than precast concrete tees. Precast planks are usually placed over precast concrete post and beam frames. The process is quite similar to the tee process just described, and also requires that both a light weight topping and a waterproofing surface be added in order to form a roof slab.

Vocabulary		
Form jacks	Stud	Framed wall
Wythe	Tilt-up panel	In-situ
Flat slab	Waffle slab	Ribbed slab
One-way slab	Two-way slab	Form pans
Composite slab	Turned-down edge	Isostatic lines
Edge twist	Punching shear	Drop panel
Shear capital	Battered wall	Load shadow
Stress concentration	Slenderness ratio	Precast tee
Precast plank	Site cast	Lift slab

REVIEW QUESTIONS

1. Under what circumstances is a slab and bearing wall system a good choice of superstructure?
2. What is the basis for selection of a material to use in a bearing wall?
3. How can the preliminary depth of a reinforced concrete flat slab, a waffle slab, and a one-way ribbed slab be established?
4. Briefly, graphically and verbally, describe the behavior of slabs and bearing walls under vertical loads.
5. List and describe the most common modes of failure for bearing walls and slabs.
6. Briefly discuss the ways in which a slab is similar to, and different from, a beam in its structural behavior.
7. What is one major construction process advantage of composite slab construction over a flat insitu slab?
8. What are "stress reversals" in a structural slab?

Figure 13-1
Charles de Gaulle airport interchange in Paris by Paul Andreu and Jean-Marie Duthilleul.

13 Trusses

GENERAL

A truss is a series of triangulated elements assembled in a single plane in order to form an "improved beam" (Fig. 13-2). Trusses are essentially very good beams. They resist loads similar to beams, but are much more efficient due to wide separation of the top and bottom chords by triangulated web members. In very long span applications the assembly of triangular elements may assume a somewhat more three-dimensional configuration; however, this actually becomes a space frame which will be discussed in the next chapter.

Figure 13-2
Student model of a pitched truss.

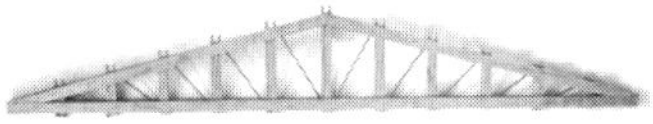

DESCRIPTION

In its most simple form a truss has three members, pinned at the joints, and is formed into a triangle. The triangle is a stable or rigid form. It cannot change shape due to external loading without changing the length (deforming) of at least one of its members. While the truss may globally provide bending resistance to external loads like a beam, the individual (local) members of a truss are in simple tension or simple compression. Bending and shear that occur in beams can be avoided in the individual members of a truss if external loads are applied only at joints.

HISTORY AND SIGNIFICANT EXAMPLES

Building examples

Wood trusses have been used for at least 2000 years. Some excellent early examples that still exist are found in early Christian churches. Trusses continue to be widely used in many different building types down to the current day.

Figure 13-3
Trussed arches at the Frankfort railroad station in Germany.

Well known early timber trusses include Santa Sabina in Rome, and Santa Apollinare in Ravenna, Italy. Because of their vulnerability to fire during the violent middle ages, trusses that supported a roof above might have a stone vault below. Later stone vaults completely replaced trusses in some areas; however, they continued to be used where extensive quantities of timber were grown. With the advent of steel much greater spans became possible. Much of the fabrication could be moved into a factory setting, and with the use of cranes erection became very rapid. The industrial age also generated the need for greater column free spans in factories, aircraft hangers, and rail stations such as the one at Charles de Gaulle Airport in Paris (Fig. 13-1). Trussing is now often used in forming other structural systems such as the steel arches at the Frankfurt Railroad Station, Frankfurt, Germany (Fig. 13-3).

Nonbuilding examples

Bridges such as the Firth of Forth Bridge, Edinburgh, Scotland, and the pivot bridge on the Mississippi River Keokuk, Iowa (Fig. 13-4) make extensive use of trusses.

Figure 13-4
Pivot bridge at Keokuk Iowa.

TYPES OR CATEGORIES

By material

The oldest type of truss is the *heavy timber* roof. Its typical detailing and configuration required traditional skill, which still has considerable visual appeal (Fig. 13-5). However, heavy timber trusses are less widely used currently than they have been in other historical periods. Some of the best examples are to be found in medium size churches. *Light weight wood trusses* are by far the most widely used wood trusses. They are normally factory made and used in residential and small commercial type buildings (Fig. 13-6). These trusses are rapidly jointed at the factory by "gang nail plates" (Fig. 13-7). Wood trusses are used for spans between 30 and 60 feet. In that span range they compete with steel beams.

At about 60 feet, steel trusses are often the system of choice. *Open web steel joists*, *long span web joists*, and *deep long span web joists* all share a fairly common configuration (Fig. 13-8). Together, the three are used for spans as short as 20 feet, and as long as 120 feet. *Heavy steel trusses* have a span capability even greater than a deep long span joist. Heavy steel trusses are usually assembled from a combination of hot rolled steel members such as wide flange, tee, angle, and channel sections. This is done because of the ease in bolting and welding such sections (Fig. 13-9). Riveted joints are now rare in

Figure 13-5
Typical heavy timber truss.

Figure 13-6
Lightweight wood trusses in a project under construction.

Figure 13-7
Close view of a "gang nail plate".

modern steel trusses (Fig. 13-10). Occasionally steel tubes and pipe sections are used, especially in very long span heavy trusses. Such pipe sections perform especially well under simple compression (Fig. 13-11). Light weight or cold rolled steel trusses are used in residential and small commercial buildings that will have walls fabricated from cold rolled, light weight steel studs and plates.

Historically heavy timber and steel members have occasionally been combined to form *composite trusses*. Iron or steel rods or cables have sometimes been substituted for trusses web members that experienced only simple tension when the truss was loaded. Currently the more common composite use of wood and steel is in fabrication of a type of open web joist. These joists have wood top and bottom chords and steel pipe web members. Known by many proprietary names, one of their significant advantages over steel web joists is that they provide nailable surfaces on both the top and bottom chord of the

Figure 13-8
Open web joist supporting corrugated steel deck above.

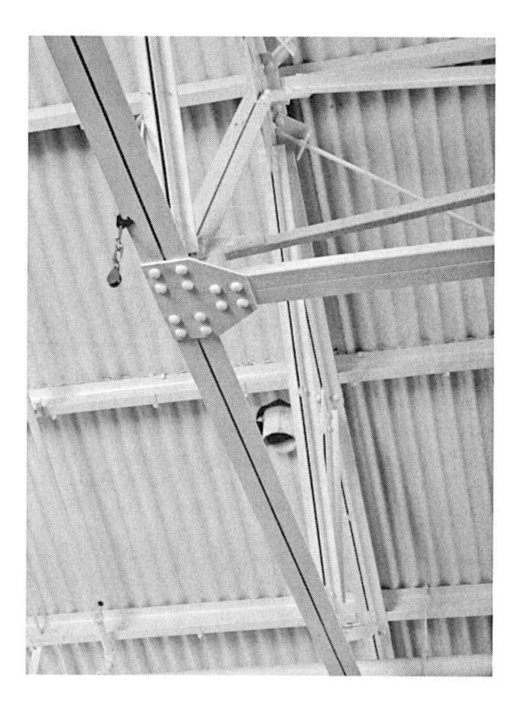

Figure 13-9
Built up steel truss.

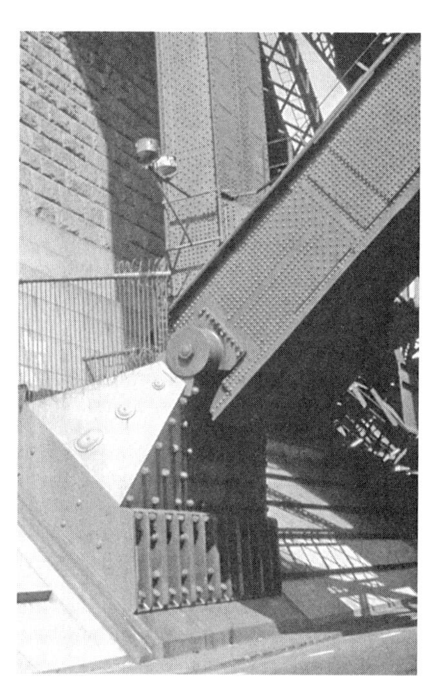

Figure 13-10
Riveted joints in a steel truss.

round pipes can be
difficult to join at
a single complex
joint

Figure 13-11
Pipe sections used to build up a steel truss.

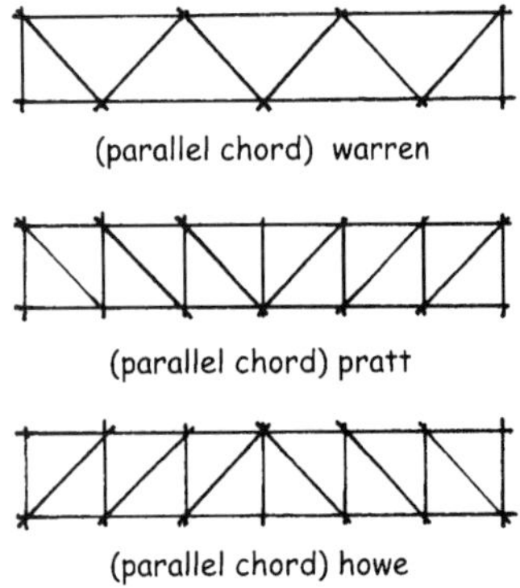
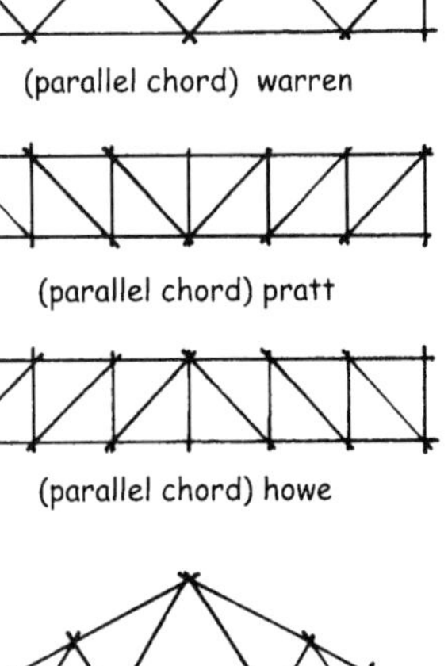

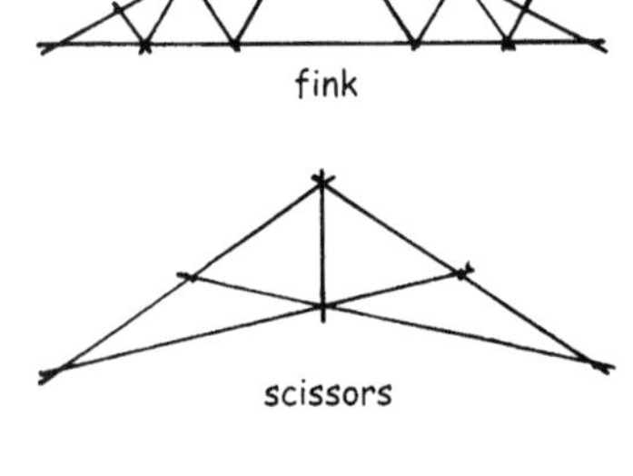

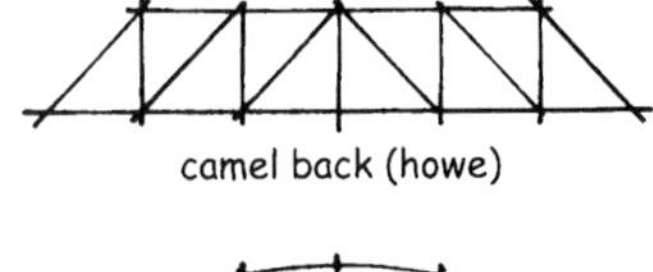

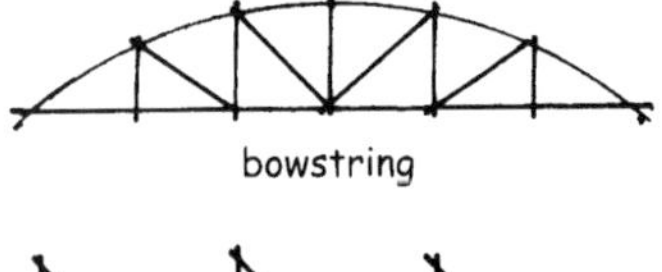

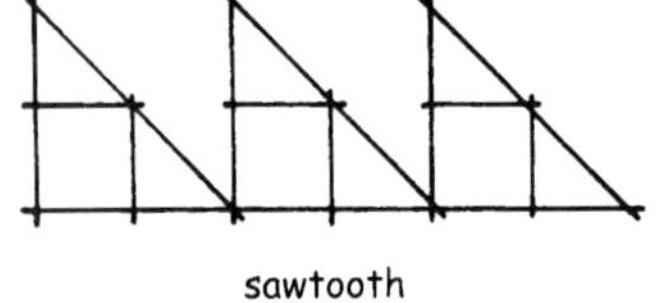

Figure 13-12
A few widely used truss configurations.

truss. This makes attachment of floor plates and gypsum board ceilings much easier in small to medium size construction.

Because the goal of trusses is to lighten the structure and because forms for concrete trusses are quite complex, reinforced concrete has not been widely used in trusses. They are, however, a bit more common in bridge construction. Reinforced concrete offers weather proofing with less maintenance than steel, and is more fire resistant than either wood or steel. As reinforced concrete evolves into a material of significantly greater strength, it may have increased potential as a potential truss material.

By configuration

A bewildering array of truss configurations has evolved over time. Most are flat two-dimensional assemblies such as the Pratt, Howe, Warren, Bow String, Saw Tooth, Camel Back, Scissors, Fan, and Fink trusses (Fig. 13-12). However, triangular and square trusses are occasionally used in very long span applications to eliminate the need for bracing between trusses (Fig. 13-13). Both triangular and square trusses may or may not have cover plates on each end.

Trusses by position

Trusses placed in the conventional horizontal position are not given special additional names, but most trusses may also be placed in a sloped or inverted position. Such positioning is normally done to achieve positive roof slope, a more aesthetically interesting building mass, or to develop an unusual internal ceiling (Fig. 13-14).

Figure 13-13
Triangular trusses on the Kemper Arena in Kansas City Missouri, site of a serious collapse.

NOMENCLATURE

Take a moment now to look at the nomenclature of a truss (Fig. 13-15). When used for a floor of a building, the *top chord* of a truss is normally used as the functional bearing surface. In bridges, however, the *bottom chord* may often be used to support the road way surface. *Web members* are used to separate the top and bottom chord, and to transmit loads between them. Web members come in several types. The vertical web members that are experiencing compression are often referred to as *posts*. This differentiates them from *diagonals,* which are web members that run between the top and bottom chord at some angle other than vertical. *Struts* are diagonal web members that experience simple compression. Each one of the triangles that form the truss is known as a *panel*, and the joints of these panels are known as *panel points*. *Panel length*

Figure 13-14
Notice the inverted position of the trusses in the Airborne Museum in Fayetteville, NC.

Figure 13-15
Truss nomenclature.

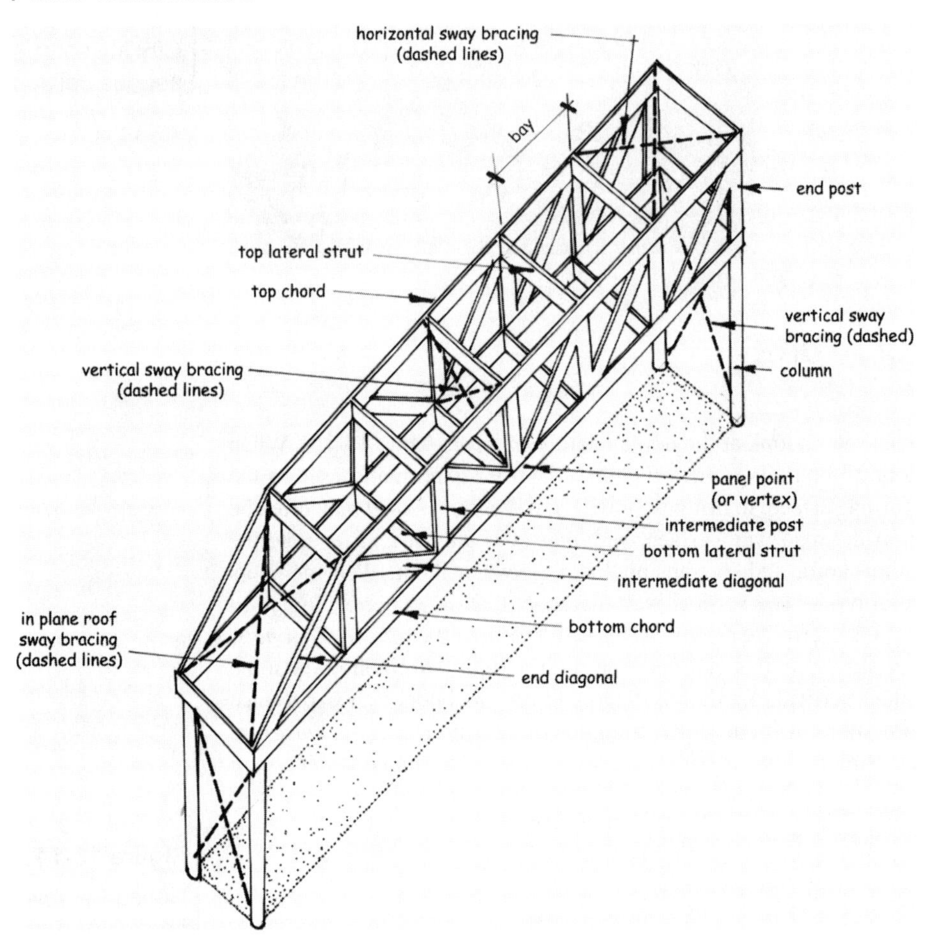

is the horizontal distance between panel points. The *overall length* is measured by the structurally triangulated portion only, although an extension of the top chord may be used to form an *overhang*. Sometimes a level return may be attached to the overhang to provide a surface to which a finished *soffit* may be attached. The *clear span* of a truss is the horizontal distance between the supports for the truss. The highest point of the truss is known as its *peak*. If the top and bottom chords are joined at the ends of the truss, that joint is known as the *heel*. The slope of the top chord is normally described in a ratio related to 12 inches. For instance, a 3-in-12 slope has 3 inches of vertical fall for every 12 inches of horizontal run. *Purlins* are small beams that run perpendicular between trusses and are used to carry the *roof decking*. *Anchorage* is the connection between the truss and the supporting structure below. *Bracing* runs between trusses and between columns for the purpose of lateral stability. At least the end bays usually receive such bracing. Small horizontal beams called *girts* are often attached to the outside of the columns. The purpose of these girts is to support the building's weatherproofing skin (both vertically and horizontally), and not contribute in a significant way to lateral stability.

COMMON APPLICATIONS

Architectural applications

As previously outlined, trusses are widely used for spans that exceed those appropriate to conventional beams. However, issues other than span may be just as important in the selection of a truss system. Unlike conventional beams, trusses allow free passage of mechanical and electrical systems such as heating ducts, pipes, and electrical wiring. In addition, open web joists, and most small trusses are factory made. This means that quality control will be better than site fabrication, and if common sizes can be used, it is likely that they will be cheaper. Open web joists are often used in medium to large office buildings and large retail stores. Heavy timber trusses are used in medium to large churches. Cold rolled or light weight steel trusses have growing popularity is residential, and small commercial buildings. Light weight wood trusses still dominate the residential and small commercial building market. Heavy steel trusses are widely used for small to medium size bridges, large warehouse roofs, aircraft hangers, factories, train stations, and athletic facilities such as basketball arenas and gyms.

Nonarchitectural applications

Bridges are the most common nonarchitectural applications for truss systems. Whether for rail or road, trusses are used worldwide as soon as normal beam spans are exceeded.

BEHAVIOR UNDER LOAD

Configuration stability

As previously stated trusses exist because triangles are inherently rigid. The length of any side of a triangle cannot be changed without changing the size of the angle opposite. Inversely, no angle can be changed without changing the length of the side opposite it. In plain words, it is rigid. That is what gives the triangle its profound structural potential, and makes the truss system possible. Pin the ends of three small sticks together and you can physically experience this rigidity or *configuration stability* for yourself. If a fourth stick is pinned into your experimental triangle so that it becomes a pinned rectangle, notice that the form becomes immediately unstable. It is evident that there is some relationship between the number of sides and the number of vertices that cause these pinned polygons to be stable or unstable. A third possibility exists however. It is possible to pin a configuration that looks like a truss but investigation will prove that one or more of the members is playing no structural role. It is a *redundant member*, since it is carrying no load. A redundant member can be

Figure 13-16
An unstable truss.

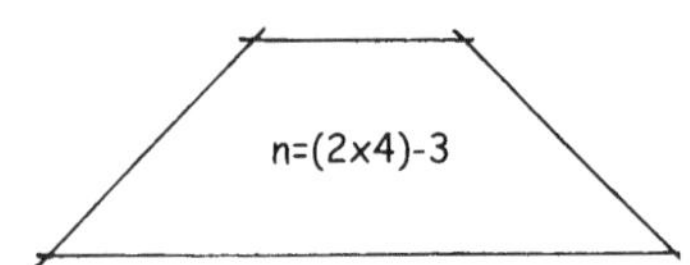

Figure 13-17
Truss with redundant members.

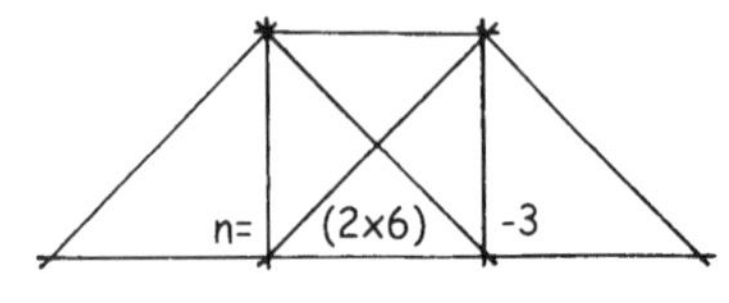

Figure 13-18
Stable truss without redundant members.

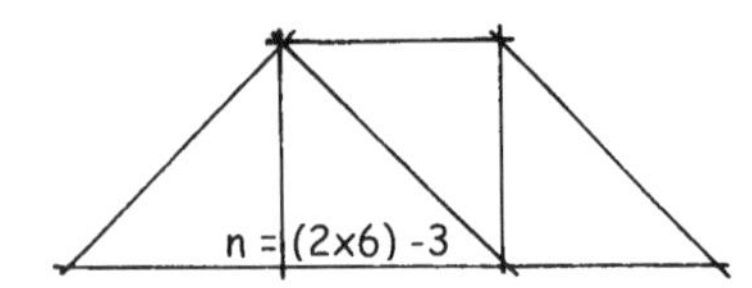

removed, and the remaining configuration can resist loads just as well without it. Engineers have evolved the following simple formula that produces a rigid truss that is free of redundant members. The number of members (N) equals two times the number of joints (J) minus 3 or $N = 2J - 3$. Take a moment to apply this formula to three potential "trusses." The first "truss" is unstable (Fig. 13-16). The second "truss" has a redundant member (Fig. 13-17). Only the third "truss" is both stable and free of redundant members (Fig. 13-18).

Path of load propagation

For roof structures *decking* will collect all applied loads, transmit these to *purlins*. The purlins then carry the loads to *panel points*, and finally the truss transmits the loads to *columns* or bearing walls.

Member stresses under vertical loads

1. *Beam-like global behavior:* As previously stated a flat truss is just a very good beam. When a truss is simply supported at each end, the top chord of the truss is in compression and the bottom chord is in tension. However, in forming a truss most of the web found in a conventional beam can be cut away since most of the beam web it only adding additional unwanted weight. Instead, only the minimum necessary web members have been used to form the truss. These web members hold the top and bottom chord separate, and transmit loads between the two chords. Ideally this allows the web member of a truss to be in either simple tension or simple compression. Since significant bending is not present in these web members, they may be much smaller and economical. In fact, bending is even avoided in the top and bottom chords, if possible.
2. *Stresses in individual web members:* To predict which web members are in compression and which are in tension first recall that a beam is simultaneously both a "bad arch" and a "bad cable structure" Since the truss is just an improved beam, this behavior can also be seen in trusses under vertical load. If we choose the simplest possible cable and arch as a starting point, two "families" of trusses can be evolved by expanding these initial basic elements into more complex and longer span trusses. A Pratt truss is initiated as a cable structure (Fig. 13-19) while a Howe Truss is initiated as an

Figure 13-19
Notice the first diagonal member at the end of a Pratt truss hangs down like a cable.

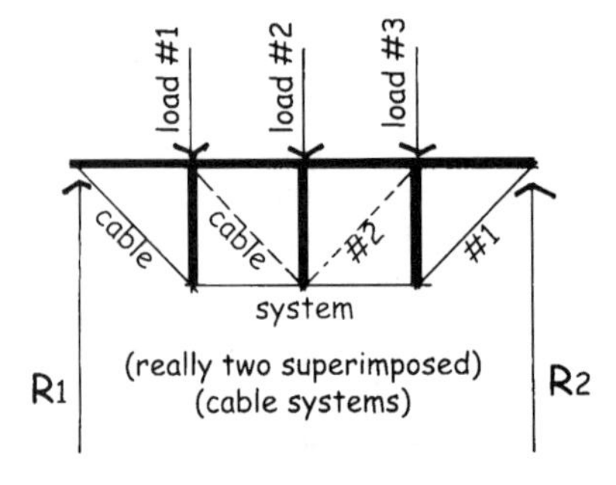

arch structure. Note that the initial diagonal web member at each end of the Howe truss is essentially in an "arch" (compression) position, while the same members in a Pratt truss are in a "cable" (tension) position. A second point to remember is that web members usually alternate between tension and compression as you proceed from one end to the other. This can be quite apparent in either of these flat trusses.

Stresses in truss supports

Bearing stress is a very significant issue in trusses since long spans collect large loads, then apply these large concentrated loads across very small areas at the supports at both ends of a truss. As mentioned in earlier reading, when concrete block walls are used to carry trusses a bearing plate and bond beam are normally required. However, it is common to place trusses on columns, since trusses concentrate loads at such supports. Unfortunately, trusses may impose very much larger loads on their columns than beams might. This is due to the much greater spans of which they are capable. It is best, of course, to make these column loads axial whenever possible. Even when truss loads are axial, supporting columns have a great tendency to Euler buckle. In addition, long span trusses often rest on long columns. (Functionally it would be very unusual to have a 120-foot steel truss that only needed to have a 10-foot column.) In factories and airplane hangers columns would be closer to 30 feet in length. Eccentricity makes the tendency of these long columns to buckle even worse (Fig. 13-20).

Stresses in joints

Members are small in trusses, and a large number of connectors may be required due to large loads. *Gusset plates* are then used to allow more connection space at the joint (Fig. 13-21). End, edge, and bolt to bolt failure are common concerns. Gusset plate buckling can also occur if all the members to

Figure 13-20
Student model of pitched trusses carried by spaced wood columns.

Figure 13-21
Leave lots of room for bolts in gusset plates of a truss & seat the members deep into the joint.

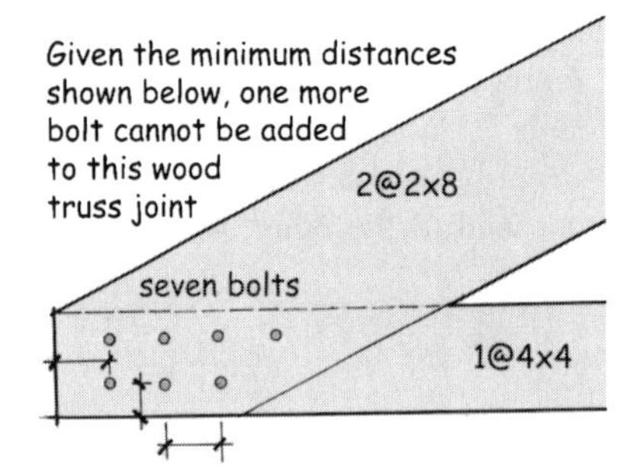

be joined are not attached deeply into the joint. Rigid (moment) connections are not usually possible between trusses and single columns. Bolt and weld failures are quite similar to those discussed in a previous chapter.

Under lateral loads

Like any deep thin beam, the truss is vulnerable to lateral bucking under vertical load, but the addition of lateral loading can increase this tendency and also introduces the tendency of the individual trusses to overturn. Lateral loads parallel to the long axis of a roof truss are well resisted by the rigid configuration of the truss itself, although the columns or walls supporting the trusses may be subject to wracking, overturning, or sliding at the base. However, lateral loads such as wind perpendicular to the long axis of the truss cause the truss to overturn. For these reasons permanent lateral bracing running between individual trusses is needed (Fig. 13-22). Some permanent bracing is often gained once the roof deck is fully in place; however, additional temporary bracing may also be used only for stability during the erection process on the building site.

The problem of uplift

The similarity of the shape and weight of trusses and airplane wings should not escape the reader. Winds racing over a truss roof can produce "lift" on the roof just as they do on an airplane wing. Like the airplane wing the truss is relatively light, compared to other structural systems. If not adequately secured to the wall support below, the truss roof may begin to lift up.

Figure 13-22
Steel cable cross bracing is often used between trusses for lateral support.

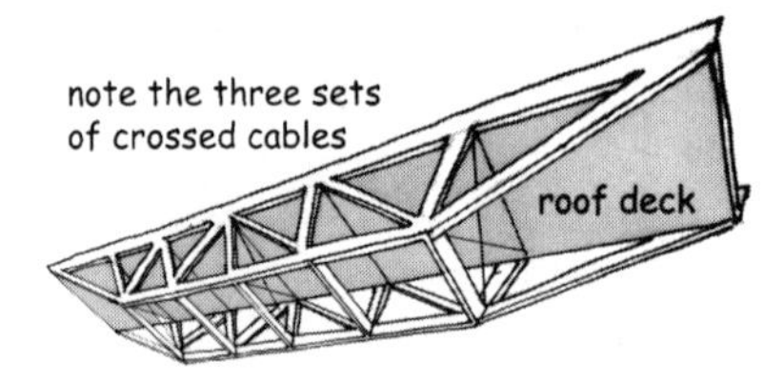

The problem of expansion

Building materials shrink and grow with temperature changes. Some materials change size with temperature more than others. To account for this they are given a *coefficient of thermal expansion.* This coefficient identifies how much 1 inch of a selected structural material will change size if the temperature changes 1 degree Fahrenheit. Obviously it is a big concern in climates where large temperature swings take place. But thermal expansion and contraction are also a particular concern in long span structures where you have lots of inches of material, each changing according to its thermal expansion coefficient. Special joints at the ends of trusses must be used to allow this movement to take place.

FAILURES

Beam-like failures: Since a truss is in many ways like a beam, it is not surprising that trusses experience failures similar to beams. Beam-like failures such as bending failures and excessive deflection are of concern near the mid-spans, and shearing failure is of concern near supporting beams or walls. However, bending failures in a truss may be expressed as either a strength failure in compression on the top chord, or a strength failure in tension in the bottom chord. But it is more complex than that. Every joint and every connection in a truss is tested when the truss as a total accepts vertical loads. Every compressive web member is acting like a column under compression, so it may fail in any way discussed concerning columns in the post and beam chapter. Every web member in tension can fail in all of the ways discussed in the cable structure chapter. Any top or bottom chord member can fail locally in bending if roof decking, ceilings, or purlins rest anywhere on them other than at panel points. Every bolted joint can fail in bearing or tearing through an end or edge of a plate or member, between connectors, and in rotation. Any of the bolts in the joint might fail in shear. Since truss members are joined at angles, calculation of such failures has greater complexity than most post and beam connections.

Stability failures: Beam-like stability failures such as rotation and buckling were previously discussed. However, since flat trusses are thinner and deeper than beams, they are particularly vulnerable to such instability failures. The reader should also not forget that a second type of stability failure is global configuration distortion due to inadequate *form stability*.

Excessive deflection: Since trusses are significantly longer than beams, normal rules-of-thumb concerning deflection become less applicable. Even if the relatively conservative building code rule of "member span divided by 360" is used, it may still lead to dangerous "ponding" and subsequent structural collapse. Take a moment to understand this failure scenario. If a truss has a 360-foot clear span, by the rule just stated, a pond of rain water at mid-span would be allowed to become 1-foot deep (because 360 feet of truss span divided by 360 is equal to 1 foot). Water weighs about 62 pounds per cubic foot. The weight of that "pond" causes additional deflection in the long truss, which causes the pond to become deeper, which lead to additional deflection, which leads to.structural collapse. This is the *ponding scenario* for long span structures, and it is a serious concern in trusses. One of the most famous truss failures occurred in 1979 at the Kemper Arena in Kansas City. Metal fatigue in hanger joints was cited as the cause of a dramatic 200 foot by 215 foot area of the roof collapsed following a heavy rain storm (Levy and Salvadori 1992).

Lateral load failures

Wind pressure

Trusses form such a large moment arm against the small joints that failure in joints is fairly common if lateral support is not well considered. Such lateral support usually includes bracing between trusses, bracing in the roof plane, and lateral bracing in the walls (Fig. 13-23). Lateral bracing of truss buildings is made even more difficult by the presence of large doors. For example, a large aircraft hanger is a very common truss building. Large doors in at least one side of the hanger will be necessary. Lateral bracing of that side will be very difficult indeed, because normal cross bracing using cables is not possible because they would obstruct passage of the airplanes through the door opening.

Roof loss

As previously discussed strong winds cause a truss roof to begin to behave like an airplane wing, and start to lift. When the wind then finds its way under the slightly lifted edge of a roof, rapid rotation of the roof, and sudden flight of the roof is both dramatic and inevitable. Roof loss can be avoided if it is sufficiently secured to the supporting columns below, then the columns are firmly attached to the foundation below. In disaster reconnaissance conducted following tornados, it is quite clear that current code requirements for these joints are quite inadequate, and can be profoundly improved with the use of "hurricane straps". A second problem often found is that the nuts and washers that attach columns or walls to foundations are simply not put in place and tightened. The ultimate

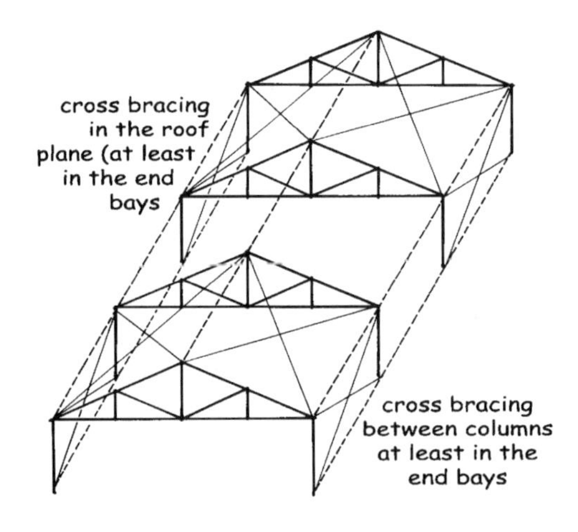

Figure 13-23

Bracing is needed between columns, trusses, and in the roof plane.

Figure 13-24
Roof lifted off in a tornado in the Midwest.

result of uplift failure is that portions of the roof, the total roof, or the total building will be found several hundred feet down wind (Fig. 13-24). Once the roof is lost, form stability of the remaining portion of the building is also lost.

Local and global failures

A local failure of a structure is the failure of one of the members or joints in a structural system. A *global failure* is a collapse of the total system. One serious concern in a truss system is that a local failure may "go global". Here is a typical scenario of this type. Point loads should be applied only at joints in the truss if possible. Such point loads might be purlins collecting and concentrating roof deck loads at panel points in the top chord of the truss (Fig. 13-25). It might also include suspension of point loads such as mechanical and electrical components from panel points in the bottom chord of a truss. Mistakes in the bottom (tension) chord may "stay local" causing only permanent deformation of a single steel member; however, such a mistake in the top chord will cause not only that single chord member to fail in bending, but the whole top chord to fail in buckling because it is in compression as well as bending. This will lead to a global collapse of the total system, or "go global".

Long span collapse and large occupancy

Many long span buildings have a very large number of occupants under the roof. A 30, 000 fan basketball arena might well have a truss type roof. If such a roof fails globally, the failure is potentially several thousand times more serious than that of a post and beam office occupied by only two or three people.

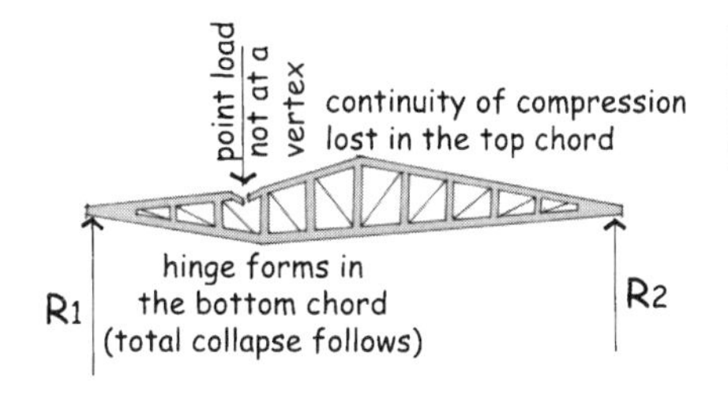

Figure 13-25
A local failure "going global".

Trusses and fire

Steel trusses and light wooden trusses are particularly vulnerable to structural weakening and collapse due to fire. Various building codes make differing provisions for fire. These are beyond the scope of this book, but the reader is well warned that fire is a serious issue in the use of small member trusses. They can weaken, to collapse in an amazingly short time, perhaps even before occupants have time to escape. Appropriate design may be more than just satisfying the minimum requirements of the building code.

OPTIMUM CONFIGURATION

Total system

Depth to span tables and rules of thumb are commonly used during early preliminary design to gain a crude estimate of the approximate depth of truss that will be required. It matters if the truss is made of steel or wood, and what configuration it is; however, a typical crude rule of thumb ratio for trusses is that the depth of the truss will be about a tenth of the span. So for a 100-foot clear span, the truss might become 10 feet deep. Yes, much can be done to reduce this depth, but it is going to be deep. Usually the designer begins with the applied loads, works down through the roof decking to the spacing of the purlins, and the location of the panel points. Beginning from below, we know that we would like to have point loads such as heating and cooling ducts, electrical conduits and lighting, plumbing and drainage pipes also be hung from panel points. The slope of the truss will be based on several factors, but snow and rain loads are certainly two of the most important criteria. Generally the designer will want the truss to be deepest where the tendency to bend is the greatest. This is at mid-span if the truss is simply supported at both ends. However, if floor trusses are to be used it is likely that both the top and bottom chords must be flat to produce a walking surface on top and a flat ceiling below. In these cases a parallel chord truss must be used instead of one with a pitch. An urge to use cables for web members in a truss must be tempered by a full investigation of stress reversals experienced during all of the possible load combinations (i.e. dead load + wind load + snow load, etc.)

Spacing for trusses varies with type, material, and span; however, the length of roof decking sets the maximum distance that can separate purlins. Similarly, the size of ceiling module to be used directly influences the spacing of the bottom chord. Today, many configuration choices are set by multiple runs of computer models using different variables. Although economy can be judged by such models, other significant criteria such as function, aesthetics, and safety cannot.

Members

Purlins can be sized as beams during preliminary design, because that is how they will behave. Beam tables and rules of thumb are often employed for this purpose. Adjustments will inevitably be required during final design. Purlins on a parallel chord truss are deeper than they are wide. If these purlins are mounted on a sloped truss, conceptually they should become more square.

Girts also behave as beams that are loaded in two axes. The weight to the building skin exerts vertical loads on the girt. Simultaneously, wind places lateral loads on the girt. Because of this double loading girts, like purlins, tend to be more square in section than rectangular beams experiencing only vertical loads.

Joints

Vertical load continuity: Trusses are long span systems. Each truss collects a very large roof load along its considerable length, and focuses that large load across a profoundly small bearing area at each end of the truss. It is structurally logical to continue to carry these large point loads down vertical straight lines such as columns. It is difficult, and not structurally logical, to attempt to diffuse this load widely across a bearing wall if it can be avoided. Remember that in general, failures of members are often less damaging than failures of joints.

Lateral load resistance: While continuity of vertical load propagation is assured by resting a truss directly on a column, lateral wracking of the total building may still destroy that joint. When a tall column joins a long span truss, long moment arms are formed. When the building is loaded laterally, these long moment arms work against the very small joint between them much like a claw hammer is used to pull a nail. This load concentration is sometimes avoided by bearing a horizontal truss on vertical trusses at both ends (Fig. 13-26). This is a

Figure 13-26

Horizontal trusses resting on vertical trusses instead of a single long slender column.

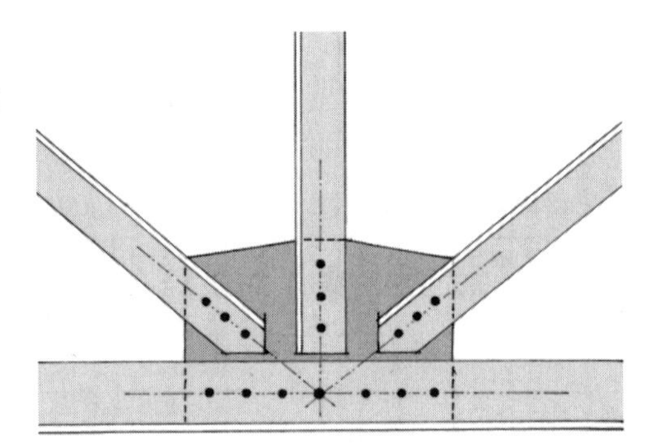

Figure 13-27
Members that are joined at a truss connection should converge on a single point.

logical solution; however, lateral stability must still be established perpendicular to long axis of the truss. Also remember that failure of a single column often causes more damage than the failure of a single truss.

Connector space: As previously discussed it is best to give truss joints as much connector space as possible. The minimum number of bolts, nails, or welds at each joint will have to be calculated, but it is essential during preliminary design to give the joint the maximum amount of space possible. *Gusset plates* allow sufficient end distance, edge distance, and bolt to bolt distance. If these distances become too small, there is a considerable tendency for the metal to tear, and the joint to fail. Such space will also be important during actual building erection in order to have enough construction space to work wrenches, hammers, and welders. Good truss design has the centerline of each member to be joined at a single joint to converge at a single *point of concurrence* (Fig. 13-27).

Soil and foundations

The large loads collected and focused by trusses will require considerable support from the soil. Soils of sufficient strength will probably not be found at the ground surface. This means that a deep point type foundation such as drilled pier will usually be appropriate for long trusses. This foundation can reach down to stronger soils or bed rock.

Related lateral support system

Other lateral support systems may certainly be used, but cross bracing using cables is by far the most common choice. This bracing is required at least in the end bays of the walls, and the end bays in the roof plane. Some type of lateral sway bracing is also critical between trusses (Fig. 13-28). This bracing prevents rotation of the trusses out of the vertical plane.

Related envelope

The distance between trusses is usually considerably greater than those used in post and beam structures. This implies larger weather enclosure panels than

Figure 13-28
Bracing between trusses in the Viking Ship Olympic stadium in Hamar Norway by Nils Torp.

post and beam. Prefabricated "sandwich" panels are common in warehouse and industrial applications. This type of panel captures some type of rigid expanded foam insulation inside of a sheet metal "sandwich". Considerable expansion and contraction due to temperature must be considered in joints and connections in not only the truss structure, but also the envelope that encloses them. Generally use of large envelope panels means fewer panel connections. Fewer connections will require less labor, and less labor implies less cost. Unfortunately, fewer seams and joints provide fewer opportunities to absorb expansion and contraction within the joints. As a benefit, large panels also provide fewer opportunities for water and wind leaks through the building skin.

FUNCTIONAL FOOTPRINT

Most commonly, truss systems generate large rectangles. It is also true that trusses can, and are, occasionally arranged radially. This yields a round functional footprint.

PATTERN OF GROWTH

Growth in length in a truss system takes place by bay similar to post and beam systems. The critical dimension in this growth is the "center-to-center" distance between trusses. Growth in width often takes place by attaching a second building or room by connecting at a shared edge or face of the existing parent truss building. This method allows more freedom in dimensions and shapes in the new building than growth alternatives that directly load the earlier building with an unexpected new additional load. For this reason growth up and down is usually not done. It is possible to place a second truss system above an older truss system by offsetting a new row of columns with the same or different spacing. Growth may be better served by attaching a completely different system outside the original supporting columns, or walls. This would happen if a small maintenance room were to be added to an existing trussed airplane hanger.

DESIGN METHODS

As with post and beam structures, preliminary design usually makes use of span tables found in the building code, or rules-of-thumb. Ultimately standard truss calculations must be completed for final design. If standard truss configurations are used, most of these final calculations will be easily completed by standard computer software that has become widely available. Spacing and integration of the truss structure with mechanical and electrical systems can be much easier than post and beam, since even fairly large heating ducts can pass between the web members of a truss. As with post and beam, such coordination of systems and the building envelope often leads many designers to begin their design on graph paper with a selected grid size. Again, be aware that this approach normally leads to design of great unity and as noted in post and beam design, they can sometimes be criticized aesthetically as being "son of graph paper". In unusual truss designs physical scale models are built using balsa wood, small metal tubes, and very small metal plates (Fig. 13-29).

AESTHETIC POTENTIAL

It is common to expose unadorned trusses. This reduces costs and allows the structure to provide direct and honest visual expression. When exposed and adequately lighted, timber trusses are particularly appealing. It can be difficult to adequately light roof trusses, and special design attention will be required. Surprisingly, the beauty attributed to the timber may also be the beauty of the steel, of the bolts, and plates used in the connections. Placing circulation paths for building occupants near these truss joints can make the most of the visual interest inherent in these connections. Often the balcony of a large church can get occupants much closer to both the wood and the steel bolt plates.

Given the large size of trusses as a structural member, a visual expression of power may be appropriate. A 12-foot deep truss with a span of 120 feet is unarguably powerful in its raw size. Power may be the only choice if pedestrian circulation passes close to such a truss.

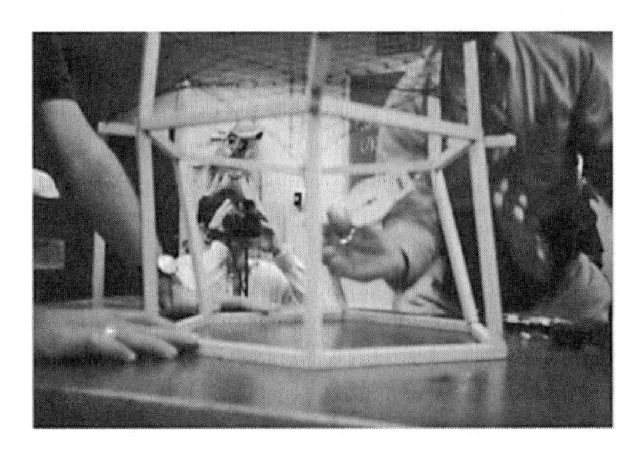

Figure 13-29
Even informal tests of structural models can yield useful insights.

Human scale is normally possible with timber trusses, but large steel trusses require machine construction, use amazingly strong steel material, and often house very large functions. This means that human scale will normally be lost. Human scale is the ability of a human being to measure or understand the size of a building using his or her body as the unit of measure.

Like post and beam superstructures, rhythm is an inherent visual potential of trusses. However, the truss spacing may be so great that such rhythm may have more vehicle appeal than pedestrian appeal. More explicitly, when passing in an automobile, the viewer may be more aware of the rhythm of the structure than when slowly passing on foot.

In an art work, vertical lines are often used to form a "focal point" (point of greatest visual attention). Horizontal lines are used for "continuity", to tie parts of a visual expression together. Diagonal lines are said to be lines of "drama". The diagonal web members in a truss, therefore, offer an easy opportunity to generate higher excitement (or drama) in the viewer. The closer the viewer is to these diagonals, the greater the drama.

Since roof trusses usually support opaque roof decks, the play of light and shade is not as great as in shell buildings, but in buildings such as trussed green houses, a type of "spider web" appeal may be possible given the trusses backlighting by the sky outside of the glass roof.

CONSTRUCTION

Trusses are fabricated from repetitive components. This makes manufacture easy and cost effective. In all but the smallest trusses, some degree of factory fabrication is typical. Transportation from the factory to the building site limits the degree to which the truss may be factory assembled. Light wood trusses are usually smaller than 60 feet in length and can normally be fully assembled, strapped together in bundles, and delivered to the site by flat bed trucks (Fig. 13-30). Very long span steel trusses may be delivered in approximately 60 foot sections, then fully assembled at the site.

Trusses, columns, and cable cross-bracing are typically large, light, and few in number. This means remarkably rapid assembly at the building site. Time is a key issue in the use of heavy equipment. Labor time is also reduced due to this rapid erection process. Remarkably few workers can erect an astoundingly large truss building in very short order. Since labor is often more expensive than materials in industrially developed nations, this also offers profound cost savings.

An adequate space for final assembly and storage of trusses at the site must usually be considered. A single crane can often lift small trusses. To control the movement of the truss during the lift, "tag lines" are usually attached. Larger trusses will require two large cranes for both lift, and maneuver control. Adequate

Figure 13-30
Bundle of light weight wood trusses bound together for transport to the building site.

Figure 13-31
Two cranes working together to place long steel trusses.

room on the site for placement and operation of these large cranes must be preplanned (Fig. 13-31).

The need for temporary lateral support can be an essential consideration during the final erection of a truss system. Once the members of the frame are all in place, and its lateral support is completed, the system will be quite rigid. However, when only partially complete, the system is quite vulnerable to lateral loads such as wind. Small light wood trusses are sometimes overlapped horizontally resting on top plate, then rotated into vertical position one at a time, and braced.

Vocabulary		
Joist	Purlin	Girt
Panels	Panel point	Ridge
Web member	Posts	Strut
Base plate	Gusset plate	Point of concurrence
Sway bracing	End post	Intermediate post
Top chord	Bottom chord	Top Lateral strut
Bottom lateral	Sandwich panel	Center-to-center spacing

REVIEW QUESTIONS

1. When is a truss system a good choice of superstructure?
2. What is a "normal" span for a truss in timber and steel?

3. Why is a truss said to be “a very good beam”?
4. Graphically produce the configuration of several of the most common alternative truss superstructures.
5. Name and locate the elements of a truss superstructure.
6. List and describe the most common modes of failure for truss structures.
7. Briefly discuss the differences in the pattern of stresses that are usually found in trusses.
8. Briefly discuss the construction advantages and limitations for trusses.
9. How does the aesthetic potential of a post and beam, cable system, or arches differ from that of a truss?
10. What is the single greatest functional advantage of a truss structure over a cable system?

Figure 14-1
Pavilion at the Vancouver Expo in 1986.

14 Space Frames

GENERAL DESCRIPTION

A space frame is the three-dimensional equivalent of a two-dimensional truss. Like the truss, the space frame gains its rigidity and resistance to load by its triangulated configuration. In its most simple form the space frame forms a *tetrahedron* (Fig. 14-2). However, the basic module for the most widely used space frames are the *square-based pyramid* (Fig. 14-3). Typically the tetrahedral or square pyramid modules are assembled in an interlocking manner to form a usable structural plane. A number of other basic modules may also be used, and many will be discussed later in this chapter. The space frame is a very light and efficient long span structural system, with small repetitive members and joints that can be easily fabricated in an industrial setting. These members are then easily assembled on the building site. While the space frame globally provides bending resistance to external loads in a manner similar to a slab, the individual (local) members of a space frame are in simple tension or simple compression like a truss. Bending and shear that occur globally in slabs are converted into simple tension and compression in individual members of a space frame so long as external loads are applied only at joints.

HISTORY AND SIGNIFICANT EXAMPLES

Based on a fully developed understanding of two-dimensional trusses, space frames began to evolve in the late 1880s as an intellectual possibility. Alexander Graham Bell applied three-dimensionally triangulated forms to research toward development of aircraft frames. But it was not until the early 1940s that the practical joinery necessary for wide building industry use was finally accomplished with the patenting of the Unistrut and Mero systems. Examples of these systems are illustrated later in this chapter (Robinson 2001).

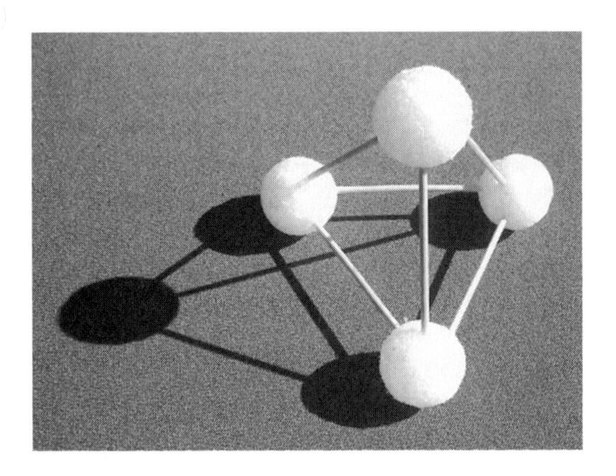

Figure 14-2
Model of a tetrahedron.

The Atomium in the Brussels Expo in 1958, the Currigan Convention Center in Denver Colorado, the Vertical Assembly Building at the Kennedy Space Center in Florida, and the Omniplex in Atlanta Georgia (Fig. 14-4) are all well-known examples of space frame buildings. Typical non-building examples of space frames are electric power transmission towers, microwave towers (Fig. 14-5), and modern construction cranes. Some feel that woven reed baskets are an early mundane example predicting space grid structures.

TYPES OR CATEGORIES

By material

Because of light weight and great strength, space frames are predominantly made from steel or aluminum; however, wood and even reinforced concrete have been used. Wood is sometimes considered for fairly small span projects,

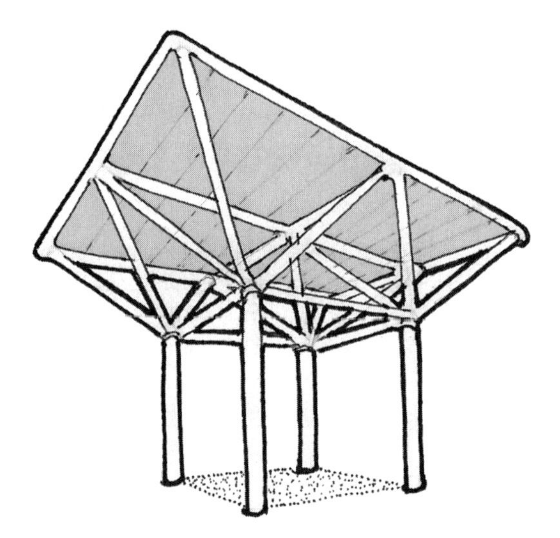

Figure 14-3
Square base pyramid type space frame.

Figure 14-4
Omniplex in Atlanta Georgia.

and reinforced concrete might be considered in larger span projects where fire is a serious concern. Steel and aluminum are vulnerable to rapid loss of strength due to fire, and the unusually small members typically used in a space frame accentuate this vulnerability; however, the inherent load dispersing capacity of the space frame is thought to substantially mitigate the material vulnerability of steel or aluminum. If a horizontal space frame roof structure is sufficiently high above the floor, vertically flared heat diverters are occasionally used on the supporting columns. The idea is that these flared shields will more widely diffuse heat rising from any fire away from the critical space frame area immediately above the column where vertical loads are concentrated.

Figure 14-5
Global failure of a microwave tower in the wake of a tornado in Tulsa Oklahoma.

Figure 14-6
Typical space truss at a shopping center in Oslo Norway.

By configuration

Many sources recognize that a wide range of frames are triangulated in three dimensions. All such configurations technically belong to this family of superstructures. The best known member of the family is the *space truss* (Fig 14-6). Space trusses can be warped to *trussed arches* (Fig 14-7), *trussed vaults* (i.e., Law Faculty by Norman Foster, Cambridge, England), and geodesic domes (Fig. 17.10 in Chapter 17).

Tensegrities: Any triangulated structural form that can transfer loads three dimensionally belongs to this family. Even the most abstract, inventive, and free-form *tensegrities* belong to this family. A tensegrity structure relies on the continuous juxtaposition of push and pull to maintain its geometric configuration, and to support loads (Fig. 14-8 and 14-9). Such configurations have considerable

Figure 14-7
Arched space frame at the Biaritz train station shelter in France.

visual interest and have attracted sculptors like Kenneth Snelson to consider their use. Structurally, tensegrity has been used in very long span domes such as the Georgia Dome in Atlanta.

Figure 14-8
Tensegrity sculpture in London.

Geodesic domes: Initially explored by Buckminster Fuller, geodesic domes might be seen as a member of the space frame family. In general practice they are more often placed in the dome family, just as those space frames that are warped into vaults are usually placed in the vault family. Within those families they will be given names like trussed arch or triangulated vault. Because of this poplar market place use, triangulated vaults, trussed arches, and geodesic domes have been placed in other chapters in this book even though they might also have been considered here.

Space truss: In classifying the most widely used form of space frame, the space truss, it is the geometry of the top and bottom mat (chord, or layer) that first differentiates them. Then it is the specific type of joinery that most dramatically classifies them.

1. Many polygons may be used or combined to form the *top and bottom layer* of a space frame (Fig. 14-10). Only the most widely used top and bottom mat configurations that are commercially available have been presented here. Triangular, square pyramid, and hexagonal top and bottom mats are widely sold, and fairly inexpensive to transport.
2. *Joint mechanism:* Several patented systems of joinery have been developed. The Unistrut (Fig. 14-11) and the Mero (Fig. 14-12) systems are probably the most widely used. Therefore they are presented at this time.

By position

Space frames are most widely used as roof systems. The vast majority of these are space trusses that are flat and horizontal. However, space trusses can be sloped for removal of rain water (Fig. 14-13). It is possible to use space trusses as a structural floor or wall system as well. One well-published example of a space truss placed in vertical position is found in Parc de le Villette, Paris, France (Fig. 14-14). They can even be distorted into extraordinary forms (Fig. 14-15). Use of a space truss for a floor system allows more space in office buildings for the abundance of wiring needed to support computers and other equipment. Very heavy point loads are not normally placed on such a floor.

NOMENCLATURE

Space truss

Take a moment now to look at the nomenclature of a space truss. Each interlocked pyramid module in a space frame has a *base* usually a triangle or a rectangle, and a point at the top referred to as the *apex*. Each module is sometimes known as a *section*. When assembled into a flat space truss configuration

Figure 14-9

The Mountjuic tower in Barcelona by Santiago Calatrava shows some characteristics of a tensegrity.

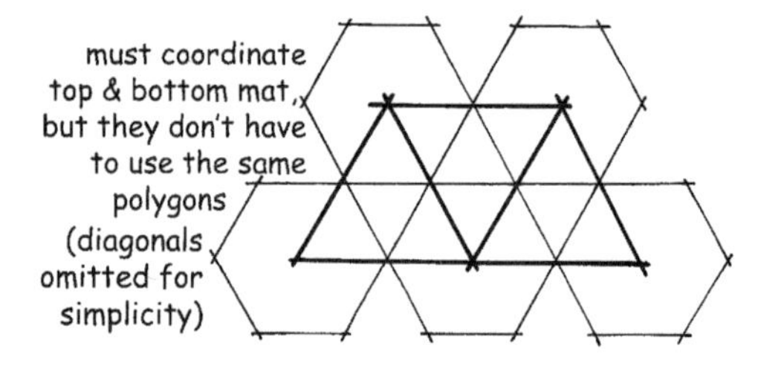

must coordinate
top & bottom mat,
but they don't have
to use the same
polygons
(diagonals
omitted for
simplicity)

Figure 14-10

The top and bottom mats of space trusses are a series of adjacent polygons.

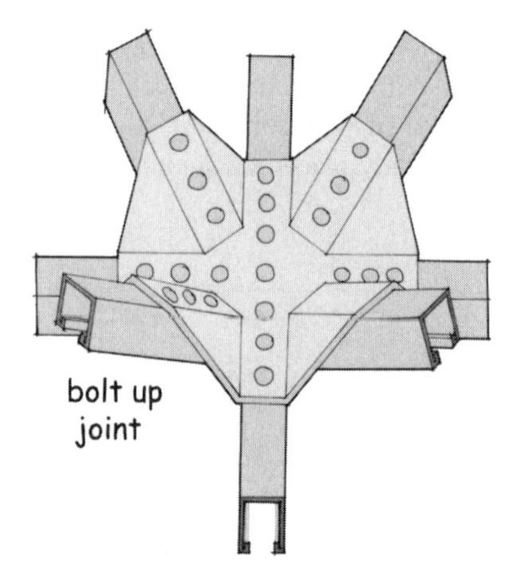

Figure 14-11

The Unistrut system.

Figure 14-12
The Mero system.

Figure 14-13
Inclined space truss adjacent to the Thames river in London.

Figure 14-14
A vertical space frame in Paris by Adrian Fainsilber.

the top surface or mat is usually called the *top chord* and the lower surface is known as the bottom chord. *Diagonals* are used to connect the top and bottom mats or chords. If a diagonal is in compression it is a *strut*.

Tensegrity structures

A *tensegrity* structure is an assemblage of cable *tensors* and rigid *struts* in a widely imaginative range of structural forms. External loading to a single member of a tensegrity will cause these structures to expand and contract as a total system rather than to yield as a single member.

Figure 14-15
One of Bernard Tschumi's folleys at the Parc de la Villette in Paris.

COMMON APPLICATIONS

Architectural applications

Space frames of all types have very long span capability. Therefore space trusses are widely used; as a roof for exhibition halls, athletic areas, aircraft maintenance facilities, field houses, large single story schools, large warehouses, and major airports such as Stanstead Airport in London (Fig. 14-16). When very large sheets of glass have to be hung, some form of space frame has been used in several significant contemporary buildings (i.e., Tower Bridge House, London, England) (Fig. 14-17).

Non-architectural applications

Because space frames are light and can be constructed from multiple small members in remote sites, they are used for power transmission towers. Because they offer small wind resistance and have little dead weight they are also used for radio and television broadcast towers. In this use these slender towers are sometimes externally guyed against lateral wind loads. Because of their great strength in multiple axes and light weight, space frames are used both for the tower and booms of large construction cranes (Fig. 14-18).

Figure 14-16
Stanstead airport outside London by Sir Norman Foster and Associates.

Figure 14-17
An elaborate space frame used to support a wide expanse of glass.

Figure 14-18
Most construction cranes are space frame structures.

BEHAVIOR UNDER LOAD

General comments

The space frame invites even widely dispersed loads, and is vulnerable to large concentrated loads. Because of the redundancy and load-dispersing capacity inherent in the lattice of a space frame, failure in one of the small individual members is considered to be less likely to lead to global failure of the total space frame system than in planar trusses. In exhibition halls and sports arenas only the absolute minimum of columns are normally used to carry the space frame. If one of these columns fails, a global collapse of the roof will likely follow. Such a failure would threaten the large number of spectators that typically occupy such buildings.

Truss-like behavior

Like trusses, triangulation allows the members of the space frame to ideally experience only simple tension and compress. The only difference is that in a truss all of the forces act in a single two-dimensional plan, while the forces in a space frame take place in three-dimensional space. Like the truss compressive members can be vulnerable to buckling. Connection plates used in a space frame are more elaborate in shape than the gusset plates of a truss, but they are still vulnerable to many of the same modes of failure. Specifically that includes bolt shear, bolt bearing, edge tear, end tear, and bolt-to-bolt tear. All of these were discussed in earlier chapters. However, due to the more elaborate three-dimensional configuration of the connection plates, they may also distort and buckle in three dimensions under some circumstances. Space frame joints are inherently complex. This complexity is the inescapable result of the necessity of joining many members at a shared point. Eight or more diagonals, top mat members, and bottom mat members must meet at a typical shared connection. Eccentricity and buckling are encouraged if member loads are not focused on a single point.

Slab-like behavior

Now notice the similarity of a flat space truss and a two-way slab. Deflections of the flat space frame system are similar to those discussed in slabs in an earlier chapter. Therefore, forces in the top and bottom plane of the space frame are similar to those in a deflecting slab. Stresses build up at column supports similar to the punching shear found in slabs. Overhanging the end portions of a space frame can reduce deflections between vertical supports (Fig. 14-19). The reader will recall that deflections in a flat slab generate rotation at the edge of the slab. A similar tendency in space trusses requires additional attention to adequate cross bracing at their edge. Finally, take a moment to understand specifically how loads are three-dimensionally distributed across the members of a space truss. In many ways a space truss is just a two-way truss system, but it is more. In a two-way truss system, their separate action may be independent of each other in resisting vertical loads. In fact, if the span of two perpendicular trusses is significantly different, then their depth will also be different (Fig. 14-20). But the internal members of a space truss are so constructed that loads are readily shared between the two perpendicular "trusses".

Recall the illustration in Chapter 12 of a flat slab as a series of parallel planks, and that as a point load is placed on one of the planks, that plank deflects more than those adjacent to it. This illustrated that shearing force is present in a flat slab. Similar shearing loads in a space truss are transmitted to both perpendicular "trusses" in a space frame (Fig. 12.12). Recall also that if a flat slab were made of a series of parallel beams (or in this case a space truss were a series of parallel planar trusses) that those planar trusses would be forced to rotate as deflection takes place in the space truss. If a second perpendicular truss is correctly configured, it will resist the rotation of the first truss. This resistance would cause some of the load in the first truss to be transmitted to the second perpendicular planar truss (Schodek 1980) (Fig. 14-21).

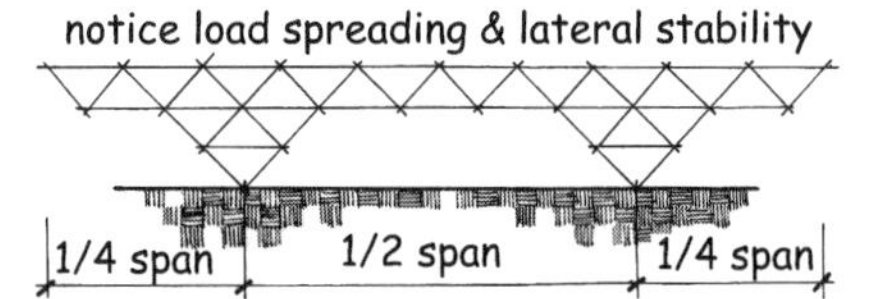

Figure 14-19
An overhung space frame.

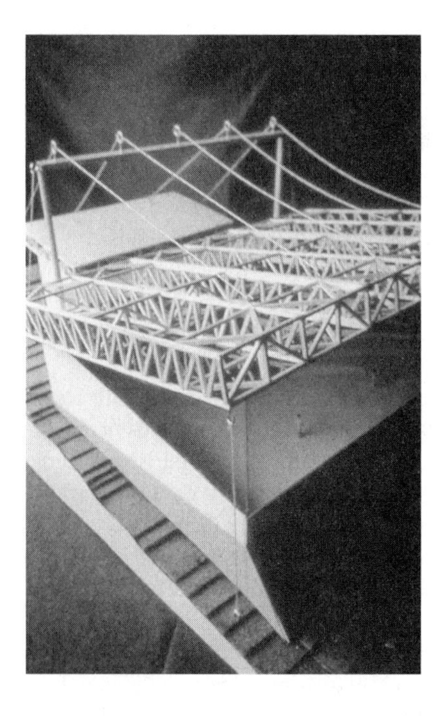

Figure 14-20
This student design shows that all two-way trusses do not produce space frame action.

Figure 14-21
Look closely to see how "shearing" loads can be transmitted from one axis to the other.

Path of load propagation

As with the flat slab, loads are collected by the space truss, concentrated above vertical support columns, and are then carried downward through those columns ultimately to the ground (Fig. 12.15). Like the slab, the equivalent of punching shear is also a threat in a space truss. In a space truss this can be partially prevented by carrying loads only at joints, just as in a truss. However, even if large loads are focused on a joint, it may exceed the capacity of the adjacent small members connected to that joint. If those members fail, usually in local buckling, a global failure of the space truss is threatened since very few columns are normally employed to support a space frame. To avoid this, vertical support for a space truss will be configured to distribute the loads widely across many joints (Fig. 14-22).

Member stresses under vertical loads

Like a beam or a planar flat truss, the top chord of a space truss will be in compression if it is simply supported at the corners. The bottom chord or layer will be in tension. Diagonal members that transfer the loads between the upper and lower mats will be placed in simple tension or compression similar to diagonals found in a planar truss. Ordinarily the relatively slender diagonal struts in a space truss will fail in compression before other diagonals can fail in tension. This is because of the slender strut's inherent vulnerability to buckling. The reader will remember having read in the chapter on columns that a pipe shaped section is the most resistant to buckling under compressive load. That is why

Figure 14-22
This elevator tower in Hamburg spreads vertical loads across many joints in this space frame.

space trusses make use of pipe sections, or a close equivalent, as their standard member. Recognizing that it is better to have the most heavily loaded diagonals in tension than compression, one can now see why the point load of a column is often carried up to a joint in the top mat, rather than resting in a similar joint in the bottom mat.

Stresses in space truss supports

Bearing stress is a very significant issue in space trusses since long spans collect large loads, and then apply these large concentrated loads across very small areas at the supports of the space truss. For this reason, and for reasons of redundancy, it is often better to rest space trusses on long walls rather than on isolated columns. Because of significant load concentrations even walls may require a bond beam similar to those found in use under open web joists or steel trusses.

Because of the great loads associated with long span systems, any columns that are used for support must be resistant to Euler buckling. Long span space trusses often rest on very tall columns. Functionally it would be very unusual to have a 200 foot × 200 foot steel space truss that required only a 10 foot column. In exhibition halls and airplane hangers such columns would be 30 to 60 feet in length. This additional length and any eccentricity of loading would make the tendency to buckle even more serious.

Under lateral loads

The space truss itself is quite resistant to lateral loads. It is lighter than many roof frames, and is therefore more earthquake resistant than a heavier system. Its inherent shape stability and rigidness also make it quite resistant to wind. The lightness of the space truss does make it a bit vulnerable to wind uplift, however. The real lateral load problems occur in the vertical support system under the space truss. It is quite possible to support a 200 foot × 200 foot steel space truss on only four supports. However, the distance between these supports will be so great that cross bracing with steel cables between these four supports is quite unlikely. Instead, each support must be made independently stable against lateral loads. Additional bending stresses are likely to be transmitted to the horizontal space truss above as part of this stabilization. Continuation of the space truss construction downward to form its own vertical support can provide significant resistance to lateral loads and spread vertical loads across many joints (Fig. 14-19).

The problem at the foundation

The great loads due to long spans space trusses, thus focused into very few vertical supports will produce extraordinarily large point loads on the foundations and the bearing soil. Weakness in the soil may increase the number of columns to be used even if the internal function of the building does not welcome them. Such soil problems may be further compounded if lateral loads cause load eccentricity and potential rotation at the base of each column.

In small footprint building, it is more likely that each column will rest on similar soil conditions, but in long span buildings there is a greater chance that diverse soil conditions may be encountered. Certainly such differences may be technically resolved, but should not be conceptually ignored during early preliminary design.

The problem of expansion

As noted in an earlier chapter, building materials shrink and expand with temperature changes. Recall that each building material has a coefficient of expansion that reflects relative rate of this expansion compared to other building materials. However, no matter what the building material and its coefficient, long spans of this material expand a lot more than short spans of the same material. Space trusses are a very long span system, and will have very significant expansion. Expansion joints and other adaptations will be a significant practical consideration in any space truss system. When considerable difference between interior and exterior temperatures exists, thermal expansion is a particularly complex issue.

FAILURES

Excessive deflections

Recall the roof ponding scenario outlined in the chapter addressing trusses. Excessive deflection, particularly when experiencing unpredicted snow loads or roof ponding, has also led to space frame collapses.

Stability failures

Failures due to lateral loading was briefly discussed above citing the more limited range of lateral support alternative that are available to the designer when making use of a space frame. Also previously emphasized was the sobering threat posed by the lack of numerous redundant columns inherent in most space frame applications (i.e., a basketball arena).

Member buckling

Since most of the top mat or layer and about half of the diagonals that separate the top and bottom mats are in compression, buckling failure is a serious threat to these relatively slender members. Lateral buckling in the direction of the weak axis was explained in the chapter on columns. That is why the circular pipe section is often used, since it has no "weak" axis. However, two other types of unusual buckling failure should now be mentioned. *Torsional*

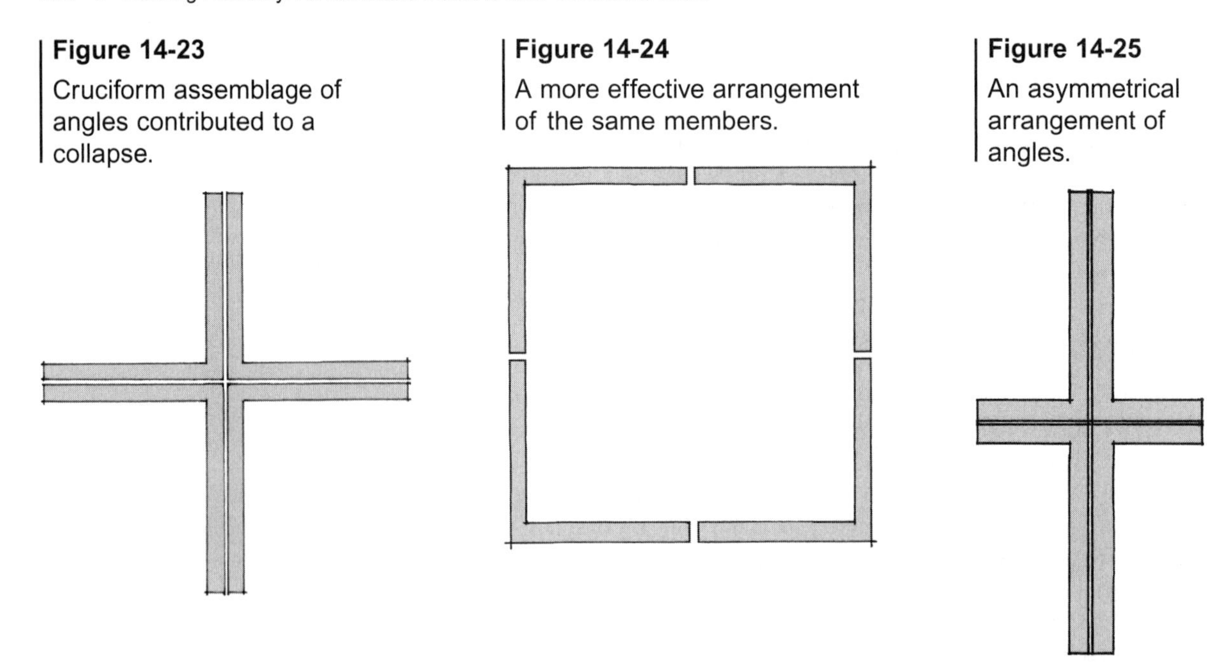

Figure 14-23
Cruciform assemblage of angles contributed to a collapse.

Figure 14-24
A more effective arrangement of the same members.

Figure 14-25
An asymmetrical arrangement of angles.

buckling is possible if an inherently weaker cross section is used in fabrication of space frame members. Metal angles were aggregated into cruciform pattern (Fig. 14-23) in the Hartford Civic Center Arena, which collapsed in 1978. This arrangement is inherently more vulnerable to torsional buckling than the same members arranged into a tube (Fig. 14-24). If the Hartford arrangement had been asymmetrical in its two axes (Fig. 14-25), it might have experienced a third type of member buckling known as *flexural-torsional buckling*. This type of buckling combines the effects of both lateral and torsional buckling (Martin 1999).

Wind failures

Wind uplift failures are possible with space trusses because they are so light. Such uplift failures are an increased concern when substantial external overhangs of the space truss are part of the building's preliminary design. This does not imply that dramatic overhangs should not be used. They are a wonderful potential of this type of structure with significant functional, climatic, and visual benefits. Just exercise respect for the wind implications and engineer them accordingly.

Local and global failures

A local failure in a single slender member of a space frame is very easy to produce if point loads are applied to that member anywhere other than at its joints. This said, this local failure is a bit less likely to "go global" than a similar failure in a truss. This is because the space truss has greater redundancy. This is less true for failed members that are near major support columns.

Failure during a fire

Fire egress of the large number of people that habitually occupy space under one of these large structures will need lots of exits close at hand, and as much warning and escape time as possible. Yes, these areas can be given fire sprinklers and heat deflectors, but space frames are rarely fire insulated like many other structures. They are usually exposed. This issue is not to be taken lightly.

OPTIMUM CONFIGURATION

Total system

The ideal global shape of a space truss is dictated by the local shape of its single module. Tetrahedron modules try to grow into triangular or hexagonal global forms, while square pyramid modules want to grow into square forms; however, your pragmatic design freedom is much greater. A space truss is not restricted to a single plane. It doesn't have to have long straight edges. It doesn't even have to remain horizontal. In fact, it is a shame not to exploit this considerable design freedom. It is wise to conceptually try to be sure that all vertical supports have an equal tributary area, but even this can be avoided as long as larger and smaller supports are used to address variations in tributary area. For structural logic to be served, a column that is carrying four times the tributary area of another column will need to be four times as big.

The depth to span ratio for space frames is about half that for trusses. That is because a space frame may be conceptually considered a special type of a two-way truss. Recall that depth of a steel truss is about 1/10 of its span. So the depth of a steel space frame is about 1/20 of the span. The practical span range for space frames ranges from about 30 feet to about 120 feet. Some of the variation of its span potential is rooted in the type of support that the space truss is given. Wall support may give you a longer potential span than columns.

Members

For manufacturing economy it is best to design in such a way that standard "off the shelf" commercial members may be used. If you have an unusually large building, you may be able to have "custom" joints and members manufactured. Given a bit of thought, this is normally not necessary.

Supports

In general three types of supports are used to carry space frames. For small spans simple columns are usually used. Note that these columns may bear on a joint in the lower chord, but there are some structural advantages to bearing on a joint in the upper chord.

Joints

Like trusses, good space frame design has the centerline of each member to be connected at a single joint, converge at a single "point of concurrence". Though inherently complex forces are joined in space frames, these individual details can be elegant in their simplicity if carefully considered. The glass pyramid covering the addition to the Louvre in Paris by I. M. Pei is supported by a space frame structure. This clean solution is particularly important since viewers pass within a few feet of the joints (Fig. 14-26).

Envelope

If the space frame itself is to receive a weatherproof envelope, it is a bit more difficult than say post and beam buildings. It usually involves panels that are triangular and sloped. Assuring against wind-driven water penetration between the panel edges requires care both in design and execution. Although it flies in the face of structural logic, a rectangular vertical facade is sometimes attached to the outside of the space frame to ease the envelope challenge, and to carry commercial advertisement for its occupant. The walls and windows used under a space truss roof may be very conventional indeed. Remember that it is possible for a space truss roof to be several hundred feet long in any direction. Some type of expansion and contraction of joints will probably be needed in the roof membrane to accommodate thermal expansion and contraction. Such joints can interrupt or impede the flow of rain water from the roof. Since a space truss roof is often essentially flat, shedding rain water from the areas between these joints may require design attention.

Figure 14-26
Louvre Museum addition space frame detail.

Functional footprint

Most designers think immediately of square or equilateral triangle footprints for this structure. They are the conceptual ideal. Both footprints are normally very large because the span capability of a space frame is even longer than for trusses. But as noted above, space frames inherently provide considerable design freedom that extends well beyond these limits.

Pattern of growth

It is easier for a space frame to grow than almost any other system. A few modules can be often added or subtracted once the math is verified. More importantly large new sections of space truss may be attached in the same plane directly to an existing one. All that is required is that the new space frame has a shared edge, shared module, and does not place weight on the older system. This is easily done by providing the addition with its own independent vertical supports.

DESIGN METHODS

As with post and beam structures, preliminary design usually makes use of span tables found in the building code, or rules of thumb. Ultimately standard space frame calculations must be completed for final design. In the recent past the massive number of members used in a space truss required an extortionate expenditure of engineering calculation time. It also implied the use of very simple shapes. Now with computers, necessary calculations can be accomplished with great speed. This has also led to greatly increased sculptural freedom available to designers (Fig. 14-27). If standard commercially available configurations are used, most of these final calculations will be easily completed using standard computer software that has become widely available. Integration of the space frame structure with mechanical and electrical systems is one of the easiest in architecture, since even fairly large heating ducts can pass between the diagonals connecting the upper and lower mats. Coordination of the space frame, mechanical and electrical systems, and the building envelope often lead

Figure 14-27
Student designed and erected space frame completed under Brad Black.

many designers to begin their design on graph paper with a selected grid size. Be careful not to let this interesting building type become a dull "son of graph paper" exercise. Computer models are more easily generated for space frames with regular modules than for other types of superstructures such as shells.

AESTHETIC POTENTIAL

Space frames are so light that they can be made to seem to float in the air. In some cases this is accomplished by suspending the space truss by cables from above. It is common to directly expose the space truss if possible. When this is done, mechanical and electrical systems will inevitably also be exposed. The complex lattice of the space frame makes "interest" the number one visual appeal of this system. Yes, these frames have great underlying order because of their modular composition. But this strong underlying order tolerates a limited number of variations very well. These variations are usually changes of plane, variation of edges, and omission of a few modules in order to let in natural light. Large skylights can also be "grown" in the same way that space frames may "grow" their own vertical supports (Fig. 14-28).

CONSTRUCTION

Repetitive manufacture

Space trusses are fabricated from small, light, repetitive components. This makes manufacture easy and cost effective. In all but the smallest space frame,

Figure 14-28
Upward and downward growth of a space frame at a shopping area in Kuala Lumpur Malaysia.

factory fabrication is the rule. Transportation from the factory to the building site is one of the easiest and least expensive available.

Speed of erection

Almost all of the joints are simple and repetitive. Extensive labor training and experience is not essential. This means remarkably rapid assembly at the building site. Heavy lift equipment may or may not be required. If it is required, that portion of the erection time is very short. Labor time is also reduced due to this rapid erection process. Since labor is often more expensive than materials in most industrially developed nations, this also offers profound cost savings.

While a space frame behaves in some ways like a slab, its construction process is radically different. Most significantly, the space frame does not require formwork with all of it jacks, form setting, and form stripping. Space frames are simply bolted up.

Need for space and heavy equipment

While space frames may be erected piece by piece in the air, it is more common for the pieces to be assembled on the ground and then lifted into final position. If lifted as a single unit, multiple cranes may be required to coordinate. If only smaller sections are lifted, a single crane may be able to do the job. Either way the designer should consider the crane's size, weight, and lifting capacity. Each crane will have to stand somewhere and have an adequate reach to place the sections without letting their boom drop down too low, or get tangled with nearby power lines. If multiple cranes must be used, direct visual contact between cranes is desirable even though radios will be used for lift coordination.

Manpower requirements small

Remarkably few workers can erect an astoundingly large spaces frame building in a very short order. This greatly eases supervision requirements.

Related soil and foundation

The large loads collected and focused by trusses will require considerable support from the soil. Soils of sufficient strength will probably not be found at the ground surface. This means that a deep point type foundation such as drilled pier will usually be appropriate. This foundation will reach down to stronger soils or bed rock. If the project is small or if part of the space frame rests on a wall then a different type of foundation will be required. Be alert to soil variations. In these large span buildings the loads on each foundation might well be the same, but the soil bearing capacity may not be the same under each foundation.

Related envelope

Large space frame buildings often call for large glazed areas (windows). These windows may be quite conventional, may have significant structural members to support them, or may be suspended from the frame above. Whatever the configuration of the glass, conceptually consider the procedure by which this large fragile piece of material will be moved into place. A large piece of glass under a wide overhang might be a real challenge to normal crane assist in placement.

Sequence of construction

Maintenance of balance and stability during all stages of erection may require some planning. This is particularly true in the early stages of erection by individual pieces in the air. Wind and lateral stability may be a particular problem when cranes are coordinated to lift a total space frame roof as a single unit.

Details

Sufficient working space is seldom a problem in space frame structures. Placement of mechanical and electrical systems can be accomplished by scrambling around (sometimes in awkward positions) in smaller frames; in medium-sized frames scaffolding is useful, while in very large systems temporary floors may also be placed on the lower chord to ease this work.

Vocabulary		
Tetrahedron	Square pyramid	Module
Upper chord	Lower chord	Diagonals
Struts	Unistrut joint	Mero joint
Glazing	Trusses arch	Triangulated vault
Tensegrity	Tensor	Section

REVIEW QUESTIONS

1. When is a space frame a good choice of superstructure?
2. What is a "normal" span for a steel space frame?
3. Why is the space frame sometimes conceptually considered a special type of two way truss?
4. How does a space frame behave similar to a truss?
5. How does a space frame behave similar to a slab?
6. Name and locate the elements of a space frame.
7. How does a tensegrity work structurally?
8. Compare the local to global failure potential of trusses and space frames.

9. Briefly discuss the construction advantages of a space frame.
10. Briefly discuss the erection process alternatives and challenges for a space frame.
11. How does the aesthetic potential of a post and beam vary with that of a space frame?
12. What is the single greatest functional advantage of a space frame structure over a slab?

Figure 15-1
United States Air Force Academy Chapel at Colorado Springs Colorado.

15 Folded Plates

DESCRIPTION

Folding a slab (or plate) can increase its stiffness in carrying vertical loads, and greatly increase its span capacity (Fig. 15-2). An unfolded sheet of paper will not span its own length between two supports, but if folded it can do so with ease. It can even carry a modest additional applied external load. A *folded plate* structure technically is a member of the shell family, but in the building industry it is widely treated as a separate family of its own. In part, this is because folded plates are much easier to calculate during design and to form during construction than some of the other shell family members such as vaults, domes, and antisynclastic shells. These will be described in the next few chapters. A clear understanding of folded plate behavior is built upon the knowledge gained from beams, bearing walls, and slabs. Vaults can be understood from what the reader will learn from folded plates, and domes will require an understanding of arches and vaults. That is why this order of chapters was chosen.

Figure 15-2
Typical folded plate structure.

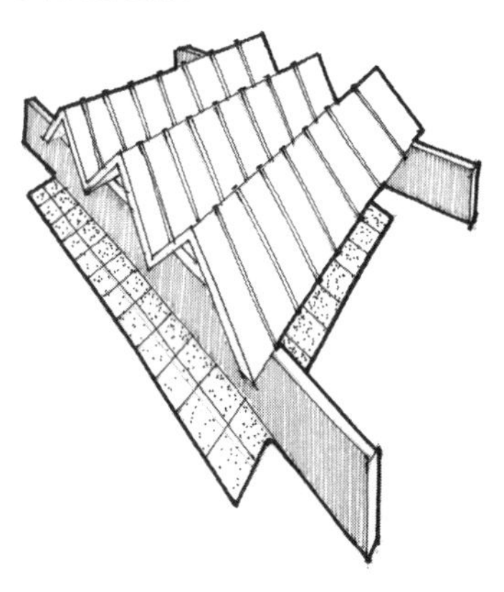

HISTORY AND SIGNIFICANT EXAMPLES

History

In his authoritative book *History of Architecture*, Sir Banister Fletcher credits Eugene Freyssinet with initiating the principle of folded plates in an air ship hanger at Orly, France, in 1916. Robert Maillart and others continued development between World War I and World War II. Box sections, currently used for many highway bridges, evolved out of the concept of folded plates (Fig. 15-3). In 1947, an article by George Winter and Ming Lung Pei entitled "Hipped Plate Construction" excited interest. Milo Ketchum and Felix Candela broadly developed the family of folded plates (Fletcher 1975).

Figure 15-3
Highway box section exposed in the collapse of the Oakland overpass.

Building examples

Selected examples of folded plates include the UNESCO Conference Hall by Breuer and Nervi, Paris, a cable railroad terminal by Pierti in Caracus, and the American Concrete Institute by Yamasaki in Detroit. "Sheninkan" in Bartlesville Oklahoma by Bruce Goff was a folded plate structure (Fig. 15-4). Unfortunately it was recently destroyed by fire.

Non-building examples

Folded plate structure is used in sandwich panels or plates used in aircraft fabrication because they are extremely lightweight and rigid (Fig. 15-5). Recall that the box girders used in bridge construction are also folded plate structures.

TYPES OR CATEGORIES

By material

Folded plates are normally made from reinforced concrete. The system may be pre-cast, site-cast, or poured-in-place. However, steel plates and wood diaphragms have also been used (Fig. 15-6).

Figure 15-4
Mr. Goff's surface treatment emphasizes the fold in the roof plate.

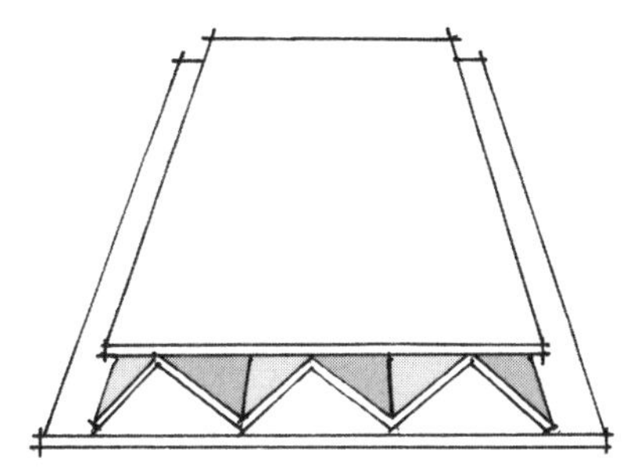

Figure 15-5
Cross section of a sandwich panel.

Figure 15-6
This wood roof at the Hamar Norway rail station is actually behaving like a folded plate.

By configuration

A wide range of alternative shapes have been evolved for folded plate systems. Of those with *parallel folds,* the more common are gabled (Fig. 15-7), three segment (Fig. 15-8), and Z-shell (Fig. 15-9). These are all "parallel fold" plates. *Tapered folded plates* are also used (Fig. 15-10). Once tapered plates are used, it is obvious that such plates can be assembled in an intersecting (Fig. 15-11) or radial (Fig. 15-12) aggregations to form two important subgroups of folded plates when a circular functional footprint is sought. In addition folded plate

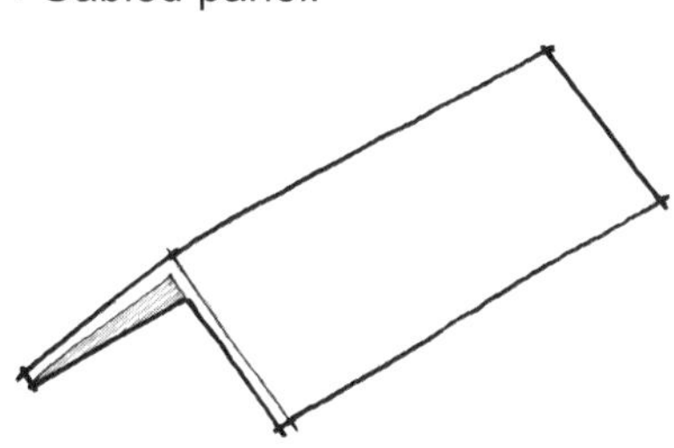

Figure 15-7
Gabled panel.

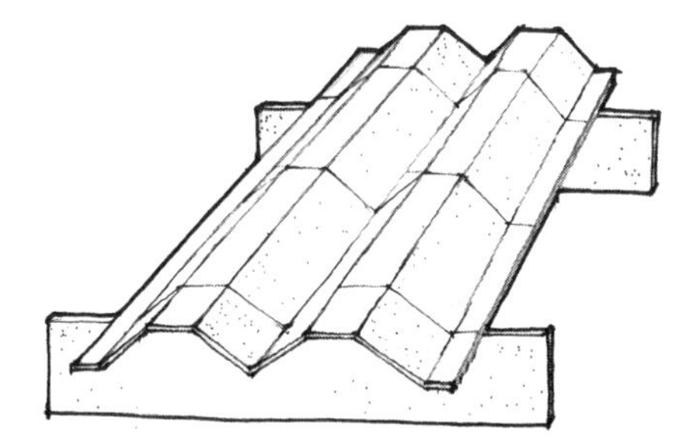

Figure 15-8
Three segment.

Figure 15-9
Z-Shell.

Figure 15-10
Tapered folded plates.

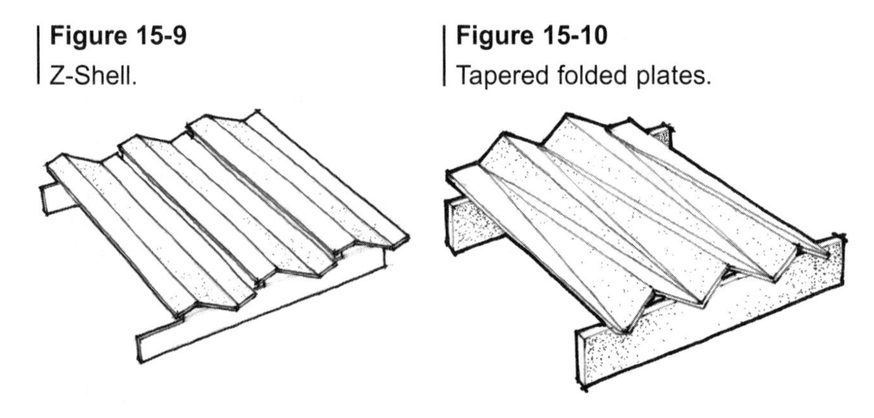

systems are occasionally grouped by their vertical support systems (i.e., continuous wall, or end frame supports) (Fig. 15-13 and 15-14). Folded plate systems require restraint against lateral spreading under load (Fig. 15-15). If *continuous walls* or *end frames* are not used to achieve this, folded plate systems may also be categorized by the alternative lateral support method used. The most widely used of these are *transverse webs* (Fig. 15-16), *tie rods* (Fig. 15-17), *moment connections* (Fig. 15-18), and *edge beams* (Ketchum 2006) (Fig. 15-19).

NOMENCLATURE

Very little specialized nomenclature is needed to describe a folded plate system. The sloped or tilted slabs are known as *inclined plates*. The upper folds are known as *ridges*, and the lower folds are known as *valleys*. If the edge of

Figure 15-11
Intersecting tapered folded plates.

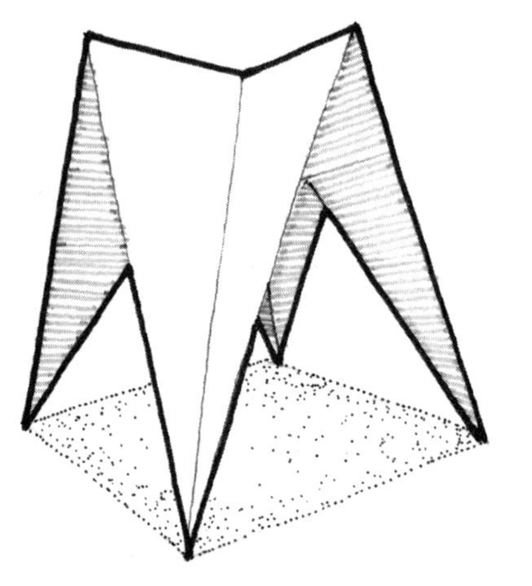

Figure 15-12
Radial tapered folded plates.

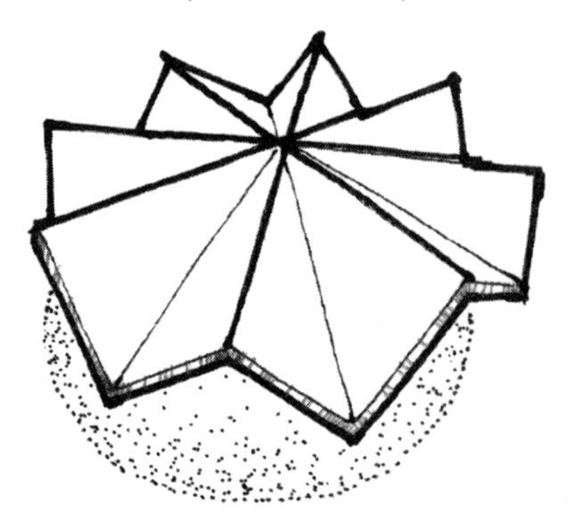

Figure 15-13
Continuous wall support.

Figure 15-14
End frame support.

Figure 15-15
Folded plates have lateral thrust similar to arches.

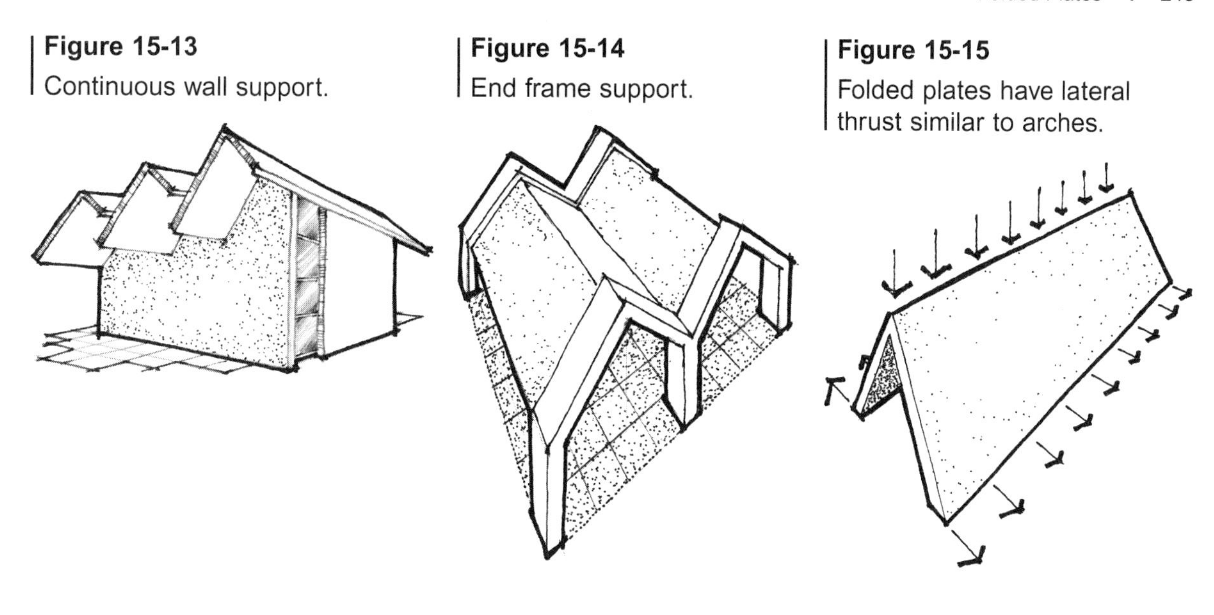

an inclined plate is folded down vertically, or outward horizontally, it is known as an *edge beam* (Fig. 15-20). An *infill panel* may be used to fill the triangular void left at the end of the inclined plates (Fig. 15-21). Occasionally a *rigid frame* may be imposed at each end of the inclined plates. *Beam stiffeners* may also be used to thicken the inclined plates over the supporting columns below (Fig. 15-22). If a bearing wall is used to carry the folded plate roof, and that wall continues upward to form an infill panel, it is known as a *continuous wall* (Fig. 15-13).

Figure 15-16
Transverse webs used to restrain lateral thrust.

Figure 15-17
Tie rods may also be used to resist lateral spreading of folded plates.

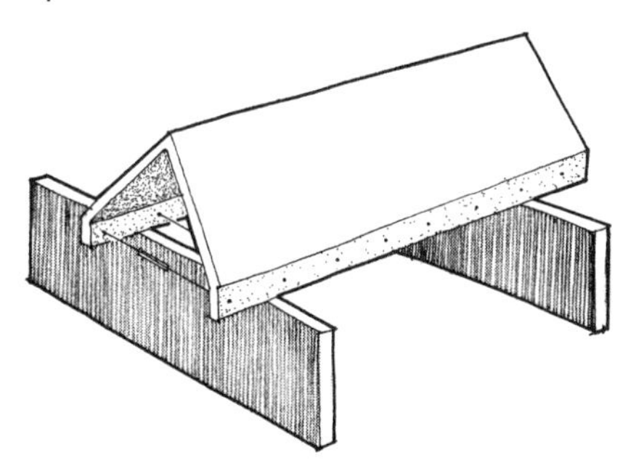

Figure 15-18
Moment connections can resist lateral thrust.

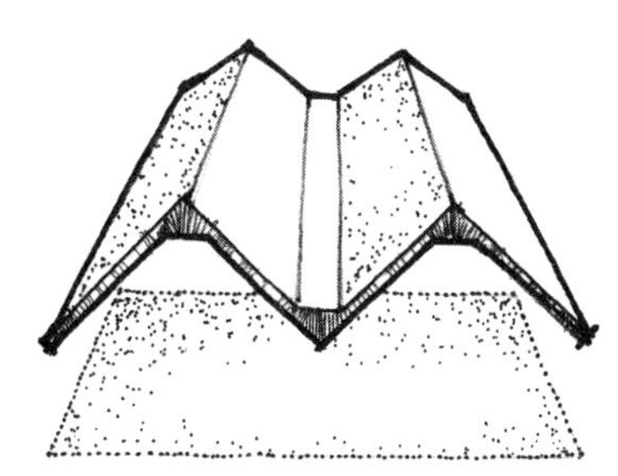

Figure 15-19
The turned down or out edge beam acts like a horizontal beam resisting lateral thrust.

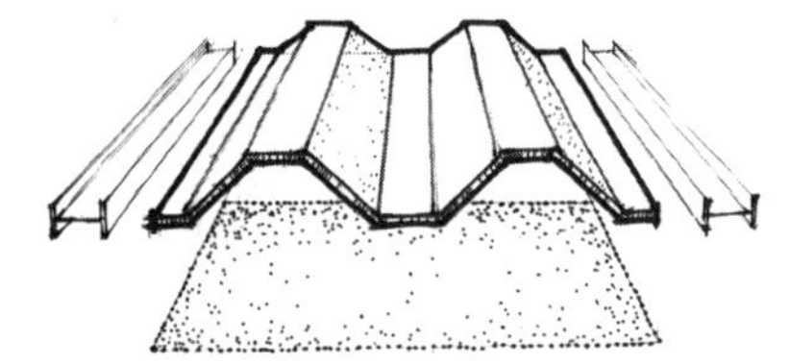

Figure 15-20
Folded plate nomenclature.

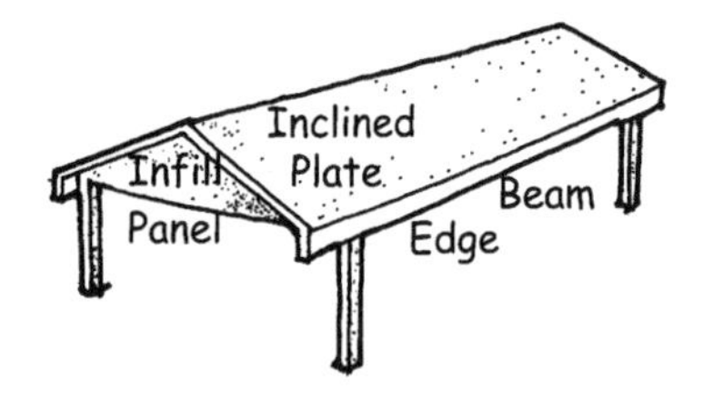

COMMON APPLICATIONS

Folded plates roofs are used for bowling alleys, elementary and middle schools, skating rinks, small medical clinics, stores in strip malls, and other building types that seek moderate span that is column free.

BEHAVIOR UNDER LOAD

The inclined plate

To understand the behavior of an inclined plate under load, first review horizontal slabs, then vertical beam. The inclined plane lies between at some angle (usually 45 degrees) and has characteristics of both the flat slab and vertical beam (Fig. 15-23). Under vertical applied loads, folded plate systems exhibit bending, shear, and buckling behavior that is similar to beams. But they also deflect, resist by "twist," and build up edge stresses like plates (slabs). They can even take on a few characteristics of bearing walls and arches. Like arches,

Figure 15-21
In this case the infill panel has been filled with glass.

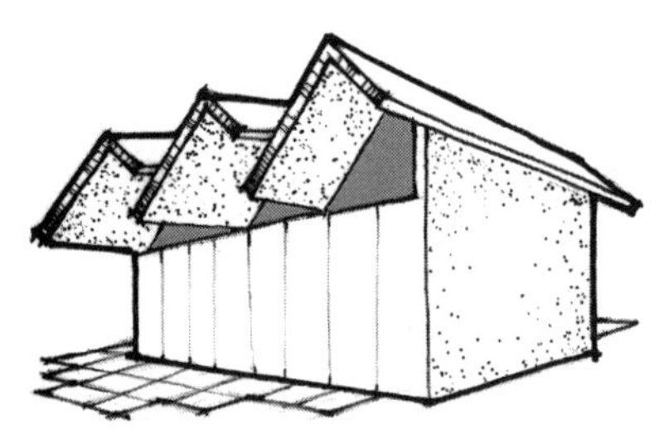

Figure 15-22
Beam stiffeners are not necessarily at the ends.

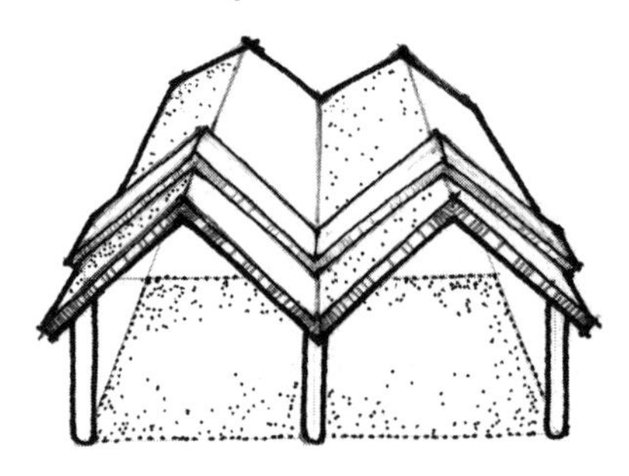

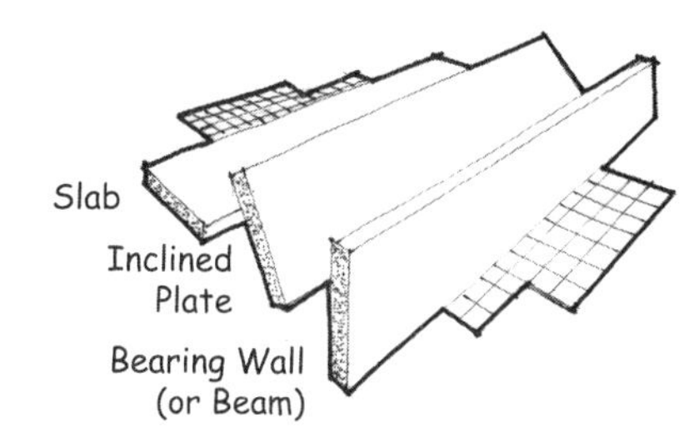

Figure 15-23
The inclined plate.

folded plates generate lateral thrust under loading. Steeply sloped inclined plates have less lateral thrust than those with less slope (Corkill, Puderbaugh, and Sawyers 1974).

Figure 15-24
Beam-like behavior of folded plates.

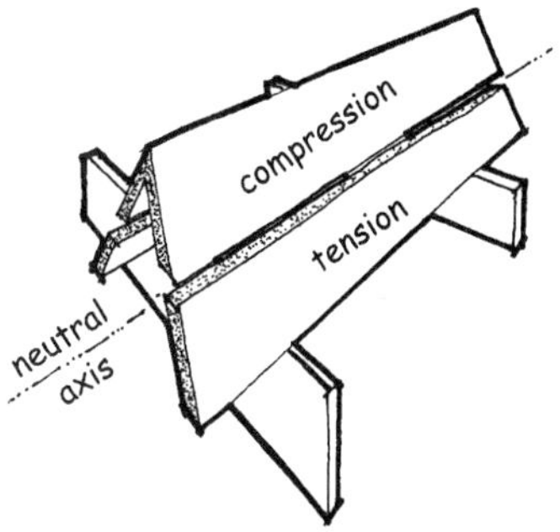

Beam-like behavior

1. *Bending:* If supported at each end the top portion of a folded plate system goes into compression, and the bottom portion experiences tension just like any other simple beam (Fig. 15-24). This means that at mid-span the bottom edge of the inclined plates have a strong tendency to develop tension tears (Fig. 15-25). Thickening that edge to form the edge beam can resist that tendency. At the apex or *ridge line* of a folded plate system there is a tendency for the thin inclined plates to buckle. However, when pitched at opposing 45 degree angles and joined into a folded plate system, the two inclined plates lose most of the lateral freedom to buckle (Ketchum 2006).
2. *Shear:* Like a vertical beam, the inclined plates also have the threat of shear at the end supports (Fig. 15-26). For this reason, and because of the bending just discussed,, the reinforcing steel in an inclined plate is similar to that found in a concrete beam. The steel reinforcing bars (rebar) are near the top chord (ridge line) at the supports and near the bottom chord (edge) at mid-span (Fig. 15-27). If the inclined plates are supported by edge beams or a rigid frame at each end (see nomenclature above) then an especially strong tendency to vertically shear exists adjacent to the supporting member (Fig. 15-28).

Figure 15-25
Reinforcing against tension tears is required.

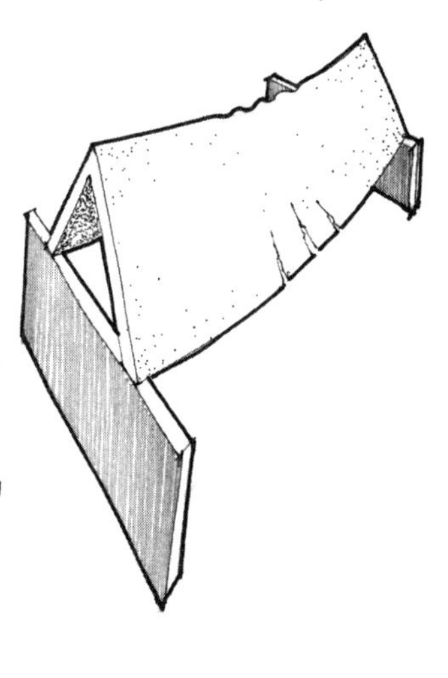

Figure 15-26
Like beams folded plates want to shear at the end supports.

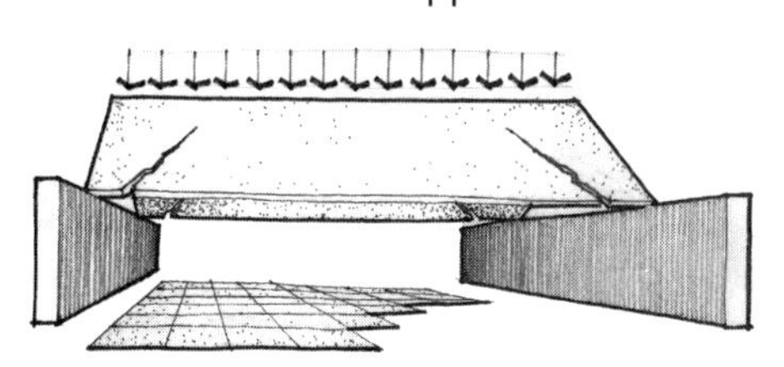

Figure 15-27
Internal steel reinforcing in the inclined plates is similar to that found in concrete beams.

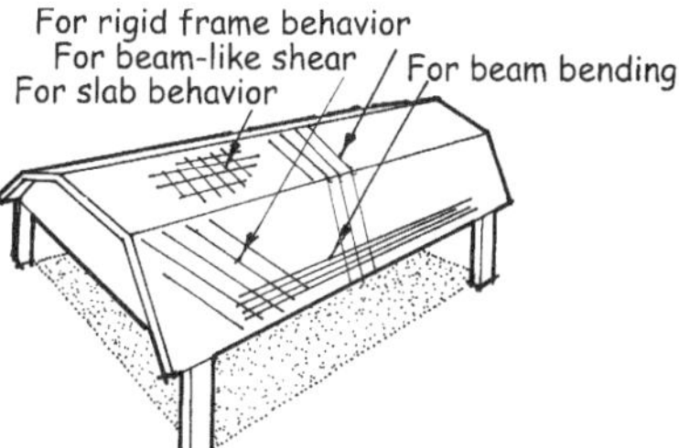

Figure 15-28
Shear immediately adjacent to edge beams is particularly significant.

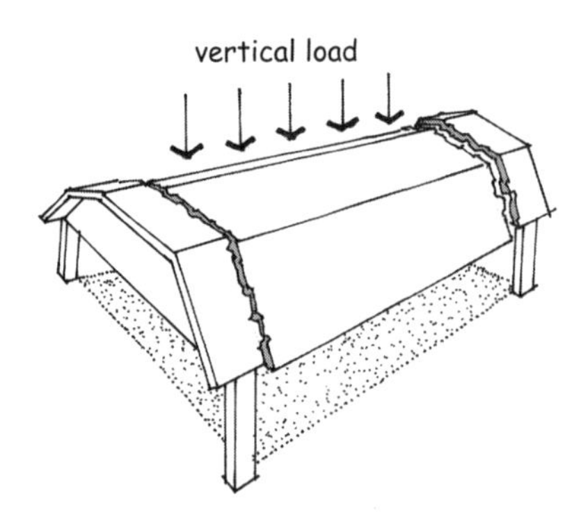

Figure 15-29
Buckling similar to an overly slender bearing wall is a conceptual issue.

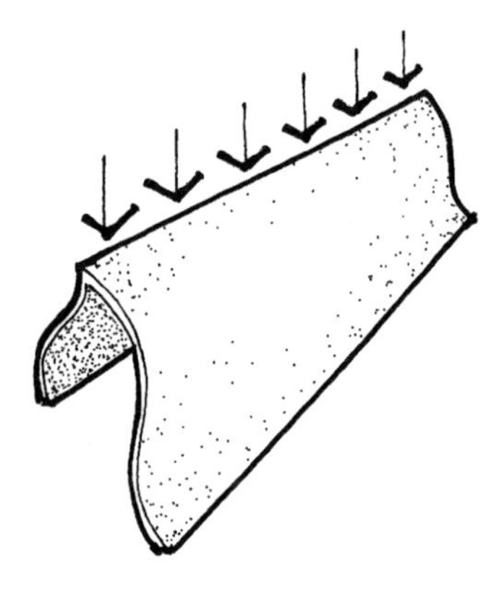

Figure 15-30
Slab-like deflection of an inclinded plate due to vertical loads.

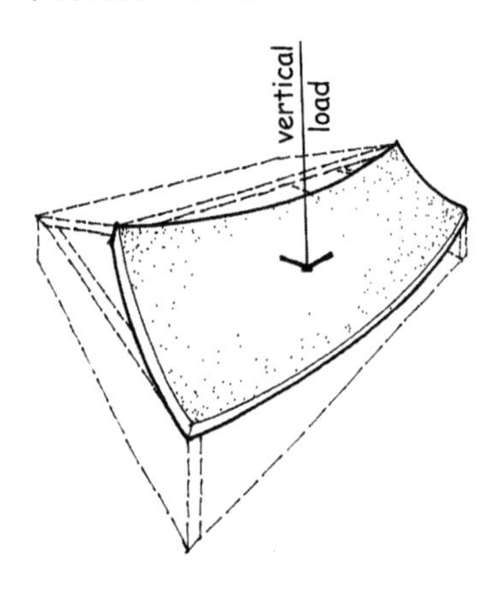

3. *Buckling:* The reader will recall that the thin web found in steel wide flange beams faces the threat of buckling. The thin inclined slabs of the folded plate systems have some of that same tendency under vertical loading (Fig. 15-29).

Slab-like behavior

But the inclined plate also simultaneously has some of the behavior of the horizontal flat slab. Remember that flat slabs deflect. So do inclined plates (Fig. 15-30). At the apex or ridge line this deflection is resisted in part by being joined to the adjacent inclined plate. However, the bottom edge is free to deflect. This is a second reason for attaching an edge beam. In this role the edge beam of a folded plate is similar to the thickened or turned down edge sometimes found on horizontal flat plates.

Bearing wall behavior

Like thin bearing walls the tendency to laterally buckle may be driven by the lateral load of winds. This buckling tendency (similar to long bearing wall) is added to the deflection tendency (similar to the horizontal plate). At the ridge fold the inclined plate is restrained against lateral displacement due to both of these tendencies by being joined to the adjacent inclined plate. Similarly, the edge beam at the bottom chord stiffens the inclined plate against both tendencies (Fig. 15-31).

Global behavior

1. *Lateral spreading:* Informed by its similarities to other systems with which the reader was familiar, let us now look at some peculiarities of the folded plate system itself. The first and most profound issue is lateral spreading of the inclined plates under vertical loads. Many mechanisms can be considered to resist this lateral spreading. Horizontal edge beam can be used if they are attached to supporting shear walls below (Fig. 15-32). Spreading is prevented at the ends by attaching the inclined plates to a rigid frame, a moment connected edge beam, or a continuous supporting wall. All of these were shown above in the discussion of folding plate nomenclature.
2. *Overturning:* The *A-frame* is a special case within the folded plate family. Often used as the structure for a small cabin or house, the A-frame presents

Figure 15-31

Bearing wall-like lateral deflection of an inclinded plate due to horizontal wind load.

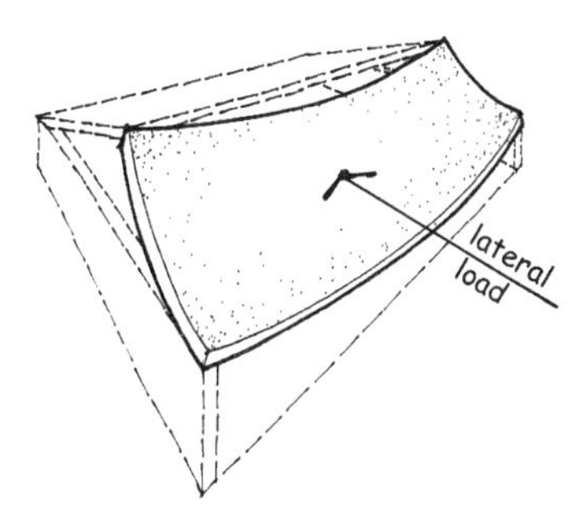

Figure 15-32

Edge beams must be attached to shear walls below in order to resist lateral spreading.

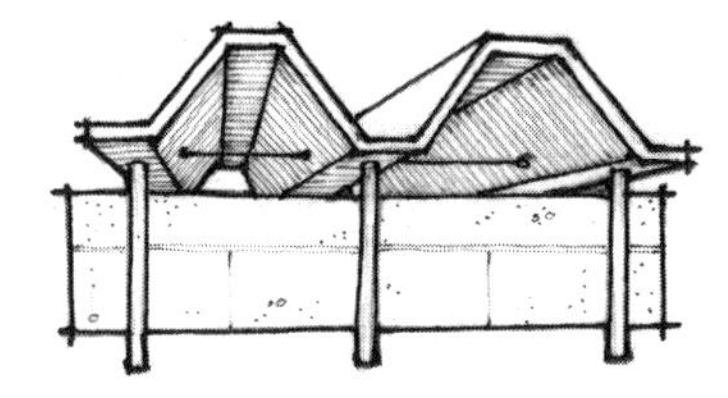

a large fairly light "sail" to any wind. This produces the threat of global overturning of the frame (Fig. 15-33).

Figure 15-33

"A" frame overturning.

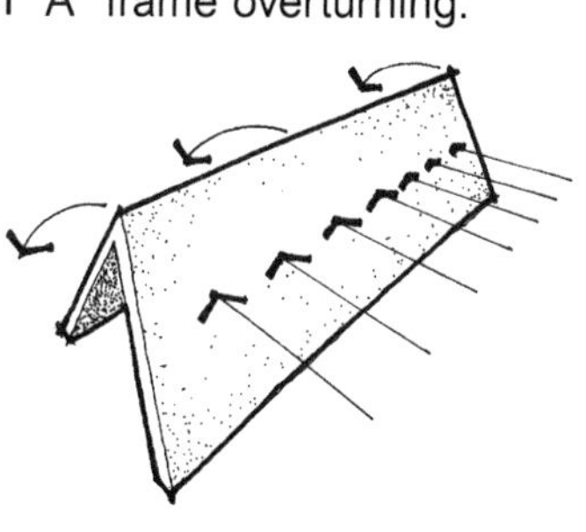

DESIGN METHODS

The most obvious design method unique to folded plate structures is the actual use of folded paper schematic and scale models (15-34).

OPTIMUM CONFIGURATION

Structural system

Folded plate systems are particularly well suited to reinforced concrete. Its flat surfaces are more easily formed than the curved surfaces of shells. The inclined

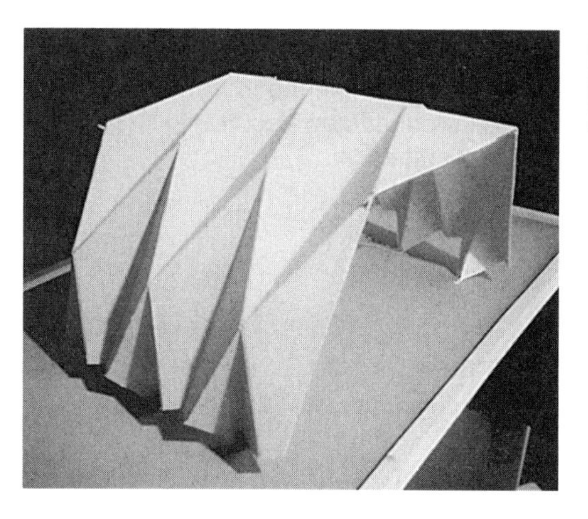

Figure 15-34

Student model of folded paper.

plate may be quite thin, (perhaps three to six inches). Spans range from about 30 to 160 feet, and are inherently resistant to fire. A crude rule of thumb depth to span ratio of about one 1: 12 might be used for early preliminary design (i.e., 10 feet deep for 120 foot span). But much depends on the building material used and the slope of the inclined plates. The plates are normally pitched at 45 degrees, but can be set at many others, particularly if the folds are not parallel. The more vertical they become, the more beam issues dominate the design. The more horizontal they become the more slab like they become, and the more lateral spreading force must be resisted (Moore 1999).

Mechanical/electrical systems

One disadvantage of folded plate roof systems is that heating, ventilation, and air conditioning systems cannot be roof mounted. A different alternative must be selected. Major ducts should be planned to run parallel with the ridge and valley folds, as opposed to perpendicular to them, if possible.

Openings

Because of the nonrectangular voids generated by folded plate, triangular infill panels of some type will usually be needed in order to close the envelope of the building. This presents a natural opening inviting glazing as a window (Fig. 15-35). Such windows supply considerable daylight at both ends and have the additional benefit of being located high in the envelope wall. Perforations for windows, mechanical systems, or other reasons are avoided in the folded plates themselves because they interrupt the continuity of the flow of force in the inclined plates of the system. Large vehicle doors and large rectangular windows can best occur under the longitudinal edge beams used to support the bottom free edge of an outside inclined plate (Fig. 15-36). Small doors through supporting walls will cause less intrusion to structural continuity if located in one of the triangular stress voids. The stress voids will require further discussion below.

Figure 15-35
Holes anywhere in the inclined plate introduce unwelcome discontinuities.

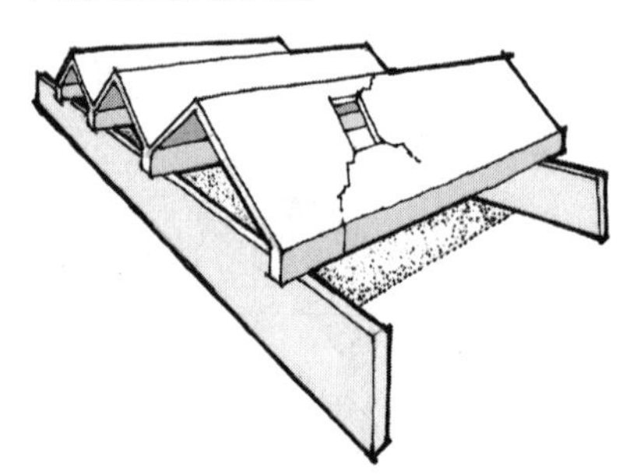

Figure 15-36
Large doors may require a long beam perpendicular to the plate folds.

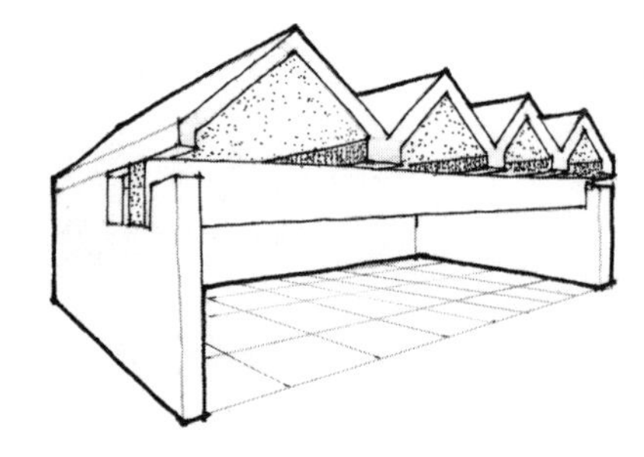

Foundations

Surprisingly the location of windows can affect the foundation loads in a folded plate system. If we ignore all lateral load and spreading issues, the vertical loads are concentrated at the bottom or valley folds of the system. Since the vertical loads are concentrated along that line, a continuous bearing wall under the valley fold is the most appropriate vertical support, and a continuous footing of some type would be used (Fig. 15-37).

Figure 15-37
Bearing walls under the valleys fold are very logical.

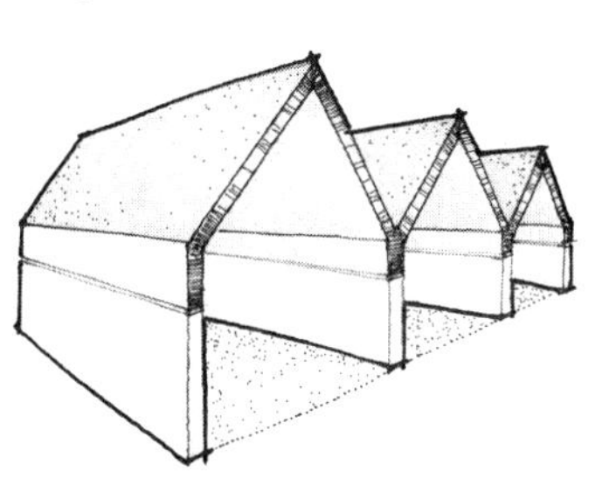

As a second alternative it is possible to place columns under each end of the valley folds, if tie rods or other mechanisms are used to resist spreading. Drilled piers would probably be used under these columns due to the inherently large loads associated with long span structures. Column support under the folded plate system would still be vulnerable to lateral loading. A reinforced concrete folded plate that rests on columns would be particularly vulnerable to earthquakes. Considerable additional lateral support will be needed (Fig. 15-38).

Figure 15-38
Lateral instability is a threat for folded plates elevated only on columns.

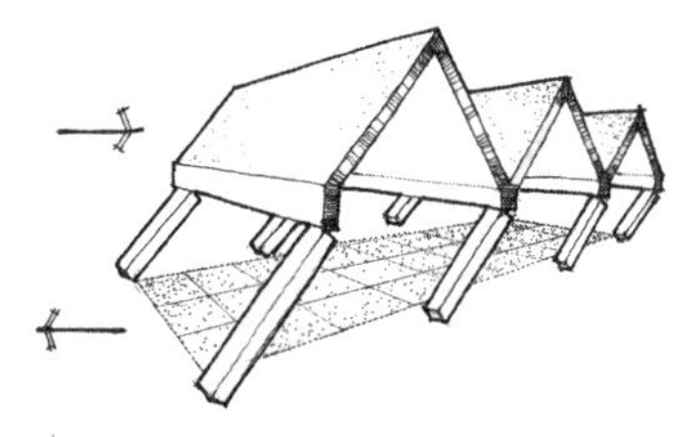

A third alternative is the use of bearing walls perpendicular to the folds of the inclined plates. Such walls can not only carry the vertical loads, but can inherently provide better lateral support than the columns just discussed. Take a moment to look at the load propagation in such a wall (Fig. 15-39). Notice that a special opportunity for a second natural window opening is generated by the absence of force in triangular portions of the wall (Fig. 15-40). If combined with the in-fill space between inclined plates a unique diamond shaped opening becomes possible. Notice that if the wall is quite tall, the loads will distribute fully across the total wall inviting some type of continuous footing, if soil conditions are adequate. If the wall is not so tall, loads may become more focused at some points along the footing. A grade beam with drilled piers might address this circumstance if the piers coincided with the focused loads.

Joints

As with other long span structures, thermal expansion and contraction must be respected in a folding plate system. A typical solution with Teflon coated, cast-in steel plates has been used. In seismically active areas, such joints must restrict the direction and extent of movement that will be allowed. Since they are inherently heavier than space frames, folded plates are more vulnerable to earthquake movements.

Figure 15-39
Familiar bearing wall dispersion of point loads.

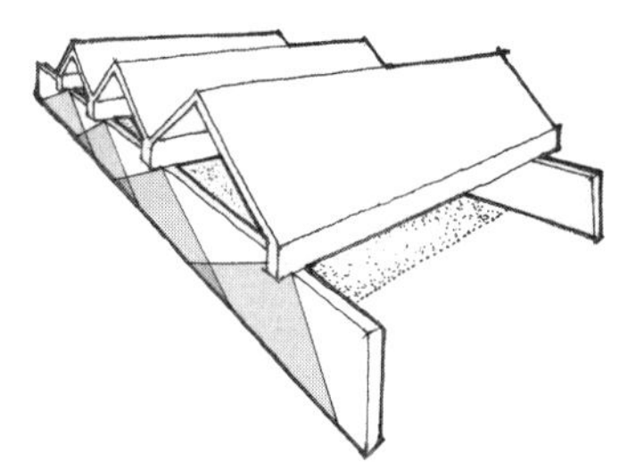

Related soil and foundation

Greater soil bearing capacity is needed for long span structures than for small buildings. Long spans also increase the probability that diverse soil conditions will be encountered, and diverse soils provoke differential settlement problems.

Topography

Folded plate buildings, like most long span structures are very sensitive to significant site slope. Site leveling, or elaborate foundation stepping will be required if

Figure 15-40
Diamond shaped window opening in stress free portions of the supporting shear wall.

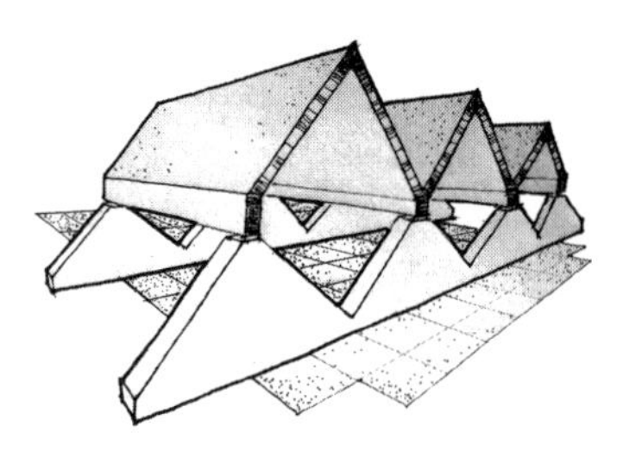

steep slopes must be overcome. For more gentle slopes the long axis of a folded plate building should be placed parallel to the contour lines forming the slope.

Related lateral support

Lateral support can be achieved in most of the ways outlined in an earlier chapter on lateral support (i.e., cross bracing). However, shear walls at each end of the span has probably been the most widely used method.

Related envelope

Other than the occasional use of triangular windows, connecting an envelope to the folded plate roof offers no significant or unusual industrial challenges. If brick or concrete block is used to form a continuous wall, a conflict of shape erupts when the rectangular masonry meets sloped concrete folded plates. Some transition must be devised. The folded plate roof requires some attention to the method of roof surface waterproofing.

Figure 15-41
Radial tapered folded plates begin to act like domes which are discussed in a later chapter.

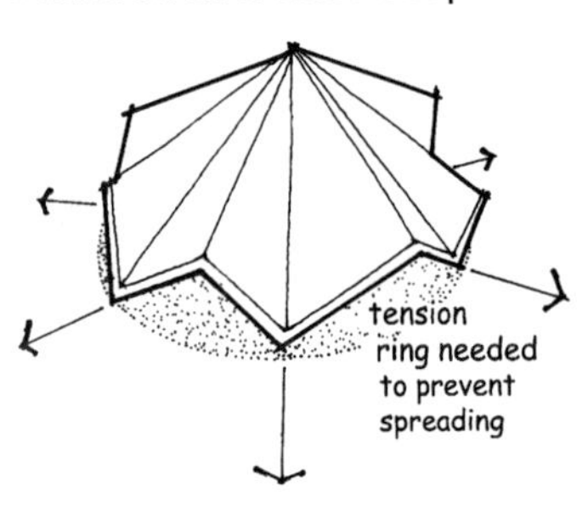

FUNCTIONAL FOOTPRINT

Given inclined panels of equal proportions and parallel folds, rectangular functional footprints will be formed. One axis of such rectangles will normally have long span dimensions (i.e., greater than 60 feet). If tapered plates are employed in a radial pattern, a circular functional footprint of considerable span is anticipated. Such radial arrangements may or may not have a vertical support at the center. In the absence of central support, the inclined planes will normally be pitched to shed rain and to exploit dome action (Fig. 15-41). In this configuration a tension ring is needed at the outer perimeter, and a compression ring at the center. Alternating tapered inclined plates may be placed side by side to form rectangular footprints (as in the UNESCO building) (Fig. 15-10). With intersecting folds and tapered plates a square footprint is optimal (Fig. 15-11). If several bays are fitted together, rectangular functional footprints are the normal goal. When several bays are connected the pitch of the inclined tapered panels is usually flattened, and the intersecting folds begin to have some of the structural characteristics of a space frame (Fig. 15-42).

Figure 15-42
Inclined plates can be arranged to act similar to space frames.

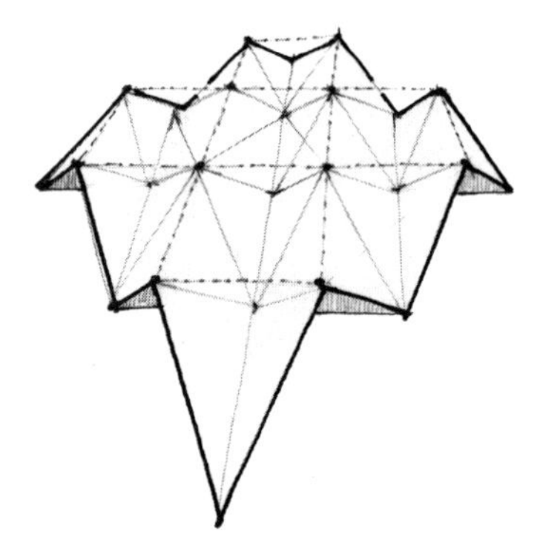

PATTERN OF GROWTH

Growth in the long dimension is very difficult in folded plate buildings. Growth in the transverse direction by whole panel is possible; however, growth of all folded plate buildings is very difficult without essentially beginning a new adjacent structure. Significant growth of radial aggregations would be the least likely of all.

AESTHETIC POTENTIAL

Folded plate structures have considerable drama due to the diagonal lines generated by the inclined planes. This drama is considerably heightened by the play of light and shade on the inclined planes. These adjacent sun and shade conditions call for a razor sharp edge at the fold. If quality control is lax at this important line, the sun/shade condition will accentuate the flaw. Unfinished concrete is usually honestly expressed on the underside of folded plates, but other finishes can be applied with relative ease. Large triangular openings at the edges can offer the sufficient "raking" light to accentuate the texture of the roof material, but they also generate unwanted glare. Because of the play of light and shade on folded plates it is common to use light colors, rather than darker ones.

CONSTRUCTION

Fabrication

Small wooden folded plate structures such as A-frame cabins are usually fabricated and erected directly on the final building site. Steel folded plates will normally be panelized with much of the fabrication done in the factory setting. These factory made components will be kept relatively small for ease in transportation to the site and handling, once there. Erection then is completed at the building site. Plywood sandwich panels can also be factory fabricated and site assembled, but this is not a wide spread approach. In part this is due to fire resistance challenges. Instead reinforced concrete has clearly been the material of choice for folded plates. Reinforced concrete folded plates may be in-situ formed, site formed, or pre-cast in an industrial setting. If in-situ forming is done, honeycombing of the inclined planes is a problem due to the slope forms, and the thinness of the plates. It is difficult to work the mix in, around, and between the reinforcing steel with correct vibration. If either site cast or pre-cast is employed, large cranes, appropriate space, and adequate surface soil conditions will be required. Site casting the folded plate sections does not normally achieve the same quality control expected in industrially pre-cast sections.

Erection

If site cast is employed, a slab on grade will be poured first in order to form an adequate casting bed for the folded plate system. Such a slab on grade may have to be stronger to support this fabrication process than will be needed later for the final functional occupancy of the building. Erection of either the columns or walls is next, and finally the folded plates are lifted into place. In-situ folded plates require a system of forms, jacks, and scaffolding under them like flat slabs. The forms for folded plates are much simpler than those that are required for vaults in the next chapter.

Vocabulary		
Three segment	Gabled	Z-shell
Sandwich panel	Plywood diaphragm	Continuous wall
Transverse web	Inclined plate	Edge beam
Infill panel	Rigid end frame	Beam stiffener
Tapered plates	Ridge fold	Valley fold
A-frame		

REVIEW QUESTIONS

1. When is a folded plate system a good choice of superstructure?
2. What is a "normal" span for a reinforced concrete folded plate system?
3. In what ways does a folded plate behave like a beam?
4. In what ways does a folded plate behave like a slab?
5. In what ways does a folded plate behave like a bearing wall?
6. In what ways does a folded plate behave like an arch?
7. What sort of site topography favors the selection of a folded plate roof system?
8. Name and locate the elements of a folded plate system.
9. Briefly discuss the construction issues that influence the selection of in-situ, site cast, or pre-cast folded plates.
10. What unique glazing opportunities are implied by the selection of a folded plate system?
11. What is a common mechanical and electrical system problem associated with the use of a folded plate roof?

Figure 16-1
Vaulted corridor in Urbino Italy by Gian Carlo DeCarlo.

16 Vaults

DESCRIPTION

Like folded plates in the previous chapter, vaults belong to the shell family. Also like folded plates, vaults have historically been used so frequently that it is common for practitioners to treat them as a separate family. If a series of arches are placed immediately adjacent to each other and fused together, a vault is formed (Fig. 16-2). By examining the resulting structure, the reader can readily predict that vaults will share some of the structural behavior of arches with some of the characteristics of folded plates.

Figure 16-2
Arches fused into a vault.

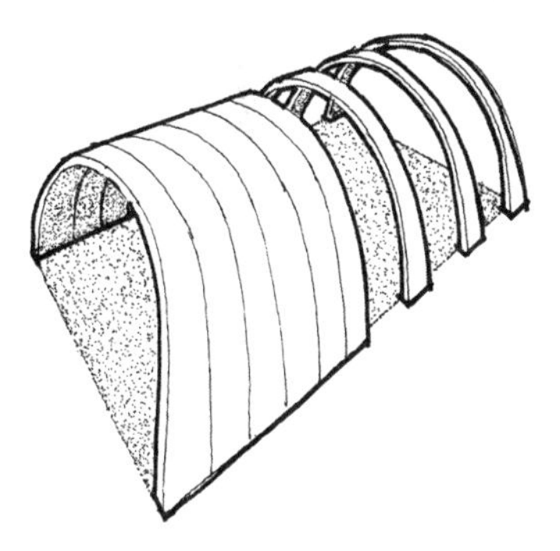

HISTORY AND SIGNIFICANT EXAMPLES

Examples in nature

In nature, caves are the most common example of vault-like structural appearance and load propagation. This has not been lost on mine and tunnel engineers, so vaults become the most wide-spread tunnel configuration.

History

Corbelled arches appear as early as the Treasury of Atreus, Mycenae, in 1325 B.C. Brick barrel vaults were used in ancient Babylonia and Assyria. However, it is in the classical tradition of Rome around the time of Christ that vaults widely dominate major buildings as a masonry spanning means. Because of the justifiable concern for fire, trusses over the naves in early Christian churches were largely replaced by barrel vaults later in Romanesque architecture (Fig. 16-3). The cruciform plan of churches formed by the intersection of the nave and transept made use of intersecting vaults. However, transepts that differed in width from the width of that nave implied the intersection of barrel

Figure 16-3
Romanesque church with a vaulted nave.

vaults of differing height. To solve this difficulty, gothic vaults of differing slope were later used in similar gothic churches. When arcades were used to form the side aisles of gothic churches, loads from the vault over the nave were concentrated in the columns supporting the arches. Groin vaults allowed greater continuity in propagation of these loads, and potential openings for high windows along the length of the nave (Fig. 16-4). This additional daylight

Figure 16-4
Typical groin vaults with light entering high in this church nave.

Figure 16-5
Fan vaults at Kings College in Cambridge England.

was welcome in the more gray climates of northern Europe. This evolution continued to the very elaborate fan vaults of such projects as Kings College, Cambridge, England (1446–1515) (Fig. 16-5). With the onset of the industrial age, iron began to be used in rib support glazed vaults such as the Galleria Vittorio Emanuele, Milan, Italy (1865–1877) by Mengoni. Such vaults were well suited to the demand for long span roofs to cover the newly evolving railroad station platforms (Fig. 16-6). This tradition extends to current day

Figure 16-6
Milan railroad station in Italy.

Figure 16-7
Hay's Galleria in London by Michael Twigg Brown and Partners.

projects such as the Galleria, London, England (Fig. 16-7). Thin shelled reinforced concrete vaults such as the Old Flower Market Hall, Pescia, Italy (1945–1951) by Saviolli, Ricci, Brizzi, and Gori sought the material limits of concrete in vault construction. Felix Candela in Mexico is considered by many to be the foremost pioneer in such applications. Skewed reinforced concrete grids were used by Nervi to form vaults over air force hanger at Orvieto, Italy, but it was unfortunately destroyed during World War II. However, such grids have more recently been used to form vaults in the Law Faculty in Cambridge, England, and the TVG Railway Station in Avionon, France (Fig. 16-8) (Fletcher 1975).

Non-building examples

Many Roman road bridges were supported by masonry vaults (Fig. 16-9). Sewers dug under the medieval cities of Europe normally used the same vaulted structure as the mine and road tunnels that are their close cousin. Even today many road culverts continue to utilize the vault structure.

NOMENCLATURE

Vaults generally utilize the same nomenclature as arches. These were fully identified in an earlier chapter. Some of the end support methods established for folded plates are also used for vaults. When they are, they carry the same nomenclature (i.e., edge beam, continuous wall, etc.)

Figure 16-8
TGV rail station at Avignon France.

Figure 16-9
Bridge from the Classical period in Rome.

TYPES OR CATEGORIES

By material

Both stone and brick have been widely used as vaults just as they have been for arches. If properly configured, very little reinforcing steel is needed to complete an optimally configured reinforced concrete vault. Thin shell vaults can be less than four inches in thickness. From the iron of the early industrial age to the more efficient aluminum and steel of today, small members can now be assembled into vaults of considerable span. Metal space frame grids may be warped into the vault shapes. In light steel construction, corrugated sheets are now used to form warehouses and farm buildings (Fig. 16-10). Its light transportation weight and ease of erection make it an appropriate selection for such applications.

By configuration

The most common cross section (or transverse) shapes for vaults are barrel vaults, parabolic vaults, and gothic vaults. Vaults may rest directly on a continuous foundation, or be elevated on bearing walls, columns, arches, or rigid frames (Fig. 16-11). In this consideration vaults have much of the structural

Figure 16-10
Corrugated steel vault storage building.

behavior of folded plates. As you will see later in this chapter, if a vault is elevated its longitudinal length significantly affects its structural behavior. "Short" vaults act differently than "long" ones. A single flat plate may be warped in only one axis to form a vault; however, as indicated in the history section above it may become useful to employ ribs. These ribs may be simple transverse ribs running perpendicular to the long axis of the vault, or groin vaults, which intersect diagonally. Vaults may also be formed from skewed grids known as lamella (Fig. 16-12). More complex organizations of ribs and infill panels have evolved such as the fan vaults. To accomplish vault action, space trusses may be warped into vaults, particularly if a very large free span is needed.

Figure 16-11
Undulating vaults, vault sections, and vaults with varying radius are also possible.

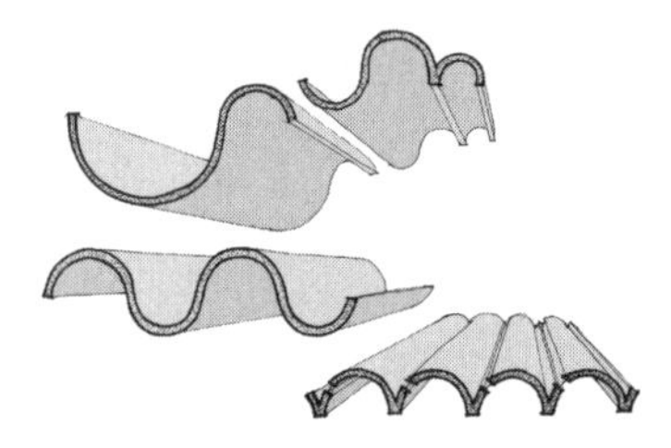

BEHAVIOR UNDER LOAD AND FAILURES

Following the earlier example set in *Structure and Architecture* (Savadori and Heller 1963), it is best to explain the complex behavior of vaults by relating them to a series of structural types with which the reader is already familiar.

Figure 16-12
Student model of a skewed grid known as a lamella.

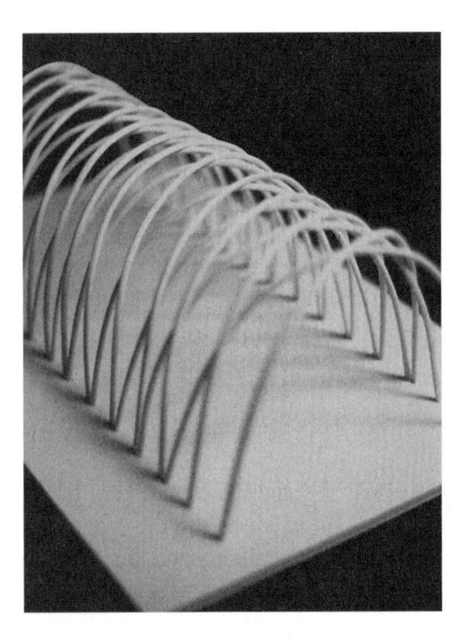

Arch-like behavior

When a vault system rests directly on the ground, they behave very much like arches. Lateral thrust at the base exists and must be restrained. It continues to be the goal to keep the compressive pressure line within the middle third of the transverse vault section, just as in an arch system. Thin shell vaults are particularly vulnerable to buckling and do not invite point loads. When superimposed vaults are used, it is traditional to place spring line directly over spring line to avoid vault buckling.

Bearing wall behavior

Recall the way in which point loads disperse across a bearing wall. Loads applied to a vault disperse in a similar manner (Fig. 16-13). Both bearing walls and vaults are able to do this because of in-plane shearing stress. Imagine a bearing wall cut into a series of closely placed columns, then one of the columns is vertically loaded. That column would be forced to slide past the columns adjacent to it (Fig. 16-14). But if the columns are then fused together, the load would be transferred to the adjacent columns. Although the vault is curved in-plane, shear still allows the same type of load dispersion to happen.

Folded plate behavior

Bending: When a vault is supported at both ends the top portion of a vault goes into compression and the bottom portion experiences tension just like any other simple beam. This is very similar to a folded plate system that we have just studied. This means that at mid-span the bottom edge of the vault has a strong tendency to develop tension tears (Fig. 16-15). Like the folded plate, the bottom edge of the vault may be thickened to form the edge beam to resist this tearing, and also the lateral thrust of the vault.

Shear: Like a vertical beam and folded plates, vaults also have the threat of shear at the end supports. For this reason and because of the bending just discussed, the reinforcing steel in an inclined plate is similar to that found in a concrete beam. The rebar is near the top chord at the supports and near the bottom chord at mid-span (Fig. 16-16). If the vaults are supported by edge beams or a rigid frame at each end (see nomenclature) then an especially strong tendency to vertically shear exists adjacent to the supporting member (Fig. 16-17).

Buckling: The reader will recall that the thin web found in steel wide flange beams faces the threat of buckling, while a thin arch must maintain the pressure line within its very thin middle third in order to avoid buckling. For both reasons the thin concrete vault is also vulnerable to out-of-plane buckling. In fact in Chapter 18 the reader will find that point loads are not invited by any member of the shell family.

Lateral spreading: Lateral thrust is resisted by all of the same mechanisms as their close cousin the folded plate. Specifically that includes tie rods; rigid moment connected arched ribs at the ends, edge beams, and continuous walls.

Figure 16-13
Arches concentrate loads along a narrow curve, but vaults disperse it across a broad surface.

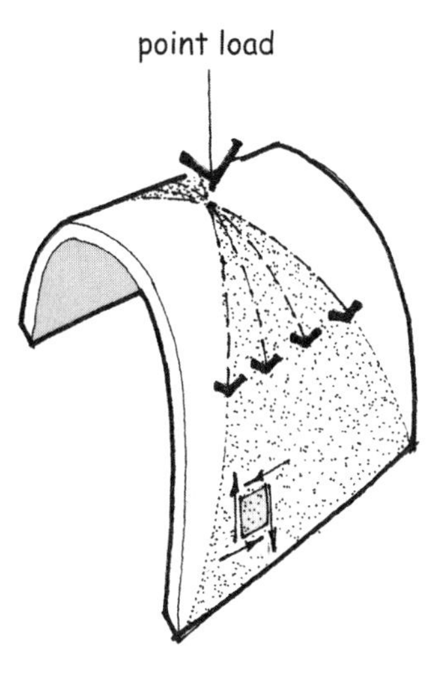

Figure 16-14
To physically feel in-plane shear rub two bricks together.

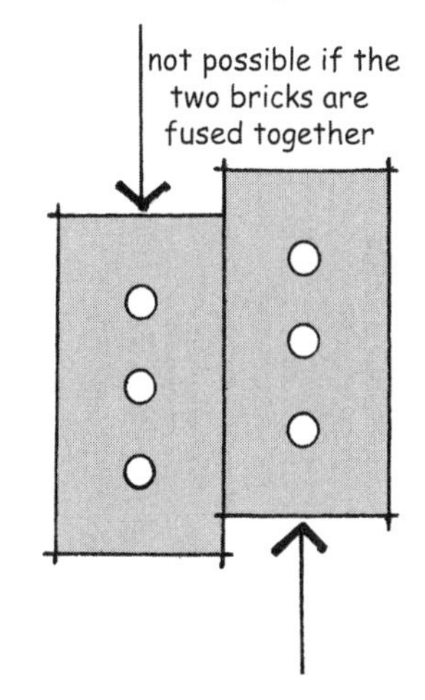

Figure 16-15

Notice the tie rods against lateral spreading, edge beams between columns, & edge stiffeners.

Short and long vaults

If a short and a long vault are separately elevated on some type of end supports, their structural behavior can be compared. In the short span vault, the loads on the vault are transferred to the end arches much as a one-way slab might. Shear near the support is a primary concern. If stiff edge beams are

Figure 16-16

Reinforcing steel placement is similar to that found in concrete beams.

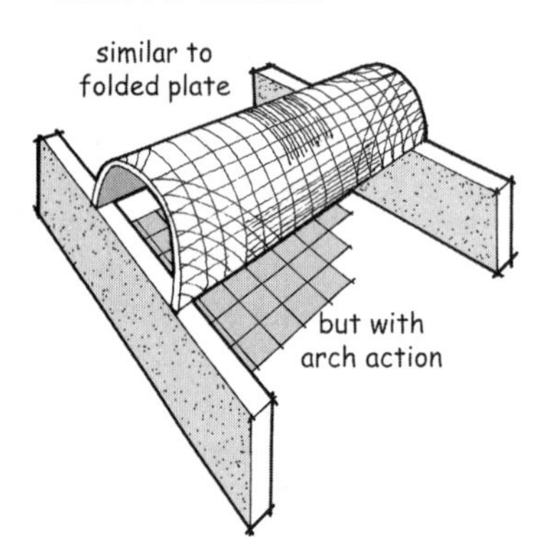

Figure 16-17

Shear near rigid frames at the ends is a threat just as it was in folded plates.

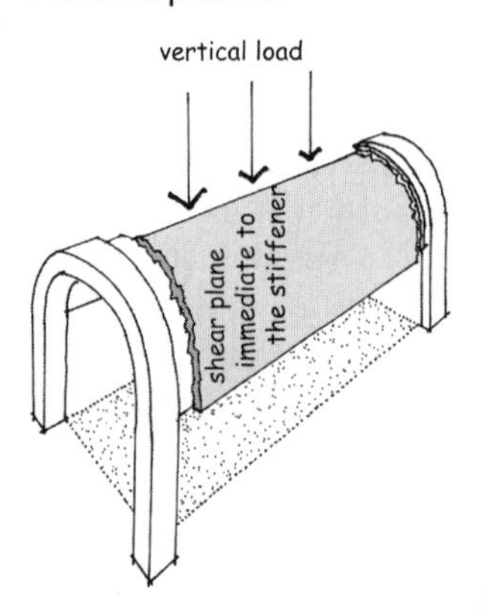

added to the short span vault the transverse arch action of the vault resting on the beams will be dominant, and the beams will carry the loads to the end supports. Longer span vaults behave more like beams with bending being the greater threat. If ribs are added down the length of a vault it begins to behave like a series of closely spaced short vaults. Still better, if the vault is continuous across the periodic ribs, the benefits of continuous "slab" action develops in the vault membrane. At this point the reader might wish to review that concept in Chapter 12.

DESIGN METHODS

Initial configurations for early preliminary design are often based on tables and rules of thumb. Scale models are easy to construct, but currently it is easier to use computer modeling. Computers also greatly ease the math calculations that inevitably must follow preliminary design.

OPTIMUM CONFIGURATION

Vaults, like folded plates, are particularly well suited to reinforced concrete. They are a bit more difficult to form during construction, however. Reinforced concrete may be quite thin, perhaps 3 to 5 inches. The preliminary span range for vaults is from about 30 to 180 feet. They are inherently resistant to fire. Like folded plates a crude rule of thumb depth-to-span ratio for barrel vaults might be about 1:12 for early preliminary design (i.e., 10 feet deep for 120 feet span). Vaults of other configurations will vary in span-to-depth ratio (Seymour Howard within Callender 1982).

Like folded plates vaults deny roof mounting of heating, ventilation, and air conditioning equipment. A different alternative must be selected. Major ducts should be planned to run parallel to the long axis of vault whenever possible.

When resting directly on the ground, a continuous foundation with lateral thrust resisting potential will normally be used. If elevated, a bearing wall directly under the long edge of the vault is most logical, although it may not be functionally acceptable. In such cases a sturdy beam may replace the long bearing wall. This beam collects all of the vertical loads on the vault and transfers them to the end of the beams, where columns may conduct the loads down to drilled piers. If elevated, some type of tie rods are needed to resist lateral thrust. Surprisingly the location of windows can affect the foundation loads in a vault system. Column support under an elevated vault system would still be vulnerable to lateral loading, particularly in a seismically active area. A third option is to use the support of perpendicular bearing walls at both ends of the vault. Such walls cannot only carry the vertical loads, but can also inherently provide better lateral support than columns. Such end walls might rest on either a grade beam with drilled piers, or even a stem wall given adequate soil conditions.

As with folded plates in chapter 15, vaults require special consideration of thermal expansion and contraction. Like many other long span structures teflon coated, cast-in steel plates may be needed to allow, but control, this movement. Vaults, like folded plates, are vulnerable to earthquake loads.

Long vaults that are elevated on columns will require greater soil bearing capacity than that needed for small buildings. Like folded plates, long vaults also increase the probability that diverse soil conditions will be encountered. As the reader has learned, diverse soils may cause differential settlement.

Because of their large footprint extensive site leveling, or elaborate foundation stepping may be required if steep slopes must be overcome. For more gentle slopes the long axis of a vault structure should be placed parallel to the contour lines forming the slope.

Figure 16-18

Rectangular glazing is not compatible with the semi-circular end openning of vaults.

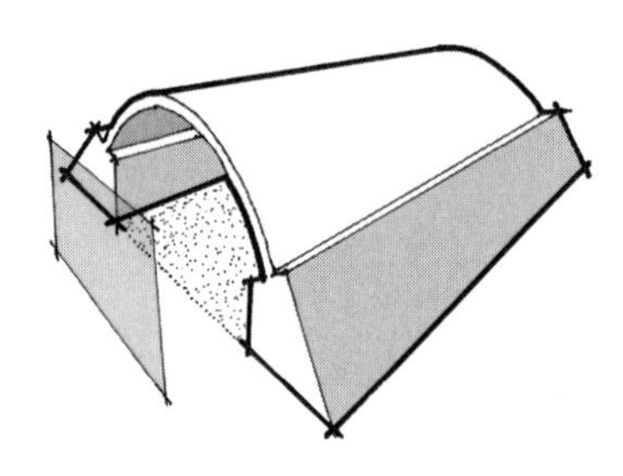

Most of the methods outlined in Chapter 5 may be used to achieve lateral support (i.e., cross bracing). However, shear walls at each end of the span have probably been the most widely used method.

Because of the semicircular voids generated at the ends of vaults, nonrectilinear glazing is often employed (Fig. 16-18). Such windows supply considerable daylight at both ends and have the additional benefit of being located high in the envelope wall. Perforations for windows, mechanical systems, or other reasons are avoided in the vaults themselves because such holes interrupt the continuity of the flow of force. Like folded plate systems, large vehicle doors and large rectangular windows are best located under the longitudinal edge beams used to support the bottom free edge of a vault. If brick or concrete block is used to form a continuous wall, a conflict of shape erupts when the rectangular masonry meets the curve of the vault. Some transition must be devised. One option is to leave a glazed gap similar to the Fort Worth Art Museum by Louis Khan (Fig. 16-19). The vaulted roof requires some attention to the method of roof surface waterproofing and rain water removal.

Figure 16-19

Notice the quality of light resulting from a small gap at the edge of this vault.

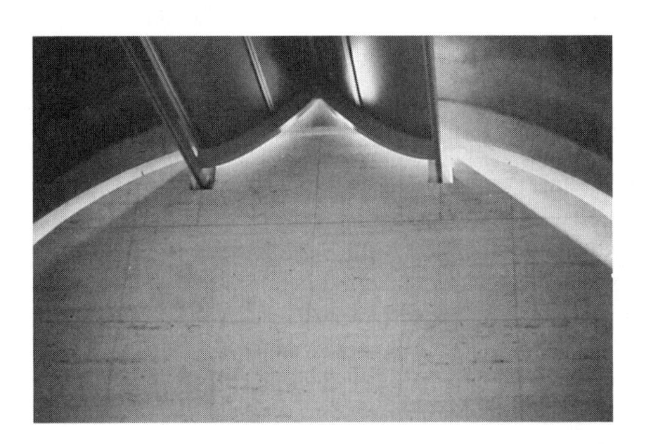

FUNCTIONAL FOOTPRINT

Rectangular functional footprints will be formed under barrel vaults. If a circular footprint is sought, tapered vault sections must be radially arranged. A fan-shaped footprint is possible if moderately tapered vaults are placed side by side (Fig. 16-20).

PATTERN OF GROWTH

Growth in the long dimension is very difficult in vault structures. Essentially a second building must be erected with matching vault edges directly abutted. Growth in the transverse direction by whole single vault section is possible; however, growth of all vaulted buildings is very difficult without essentially beginning a new adjacent structure. Significant growth of radial aggregations is very unlikely indeed.

AESTHETIC POTENTIAL

Vaults have the same "leaping ballerina" visual appeal that was identified for arches. However, vaults have much more powerfully assertive mass, voids, and sculptural appeal. While folded plates respond to sun with direct juxtaposition of surfaces in light or shade, vaults make a slow transition from light to shade. Human scale may be lost in large long vaults, but often this is not unappealing if the inside is well daylighted against gloom (Fig. 16-20).

Figure 16-20
Notice the fan-shaped footprint in this student design using a series of tapered vaults.

CONSTRUCTION

Fabrication

Small vaults are usually erected over centering similar to arches. Scaffolding and jacks may be used as part of this centering. The process of placing masonry or reinforced concrete is very similar to that discussed in the chapter on arches. Occasionally a single reusable barrel vault form will be constructed from wood. This single form will have internal jacks that can expand outward, and be collapsed inward. The system may even be mounted on tracks like a railroad. The form is jacked out, reinforcing steel is placed, and concrete is poured, vibrated, and allowed to cure. The form is withdrawn, moved a distance down the track, jacked out, and the process begins again. This is used when a long single vault such as a tunnel is to be completed. Pre-cast vault sections are less likely to be used than in folded plate solutions. Site cast over earthen, or wood forms may be preferred to pre-cast sections due to the difficulty of transportation to the site. If site cast is used heavy lift equipment must be anticipated.

Vocabulary		
Barrel vault	Groined vault	Ribbed vault
Lamella		

*Because the vocabulary needed for vaults shares much with arches and folded plates, it is recommended that the reader fully review the nomenclature given in Chapters 9 and 15.

REVIEW QUESTIONS

1. What is a "normal" span for a reinforced concrete vault system?
2. In what ways does a vault behave like an arch, a beam, a slab, a bearing wall, and a folded plate?
3. What sort of site topography favors the selection of a folded plate roof system?
4. Briefly compare the structural behavior of long and short span vaults.
5. Why is the folded plate system easier to cast in place than a vault?
6. What unique glazing opportunities are implied by the selection of a vault system?
7. What is a common mechanical and electrical system problem associated with the use of a vaulted roof?

Figure 17-1

Dome on the Prague Opera House in the Czech Republic.

17 Domes

DESCRIPTION

Like folded plates and vaults, domes belong to the shell family. Specifically a dome is a *synclastic* shell, meaning it curves downward in two perpendicular axes. This is discussed more in the next chapter. For now, the shape of a dome may be traced by rotating an arch (Fig. 17-2). Much of its structural behavior is predicted by this simple statement. Domes have many of the same structural attributes as an arch, but offer the added advantage of greater stability in three dimensions. It is a *form resistant* structure that gains its strength as much from its shape as from the material with which it is made.

HISTORY AND SIGNIFICANT EXAMPLES

In nature dome structures are found in birds' eggs, clam shells, and the seeds of the sweet gum tree (Fig. 17-3). Kitchen cups, bowls, water tanks, and radar domes (Fig. 17-4) are non-building examples of dome structures. Domes have a long history in buildings; however, it was during the Roman Empire that domes were perfected. The Pantheon in Rome was erected in about 120 A.D. Constructed in concrete, it is a hemispherical shape with a span and height of over 140 feet. In what is now Istanbul the great dome of Hagia Sophia was constructed in about 335 A.D (Fig. 17-5). It was constructed of hollow clay tiles to lighten the weight of this shallow dome, and its considerable lateral thrust is buttressed by *hemi-domes* (half domes) and adjacent building masses. The lost technology of dome structures was rediscovered by Brunelleschi in his famous dome in Florence, Italy, in 1420 (Fig. 17-6). In 1590, Michelangelo and others placed the great dome at Saint Peters in Rome. Great domes like that of Saint Paul in London by Sir Christopher Wren stretch down to the current day (Fig. 17-7). The most profound recent development in dome evolution is the geodesic dome by Buckminster Fuller (Fletcher 1975).

Figure 17-2
The shape of a dome is defined by rotating an arch.

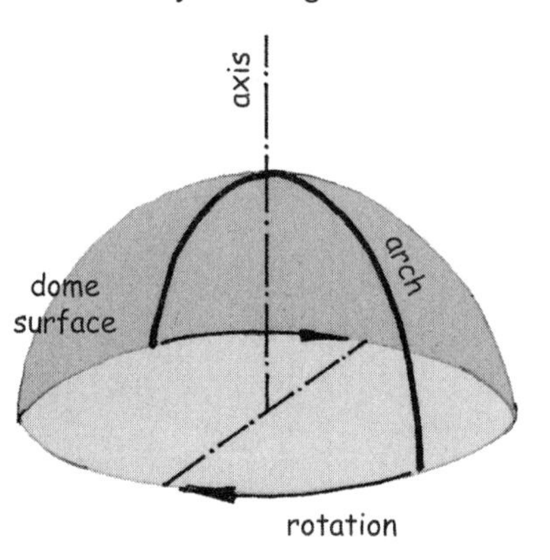

Figure 17-3
Seed from the sweet gum tree.

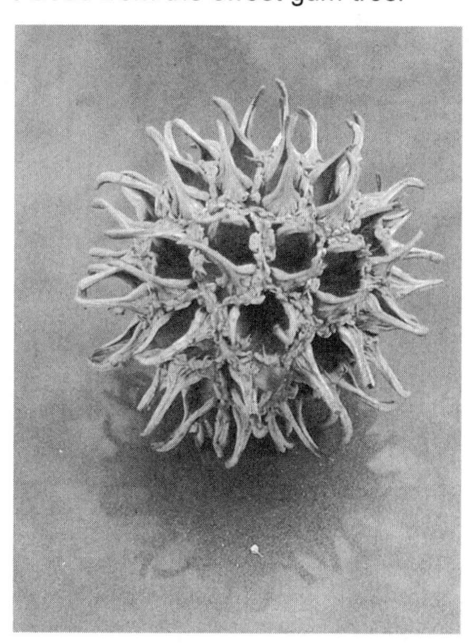

Figure 17-4
Typical dome for a weather radar.

Figure 17-5
Dome from Hagia Sophia in Istanbul in Turkey.

Figure 17-6
Dome of the Florence cathedral in Italy.

Figure 17-7
St. Paul's cathedral in London.

NOMENCLATURE

Smooth domes: A dome is a *rotational surface* about a vertical *axis*. Domes provide a column free area below known as its *span*. The *rise* of the dome is the distance from its *spring line* to its *apex*. If the smooth dome is made of masonry much of the nomenclature of arches is reapplied. Individual stones are known as *voussoirs*. This inside surface of the dome is known as its *intrados* and the outside surface is known as the *extrados*. Vertical joints between voussoirs are called *meridial joints*, and the horizontal joints are known as *hoop joints* (Fig. 17-8).

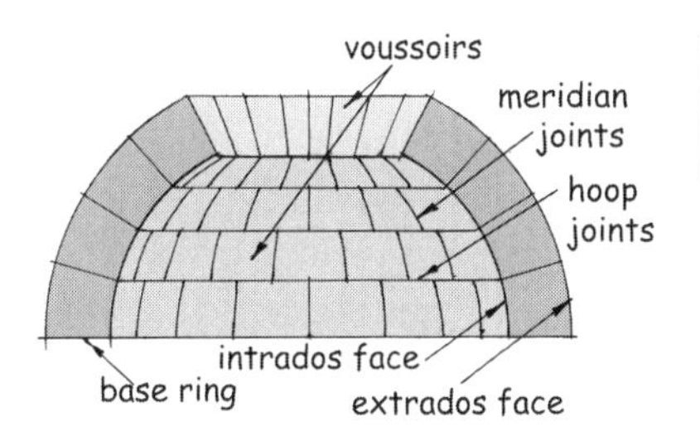

Figure 17-8
Smooth dome nomenclature.

Figure 17-9
Radial dome nomenclature.

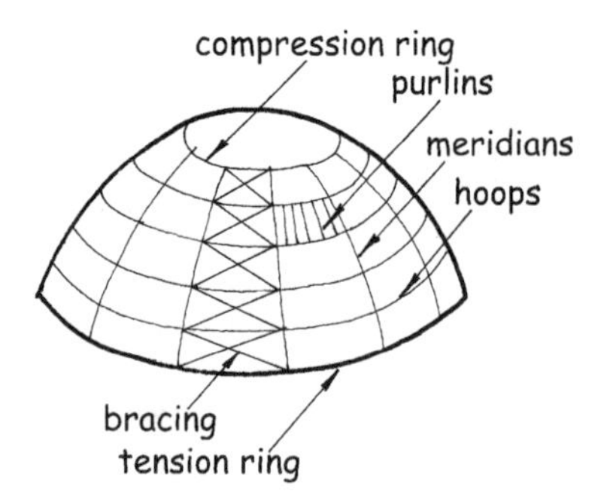

Radial domes: Radial arches with a shared apex of a dome are known as *meridians*. Horizontal *hoops* stabilize these meridians, and share loads with them. The meridians, and sometimes the hoops, may be thickened and raised above the smooth dome surface to form *ribs*. A stiff *tension ring* is needed at the base of such domes to prevent lateral spreading. A *compression ring* at the top of the dome may provide an opportunity for an opening known as an *oculus*, or may be filled in solidly. Sometimes a *cupola* is placed over an oculus opening (Fig. 17-9).

Geodesic domes: A *geodesic* dome is essentially a space frame formed of nearly equal length members, and curved into the shape of a dome (Fig. 17-10). A *great circle* is formed by cutting a sphere at any angle through its center (Fig. 17-11). An infinite number of great circles can be cut in this way. A great circle can be cut into an infinite number of straight line segments forming *polygons*. This is known as its *frequency* (Fig. 17-12). Notice that an *insphere,* an *intersphere,* and a *circumsphere* can be defined in this process. Great circles can be cut such that the pattern of their intersections form triangles and other *polyhedrons* (i.e., hexagons, etc.) on the face of a sphere. This triangulation produces structural rigidity similar to that of trusses and space frames. It is useful to make all of the members forming this lattice the same length for ease in manufacturing and assembly. Only a limited number of polyhedra can achieve this end. For very large geodesic domes this single thin

Figure 17-10
Example of a geodesic dome at the St. Louis botanic garden.

lattice is vulnerable to out of plane bending due to applied loads normal to the dome surface (also known as *snap through*). Development of a space frame between the insphere and the circumsphere gives the depth necessary to overcome this vulnerability (Pugh 1976).

Figure 17-11
Great circles.

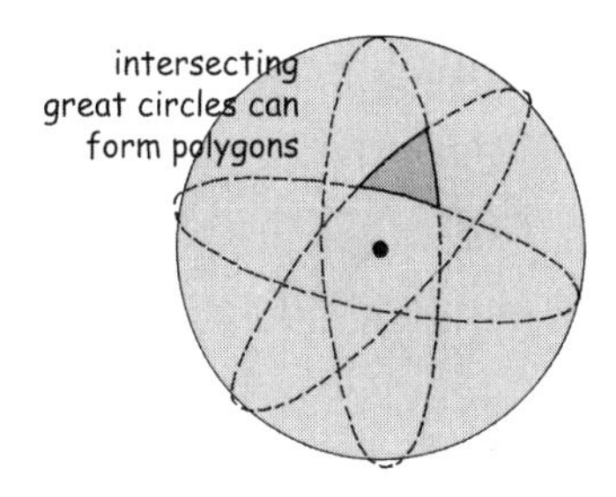

TYPES OR CATEGORIES

Masonry: Stone, brick, and hollow clay blocks have been the most widely used material in the construction of domes. Both *smooth and ribbed domes* have been made from masonry. The great challenge of these domes is in the calculation of the size and slope of the face cuts needed for each stone in the dome. In today's market few designers and masons have an appetite for this task; therefore, much of this knowledge has been lost to practitioners. Certainly the computer will greatly assist any architect that courageously decides to revive this long tradition. Tension at the base and in the lower portion of the dome is not well addressed by masonry as a material. It is therefore traditional to place a steel tension ring at the base of a masonry dome.

Timber: In the "onion" domes of Byzantine architecture from Constantinople to Moscow, tension was introduced into its meridians. Masonry does not want to be placed in tension, and timber was widely available in the Russian forest. So these domes often have an elaborate internal wooden framework in order to achieve their extraordinary external form (Fig. 17-13).

Reinforced concrete: Both smooth and ribbed domes are currently built in concrete. Some require considerable thickness, but the more funicular their form, the more *thin shell* concrete becomes appropriate (Fig. 17-14).

Metal: Iron, steel, and aluminum domes are assembled from prefabricated pieces into configurations such as the Schwedler, lattice, parallel lamella, and the hexagonal systems (Fig. 17-15). Metal members may also be assembled into *radial trusses* or *radial triangulated arch*es (Fig. 17-16). As previously described geodesic domes are also built from lattice of metal members. Kaiser geodesic domes make use of a folded plate skin instead of a member type space frame (Fig. 17-17).

Figure 17-12
Polyhedrons of different frequency can be superimposed on a great circle.

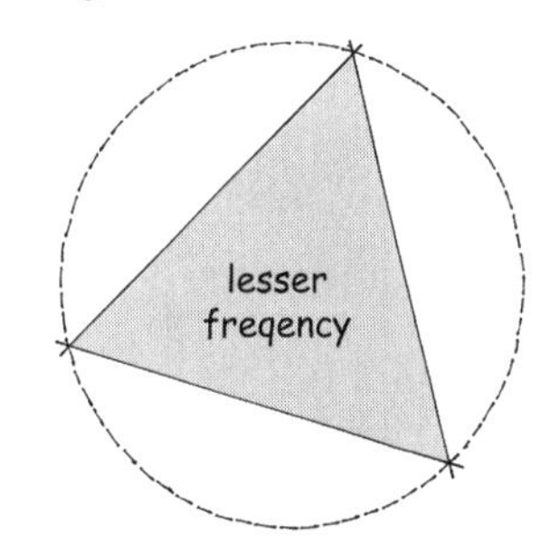

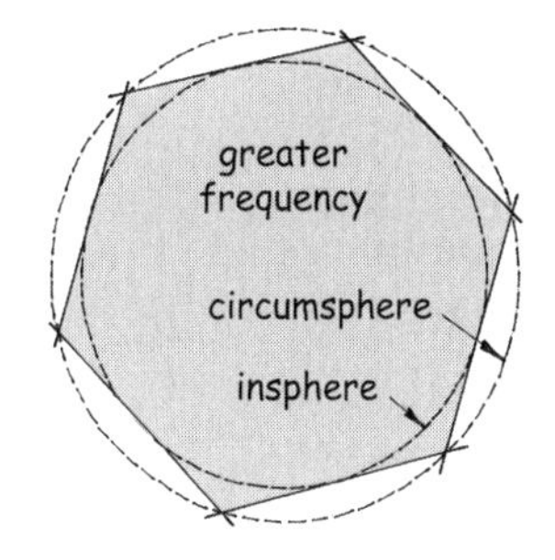

COMMON APPLICATIONS

Domes have been used primarily for religious and government buildings. Since domes yield a curved surface, they are inherently inappropriate as a flooring system. Unless they are very shallow in rise, domes produce very large, and often unused overhead space. This may be desirable when the space below is filled with a large crowd of occupants, or where a sense of grandeur is sought; however, this additional volume of enclosed space will also increase

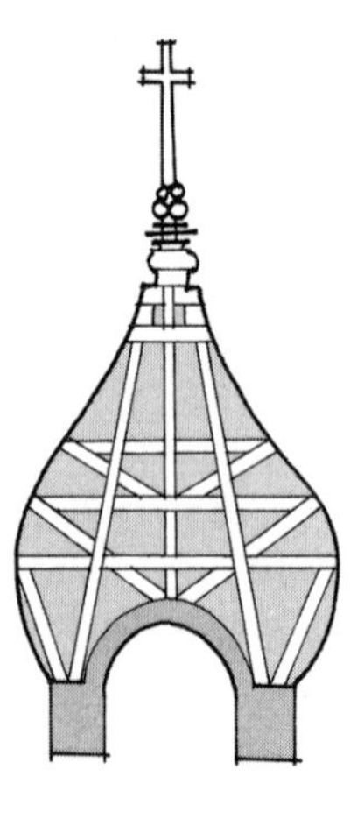

Figure 17-13
Internal timber frame in a Byzantine dome.

Figure 17-14
Funicular thin shell dome in Oklahoma City by Bruce Goff.

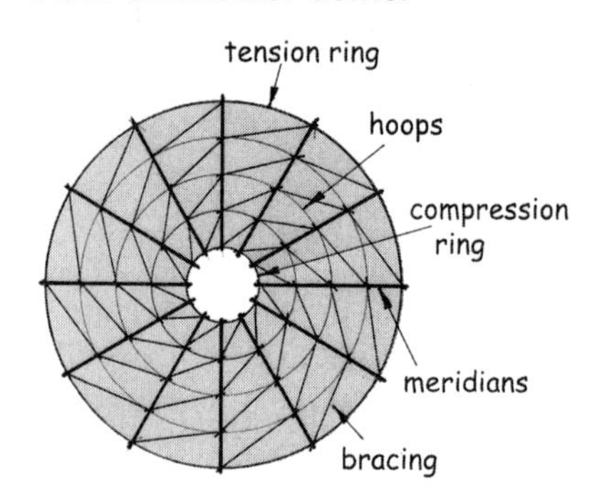

Figure 17-15
Notice the diagonal bracing in this Schwedler dome.

heating costs. In very hot dry climates, heat will rise into this overhead volume of space away from the occupants below. This accounts, in part, for the wide use of domes in mosques in the deserts of the Middle East.

BEHAVIOR UNDER LOAD

Load propagation

Ribbed domes: Vertical loads are carried down to the foundation by the meridians very much as in an arch. By shearing action in the plane of the dome loads can also be distributed to adjacent meridians, and hence across the surface of

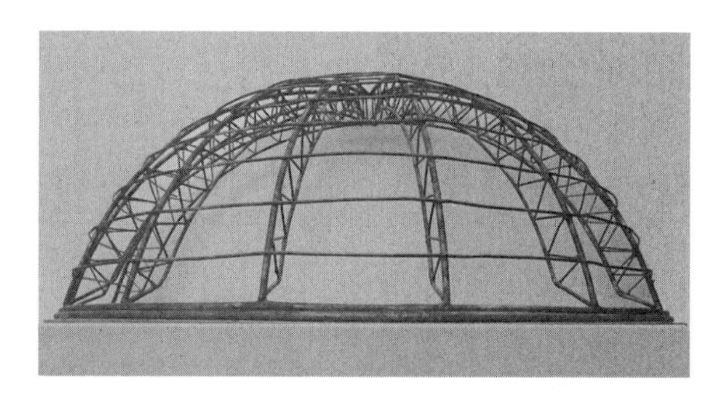

Figure 17-16
Trussed meridians in a student model.

Figure 17-17
The Kaiser geodesic dome has a structural skin.

the dome in *membrane action* (Fig. 17-18). The reader will recall that arches have strong lateral thrust at the base, and this also occurs with the meridians in a dome; however, this tendency is restrained by horizontal hoops acting as tension rings in the lower portion of the dome. This tension, or spreading tendency, is greatest at the base of the dome (Fig. 17-19). In the upper portion of the dome these same horizontal hoops act as compression rings. To visually confirm this shift from tension to compress, cut an orange in half. Carefully remove the eatable portion leaving the hemisphere of skin intact. Set the hemispherical skin on the floor and step on it. Notice that the skin will tear at the base due to tension and the skin will buckle at the apex due to compression. Since the compression in these hoops is balanced in all directions at the top of the dome, a void (oculus) can be left to let in natural light, and to lighten the weight of the dome. When this is done, thickening of the compression ring around the oculus will be needed. Similarly, thickening at the base tension ring is also appropriate.

Smooth domes: Thickened meridians have been employed in part to overcome buckling in the dome surface; however, smooth domes are quite common.

Figure 17-18
In-plane shear yields membrane action.

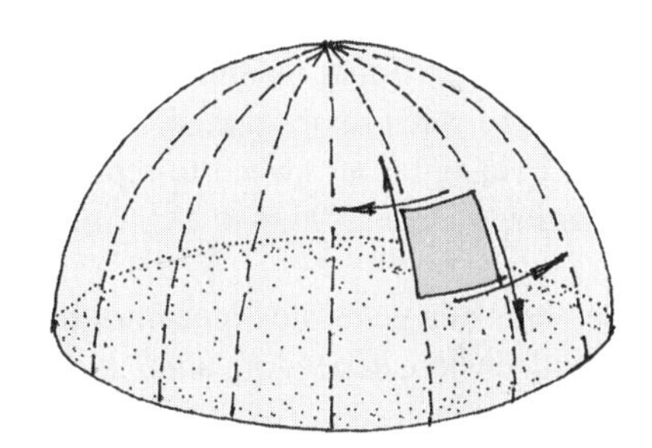

Figure 17-19
Like arches the dome wants to spread at the base due to lateral thrust.

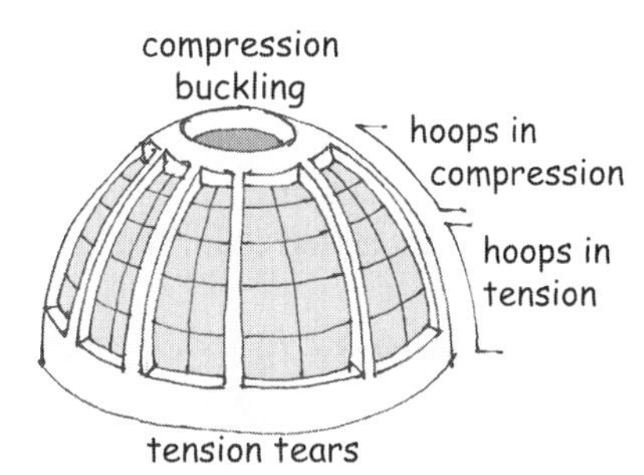

If properly designed, the skin of such domes can be quite thin. In many cases the thickness is governed more by adequate fire and weathering concrete cover for the encased reinforcing steel, than the structural stress. Smooth domes as thin as three inches have been constructed. In a smooth dome any point in the dome is simultaneously acting as meridian, hoop, and in-fill shear panel.

Geodesic domes: Geodesic domes do not respond as individual members, but rather as a global system. If one member is pushed inward, the total dome will contract. If wind suction pulls outward on one member, the total geodesic system expands. Geodesic domes act in the same manner as tensegrity structures found in the chapter on space frames. Because of their minimal use of material, the dead load of a geodesic dome is very light indeed.

Stresses

Meridians: Like arches simple compression is sought in meridians. Bending perpendicular to the meridian is unwanted. Because of their potential slenderness, meridians are vulnerable to in-plane buckling similar to buckling in a column. As compressive loads increase at the base of a dome, meridians often respond with increased thickness as they approach the base ring. Domes expand and contract with temperature. This can lead to edge disturbances and edge fatigue at the base of a dome. Applied loads can also produce similar disturbances but are usually less significant than those produced by thermal expansion and contraction. These disturbances are quickly spread across the dome by membrane action, but a bit of local stiffening and thickening may be appropriate at the base of the dome to avoid local flexure (Shodek 1980).

Hoops: As discussed above, hoops in the upper portion of the dome are in compression, and those in the lower part of the dome are in tension. Bending of hoops is possible due to external loads normal to the dome surface; however, meridians jointly share resistance to bending loads exerted on the hoops.

Dome surface: The skin of a dome can resist in-plane shear in a manner similar to vaults (Fig. 17-20). This allows loads in any direction to be transferred between meridians and hoops. It also allows loads to be spread across the broad surface of the dome. The distribution of loads across a broad surface is known as membrane action. Low rise domes have more lateral thrust than those with a higher rise. Column-like buckling in the plane of a thin skin dome becomes a greater threat in low rise domes due to increased in-plane compressive stress. In reticulated domes (those fabricated from small individual members), stress resistant in-fill shear panels may not be present between hoops and meridians (i.e., Schwedler dome). In this case diagonal bracing is introduced to replace shear resistant action of infill panels (Salvadori and Heller 1963).

Geodesic members: In general the metal members of a geodesic dome must be capable of resisting both axial compression and tension, depending upon internal and external global loading of the dome.

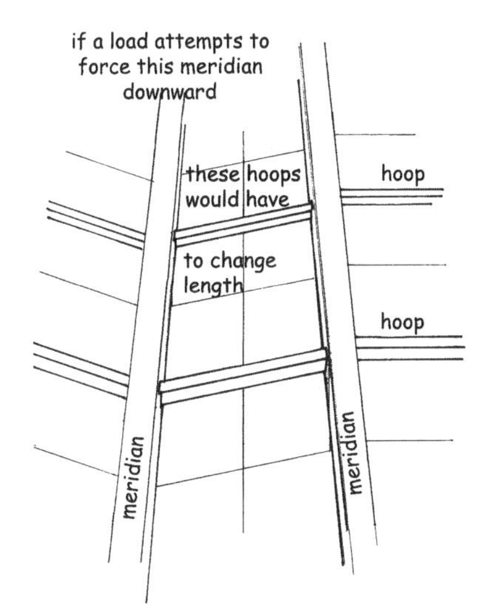

Figure 17-20
Shearing action in the dome surface.

Failures

Most dome failures happen during earthquakes or unanticipated loading. Unequal buttressing and any discontinuity in the dome surface have often been the starting point for such failures. Domes are normally quite rigid. Like arches they are vulnerable to differential settlement of its foundations. One of the unique failures which threaten domes is “snap through”. Imagine cutting a hollow rubber ball in half. Rest the resulting hemisphere on a table and press downward on it with the tip of your finger. The “dome” will locally deflect because of its vulnerability to point loads normal to its surface. Gradually the local failure increases, and then suddenly globally “snaps through”. Shortening the radius of curvature, thickening the dome surface, and assuring that the dome is both continuous and isotropic will increase its resistance to snap through (Levy and Salvadori).

OPTIMUM CONFIGURATION

Radial domes: In the absence of hoops, the optimum shape for a meridian dome is parabolic with meridians that increase in thickness as they descend onto a stiff thickened tension ring at the base (Fig. 17-1). Understand that when glazing fills the area between meridians, each meridian must act alone since adequate shear action cannot be developed between meridians. Therefore arch rules of thumb for proportioning members might be applied initially.

Ribbed domes: If both radial meridians and horizontal hoops are thickened, loads can be shared between them. A wide range of dome shapes can be utilized beginning with hemispherical and extending to elliptical and tapered domes (Fig. 17-21). Metal domes of this type have a depth to span ratio of about 1:5 to 1:8.

Figure 17-21
Dome with parabolic meridians.

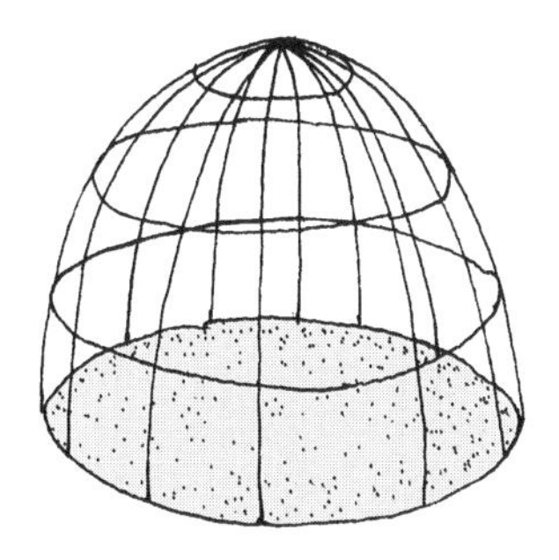

Smooth domes: Without thickened meridians and ribs, the optimum smooth dome is parabolic under its own weight (Fig. 17-14). The thickness of smooth shell domes is dependent upon the radius of curvature of the surface, and the type of material to be used. The preliminary design span of masonry domes ranges from 30 to 140 feet, the rise from 18 to 105 feet, and the average thickness is around 24 inches. Similarly, the preliminary design span of concrete domes is about 40 to 240 feet, the approximate rise is 5 to 42 feet, and the estimated thickness is from $2^1/_2$ to $5^1/_2$ inches (Corkill, Puderbaugh, and Sawyers 1974).

Reticulated domes: Radial curved trusses can be formed into dome-like configurations. To the extent that they retain only trussing action, truss rules of thumb might be used in early preliminary design. That would suggest preliminary design spans from 60 to 180, and a rise of about 6 to 25 feet (Fig. 17-22) (Schodek, 1992). If radial built-up triangulated steel arches are used to form true meridians, their preliminary design depth may be revised to 1/100 of the span (Tang, 1978). Lattice type steel domes have a preliminary design span up to several hundred feet. The rise of such lattice domes is in the range of 1/5 to 1/8 of the span, while the individual member lengths usually range from 15 to 25 feet (Semour Howard within Callender 1974).

Geodesic domes: The ideal form for a geodesic dome is a completed sphere. When a lesser portion of the dome is needed, the bottom edge will not be flat, making the bottom joint to the foundation problematic. The best way to enter a geodesic is under that bottom edge (Fig. 17-23). If the geodesic rests directly on an earthen berm, such entry is made easy. Window openings are not rectangular, but can easily be made between structural members in the dome. Stresses surface folded plate geodesics made by Kaiser Aluminum have the same geometry as space frame geodesics, but simultaneously perform both the envelope and structural role. For preliminary design estimates of individual members, lengths range from 1/25 to 1/30 of the total dome span. The space truss depth is about 1/100 of the dome span, and the range of rise is about 1/2 to 1/5 of the span (Tang 1978).

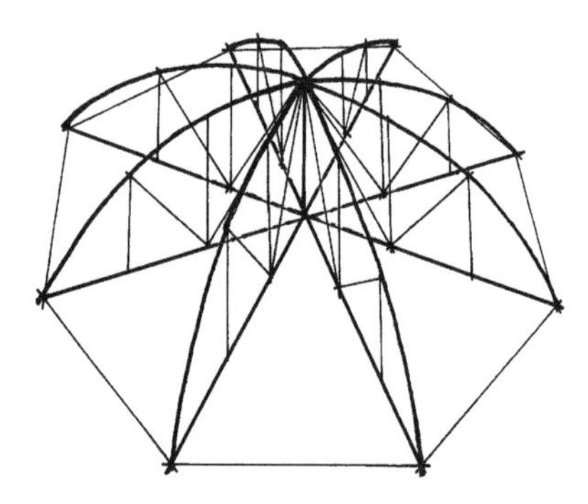

Figure 17-22

Radial bowstring trusses look, and to a certain extent can act like domes.

Figure 17-23
Irregular edge at the bottom of a geodesic dome.

Members: Meridians would theoretically be larger at the base than at the apex since the loads are greater at the base. However, for ease in fabrication uniform size meridian members are sometimes used, particularly in smaller span domes and where labor is the governing cost factor.

Related lateral support: The dome structure is inherently form stabilized against lateral loads. Only when it is resting on some other structure below (i.e., a series of columns) does lateral support become a significant concern.

Related soil and foundation: Domes are a long span system, and invite a single soil condition under the total dome. Differential soil conditions are unwelcome. The radius of a dome is usually significantly reduced when located on steep hill side slopes instead of level ground. Geodesic domes are light and will tolerate a range of foundation alternatives. Concrete and masonry domes are heavy and may invite a ring-shaped grade beam with drilled piers, particularly if clay soils are encountered.

Related envelope: Historically masonry domes have often been covered by lead plates such as at Saint Mark's cathedral in Venice (Fig. 17-24). The state capital dome in Denver, Colorado, was even covered in gold leaf. Once the role of meridians and hoops are understood, domes may even be in filled with glass between the structural members. However, openings have traditionally been placed in the *drum* directly below the tension ring of a dome, in an oculus at the apex of the dome, or in a cupola sitting over the oculus. If properly conceived the dome can perform both the structural and envelope functions simultaneously (Fig. 17-25). Concrete can be impervious to weather if properly designed and executed, but may also require an additional waterproof surface.

Figure 17-24
Notice the finished surface of St. Mark's cathedral.

Figure 17-25
Dome where the structure provides its own weather-proofing surface if the climate is right.

FUNCTIONAL FOOTPRINT

Domes normally cover either round or elliptical footprints. Occasionally a series of small domes may be aggregated together to cover a footprint of a different shape. Many mosques in the Middle East cluster several smaller domes over a rectangular footprint.

PATTERN OF GROWTH

Domes are one of the structural forms least capable of further growth. Clam shells grow by adding subsequent layers; however, this metaphor has not been applied successfully in architecture. Expansion of a dome is therefore not normally attempted; rather an adjacent building is normally added. One unexplored growth possibility for domes is to excavate additional subterranean floors below a dome roof.

DESIGN

Modeling: Scale models are perhaps the best way to study the proportions of a dome. Recall that Sir Christopher Wren constructed three superimposed domes at Saint Paul's Cathedral in London. One dome was designed to look right with the outside massing of the building, under it there was one for structural necessity, and under that one for interior appeal. Models of domes can be made by building a form in Styrofoam or clay, then using the precoated plaster cloth used by doctors to make casts for broken bones. An alternative method is discussed in the next chapter on shells. If a more refined model is needed and the technology is available, heat or vacuum forming of plastic can yield elegant results.

Aesthetic potential: Like other shell structures, domes gain much on their exterior appeal from the play of light on their sculptural form. As with Saint Peters in Rome, many designers have chosen to stress the meridians because it further emphasizes the sculptural form of the dome. The contemporary dome on the Reichstag in Berlin by Foster (Fig. 17-26) takes the opposite approach by

Figure 17-26
Hoops are strongly expressed in this photo montage of the Reichstag dome in Berlin by Norman Foster.

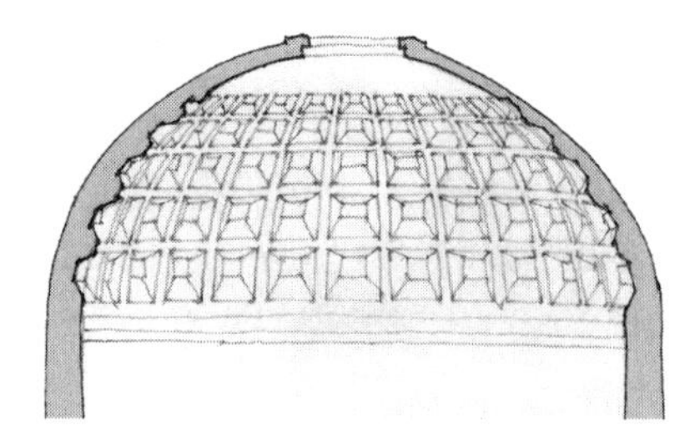

Figure 17-27
Coffers can lighten the weight of a dome.

emphasizing hoops. In part such meridian and hoop divisions are also intended to give some scale and surface pattern to the most massive of these long span structures. If an opaque dome is not penetrated by an oculus, a cupola, or windows it remains an ambiguous formless dark void. Once appropriate day lighting has been introduced, the dome's intrados may be ornamented or coffered. Coffers not only add interest to the inner surface of the dome, they also lighten the physical weight of the dome as in the Pantheon in Rome (Fig. 17-27).

CONSTRUCTION

Elements of steel and aluminum domes are fabricated in an industrial setting and delivered to the building site. Individual members or panels are then lifted by heavy equipment of assembly in place in the air. Extensive scaffolding is needed for this approach (Fig. 17-28). The huge dome at Shah Alam, Malaysia, is the largest religious domed building in the world. This aluminum dome was fully assembled on ground, and jacked up into its final position

Figure 17-28
Oklahoma State Capital dome under construction.

Figure 17-29

Base ring of the aluminum dome at Shah Alam Malaysia.

(Fig. 17-29). Smaller masonry domes have traditionally made use of wood or metal centering, but Brunelleschi's dome in Florence proves that completed hoops make such centering unnecessary.

Vocabulary		
Schwedler dome	Edge fatigue	Snap through
Meridian	Hoop	In-plane buckling
Tension ring	Compression ring	Oculus
Cupola	Coffer	Ribbed dome
Smooth dome	Geodesic dome	Great circle
Frequency	Insphere	Circumsphere

REVIEW QUESTIONS

1. In what ways does a dome behave like an arch?
2. What is the structural purpose of a hoop?
3. Briefly describe how in-plane shear develops in a dome.
4. Why is buckling a special threat in low-rise, thin shell domes?
5. Briefly describe the structural behavior of a geodesic dome.
6. Why is the closure of a hoop important in the erection of a masonry dome?
7. What are the best places to locate windows in a dome?
8. What are the aesthetic opportunities and problems of a dome?

Figure 18-1
Opera House in Sydney Australia.

18 Shells

BACKGROUND

In the last few chapters folded plates, vaults, and domes have been discussed. They are all technically shells. We have treated them separately because the unfolding of their structural behavior is easier to understand in this sequence, and because each one of these is often treated as a separate type of structure in the marketplace. In this chapter only antisynclastic shells (the last remaining member of the shell family) will be addressed. Before we begin, let's take a moment to summarize all the types of shells.

Figure 18-2
Folded plate type shell.

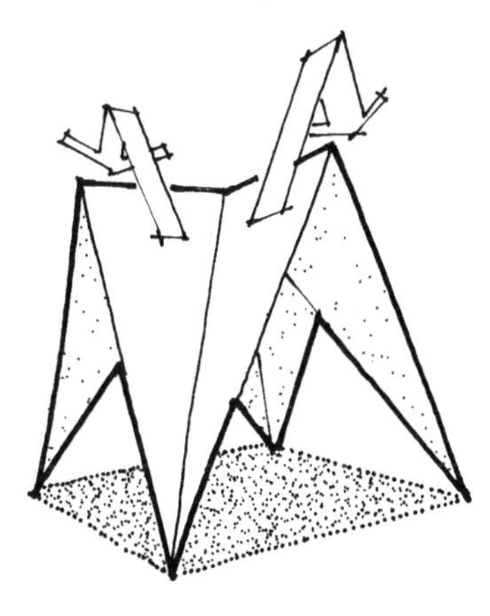

TYPES AND CATEGORIES

Shell type structures can be divided into four general subtypes by configuration:

1. *Folded plate shells* (or prismatic shells) are formed by folding or joining a series of flat surfaces. Like Japanese origami, a wide range of polyhedrons may be formed. This type of shell was discussed in Chapter 15 (Fig. 18-2).
2. *Singly curved shells* are formed by curving instead of folding a flat plate (Fig. 18-3). Further, this type of shell is curved in only one direction. The most common example of this type of shell is the vault. However, north light shells (Fig. 18-4), butterfly shells (Fig. 18-5), funnels (Fig. 18-6), cones (Fig. 18-7), and undulating, flat corrugated shells (Fig. 18-8) are all singly curved shells. Vaults were covered in Chapter 16.
3. *Synclastic shells* are doubly curved, but are curved in the same direction. The most common example of this system is a dome (Fig. 18-9). However, a torus (Fig. 18-10), spherical shells (Fig. 18-11), and elliptical parabaloids (Fig. 18-12), also belong to this group. Domes were covered in Chapter 17.

Figure 18-3
Singly curved shell.

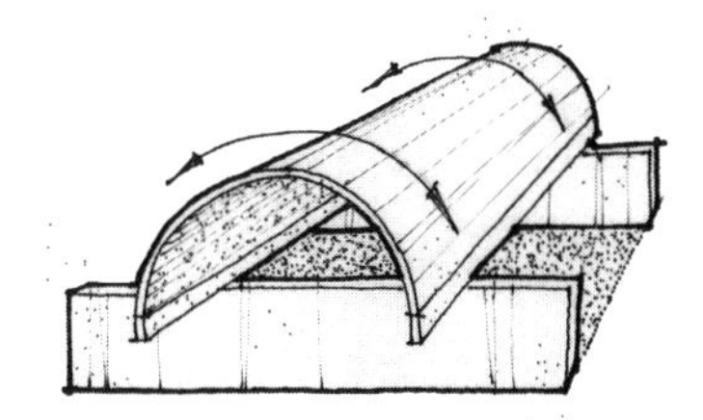

Figure 18-4
North light shell.

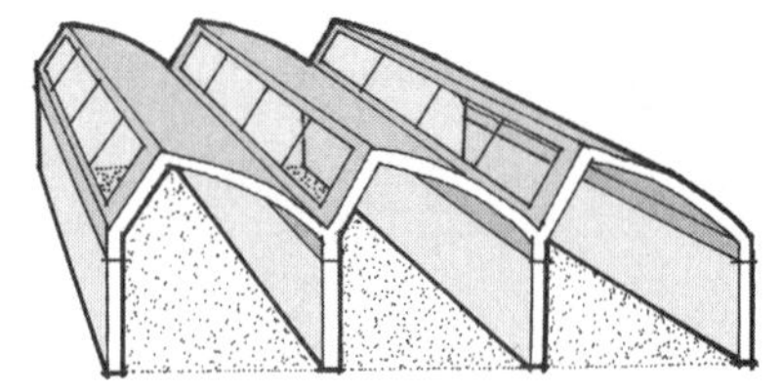

Figure 18-5
Butterfly shell.

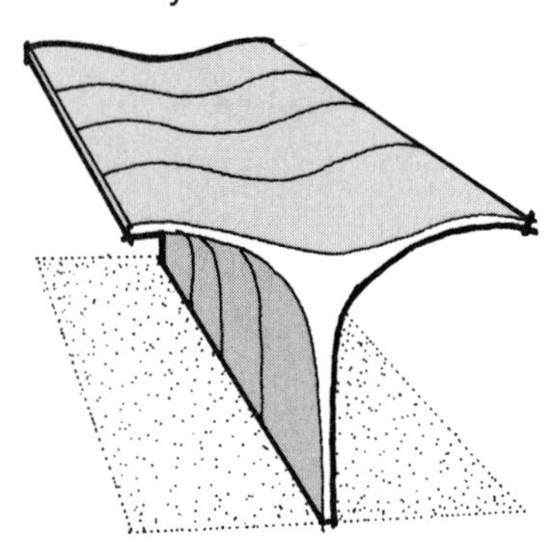

Figure 18-6
Funnel shell water tower in Santa Cruz Bolivia.

Figure 18-7
The members in this cone at a German bank are sufficiently dense & rigidly connected to act as a shell.

Figure 18-8
Undulating shell at Le Cite de Sciences in Paris by Bernard Tschumi.

4. *Antisynclastic shells* are also doubly curved; however, the two curves bend in opposite directions. Typical examples of antisynclastic shells are hyperbolic parabaloids (Fig. 18-13), conoids (Fig. 18-14), and hyperbaloids (Fig. 18-15). Antisynclastic shells are the focus of this chapter. They are incorrectly, but commonly, just called shells. We will do so in this chapter for the sake of brevity (Butler 1998).

Shells may also be categorized by thickness. Antisynclastic shells that are addressed in this chapter are usually only a few inches thick. These are known as *thin shell* structures and are made of reinforced concrete. Only a limited number of forms can be made into thin shells. There are shells which are very

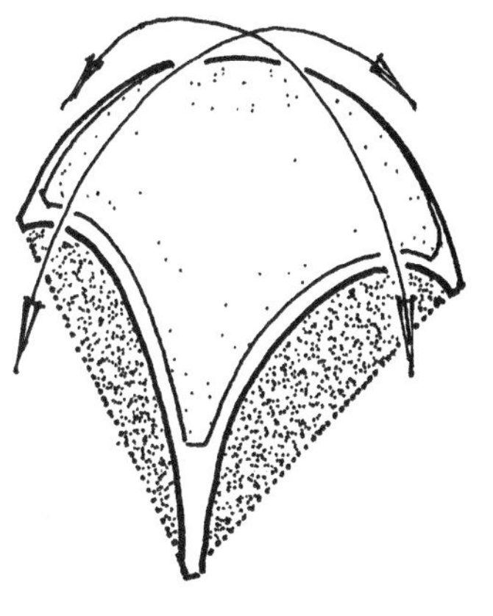

Figure 18-9
A typical synclastic shell.

Figure 18-11
Spherical shells like Le Geode at the Villette in Paris.

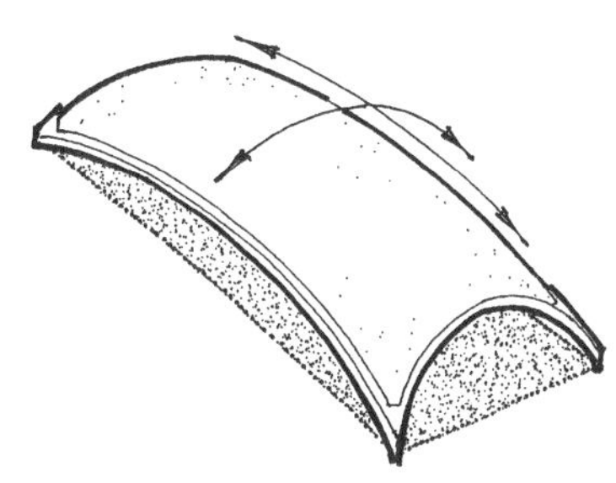

Figure 18-10
Torus.

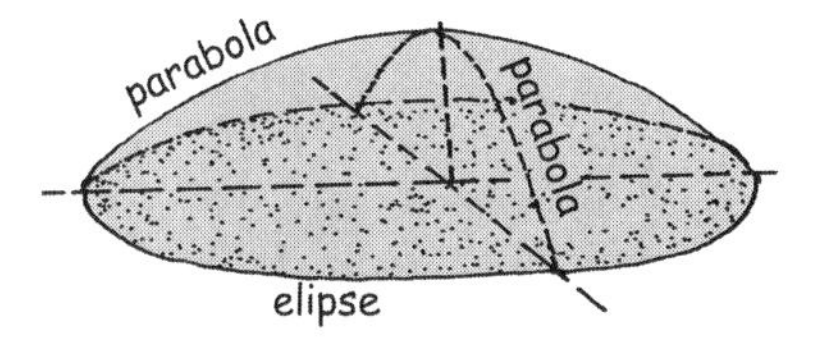

Figure 18-12
Elliptical parabaloid.

Figure 18-13
Hyperbolic parabaloid.

Figure 18-14
Conoid.

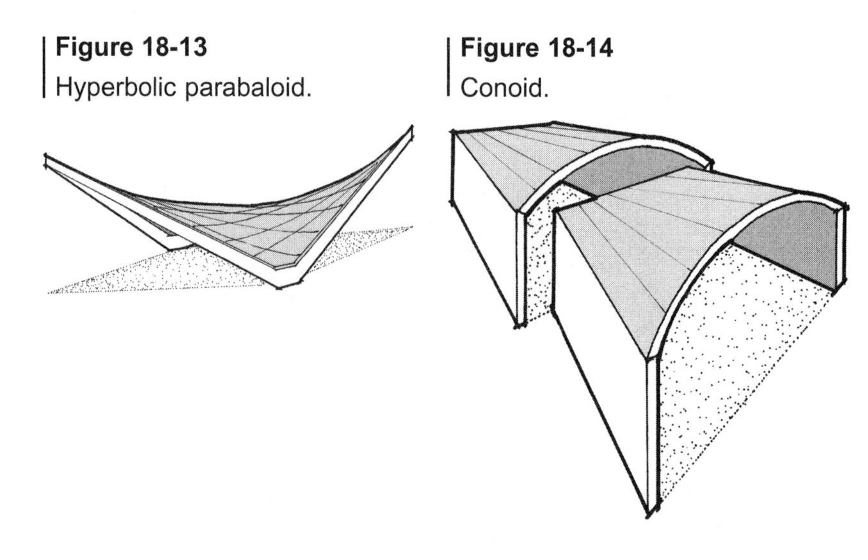

thick indeed. A good example is the TWA terminal in New York by Eero Saarinen. While it is also constructed in reinforced concrete, it is several feet thick at some points (Fig. 18-16).

As each one of the above types of shell structures behaves in a complex and significantly different manner, separate chapters have been given to them, but it must be stressed that they all technically belong to the same structural family. Now let's focus our attention on antisynclastic shells, known by the "street name", "shells", which we will use in this chapter.

Figure 18-15
Hyperbaloid.

Figure 18-16
TWA air terminal in New York by Eero Saarinen.

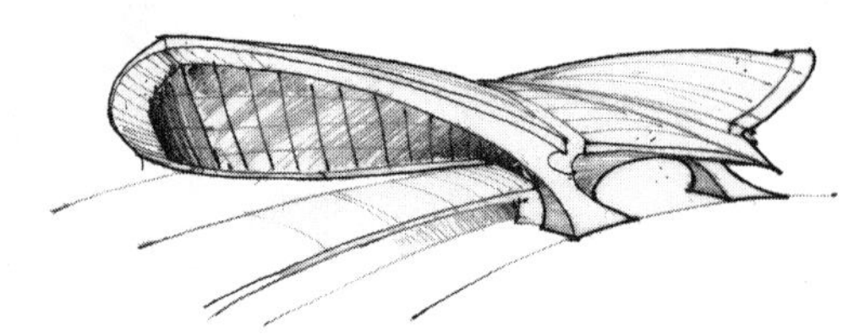

HISTORY

While folded plates, vaults, and domes have ancient origins, antisynclastic shells are relatively new creations. The evolution of thin shell concrete structures of this type offers considerable strength, impressive spans, considerable economy in material, and highly dramatic visual appeal. Pier Luigi Nervi, Eugene Freyssinet, Robert Maillart, and Eduardo Torroja have been pioneers in the development of these innovative forms. Perhaps its foremost developer, Felix Candela, recognized that shells gain their ability to resist loads primarily from their shape, not their thickness. With this insight he fabricated many of the world's greatest examples of thin shell structures in Mexico beginning in the early 1950s.

EXAMPLES

Examples in nature

Egg shells, sea shells, and nut shells are naturally occurring members of the larger shell family; however, the wings of birds in flight and manta rays in the ocean are closer to antisynclastic forms. Unfortunately their internal stresses are not. To find similar internal stress we must look to dried and warped leaves.

Nonbuilding examples

Double curvature appears in boat and aircraft propellers, some kayak paddles, and the streamlined cowling of some vehicles such as those found on some motorcycles. But the closest non-building example of an antisynclastic shell is a potato chip. In fact, many nonprofessionals refer to antisynclastic structures as "potato chip" buildings.

Building examples

The May D and F Building in Denver by I.M. Pei (Fig. 18-17), Los Manantiales Restaurant at Xochimilco, Mexico by architect: Juaquin Alverez Ordonez, and

Figure 18-17
May D&F Building in Denver by I.M. Pei (courtesy of Terry Patterson).

the Church of Our Miraculous Lady in Mexico City by Felix Candela are well-known examples of thin shell antisynclastic buildings. Mark and Milo Ketchum's website offers perhaps the most authoritative source of all types of shell structures. The Ketchum family has had national stature as structural engineers for three generations.

NOMENCLATURE

Only the nomenclature of antisynclastic shells will be cited here. The nomenclature of other types of shells has been described in the chapters on folded plate, vaults, and domes. The hyperbolic paraboloid (also called a *hypar* or "monkey saddle") is the most fundamental antisynclastic form, so it has been used as the basis for nomenclature at this point (Fig. 18-18).

As a compass is used in drafting a flat circle, all of the curves used in three dimensionally warped surfaces must have their *radius of curvature* identified. More than one radius of curvature will be present in an antisynclastic shell. A line may be drawn vertically or "normal" to the surface of the shell. Antisynclastic shells curve in opposite directions along two axes. The two main curves are defined by *lines of principle curvature*. The rest of the shell surface accomplishes the transition between these lines. Downward curves are considered *positive* curves, and upward curves are *negative*.

Developable and non-developable surfaces: Some shell surfaces are *developable*. They may be flattened out without doing violence to the surface of the curve. Vaults have a developable surface. Other shells such as domes are *non-developable*. They may not be flattened without violence to the shell. Think of the difficulty encountered when a cartographer attempts to draw a flat world map to replace a spherical globe. Antisynclastic shells must flatten out, or assume *zero curvature*, in accomplishing the transition between principle curves (Salvadori and Heller 1963).

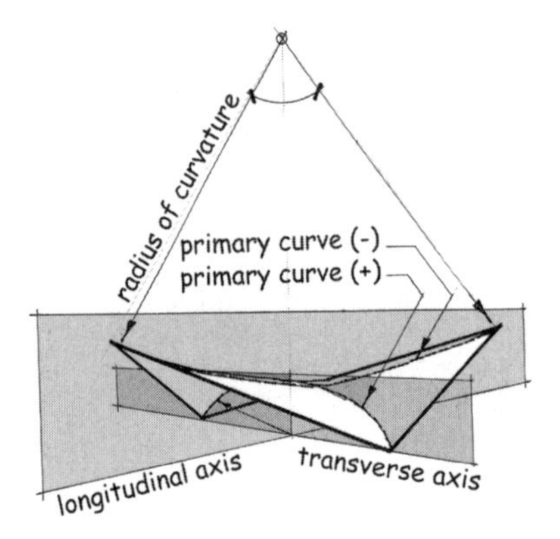

Figure 18-18
Shell nomenclature.

COMMON APPLICATIONS

Buildings that do not require interior walls to separate internal building functions are best suited to antisynclastic shells. Since shells do not inherently yield a flat walking surface, they are inevitably favored for use as roofs, rather than floors. Furthermore roof mounting of heating, ventilating, and air-conditioning systems are not normally possible shell roof systems. With these factors in mind churches, restaurants, and exhibition halls are well suited to shell roofs. Rail stations, airport terminals, and bus stations have also made good use of shell roofs.

BEHAVIOR UNDER LOAD

General observation

Before beginning any detailed discussion, first observe that antisynclastic shells are warped slabs or plates. It is no surprise that slab action is involved. Antisynclastic shells are arched in opposing directions. It is no surprise that antisynclastic shells have arch action. Finally notice that they also look a bit like intersecting vaults except that they are curved in opposing directions. Therefore it is logical that behavior similar to vaults is also involved.

Stresses

Only a few generalizations are possible given the diversity of antisynclastic shapes. The funicular configuration of many shells is similar to that of tent-type structures, and yields *membrane action* in shells. While tents are kept in tension, membrane action in shells produces compression, tension, and shear. Shearing action causes in-plane stresses to be transmitted in more than one axis. Simply put, it disperses stress across the total surface. However, while thin shell structures can distribute loads across the total warped surface by membrane action, if compressive loads in the plane of their thin shell become excessive they can still buckle. The shell roof of the Sydney Opera House (Fig. 18-1) has additional stiffeners to overcome such buckling as the shells meet the foundation (Fig. 18-19). Application of point loads such as mechanical equipment is avoided on shell roofs because they cause out of plane bending, and stress concentrations that are unwelcome in membrane action. Holes in shells are avoided because they cause discontinuities in the dispersing of stress within the plane of the shell.

The location and type of support used profoundly alters the direction and type of stress that antisynclastic shells experience. Focus your attention on the outside edge of the example shown (Fig. 18-20). If this shell is supported by a central column, the outer edge goes into tension. If supported at the corners, it goes into compression. Antisynclastic shells come in considerable variety of shapes, so sweeping generalizations are difficult to make. Each must be individually analyzed for stresses, and supports types are certainly not interchangeable.

Figure 18-19
Local stiffening of the Sydney Opera House shell.

Load propagation

Eventually the stresses flow across the total surface of the shell to the edges. Like slabs, boundary stiffeners are often used at the edge. Boundary disturbances set up where the warped shell and the stiffeners meet. If multiple shells are joined stresses may either cancel each other, or amplify each other along

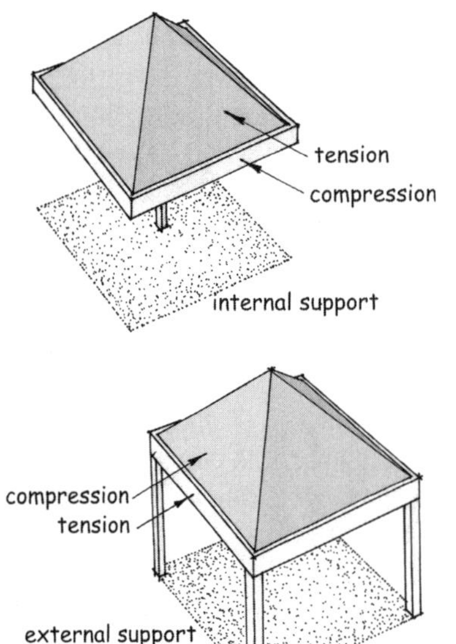

Figure 18-20
Location of support affects the character of stresses in a shell.

the joint between the two shells. A clear conceptual understanding of each specific interaction should be developed before further math analysis or aesthetic refinement proceeds.

Failures

The shrinkage that occurs in concrete as it cures can lead to cracking during fabrication of a shell. Like arches, care must be taken during the slow removal of formwork. Once a shell has cured and the forms successfully removed, thermal changes cause changes of size and shape, which must be considered. Many shells have a very limited number of supports. If one of these fails, global collapse of the total roof is inevitable.

OPTIMUM CONFIGURATION

Rise to span ratios are controlled in shells to avoid generation of excessive compressive stresses in the shell. As the ratio diminishes, lateral thrust increases, and so does compression in the shell surface. For preliminary estimates, the rise of a shell commonly ranges from 1/6 to 1/10 of the span. The thickness of an antisynclastic shell may vary from $1^1/_2$ to about 5 inches if it is rationally configured. If the shell is aesthetically conceived, the thickness can grow from inches to feet. The minimum thickness of thin shells is primarily necessary to provide fire cover for the steel reinforcing net within the shell. Remember that when two or more antisynclastic shells are joined on shared edges, forces are either cancelled or multiplied. Additional stiffening is usually necessary in the latter condition. Many shells are supported by edge stiffeners. The reader will recall that shells are warped flat plates, and that flat plates have edge rotation and edge disturbances (Tang 1978).

Shell roofs that are directly supported on point foundations must gain all of their lateral support from them. Shells that are elevated on columns are even more vulnerable. Even light thin reinforced concrete shells remain vulnerable to "hammer head" failures under seismic loading. If lateral loads are introduced, considerable moment can develop at the joints of shells and supporting columns. Many antisynclastic shells have only one vertical support (Fig. 18-21). Vertical and lateral movement must not occur at these foundations. Reliable geology and soil, as well as fairly massive foundations are typical to these structures. The lower the curvature of the shell, the greater the lateral thrust. A serious possibility of foundation rotation can be present in such configurations.

The curved edge of some small antisynclastic shell roofs can make glazing below them a difficult matter, often requiring specially fabricated windows. Very large shells have edges that will accommodate a more conventional "off-the-shelf" window or wall panel. Opaque wall panels are normally avoided under antisynclastic shells since the roof appears to be supported by a bearing wall if opaque panels are employed. This is a violation of the principle of

Figure 18-21
Umbrella type shells used inside a Paris rapid transit station.

structural integrity or truth. It also negates the impressive span that has been achieved at some risk and difficulty by the shell.

Functional footprint

For all of the sensuous space generated vertically by antisynclastic shells, most still cover a roughly rectangular footprint of some type. Free spans range from 50 to about 280 feet. The "monkey saddle" shell can cover a circular footprint.

Pattern of growth

Large single antisynclastic shells are essentially finite structural entities. They do not invite extension. It is possible to construct a series of separate but overlapping shells to extend existing interior space (Fig. 18-22). Some roofs are formed by joining multiple lesser shells along shared edges. These can easily be extended by simply adding more small shells (Fig. 18-23).

CONSTRUCTION

Little industrial fabrication is normally related to antisynclastic shells. In-situ reinforced concrete is the rule. Steel reinforcing mats and limited use of reinforcing bars are often all that can be factory fabricated. The concrete is also normally remotely mixed in batching plants. The resulting mix must be especially closely controlled due to the extreme thinness of most of these shells. The proper water content of the mix must be maintained while in route to the site, and while waiting to be placed at the site. The longer the route between

Figure 18-22

The shell overlapping in this building in Trevesio Italy illustrates the potential for growth.

Figure 18-23

Growth by shared edges.

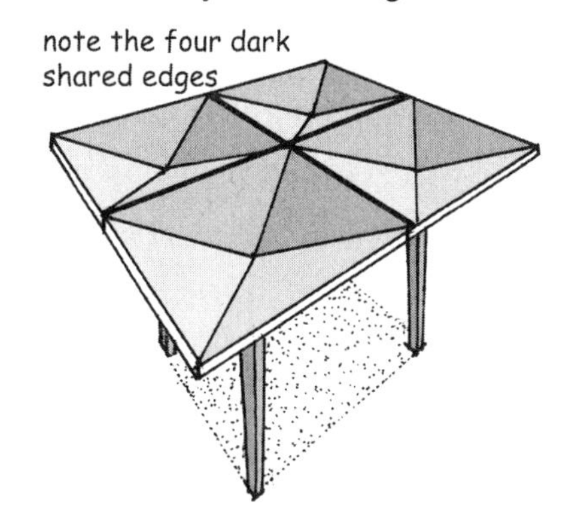

the batching plant and the construction site, and the longer the waiting time once at the site, the more severe the quality control problem. Shells are normally monolithic pours. That is, they are continuously poured until finished, without any "cold joints".

In thin shells it can be difficult to work the concrete mix around the reinforcing mats and to provide appropriate vibration. Four methods are used to form antisynclastics. The first method makes use of elaborate truss type wooden form work that is surfaced with wood sheathing. While antisynclastics do not appear so, they do contain straight lines (Fig. 18-24). Therefore, they can be formed using straight boards. In the second approach Felix Candela has successfully used earthen form work. Ground is shaped to the appropriate curvature, and then covered with a bond breaker such as Mylar plastic. Once the concrete is cured the earthen form is mined from under the structure. A third possibility is the use of a pneumatic form. This is essentially a balloon over which concrete is placed, and then the balloons are deflated. Both plastic foam and concrete have been sprayed in this way over pneumatic forms since the 1960s. Whatever formwork is used, concrete placement method varies with the slope of the shell. If the curvature is not overly steep, concrete may be pumped under pressure over the reinforcing mat and the single bottom form. At slopes over about 30 degrees concrete must be placed between two forms. Placement becomes much more difficult and cost significantly increases. One final method

Figure 18-24

Shopping center sign in thin shell configuration showing that it has straight lines.

Figure 18-25
Shell constructed over a reinforcing steel matrix.

is occasionally encountered. A steel reinforcing bar (rebar) matrix is first erected on the site. This method has been used more for synclastic shells, and yields very interesting buildings (Fig. 18-25). Mylar plastic sheets or fine wire meshes are then stretched over the rebar matrix. Plastic foam or concrete is shot under pressure against the rebar matrix with its Mylar backing. Once cured, the Mylar sheets are pulled off, and the matrix is sprayed from the opposite side of the rebar matrix. This fully encased the rebar matrix in plastic foam or concrete. In short, this is a method where the reinforcing becomes self-forming, which can offer significant cost reduction (Frolich 2002).

DESIGN

Some designers have avoided thin shell scale models because they require specific skills. In the past a clay mold was first formed, and then either paper mache or plaster cast cloth (obtained at medical supply stores,) was stretched over the clay mold. Now scale shell models can also be made by shaping two layers of aluminum or steel screen (Fig. 18-26). A Styrofoam form may assist in shaping the two layers of screen. If it is used, it should be covered with "shrink wrap". The two layers of screen are then sprayed with a commercially available surface such as "false marble paint". After several light coats have dried, the shell can be removed from the styrofoam form. Then the inside of the shell can be similarly sprayed. It is also possible to directly heat form plastic into a shell if it has a fairly shallow rise. Computer modeling and calculation have greatly simplified the process of designing antisynclastic shells.

the two screens are
joined by straight
pins

Figure 18-26
A partially completed shell model made of two screens.

Aesthetic potential

Sensuous flow of space and light provides the primary aesthetic potential of antisynclastic shells. Shell surfaces become the next focus of design concern for these structures. Any drawings and renders that are part of this process must adequately and correctly represent the space, light, and surface of these designs. For this reason graphite pencil has often been used to describe the design intentions of an architect for these buildings.

Vocabulary		
Antisynclastic	Singly curved shell	Doubly curved shell
Lines of principle curvature	Positive curvature	Negative curve
Developable	Non-developable	Radius of curvature
Edge disturbance	Membrane action	

REVIEW QUESTIONS

1. What are the four main types of shell structure?
2. Name three common types of antisynclastic shells.
3. What is a typical span range, and rise-to-span ratio range?
4. What methods are used to form shell type structures?
5. Briefly explain "membrane action."
6. Why is foundation movement a serious threat to thin antisynclastic shells.
7. Why is it unwise to perforate thin shell structures with holes?
8. What are the construction disadvantages of highly sloped antisynclastic shells?

Figure 19-1
Dynamic Earth Center in Edinburgh Scotland by Hopkins and Partners.

19 Tents

DESCRIPTION

A tent structure is a membrane placed into tension so that it may support external loads. These minimal surfaces are quite efficient and require much less material than most other systems. Since the membrane will not support bending like a beam and does not suffer buckling due to axial compression like a column, these systems are quite light. In fact the pseudohyphen struts that carry tents are often equal in weight to the total membrane being supported. While pneumatics (discussed in the next chapter) place a membrane under tension by internal air pressure, tents are supported by rigid members such as struts, guying, and arches. The reader will recall that cable systems also rely on tension; however, they concentrate loads along thin lines, while tents spread tension across a broad surface.

HISTORY AND SIGNIFICANT EXAMPLES

Nomadic people have made use of tents for thousands of years (Fig. 19-2). This is a tribute to the light weight of this structural system, and to its efficient use of limited materials. About 2000 years ago the Coliseum in Rome was believed to have been covered by a moveable fabric tent using technology that was developed for ships' sails. More recently larger tents have been used to shelter exhibitions such as the circus. But serious use in architecture really begins to emerge with the work of Frei Otto and others in the wake of World War II. Otto systematically searched for architecture that used a minimum of material. Using soap bubble models in a very rational and thorough approach, he opened architecture to the use of both tents and pneumatics (Fig. 19-3).

In nature tree leaves, the webbed feet on frogs, and the wings of bats all resemble tents. Non-building uses of tent-type structure includes hammocks, fishing

Figure 19-2
Native American tepee.

Figure 19-3
Soap bubble modeling was used by Frei Otto.

nets, kites, sails, hang gliders, trampolines, and umbrellas (Fig. 19-4). Some of the best known architecture with tent structure includes the Munich Olympic stadium and halls by Frei Otto and others (Fig. 19-5), the Dynamic Earth Center in Edinburgh by Michael Hopkins and Partners (Fig. 19-1), and Canada Place constructed for the 1986 Expo in Vancouver, Canada (Fig. 19-6).

Figure 19-4
An umbrella is a very simple form of tent structure.

Figure 19-5
Munich Olympic Stadium by Frei Otto and others.

Figure 19-6
Tents are perfect for temporary buildings like those found at the Vancouver Expo.

TYPES OR CATEGORIES

By tightness of weave: Tents may either be made of fabric membrane, or be a surface formed by a cable net. *Fabric membranes* simultaneously provide both the structure and waterproofing envelope, but can only span a limited distance of perhaps 150 feet. *Cable nets* can only provide structural support, but they can cover very large spans up to several hundred feet.

By stressing mechanism: There are basically two types of tents based upon the nature of their internal stresses. *Sagged cable nets or membranes* are stretched only by their own weight. A hammock belongs to this group. *Prestressed cable nets or membranes* are purposely stretched into tension prior to being asked to resist external loads such as snow and wind. An umbrella belongs to this group.

By proportion: Tension structures can generally be divided into three groups based upon their dimensional relationships. *Linear* systems include cable structures discussed in an earlier chapter on cable structures. These may be strengthened by prestressing, or acquire "funicular" shape by sagging (Fig. 19-7). *Surface membranes or nets* can be subdivided into several subgroups. Flat membranes/nets may rest in any position (horizontal, vertical, or inclined). They may also assume all the same shapes as the shells discussed in the previous chapter, specifically singly curved, synclastic, and antisynclastic configurations (Fig. 19-8). Both shells and tents make use of stressed surfaces to achieve these shapes; however, shells experience in-plane compression and shear, while tents experience only in-plane tension. *Space structures* are three-dimensional structures that include pneumatics (to be discussed in next chapter), and tents with two or more membranes (Fig. 19-9).

Figure 19-7
A hammock is actually a sag type tent structure.

Figure 19-8
Different types of single membrane tents.

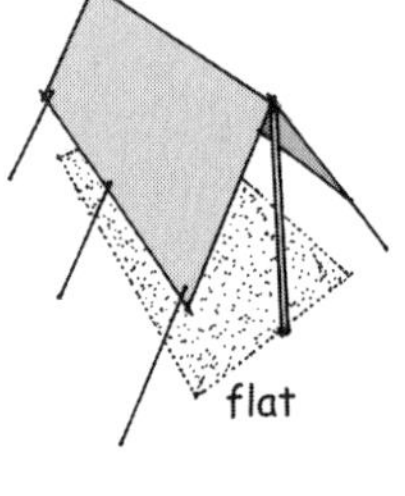
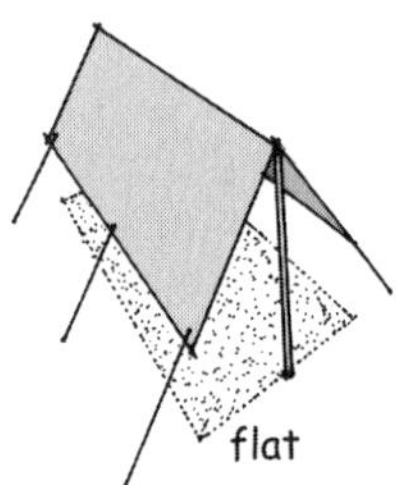

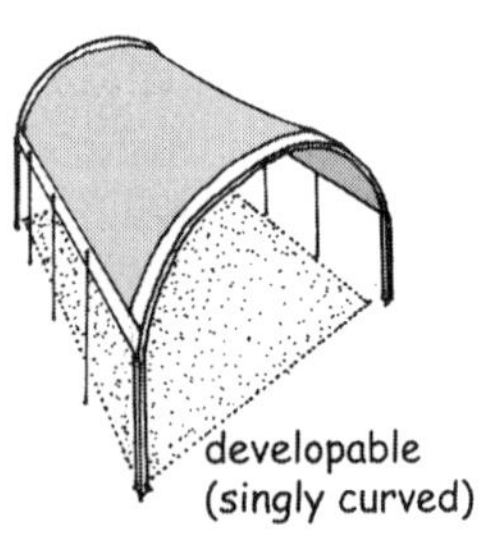

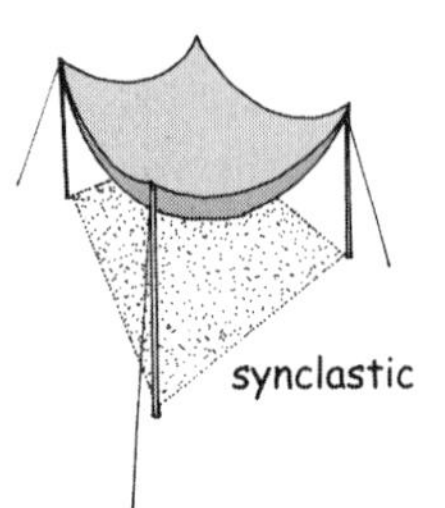

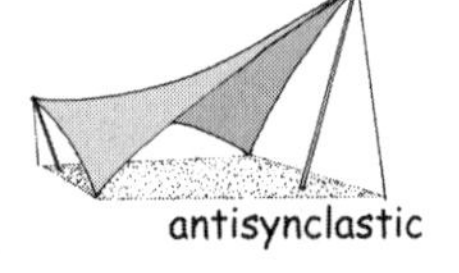

By configuration: Whether cable net or membrane, Frei Otto has divided tents into a series of groups based upon their shape and/or support methods. These classifications include: anticlastic or "saddle shaped" (Fig. 19-10), undulating (Fig. 19.11), arch supported (Fig. 19-12), and humped (Fig. 19-13) (Roland 1970).

NOMENCLATURE

Not surprisingly much of the nomenclature for tents such as "masts" and "booms" comes from the rigging on sailing ships (Fig. 19-14).

Figure 19-9
Model of a multiple membrane space structure tent.

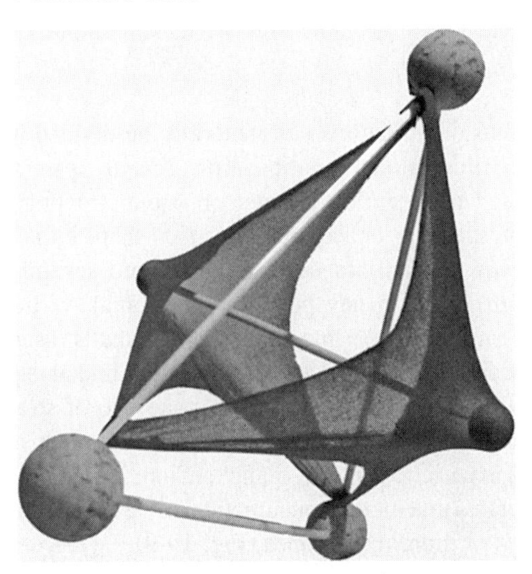

Figure 19-10
Saddle shaped tent.

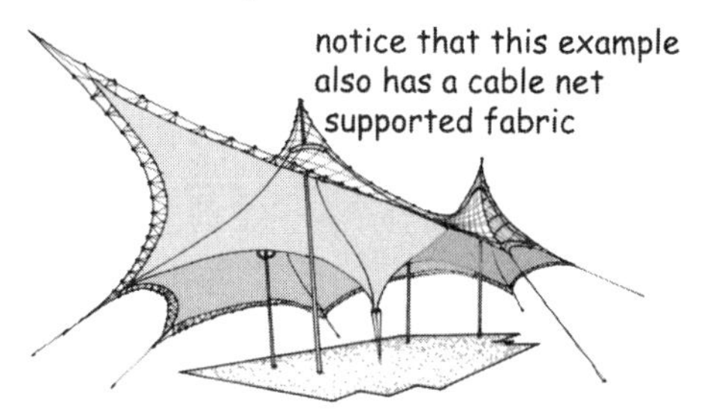
notice that this example
also has a cable net
supported fabric

Figure 19-11
Undulating tent.

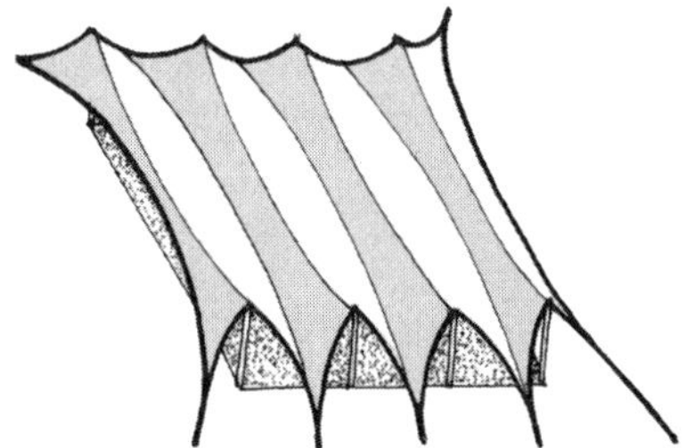

COMMON APPLICATIONS

Tents still see wide use as a temporary structure for exhibitions, markets, and shelters in parks (Fig. 19-15); however, they are also used for more permanent structures such as airport terminals, museums, and even laboratories. They are not normally used for buildings of more than one floor, since by their nature they cannot form a conventional floor system. Tent membranes are difficult to insulate, so they are more widely used in areas with a moderate climate. Being light weight, they are an excellent structural choice for seismically active areas. Indeed, following most earthquakes survivors move into tents away from heavier compressive buildings (Fig. 19-16). Later these same survivors inexplicably reconstruct heavy compressive buildings (similar to the ones that have just collapsed), and happily move back in to await the next earthquake. Tents are significantly less appropriate in areas where high winds are a regular occurrence. Their weight and configuration is suspiciously similar to that of kites.

Figure 19-12
Arch supported tent in Cologne Germany.

Figure 19-13
Humped tents like the new Denver Airport.

Figure 19-14
Tent nomenclature.

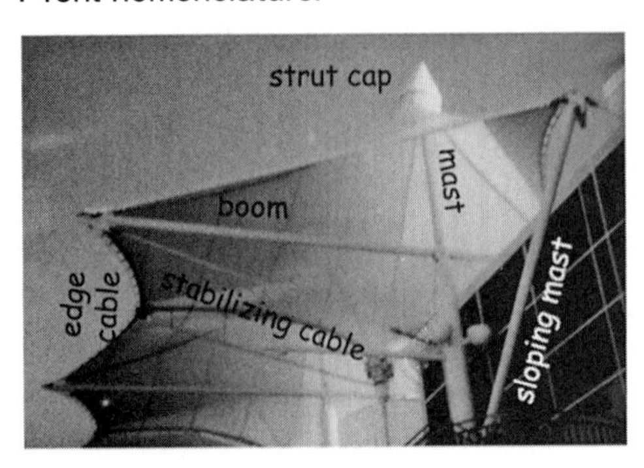

Figure 19-15
Small band shelter in a public park in Norman Oklahoma.

BEHAVIOR UNDER LOAD

Load propagation: The diversity of tent forms is so great that it is not possible to fully explore their structural behavior in this introductory text; however, the basics of all tent systems can be adequately introduced using only the anti-synclastic membrane or net as a vehicle. Begin with two cables intersecting at right angles. Let's call these two cables *primary axes*. The ends of one cable pull downward, while the ends of the other cable pull upward (Fig. 19-18). This simple two cable system has been prestressed by the pull at all four ends. The point of intersection of the two cables will not move if the pulls up and down, left and right, in and out are all equal. It is static. If this prestressing is adequate, additional external loads may be applied to this system without a profound change in the system's shape. The more flat the intersection of these two cables become, the less this is true. Downward snow loads are borne by the upward bending cable (or *carrying axis*). Wind suction upward is resisted

Figure 19-16
Tents used as temporary shelter in a park in Kobe Japan following a particularly destructive earthquake.

by the downward pulling cable (or *stabilizing axis*). This *antisynclastic action* is at work simultaneously at every point in a saddle-shaped tent (Fig. 19-17). If slackness is developed at any point in the membrane due to either the applied loads or inadequate prestressing, then undesirable wrinkles and *oscillation* can develop in the tent. This oscillation or "flutter" will be quite familiar to campers caught in their tent during a storm (Roland 1970).

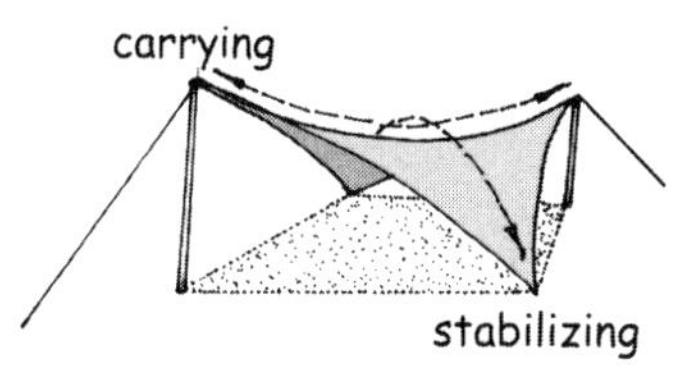

Figure 19-17
Primary axes of a tent.

Stresses: A short radius of curvature (Fig. 19-19) along the two primary axes is desirable. The tighter this curvature, the more stable the membrane, and the less stress induced in the membrane. Minimum membrane surface can be found by soap bubble modeling in the tradition of Frei Otto. Short tight radii also limit the extent of flat surfaces developed, which limits opportunities for *perched* snow and rain that may gather in small depressions in any flat surface. Membrane structures do not welcome point loads. Humped membranes may be thrust upward on struts or pulled downward by guys or tie downs. In either case, undesirable stresses are concentrated in small areas of the membrane. Some mechanism to spread these stress concentrations across a broader surface of the membrane is needed. Edge cables (Fig. 19-20), cable loops (Fig. 19-21), rigid and semirigid rings (Fig. 19-22), strut caps (Fig. 19-23), and buttons (Fig. 19-24) can be employed toward this end (Roland 1970).

Figure 19-18
Anticlastic action can be seen in the crossing of these two cables.

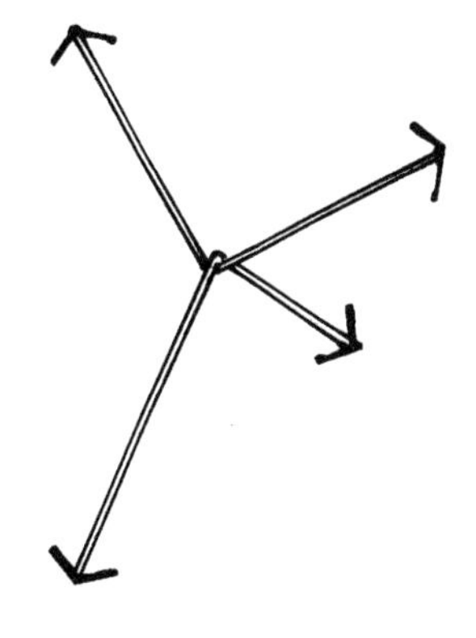

Failures: Wind uplift is a primary threat to tent structures, particularly when the skirt, or area under the outer edges, is not fully enclosed. In such circumstances not only does wind suction exist above the tent (similar to the lift on an airplane wing), but also wind can get under the canopy and uplift the very light tent membrane (Fig. 19-25). Tents will generally fair well if loads can be evenly distributed across the total membrane; however, stress concentration can lead to strength failures, particularly at seams. The more flat the membrane, the greater pre-stressing forces must be. This leaves less residual strength in the tent fabric to be used to support any additional applied loads. Therefore strong short radius curves are preferred along the primary axes of membranes. It is also the reason that longer spans cannot be simple membranes, since current fabrics simply do not have sufficient inherent tensile strength. Wind oscillations of a tent structure tend to amplify with longer durations, and can also produce impact loads when the canopy "pops" with sudden wind gust reversals. Perhaps you have seen a kite destroyed in this way.

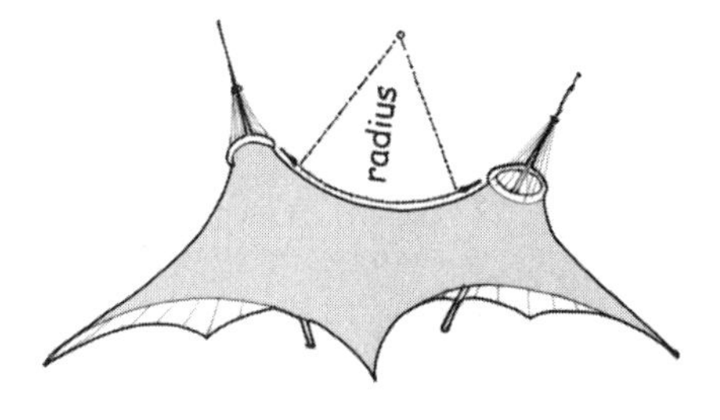

Figure 19-19
Radius of curvature in a tent.

Figure 19-20
Edge cables on a membrane tent at the Lyon airport.

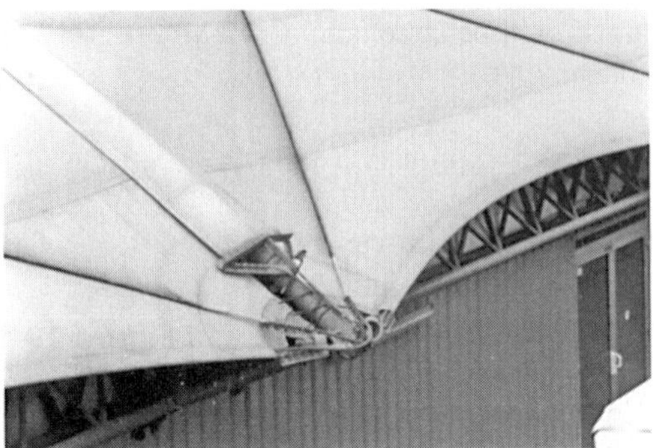

Figure 19-21
Cable loops at the Munich olympic stadium.

Figure 19-22
Rigid ring and laces in the fabric of the Munich olympic swimming hall.

Figure 19-23
Tent model using strut caps to avoid stress concentrations.

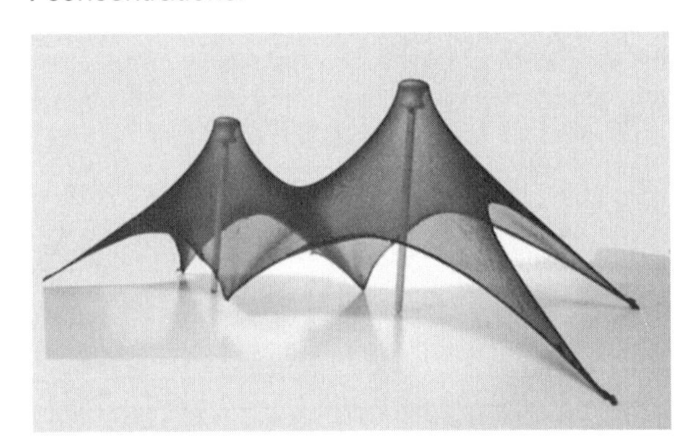

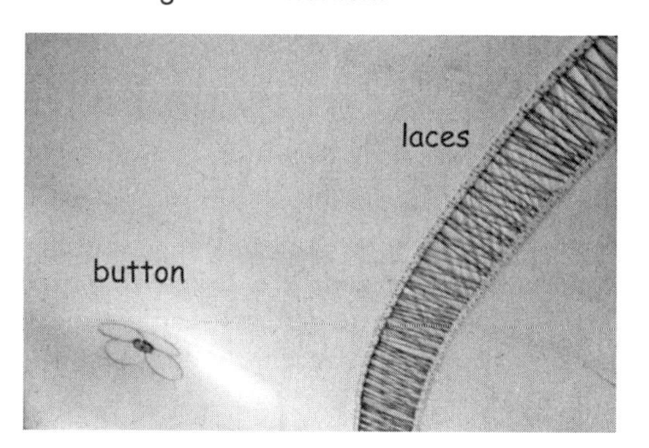

Figure 19-24
Button and laces in the Olympic swimming hall in Munich.

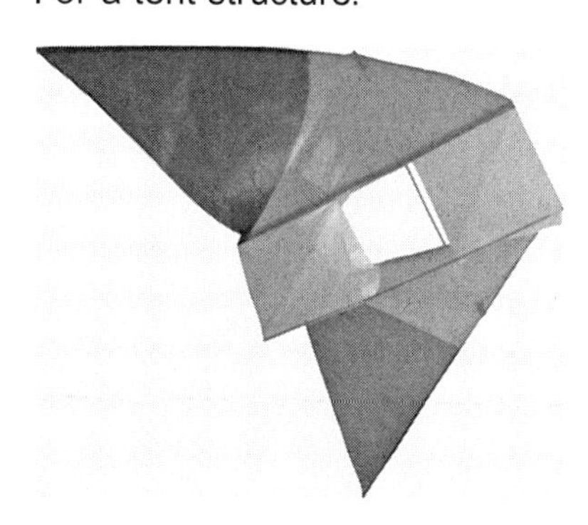

Figure 19-25
A kite is also a very light form of a tent structure.

OPTIMUM CONFIGURATION

System: Tents are used to span from a few feet to several hundred feet. The depth of tents ranges from about 1/2 to 1/5 of the span. Thickness with respect to span is negligible. (Tang 1978) antisynclastic tents should be given a short radius of curvature in both of its principle axes, maintain equal stress throughout the net or membrane, and use the minimum amount of material. Unfortunately to maintain such curvature for a large span tent may require excessive head space. It may be more economical to group several smaller, but very strongly curved, membranes together (Fig. 19-26). Arch support tents may provoke a similar concern, but undulating membranes and multiple-strut hump tents do not suffer from the head space problem. If additional height for rain drainage is needed at mid span in a tent, and an additional vertical strut will interrupt the function below (i.e., a skating rink), a flying strut can be introduced (Fig. 19-27).

Members: Fabric membranes will normally be cut into unusual shapes such as "fish belly" and tapered panels. Cable nets may also be divided into panels of unusual shape for ease in transportation to the site. Membrane panels are jointed by seams with interlocking rolls, and then glued and/or stitched. These multiple layers provide additional strength. As these thickened seams converge on the apexes and valleys in humped membranes they indirectly strengthen the

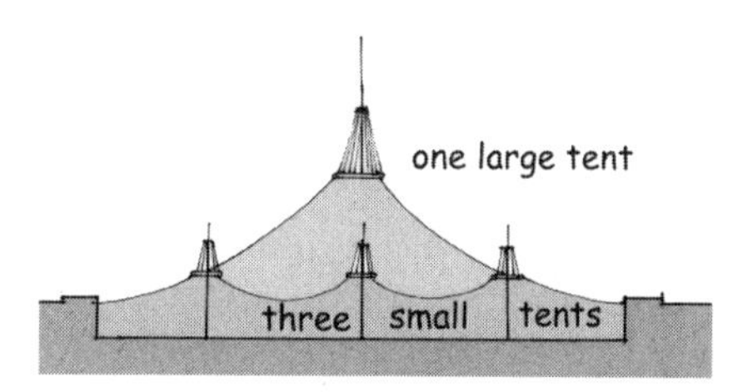

Figure 19-26
Grouping small tents to reduce head space.

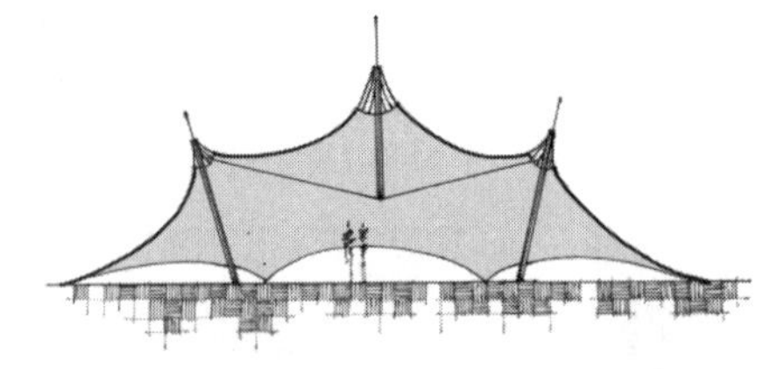

Figure 19-27
Use of a flying strut.

membrane against the stresses concentrated at those points. *Cable nets* normally contain joints that can rotate. This allows the net to be a *developable surface*. Like the chain mail armor of a medieval knight, a developable cable net may be laid flat on the floor, then assume an extraordinary shape when put into service. Cables are often doubled for ease in attaching adjacent panels together (Drew 1976) (Fig. 19-28).

Joints: Cable joints for an individual tent structure require considerable study, and adequate time and budget must be set aside to that end. Much insight can be drawn from what is already known from the rigging on sailing ships, suspension bridges, construction cranes, and the like. Common concerns include the complexity of joining multiple cables at unusual angles, removal of rain drainage from any low point in structural joints, and control of material stresses resulting from applied loading. Full scale mockups (Fig. 19-29) of such joints will ease construction problems, and facilitate lab testing. Considerable "tuning" or adjustment will be necessary in tent structures in order to achieve proper prestressing, adequate weather enclosure, and to provide necessary construction tolerances. To obtain these results membranes often contain laces (Fig. 19-30), turnbuckles, and threaded end adjustment devices (Fig. 19-31). As a long span

Figure 19-28
Details of the cable net at the Munich Olympic Stadium.

Figure 19-29
Full scale mockup.

Figure 19-30
Fish belly membrane panels with laces between at the Munich olympic swimming hall.

Figure 19-31
Example of cable adjustment devices.

Figure 19-32
Cast concrete weights may be lifted in sequence as stresses in the tent increase.

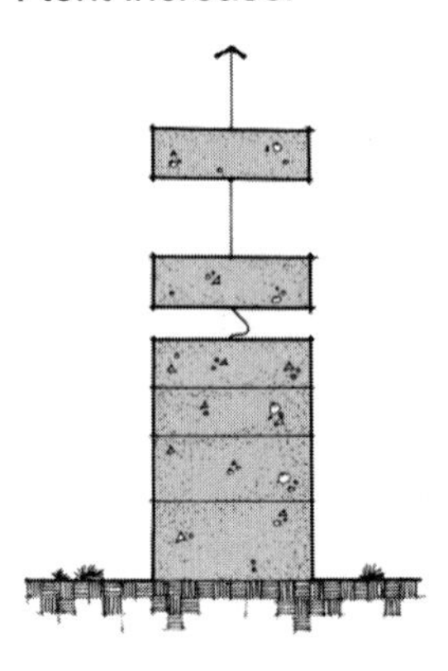

structure, thermal expansion and contraction can produce unacceptable variation in stresses in a cable net. Sometimes a tent can simply change its shape or curvature to accommodate changes in loading, but it is also possible to overcome these variations by replacing rigid tie-down connections with cast concrete weights at the ends of the cables (Fig. 19-32). As stress increases more of the blocks are lifted allowing the stress in the cable to be controlled within an acceptable range.

Related lateral support: Most tent structures are stabilized against lateral loads such as wind by external guying. These guys are often necessary to prestress the tent membrane anyway, and can do double duty as the favored means to retain lateral stability. The reader will recall that lateral stability has special importance for arches. If an arch is used as a rigid support under a tent structure, the tent membrane will inherently supply continuous lateral support for the arch against out-of-plane bending or rotations (Fig. 19-33).

Related soil and foundation: Conventional gravity foundations resist the downward thrust of compression structures resting on the soil. Conversely, tents pull upward and at an angle. This calls for unusual foundation configurations. Temporary tents may either use heavy weights at the ground surface, some type of driven pile, or an auger. More permanent tents use a buried "dead man" type foundation (Fig. 19-34), or a buried canopy similar to a sea anchor. In rock several types of expansion bolts are normally used.

Related envelope: Fabric tents form their own weatherproof envelope, but cable nets do not. The envelope for a cable net may either take the form of infill panels within the net (Fig 19-35), or a separate fabric membrane may either overlay, or be suspended below, a cable net. When either a membrane or cable net roof requires an enclosing wall below, serious design conflicts emerge. Several concepts and varied details have been used at this joint between roof and wall. The

Figure 19-33
Arch that has been tent stabilized.

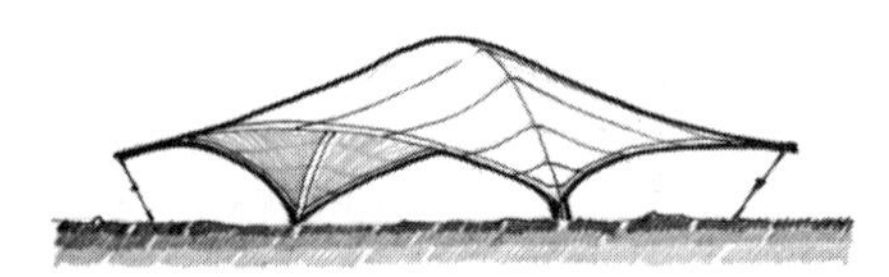

Figure 19-34
Soil has to resist upward, rather than downward force in tent foundations.

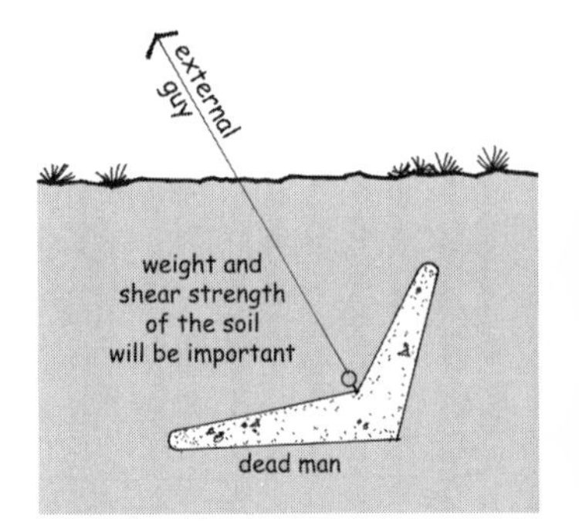

Figure 19-35
Separate infill panels within a cable net at the Munich olympic stadium.

roof membrane may simply be secured directly to the ground, or the roof membrane may be pulled over some rigid edge ring and stretched downward to form a wall. The roof membrane may be pulled tightly down on the top of a rigid wall by use of external guys (Fig. 19-36), or the tent may only be an enclosing membrane stretched over a more convention compressive frame (Fig. 19-37). Finally, a transitional element may be placed between a conventional rigid enclosing wall, and the more curved and flexible tent roof (Fig. 19-38).

Functional footprint: Tents can cover the widest range of spans and the most varied footprint shapes of any known structural system. However, the aesthetic shape of the tent is controlled more by the physical forces that are at work than by the whim of the designer.

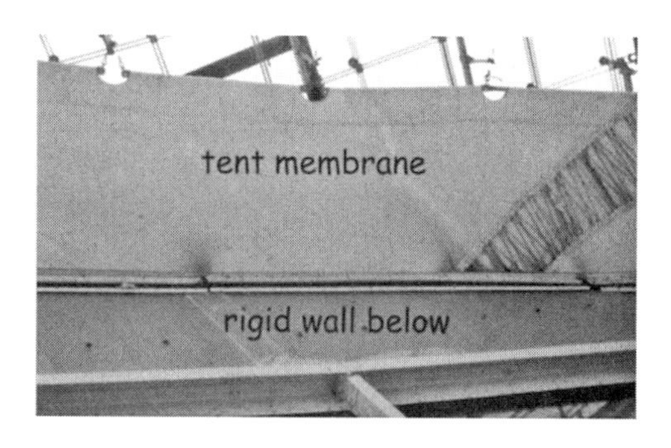

Figure 19-36
Tent pulled down over a rigid wall (in this case without guys).

Figure 19-37
Le Zenith in Paris.

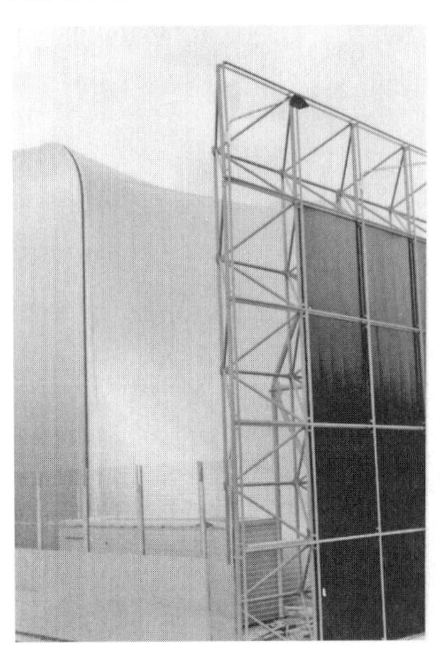

Figure 19-38
Notice the transition element between tent and a more rigid structure.

Pattern of growth: Tents grow by addition of an adjacent tent or rigid structure. They may easily abut or overlap (Fig. 19-39); however, if two tents are directly joined the forces at work in both tents will be profoundly modified. Such joining is therefore possible, but unusual. If it occurs it may be at a shared point, along a shared line, or at a shared surface.

CONSTRUCTION

Fabrication: Fabrics are either *isotropic* (equally strong in all axes) or *anisotropic* (stronger in one axis than another). Because of the material selected and the shape of panels that are cut, developable or non-developable surfaces may result. This has transportation and erection sequence implications. Once at the site special cuts and panels of unusual shape must be correctly joined.

Sequence of construction: Because of the diversity of size, shape, and type of tent structures no one sequence of construction can be defined. Generally construction on the site can be divided into three types, or some combination of the three. Smaller membranes and nets are precut at the factory and delivered in panels to the site. The panels are assembled on the ground and then hoisted

Figure 19-39
Student design with overlapping tent structures.

into place. If a canopy is too large for this method, panels may be partially assembled into sections on the ground, and the sections lifted for assembly in the air. Very large cable nets may be fully assembled from single cables and single panels in the air.

Assembly of membranes and cable nets requires detailed minute-to-minute planning and structural study. The reader will recall that cable structures change shape dramatically with altered loads and supports. This situation does not change when cables are woven into the nets. A pull on this side, has profound structural implications on the other side. Most tents will rely upon prestressing for final stability; however, when partially erected, such balanced (antisynclastic) stabilization is not yet present. During construction, membrane tents are also quite vulnerable to even moderate winds (Drew 1976).

DESIGN

Methods: The use of sag nets (Fig. 19-40) and soap bubble models (Fig. 19-41). are excellent for building an initial understanding of tents. They can be used to determine funicular forms with minimal surfaces that are under equal tensile stress throughout the membrane (Otto 1969). However, more permanent models will be needed to study architectural form during the design process. For rapid investigations of alternative tent forms nylons stockings are often the first choice (Fig. 19-42). Metal screens made with joints that can rotate can be shaped into synclastic and anticlastic forms for tents, just as they were for shells.

Figure 19-40
Sag net design method.

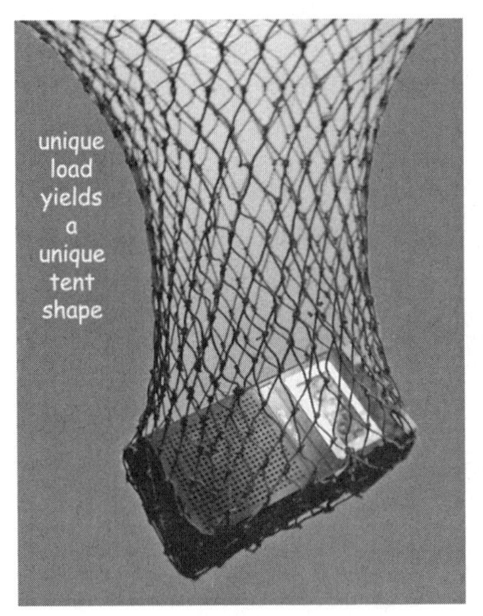
unique
load
yields
a
unique
tent
shape

Figure 19-41
Soap bubble model design method.

Scale models of details and full scale mock ups may be needed, to include lab testing. Since wind is a critical issue, wind tunnel models may be required. While the general intended shape of a tent may be fairly easily evolved with the use of the above types of models, specific mathematical structural analysis and evolution will be necessary beyond initial preliminary design.

Aesthetic potential: The beauty of tents comes from the sweeping curve of its surfaces and edges (Fig. 19-43), the translucence of its fabric (Fig. 19-44), and the possibility of vivid or subtle color. Because of its large span capability, tents can greatly exceed human scale. A single human being is particularly dwarfed when a crowd of spectators is not present in a large tent type arena (Fig. 19-45). Small versions of tents are often used as canopies at the entry of stores where they provide individual commercial personality at very little expense. Texture and pattern plays a strong role in the beauty of cable nets. Consider the net veil sometimes employed on ladies hats at the turn of the last century. It was intended to add a bit of mystery to the ladies face that it partially concealed. The warp and weft of cable nets intensifies the perceived curvature of a tent surface.

Buildings are expensive, slow to build, and we don't do very many of them. For this reason architects sometimes look at the evolution of lesser objects in order to leap ahead in building aesthetics. For example, lamp shades are tent-like structures. At a cost of a few dollars furniture designers can explore hundreds of alternatives in a few days. It is possible to learn something useful from studying small objects (Fig. 19-46).

Figure 19-42

Student model using a nylon stocking.

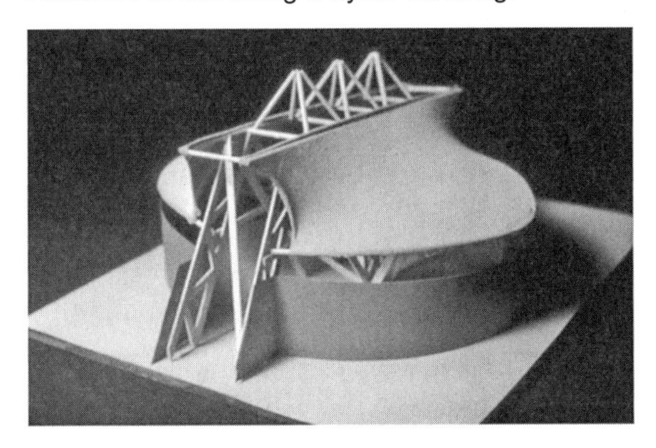

Figure 19-43

Notice the sweeping lines of the tent edge at Canada Place at the Vancouver Expo.

Figure 19-44

The inside of tents have a unique type of light.

Figure 19-45

At this scale you can't even see four people in this photo.

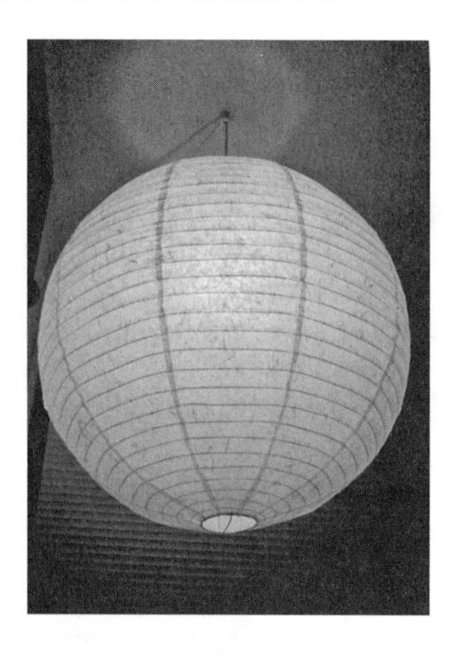

Figure 19-46
This lampshade is really a small tent.

Vocabulary		
Membrane	Cable net	Antisynclastic action
Sagged cable net	Humped tent	Undulating tent
Arch supported tent	Dead man	Mast

REVIEW QUESTIONS

1. Why can tents span such a great distance with so little weight?
2. Why is a tent a good structure in a seismic area, and less desirable in an area with strong winds?
3. What are the main differences between a membrane tent and a cable net?
4. What are some of the challenges in erecting a tent-type structure?
5. Compare the behavior of tents and shells when external loads are applied.
6. Why is some method of adjustment always an important part of tent structure design?
7. What is one advantage that a scale model has over a computer model during the design of a tent structure?

Figure 20-1
Air supported structure at the Vancouver Expo 1986.

20 Pneumatics

DESCRIPTION

A pneumatic structure is a flexible membrane placed in tension by the difference in internal and external pressures. Air, gas, water, or other fluids may be used to achieve these differential pressures.

HISTORY AND SIGNIFICANT EXAMPLES

History: Animal skin water bags were used in Old Testament times in the Middle East. Today we see pneumatics in soap bubbles and bicycle tires. Hot air balloons were used as early as the American Civil War (Fig. 20-2). Inflatable life rafts have been widely used since World War II. However, real interest in use of pneumatics as a building structure began to emerge in the early 1960s writings of Frei Otto. His larger interest was in all tensile structures, particularly tents. A part of that interest was addressed to the potential of pneumatic structures. The real watershed moment for pneumatics came with the 1970 Osaka Expo where many innovative pneumatics of considerable size and significance were constructed. Three of the most important architectural examples at Osaka were the Fuji Pavilion by Yutaka Murata (Fig. 20-3), the Floating Theater by Yutaka Murata, and Mobile Roofs by Tanero Oki and Associates. More recently pneumatics have been used as temporary formwork for other types of structure such as shells.

TYPES OR CATEGORIES

Pneumatics can be classified in more ways than any other type of structure. A brief summary of that exploration includes the following categories. *Single* or *air supported* membranes are perhaps the most widespread in use. Only a single

Figure 20-2
Hot air balloon is really a mobile structure.

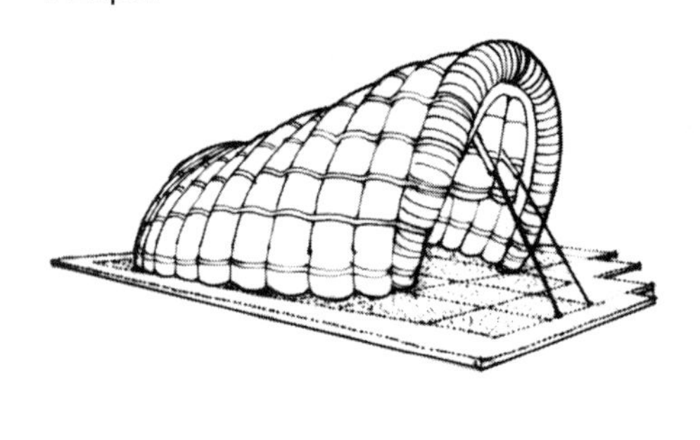

Figure 20-3
Fuji pavilion at the 1970 Osaka Expo.

layer of fabric is placed between the inside and outside pressures in order to form a weatherproof envelope and to resist external loads. The simplest example is a child's balloon. Single membrane pneumatics require fairly continuous mechanical inflation, or they will slowly collapse. *Double* or *air inflated membranes* are more like inflatable pillows or air mattresses used in camping (Fig. 20-4). They are closed systems that partially lock in internal air pressure.

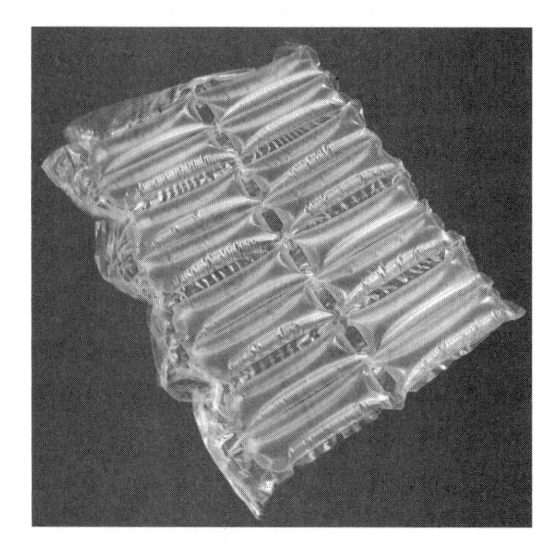

Figure 20-4
Bubble wrap is really an air inflated structure.

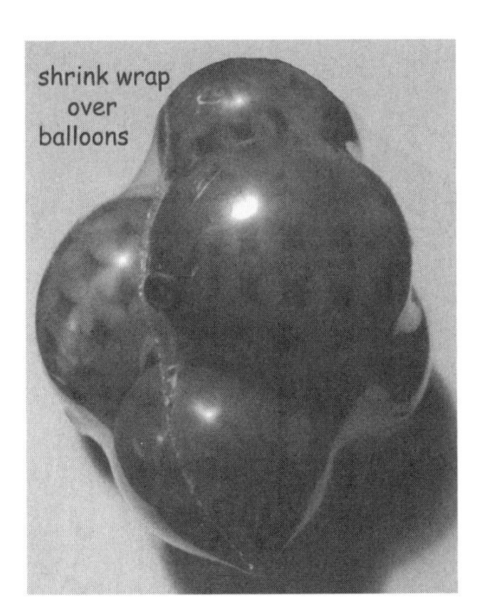

Figure 20-5
Model of multiple membranes with one pneumatic inside another.

The air trapped in dual membrane systems has thermal insulating advantages over single membrane systems. *Multiple membranes* can also be used. Like the double membrane pneumatic, this may involve superimposition of one skin over another; however, this may also involve placing lesser pneumatic structures inside a larger pneumatic (Fig. 20-5). *Open membrane* pneumatics gain structural advantage from differential pressure on two sides of a membrane, but do not capture and hold pressure internally. Ships' sails and parachutes are simple examples. *Closed membranes* do gain structural form and usefulness by capturing and holding internal pressure or vacuum. Soap bubbles and automobile tires are closed membrane pneumatics. If you open a bag of party balloons, several shapes of balloons will normally be found. Some are long and slender like the wieners used in hot dogs. Such pneumatics are said to have *one dominant dimension*. Air-inflated camping pillows are said to have *two dominant dimensions*, while spherical balloons are said to have *three dominant dimensions*. Like shell type structures, pneumatics may have membranes that are *singly curved*, *synclastic*, and *antisynclastic*. *Low pressure* pneumatics are usually large structures that require relatively less internal pressure to maintain their shape than small diameter pneumatics that require relatively *high pressure*. Bicycle tires give us an incorrect intuition concerning the relatively small differential pressure required to support the roof of an exhibition hall. Both pressure (+) and vacuum (–) can be used to prestress the flexible membranes of a pneumatic (Fig. 20-6). The *single bulged surface* is the simplest form of aggregation, having only one pneumatic element. Two or more pneumatics can be assembled into *concentric*, *radial*, or *clustered* groups. Just as soap bubbles may be stretched between a variety of rigid elements, so can architectural pneumatics. Some of the more widely used rigid elements have been rings (Fig. 20-7), buttons (Fig. 20-8), cables (Fig. 20-9), foundation walls, and ribs like the wings of hang gliders and Chinese junks (Fig. 20-10). Most architectural pneumatics are filled with air, but when filled with a gas such as helium

Figure 20-6
Both pressure and vacuum may be used in pneumatic structures.

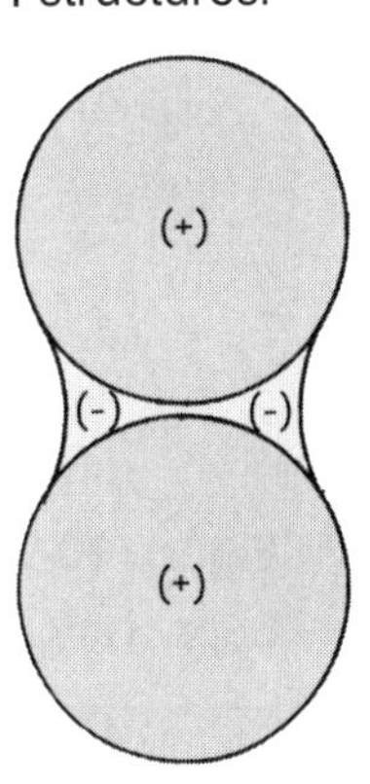

Figure 20-7
Rigid rings.

ring

Figure 20-8
Stabilizing buttons.

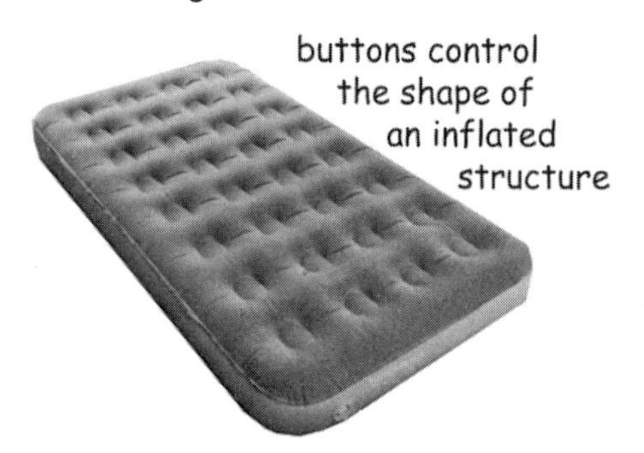
buttons control
the shape of
an inflated
structure

dead loads can be greatly overcome. The Goodyear blimp is a clear example. Filling a child's balloon with water can stress its skin as surely as if it were filled with air. This can have several practical applications. Gasoline can be placed in large mobile "fuel blatters" for temporary storage. In flat terrain, one dominant dimension tubes have been filled with water to form temporary dams related to agricultural irrigation. In very wet and swampy terrain, earth filled "blatters" have been used to form a stable road base. Even the human digestive tract contains examples of this form of adaptive membrane structure. The mobile fuel blatters introduced above are *temporary* pneumatics. So are the pneumatic forms used to produce some polyurethane foam or concrete shells. The largest grain storage facility in the world is a pneumatic located in Kansas. It is a *permanent* pneumatic structure. A *semipermanent* pneumatic will assume the same ultimate form, but be moved from site to site. Carnivals sometimes have pneumatics of this type to entertain children (Fig. 20-11). Pneumatics can be used to form other structural shapes with which the reader has already become familiar (i.e., arches, columns, and vaults) (Herzog 1976).

Figure 20-9
Supporting cables.

Figure 20-10
Supporting ribs.

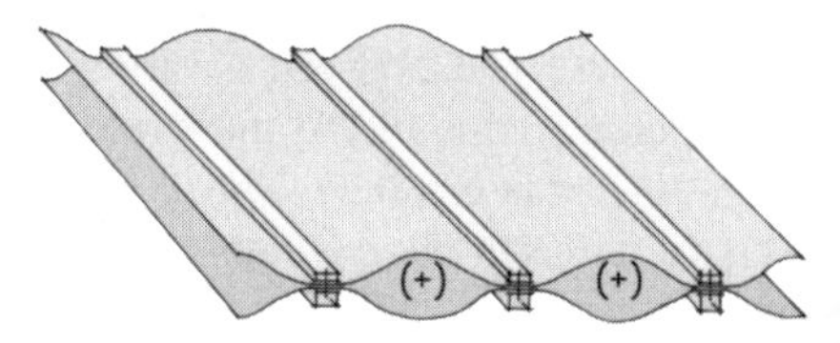
(+)
(+)

Figure 20-11
Inflatable carnival amusement.

COMMON APPLICATIONS

Many of the applications for pneumatics have already been identified. Their most common specific architectural uses are exhibition halls, athletic arenas, and warehouses. One potential use that should be more widely recognized is the use of pneumatics as temporary hospitals and shelters for those displaced victims of seismic disasters. Because they are light weight and resilient pneumatics present little threat if collapsed by subsequent earth tremors, and they are quite transportable. In fact, architects should do much more to recognize the value of both tents and pneumatics as permanent structures in seismic zones. Because they are light weight and easily deformed they are a relatively poor choice where strong winds are expected.

BEHAVIOR UNDER LOAD

Basics of pneumatics: Before describing the response of pneumatics to external architectural loads, it is wise first to become more familiar with some basics of pneumatic structures. As briefly mentioned above, the best way to build this introductory understanding of pneumatics is to observe soap bubbles and balloons (Fig. 20-12). If a large diameter and a small diameter soap bubble are placed together, often the smaller bubble will collapse into, and further inflate, the larger bubble. This is because the pressure inside the small diameter bubble is greater than that of a bubble with a greater diameter. This becomes important when adjacent pneumatic rooms are to be joined. When several bubbles are close-packed on a smooth surface such as a mirror, the internal bubbles in a group will form straight-walled hexagons. Only the outside bubbles will continue to have rounded outside surfaces (Roland 1970). This becomes important when closely packed pneumatic rooms are being considered (Fig. 20-13). Architectural pneumatics require nearly continuous or at least frequent periodic refilling to maintain the necessary pressure differential.

Figure 20-12
Student model using balloons.

Figure 20-13
Close packing of pneumatic structures.

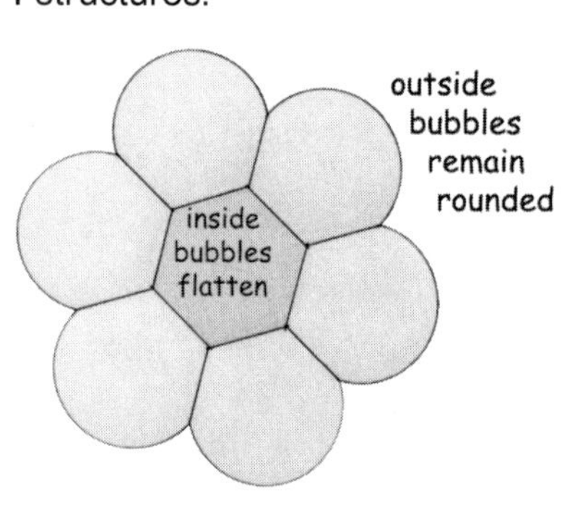

If forced air is used for heating, ventilation, and air conditioning, its pressure may be sufficient to support a pneumatic roof. Fire is a particular vulnerability of all fabric structures. In fact, most commercial membranes must be periodically replaced due to oxidation from the sun and ozone attack.

Vertical loads: Like tents and pneumatics do not invite point loads. Take a pin to a child's balloon if a demonstration is needed. Mechanical and electrical equipment is often suspended from other structures such as trusses, but that is not done in a pneumatic. Soft flexible heating ducts and soft plumbing lines are more compatible with pneumatics, than more conventional rigid ones. In fact pneumatics can, and should, bring a revolution of "soft body architecture" into existence. Internal partitions, stairs, and upper floors have traditionally required the introduction of a second more rigid type of structure (Fig. 20-14).

Lateral loads: In areas with strong winds a lower profile is appropriate. Lift and deformation due to wind pressure on the windward side, and suction on the leeward side, can deform the intended shape of pneumatic structure. This can

Figure 20-14
Student drawing with second rigid structure inside the pneumatic shelter.

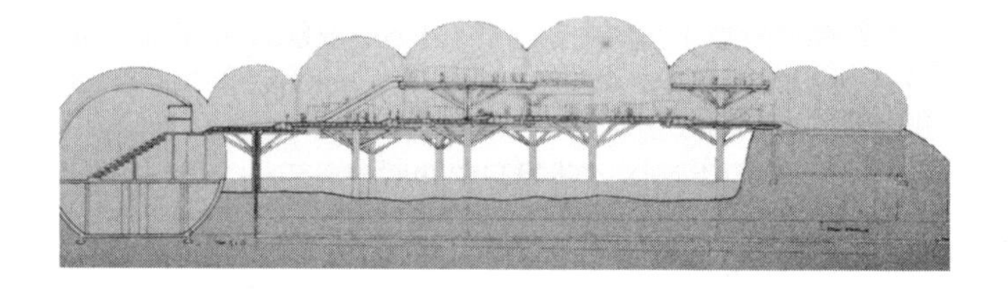

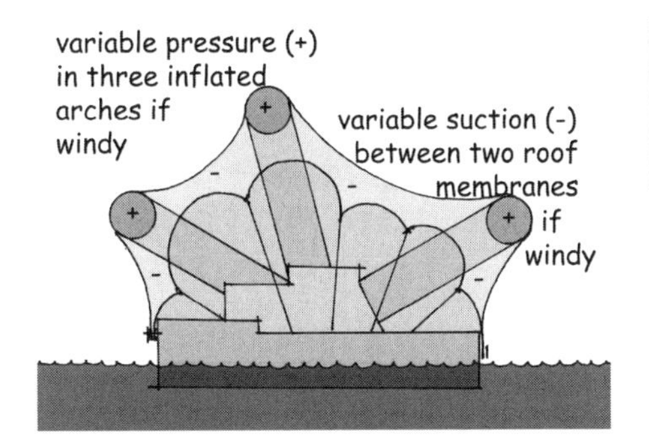
variable pressure (+)
in three inflated
arches if
windy
variable suction (-)
between two roof
membranes
if
windy

Figure 20-15

Simple pressure compensation in the Fuji Theater at Osaka in 1970.

lead to overpressurization and stress concentrations. To overcome this deformation, the air pressure in the roof element of the Fuji Theater mentioned above was varied (Fig. 20-15). Higher air pressure simply pressed the water down a bit more (Taiyo Kogyo 1970). Adequate anchorage at the base is an obvious need when high wind is expected, be aware that stress concentrations will be focused at such anchorages (Fig. 20-16). Under seismic loading these light weight, resilient, soft body structures are among the very best. Caterpillars don't die in earthquakes unless something heavy and rigid falls on them.

Stresses: Like tents, pneumatics will spread loads across the total surface of its skin if it can. However, construction seams, wrinkles, and discontinuities formed where membrane joins a rigid surface or member can cause stress concentrations.

Failures: One of the most common pneumatic failures is from snow loads. The pneumatic begins to deform as snow loads build up. These "dimples" or depressions collect even more snow. This type of load concentration has led to the collapse of single membrane/single bulge pneumatics (Fig. 20-17).

OPTIMUM CONFIGURATION

General shape: If large doors will be necessary for truck or equipment entry, a double membrane air mattress type pneumatic is the likely structural choice. For low profile cable supported single membrane pneumatics, a span range

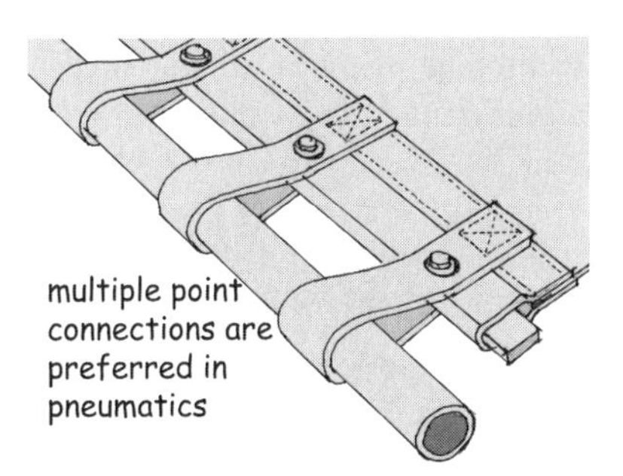
multiple point
connections are
preferred in
pneumatics

Figure 20-16

Joints in pneumatics must avoid stress concentrations.

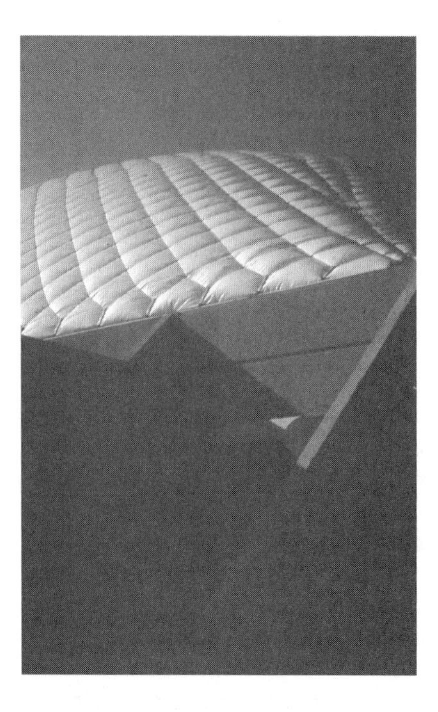

Figure 20-17

This cable supported field house in Okalahoma City that failed under snow load.

upto 8000 feet is possible, but spans from 60 to 600 feet are more common. The span-to-rise ratio is often between 8:1 and 13:1. Cable spacing is from approximately 18 to 36 feet (Geiger 1975). Internal pressures in such systems are often as little as 0.05 to 0.25 pounds per square inch (psi). As spans for the pneumatic roof increase, *restraining cables* can be introduced. These cables often assume a lamella configuration. Cable diameters and placement are a matter of mathematic calculation after completion of preliminary design (Tang 1978).

Joints: Joint configuration is of particular importance in pneumatics. Joints must distribute loads across the maximum possible membrane surface to avoid tears. Of course escaping air will build the need for greater pressure differential in order to sustain the roof configuration.

Membranes: Polyvinylchloride (PVC) or teflon-coated glass fiber fabrics are used to construct pneumatic membranes. The cutting of panels for pneumatics is much more simple than tents, often having parallel sides. The design of membrane seams usually involves interlocking folds (Fig. 20-18). Sometimes a reinforcing plate can be captured in the seam by being sewn, glued, bolted,

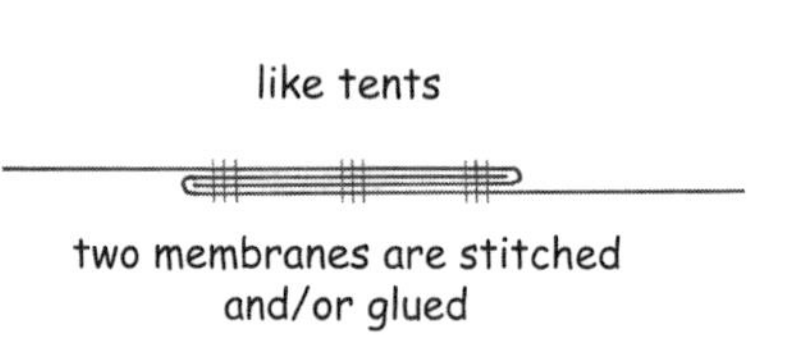
like tents
two membranes are stitched
and/or glued

Figure 20-18

Pneumatics membranes require interlocking folds.

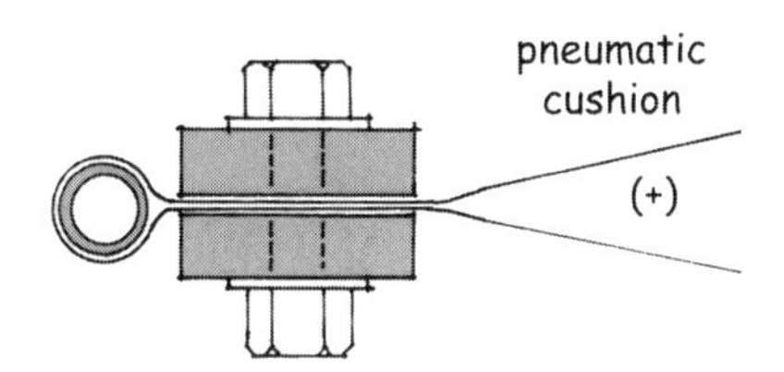

Figure 20-19
Reinforced joint with bolts and plates.

clamped, or some combination of these methods (Fig. 20-19). Leaks and tears are always a concern in pneumatics (Dent 1972).

Details: Many pneumatic connection details are reminiscent of tent details (Fig. 20-20).

Doors: Entry doors into single membrane pneumatics must limit air loss. To accomplish this, sealed-revolving doors, air-locked doors, or organically inspired lip or cushion doors have been used (Figs. 20-21 and 20-22).

Anchorage: Pneumatic structures have two types of anchorage. A large number of low strength anchors are normally sought in either case. *Gravity anchors* rely on their own weight rather than soil strength. A water-filled base ring, concrete base ring, or even a buried net filled with stone may be considered. *Soil anchors* of various screw and expansion types are also possible, but rely on the soil shear strength.

Pressurization: Depending on the type chosen, air leakage at the membrane base is a related concern. Instrumentation and mechanical systems support is needed to maintain appropriate pressures within a pneumatic. Fans for this purpose are mounted on concrete pads outside the membrane.

Figure 20-20
Notice the similarity of tent and pneumatic details.

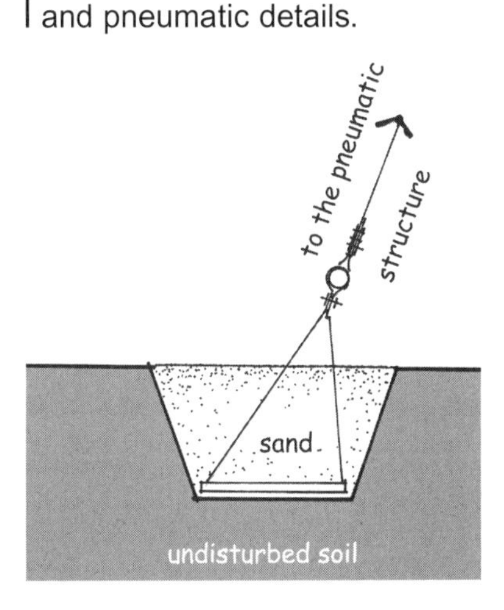

Figure 20-21
Slip-through door.

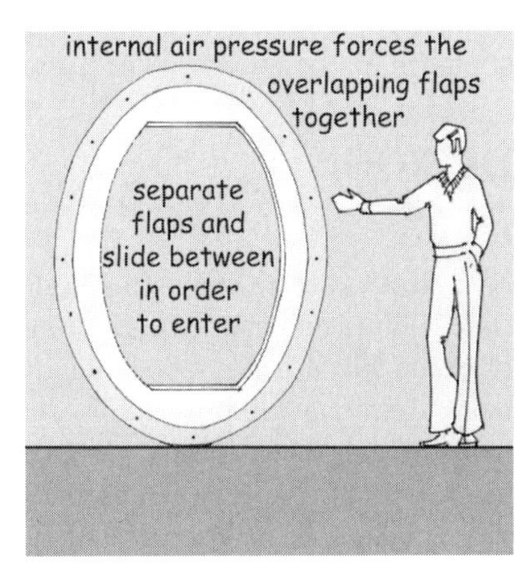

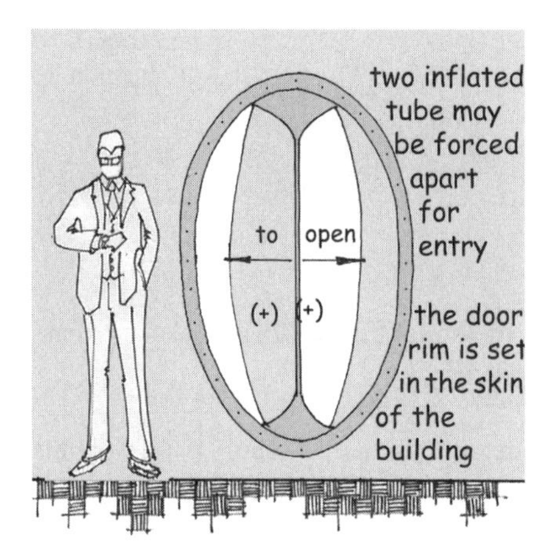
two inflated tube may be forced apart for entry
to open
(+) (+)
the door rim is set in the skin of the building

Figure 20-22
Cushion doors.

Functional footprint: Because of the organic nature of pneumatic structures, almost any footprint and the widest possible range of spans can be managed with a bit of care and imagination.

Pattern of growth: Since stabilizing pressure must be maintained, it is easiest to simply place new pneumatic cells adjacent to old existing pneumatics. This avoids the issues of different pressures in the old and new cells. Then only air-locking doors between the two will become an issue.

CONSTRUCTION

Air-inflated pneumatics have the potential of being "self-erecting". Large air-inflated structures are inflated one cell at a time, often on the ground, then lifted into place and secured to other cells. If so designed, air-inflated pneumatics may be fully self-erecting by filling superimposed cells one at a time, with no lifting equipment being required (Herzog 1976). Air-supported membranes are usually fabricated in long rolls at the factory and transported to the site. After placement of a base ring, an air-supported membrane will be fully stretched on the ground, joined, and then inflated (Geiger 1975).

DESIGN

Methods: In the beginning the best pneumatic study models will make use of soap bubbles and balloons. These can be used to acquire a basic understanding of pneumatic structures. To build a scale study model of a pneumatic, a form is made from clay, Styrofoam, or common object (i.e., tennis ball, egg crate, or balloons, etc). Then "shrink wrap" can be shaped over such a form into an excellent pneumatic structure representation. To progress beyond preliminary design the computer becomes useful. If previously developed and tested joint and seam configurations are not to be used during actual building construction, it is wise to generate and test full scale mock-ups of each detail being considered.

Aesthetic potential: Organic forms, exploitation of light translucence, and strong color have typified most pneumatic designs. Where the visual intent for the design is playful or pragmatic, pneumatics can pursue interesting but not traditional appeal. Pneumatics potentially possess some of the fascination produced by thumbing through the pages of an anatomy book. Soft body architecture offers not only considerable structural potential in the current age, but also a new type of aesthetic hardly explored by traditional and contemporary theorists.

Vocabulary		
Air-supported	Air-inflated	Multiple membrane
Open membrane	Closed membrane	One-dimensional
Single bulged	Blatter	Low pressure
Vacuum	Ballast	Semipermanent
Self-erecting	Gravity anchor	Soft body architecture

REVIEW QUESTIONS

1. Briefly list the many ways that pneumatics are classified.
2. Why are cables sometimes added to pneumatic structures?
3. What are two disadvantages to pneumatic structures?
4. What is the typical span range for pneumatics?
5. What are some unique challenges of pneumatics given strong wind loading?
6. Briefly explain the sequence of erection for large pneumatic structures?
7. What types of material are used for the skin of pneumatic structures?
8. How are most pneumatic buildings pressurized?

Figure 21-1
Millennium Dome in London by Richard Rogers Partnership.

21 Hybrids and Exotics

DESCRIPTION

Hybrids

Thus far, a wide range of traditional alternative superstructures has been presented. While most buildings normally select from these traditional alternatives, many contemporary buildings combine aspects of two or more of these systems. In part this is due to the widespread use of computers, which has made the inherently complex computations related to such combinations much easier and more reliable. A good contemporary example of a *hybrid* structure is the Millennium Dome in Greenwich, England. It combines characteristics of a cable system, a tent, trusses, and a dome (Fig. 21-1).

Exotics

The body of knowledge in structures continues to be expanded beyond traditional alternative structural systems by new one-of-a-kind structures. Like all explorers, the designers of these innovative *exotics* expand future possibilities for those that design structures. The term "exotic" has been selected for use in this text for want of a more widely used term. It is not a commonly used term within the structural engineering community (Fig. 21-2).

HISTORY AND SIGNIFICANT EXAMPLES

Examples in nature

Exotics: If Darwin's theory of evolution is correct, each chance deviant within a species is tested by its environment, and the fittest survives to procreate. Structural exotics in architecture differ only in that they are not "chance" deviants, but are the product of carefully calculated design.

Figure 21-2
Swiss Re Headquarters in London by Foster and Partners.

Hybrids: Calculated animal breeding programs seek to combine the characteristics of different animals to produce some new creature that has the beneficial characteristics of both its parents. This analogy suggests a real concern in combining structural systems. Interbreeding of animal not only integrates the beneficial characteristics of two animals or plants, it also integrates the undesirable characteristics of the two. It is wise to study both the advantages and disadvantages of all systems to be combined. Particular watchfulness is needed in the search for weaknesses or disadvantages that may be reinforced, or magnified by the combination.

Building examples

A well-known historic example of a *hybrid* structure is the Tower Bridge in London. It combines aspects of cable, arch, and bearing wall structures. Each of the traditional alternative superstructures that have been presented earlier in this book was at one time an *exotic*. A more recent example is the geodesic dome by Buckminster Fuller. There was always that first designer, who had to conceive the first of its type. That first innovative individual structure became popularized, widely used, and a wide range of variations within that type of structure were evolved. Like all evolution, all individual exotics do not meet with success. Some find wide relevance within the circumstances of given historical conditions, while others are tested and found wanting in some significant aspect that prevents their wider use. In some cases the skilled labor or structural material needed was not widely available. In other cases the courage, knowledge, and skill of the designer was unique within the design community of that period. Other less capable designers have been unable, or unwilling, to follow. Antonio Gaudi used structural modeling methods that yielded powerful structural results such as the Sagrada Familia in Barcelona, Spain (Fig. 21-3). Even with its clear benefits, this powerful example has never been widely followed. Occasionally the functional needs of a specific project or uniqueness of building site offered opportunities and demands that were seldom, if ever, encountered again. In contrast, the commonly used alternative structural systems that dominate this book evolved because they met common functional requirements on commonly encountered site conditions. It has also occurred that structural insight was lost to history and had to be rediscovered as with the Dome on the Cathedral in Florence, Italy, by Brunelleschi.

Figure 21-3
Sagrada Familia in Barcelona by Antonio Gaudi.

CHOICE BETWEEN TRADITION AND INNOVATION

The designer is always confronted with a choice between innovation and tradition. Neither is inevitably appropriate. It is an unavoidable choice on every project. If common functions and typical site conditions are encountered, tradition is likely the appropriate choice. If extraordinary functions, site conditions, or design constraints are encountered, innovation will probably be needed. The designer should be aware of the baggage that either of these choices carries with it.

Tradition

If a designer chooses from traditional alternatives as a basis for the solution for a specific project, he or she is "mining" in the commonwealth of knowledge within the profession. The designer's first responsibility in reliance on tradition is to fully understand, and fully exploit, all that a tradition holds. This responsibility exists because many designers have previously polished our understanding of that alternative system. Any mistake or ignorance in applying that tradition is less forgivable than in developing an innovative new one-of-a-kind solution. The second implied responsibility is to further that design tradition in some small way. Like taking a loan at a bank, a designer should give a little "interest" back to the commonwealth of knowledge from which he or she has borrowed. What we know of the traditional alternative structural system that was used for an individual solution should be made greater in some small way by some aspect of the designer's current project. The Millennium Bridge by Arup and Foster Partners in London is a well done current example of a contemporary structure that springs from the cable structure tradition (Fig. 21-4). While it fully exploited that tradition, it also significantly extends that body of knowledge.

Innovation

Choosing the route of innovation also has implied responsibilities. Innovation has the inherent risk of exploration. When a designer enters the unknown, he or she is largely unsupported by the insights of earlier designers. The greatest risks are often those issues that a designer fails to recognize or consider, rather than

Figure 21-4
Millennium Bridge by Arup and Foster Partners.

those that are wrongly considered. Even more profound are those secret issues that are introduced for the first time by the innovative structure. These new issues may have no precedent in any of the earlier alternative structural systems. All that we currently know about structures was evolved at real cost. Careful study of structural failures has greatly expanded our understanding of structural behavior, but only with loss of life and property. While we conscientiously avoid even the smallest structural shortcoming and profoundly abhor structural collapse, it is a historical reality that such problems were often unavoidable. The innovative structure was built, tested, and failed in a completely new way that could not have been predicted by knowledge of earlier traditional systems. Failure in any field has been a necessary companion to innovation. This hard reality should be weighed seriously before embracing the route of innovation, particularly in the extreme litigation environment found in today's practice. Even after accepting this fact, the genuine need for innovation is still going to confront all designers. Additional time, care, and cost are needed to minimize the risks presented by innovation. It is a wise practice to have competent independent professional review of all innovative solutions. Objective independent reviewers will see the solution from a different viewpoint. The chance of unrecognized or unconsidered issues will be reduced by review from diverse viewpoints. Client may bring unique functional needs, radical site conditions, or other peculiar design demands; but they cannot also present time and budget constraints that will not allow sufficient care in minimizing the very real risks presented by innovation. The TGV Rail Station at Lyon by Santiago Calatrava is an excellent contemporary example of an exotic that has produced profound aesthetic and technical impact without sacrificing safety (Fig. 21-5).

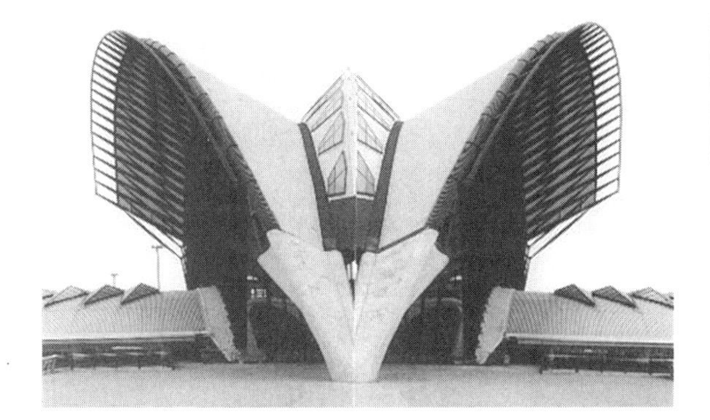

Figure 21-5
TGV rail station at the Lyon airport by Santiago Calatrava.

TYPES OR CATEGORIES

Exotics

One way to classify exotics is by the source of their innovation. High rise structures evolved because of developments in steel as a structural material and the development of the elevator. This is innovation arising *from new materials or technology*. Suspension bridges evolved because of the need for extraordinary spans for road and rail. This is innovation arising from a *new functional need*. Threat of war, extreme slopes, extremely poor soil conditions, extreme seismic and wind threats, and an extreme shortage of buildable land have all led to structural innovation based on *extraordinary conditions in the building context*.

Hybrids

Combination structures are more difficult to classify, but at least two groups can easily be seen. The first, such as the Tower Bridge in London, occurs in the face of rapid technical development. The second, such as the Millennium Dome also in London, is a more calculated effort to integrate well-established alternative traditional structural systems to a specific purpose.

COMMON APPLICATIONS

In addition to the circumstances and motivations that drive the development of exceptional structures, one more type of project should be noted. Hybrids and exotics may be deliberately introduced in very small or modest projects with the clear intention of using them as a testing bed. A small residence may be used to try a radical new structural idea, not because it is demanded, but because the risk exposure is relatively minor and the financial cost of the experiment is limited. The small spans, light loads, and limited number of occupants profoundly limits the human costs presented by the experiment.

Figure 21-6
Guggenheim Museum in Bilbao Spain by Frank Ghery.

One other provocation for innovation in contemporary structures is the desire to achieve a specific type of aesthetic appeal. The Guggenheim Museum in Bilbao, Spain, by Frank Ghery at first appears to have the potential to be a shell-type structure (Fig. 21-6). Actually a complex space frame is used to support and mitigate between the external skin of the building, and the necessary interior functional configuration.

BEHAVIOR UNDER LOAD

Exotics

The development of a truly innovative "first-of-a-breed" is like finding a new species of creature cast up by the ocean on a beach. It may look like something that you have previously known or experienced, but that similarity of appearance may have no bearing on its structural behavior. If it did, then the ancient Egyptian obelisk, which looks a good bit like a modern rocket although made of stone, might be expected to be able to fly.

Hybrids

The "devil is often in the details" in hybrid structures. It is in the joints that connect different systems that strange (nontraditional) things may begin to happen. Particular care is needed at these joints. Traditional structural concepts and traditional analysis methods may not apply at the joints, although it may appear so. The other glaring challenge to both conceptual understanding and numerical analysis is in the combined global hybrid system. We may understand how a giraffe dances, and we may understand how a hippopotamus dances, but we had best not assume that this directly predicts how a "giraffe-amus" or a "hippo-raffe" dances. While computer modeling is currently popular, the author recommends that it be combined with physical models, and laboratory testing in structural design of hybrid structures.

Both exotics and combinations

Of course, all exotics and combinations must be tested against not only all single predictable type of loads, but also all potential load combinations. No building code will demand less; however, such codes may not provide sufficient guidance in such evaluations. Worse yet, such codes cannot require tests, or evaluations, that are not predicted by prior traditional structural systems. As an analogy, imagine the problems confronted by a conventional biologist or medical doctor that encounters an alien species that appears to have a few organs made of an unknown metallic substance. Unusual tests beyond their prior experience may be needed. The character, need for, and validity of such new tests may excite intense scrutiny and even dispute. In unusual structures we should warmly welcome such external scrutiny and discussion. This scrutiny must focus both separately and jointly on each individual member or joint, each subsystem, and the global structure. Do not expect the questions presented by these unusual structures to have normal multiple-choice traditional answers. This is a dangerous presumption even with well-evolved alternative traditional structural systems.

OPTIMUM CONFIGURATION

Since exotics and combinations are so individual, it is difficult to make generalizations on optimum configuration; however, two comments can be made. The exotic structure should be configured to perform better than any traditional system, or perhaps a traditional system should have been used. Similarly, the performance of the total hybrid structure should be greater than the sum of its parts. Both exotics and combination structures should be expected to conform to the structural principles discussed in an earlier chapter (i.e., structural logic, integrity, continuity, and economy).

FUNCTIONAL FOOTPRINT

Extraordinary footprints justify extraordinary structures. Traditionally common functional footprints probably do not.

PATTERN OF GROWTH

One of the most neglected aspects of these extraordinary structures is the potential for future growth. The design of an unusual structure is so consuming that the potential for future growth is sometimes inadvertently neglected.

AESTHETIC POTENTIAL

Once again it is difficult to make general comments on structures that are so individual. Let's resort to the discipline of art, which seeks as a goal to produce innovative one-of-a-kind products. It is said that every work of art is a universe unto itself, governed by its own rules. The least it can do is obey its own rules. While it is open to dispute that a structure, no matter how individual, is indeed a universe unto itself, it does seem reasonable that the designer should seek an understanding of the rules governing the unique structure he or she has created, and make an effort to consistently conform to them.

CONSTRUCTION

Integration of unique structures with conventional building envelopes, mechanical, and electrical systems often presents profound problems requiring special study beyond that required for more traditional structures. Even the structural details may require more attention than traditional structural solutions. Unusual or unique details may be required (Fig. 21-7).

Past experience in traditional fabrication and erection of buildings may have relevance in individual components, or even subsystems of a radical new structure; however, truly innovative structures usually imply truly innovative means of fabrication, delivery, and erection. The design of a structure includes the design of its construction process. Innovative structures may also require unusual skills in their fabrication and erection. While the designer may have a very open mind in his or her search for relevant skilled labor, labor unions and traditional contracts may impede this search.

Unusual buildings are rarely fabricated from "off-the-shelf" components. Unless the project is very large, it will involve short runs of a few parts on industrial assembly lines. This means increased costs. Also the unique construction

Figure 21-7
Entry to Lloyds of London by Richard Rogers Partnership.

methods that often accompany unique buildings will require more training, time, and control than traditionally constructed structures.

Vocabulary	
Structural hybrid	Structural exotic
Tradition	Innovation

REVIEW QUESTIONS

1. Under what circumstances is structural innovation appropriate?
2. What implied responsibilities do designers have when exploiting tradition?
3. What implied responsibilities do designers have in seeking innovation?
4. What are some barriers to innovation in the current building industry?
5. Why are innovative buildings often more expensive, or at least less predictable in their cost?
6. Why might traditional design methods and building codes be inadequate to assure the safety of truly innovative structures?

Figure 22-1
Spruce Tree House at Mesa Verde National Monument in Colorado.

22 Structural Selection

BACKGROUND

Remember that a structural system has five critical components: loads, superstructure, lateral support system, foundation, soils, and geology. In the preceding chapters a concerted effort has been made to acquaint the reader with selected important concepts and choices related to each of these five components. Building on this knowledge, this chapter focuses attention on examples of typical types of issues and concerns that commonly influence these choices. No assertion should be made that the following discussions are complete or comprehensive. Neither should the sequence used be interpreted as implying any special hierarchy of importance within the issues that have been selected for this discussion. For the most systematic and detailed exploration available, the reader is directed to *Tanguage* (Tang 1978). Because of the extensive and diverse nature of these issues and concerns, the rest of this chapter is organized under several subcategories such as "functional issues" and "economic issues". In this chapter structural design issues are treated in a rational manner. However, since design also includes creative use of the intuitive mind, a subsequent chapter will also discuss "structural creativity".

FUNCTIONAL ISSUES

Spatial aspects

The structure selected must provide overhead shelter for the most appropriate functional size and shape for each room below it, when seen in *plan view*. Many architects also use some type of checklist to systematic program specific requirements for every space in the building that is to be designed. Buildings such as exhibition halls that will have multiple tenants over their life span will often require wide column and barrier free flexibility, rather than functional "tailoring". While plan view tailoring is certainly an important aspect of appropriate response to the functional requirements of a building, it is still only a two-dimensional response to a four-dimensional problem (Fig. 22-2).

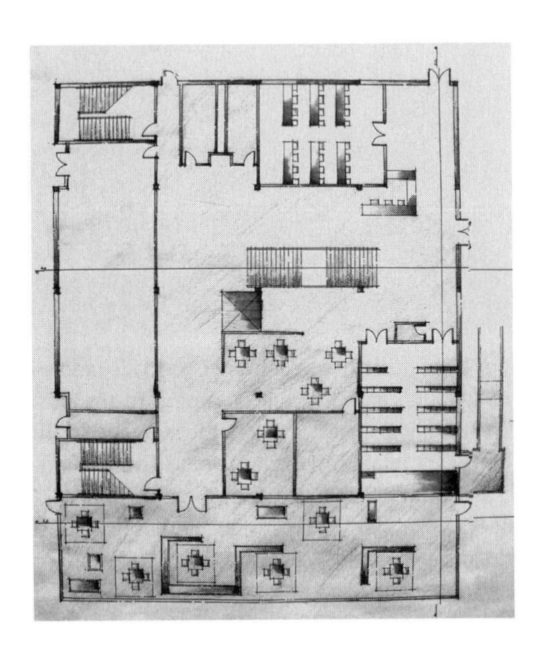

Figure 22-2
Student plan view drawing.

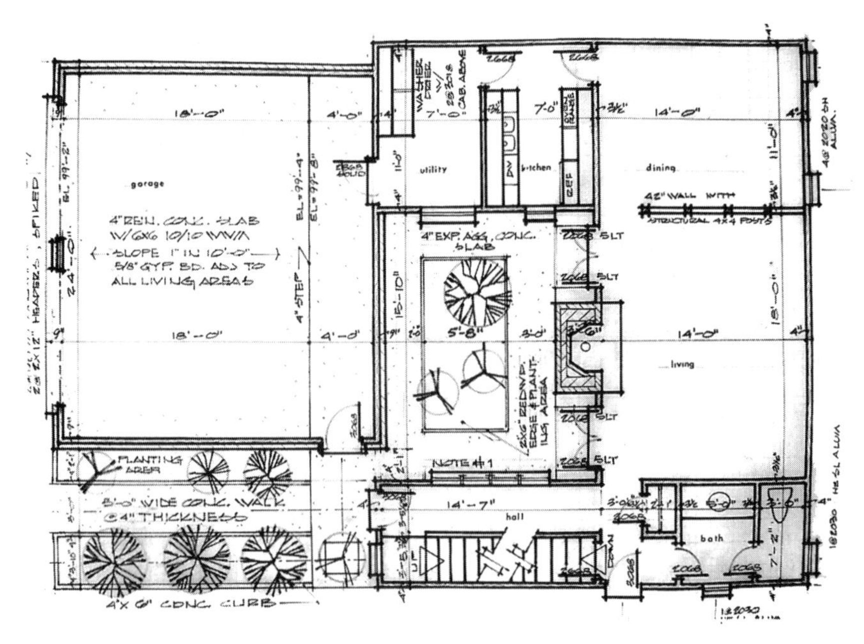

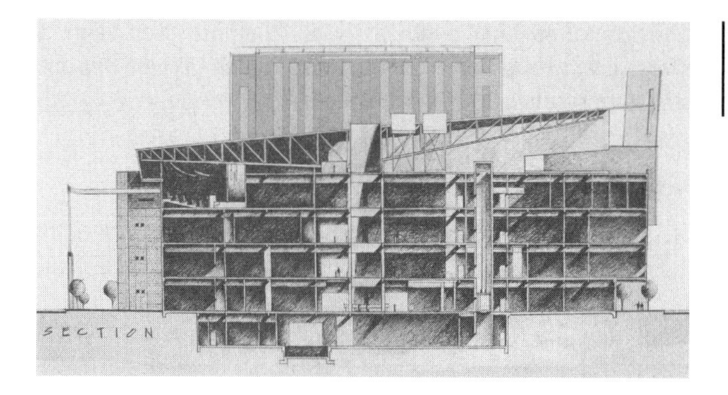

Figure 22-3

Tyical section view drawing in a student's project.

In the *section view* real integration of structure and function can normally be seen. In a multifloor building section view response to functional space requirements may take precedence over plan view response. This is because great savings can be obtained if "floor-to-floor" height can be reduced. This is also the view in which integration with other building systems can be most easily visualized (Fig. 22-3).

Occupancy loads by functional use

As noted in an earlier chapter entitled "loads", building codes are widely used to define minimum loads that must be used in design of structures. When possible, the principle of structural logic implies that the heaviest occupancy loads should be located low in a building, while lighter loads may be located on higher floors in a building. While other influences may take precedence over this optimum structural configuration, it is still helpful to recognize the optimum condition.

Probable future use

While it is not always possible to see far into a building's future, a genuine effort is usually made to predict a building's future occupancies. As just discussed, building codes will require reconsideration of structural loads when a building changes use or occupancy. It is usually easier to design in extra strength for a probable future use at the time of initial construction, than as a rehabilitation project at a later time. Do not omit consideration of profound changes to mechanical and electrical systems, additional fire exit ways, or at least the rerouting of exit ways that would probably accompany any predictable changes in future building use.

CIRCULATION

Minimum size for fire egress routes

Building codes define the minimum legal dimensions for fire egress (escape) routes. Final design dimensions will often be larger. These dimensions include hallway length and width, stair and landing sizes, and doorway locations, sizes, and proportions. All of these openings can present violations of the structure's "integrity" or wholeness.

Code loads in hallways

A quick look at any building code will confirm that hallways usually must carry heavier loads than the rooms that are connected to the hallway. This heavier estimated load is because people tend to pack pretty tightly together when they are fleeing from a fire down such routes.

Support for stairs and elevators

In the route of escape in multifloor buildings these heavy horizontal hallway loads continue on into stairs. A stairway collapse can be disastrous during evacuation of a building. Although it exceeds the scope of this text, it should be noticed that stairs are sloped. This means that more than just vertical loads must be supported.

Elevators require the structure to support heavy point dead loads presented by lift equipment. However, equally important is the fact that elevators also place inertial loads on the structure as elevator cars start and stop.

Location, size, and shape of circulation openings

So hallways, doors, elevators, escalators, and stairs all cut holes in the fabric of a structural system. These vertical and horizontal holes are violations of the principle of structural integrity (wholeness). They can profoundly weaken the structure, build up stress concentrations around them, and will probably require at least edge reinforcement around the holes. Careful placement of these wounds can limit their ultimate impact on the structure.

SITE CONTEXT

Physical setting

Site size and shape

Small urban sites purchased with the intention of producing a large amount of commercial space lead directly to the need for high rise structures. Don't forget that the building site is first a factory for the production of a building. In an automobile plant a very large factory produces a relatively small product—a car. However, the footprint of a high-rise is a relatively small factory that produces a huge product—the building. Limiting space on the site for the construction process can greatly impact the choice of a structural system. As a second example consider tilt-up bearing wall construction. There must be room on the site not just for the building, but also for the walls before they are tilted up, and for the heavy lift equipment beyond the wall panels that are to be tilted up. On a small site, it may mean that a tilt up bearing wall system is just not possible.

Extraordinarily narrow and deep sites can profoundly affect the lateral support challenges that must be confronted by a structure. Building sites with unusual shapes such as a very acute triangle can directly contribute to global torsion experienced by a building when it is wind loaded.

Site location and access

Heavy equipment access to the bottom of an excavation can profoundly effect the selection of foundation type. Narrow urban streets with tight turns may completely rule out the use of long precast concrete elements in the structure just because they cannot be brought to the site on flat bed trucks.

Geology and soil adjacent to, and under the building

A full chapter has already been given for the geology and soil upon which a building is to be erected. It is also important to consider the geology and soil of sites adjacent to the construction site as well. This can significantly affect the need for temporary shoring and underpinning. It may also lead to the need for permanent structural retainage against subsurface water or adverse adjacent soil conditions.

Topography

Generally speaking the greater the slope of the proposed building site, the greater the structural design difficulty. By implication, extreme slopes also lead to greater litigation exposure. Steep sites must usually be overcome by such structural measures as stepped foundations, excessive excavation, extensive retaining walls, or tall piers (Fig. 22-4).

Climate

Consideration for heavy snow loads and strong wind loads were discussed in an earlier chapter. Don't forget that deep frost line also means a deeper foundation. More subtly, mild climates such as in California encourage very large expanses of windows, and multiple doors. This often directly reduces the lateral support capability of the structure in an area prone to strong earthquakes (Fig. 22-5).

Adjacent structures

Support for adjacent buildings should be anticipated during the erection of a structure in a tight urban setting. This topic was engaged in an earlier chapter. Here it is important to see that shoring and underpinning can profoundly obstruct

Figure 22-4
Challenging topography at Machu Picchu in Peru.

Figure 22-5
Difficult climate at the summit ofTrailridge Road above Estes Park Colorado.

workspace in the building excavation. If this same excavated foundation area is to serve as a factory for the erection of the rest of the building, any obstruction of workspace may significantly limit the selection of a feasible structural system.

Probable natural disasters

In California lateral support systems become robust due to earthquakes. In Florida lateral support systems become robust due to hurricanes. On the Gulf Coast buildings are elevated on piles in response to potential storm surge. Snow slides threaten buildings in the Rocky Mountains, and flooding must be reckoned with in river valleys.

CULTURAL SETTING

Local cultural tradition

The local architectural history and social tradition may influence the shape of a structure beyond technical necessity (Fig. 22-6).

Figure 22-6
Small temple in Hachiman area of Japan.

Construction annoyance

Blasting is accepted in a western mining town, but it is a problem in a down town commercial district. Shallow bedrock may carry such annoyance as baggage to the foundation system that is chosen. Traffic obstruction during construction may generate sufficient annoyance within the immediate area to justify selection of a very rapidly erected structural system.

Code constraints

A structure that is possible in one community may not be possible in a different community due to code differences. Chain stores that use a standard design have encountered significant difficulties with such variations in code requirements. Also, codes are interpreted by building inspectors. Interpretations may vary from one municipality to another, even when they are using the same building codes.

Zoning constraints

Such issues as required parking are addressed in zoning ordinances. If extensive parking will be required, it may have to be placed under the proposed building, or may require a second multistory parking garage. If parking is placed under a building, it will profoundly modify the modular size of structural bays to be used in the building. Zoning also influences the fire protection required in a structure, and access to the building for fire fighting equipment. Zoning has a direct impact on the height and shape that many larger buildings may become.

Land ownership

Air, surface, and subsurface rights are all in question when designing a structure. For example some cities will allow a structure to overhang the adjacent city sidewalk under certain circumstances, while others may not. Similarly, some cities will allow temporary shoring of excavations with tiebacks that run out under city owned streets, while others will not. In areas where mining and petroleum extraction are common, subsurface rights to the land may be in question. It is certainly worth checking. In addition, your structure may have to span certain types of easements in order that they may be properly maintained.

Probable man-made disasters

Recent events have made designers more aware of the structural implications of terrorists, riots, and wars. However, the general public is far less aware of the wide spread occurrence of criminal arson than it should be. Each of these types of man-made disasters requires a uniquely different structural response. One size does not fit all.

ECONOMIC ISSUES

Initial costs

Materials

In general, use of local building materials provides great initial cost savings. If more remote materials are to be used, some consideration should be given to their volume and weight, since these will affect the cost of transportation.

Labor

In the United States the cost of labor is often of greater concern than the cost of materials. In developing countries, the opposite is often the case. In either case, less labor is cheaper than more labor of the same type. A very good reason must justify the selection of a labor-intensive structural system. The requirement for highly skilled or specialized labor can be the source of surprise cost over-runs, since the impact of labor strikes will be more severe. If specialized labor is needed for the structure that is selected; it is an obvious initial step to make certain that it is locally available before making a selection based upon it (Fig. 22-7).

Equipment

It is similarly wise to explore the local availability of construction equipment before selecting and designing a structure that requires it. This is a particularly significant consideration when very large precast or prefabricated elements are anticipated. If large forms for cast-in-place concrete are to be reused, they can be just as significant a problem.

Figure 22-7
Two skilled craftmen at work in the University of Oklahoma model shop.

Experience

If a specialized type of structural system is selected such as lift slab construction it is wise to first explore the experience of local contractors to be certain that sufficient experience exists. Inexperience can be overcome by money, but worker safety often cannot.

Profit

Market analysis

The client should have conducted a proper market analysis prior to approaching the architect and engineer. Such a study should identify genuine unmet needs within the "catchment area" for the proposed project. This analysis should also profile the "competitive context" for the project. It should specifically lay cost goals for the project.

Important, but not included in such studies is the client's financial ability to engage in the project. Cutting corners once the project has begun is an annoyance when aesthetic goals are sacrificed; it can become criminal negligence when minimum structural goals are not met. One type of evidence of a client's financial capability to engage the project is prior successful completion of several similar projects.

Short- or long-term profit

Frank discussions with the client are needed to identify true financial goals for the project. Short-term profit usually implies absolutely minimum initial cost of construction. This extends to the structure, although the structure is often not a particularly expensive part of the building's final cost. Long-term profit may allow selection of a structure with more initial cost, but which requires smaller total life cycle costs.

Cost/profit ratio

Responsible designers seldom discuss cost by itself. Usually value is a more important measure. Cost is what you pay. Value compares what you pay, with what you get. Structural designers cannot, however, ignore the ratio between cost and profit. If it is ignored, the project will not be pursued.

Investment attractiveness

In reviewing the cost/profit ratio above, one of the most decisive issues is its comparison to other competing types of investment. A client may not be just comparing this building design to another building design. It may involve an investment choice between real estate, bonds, commodities, or stocks. There are many places where the investor can invest the same money.

Life cycle costs/profits

1. *Operation:* Superstructures that may have substantial overhead space such as vaults and domes may require more heating and cooling during the buildings' total life span than may be functionally or aesthetically justified. Similarly, windows may be logically located structurally in order to avoid interruption of the continuity of load propagation, but may be functionally difficult and expensive to clean.
2. *Maintenance:* Structures fabricated from materials that are inherently vulnerable to deterioration will require more extensive maintenance. Termites, wood rot, and rust are examples of such deterioration. If such maintenance as periodic inspection and maintenance is required, sufficient additional space must be designed within the structure to allow it to take place.
3. *Modifications:* Modifications to structures are most often required by a change of use for the building. Radical changes in technology can also raise a need for structural modifications. For example, the extensive use of computers has caused several office buildings to be remodeled with a raised floor over the existing slab in order to allow flexible distribution of electrical and data link wiring. Only sufficient initial floor-to-floor space in the original structure made this change possible.

Financing

Window of opportunity

A decision to build is often dictated by the favorable intersection of several conditions. For instance, if financing availability is falling while labor and material costs are rising sharply, a small "window of opportunity" may occur when the project may be financially viable. If that window is missed, the project may be aborted. In such conditions, design of the project must be completed within very strict time constraints. In this case timing may be a primary force in selection of the structural system.

Time of delivery

In many commercial projects every month, that the project is under construction, is a month of lost rent. This loss can be very significant in very large structures. Structures that can be rapidly designed and erected will be favored in such cases.

Reliability of time of delivery may also be an issue in the selection of a structural system. For example in the design and erection of a sports stadium, clients might demand project completion in time for the first game of the season. Innovative structural systems are inherently less predictable than more traditional alternatives in such circumstances.

Consultant fees

Tradition vs. innovation

Traditional solutions require less design time than more innovative ones. Design of details will be an important part of that additional design time. Structural consultants will also have to spend more job observation time since workman on the site will be less familiar with both the general construction of the system, as well as its many new types of details.

Liability exposure

More traditional structural choices are inevitable in an environment of intense litigation. Some structures such as long span systems are sufficiently vulnerable to litigation that it may be advisable to employ two separate firms to simultaneously do two identical separate structural designs. In this way the two solutions can be compared in order to confirm its final correctness.

Extensive detailing

Some structural systems just have more details than others. In general, those with lots of joints are likely to join this group of structures. Unfortunately this is less than a universal rule. Some types of structures such as space frames may have a large number of joints, but may not require an excessive number of details since many of the joints will be identical. Conversely, some systems have relatively few joints, but each one is unique and requires extensive detailing (Fig. 22-8).

Salvage rewards

Quarrying in the twentieth century

If the population of the United States stabilizes, then the number of new buildings that are required will decline. Remodels will become the more typical architectural project, as they have in many parts of Europe. It is both likely, and advisable, to reuse parts from older buildings rather than to remanufacture

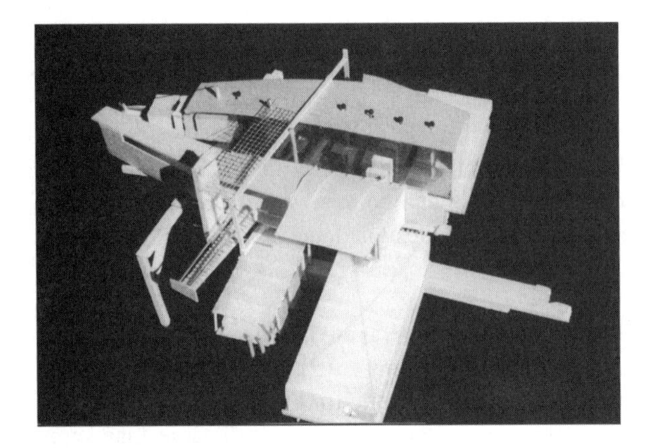

Figure 22-8
This student design by Adam Lanman need more detail than some others.

similar new parts. Since most of the buildings in the United States were built in the last century, they are the ones that are most likely to be "quarried" for components for new structures. The local and timely availability of quarried parts should become an important consideration in the design of new and remodeled structures (Fig. 22-9).

Reusable parts

In an age of sustainability, any new design should certainly recognize the importance of standardized, and reusable, structural components. Steel members are already often directly reusable, given some design imagination. In-situ (cast-in-place) reinforced concrete structural components usually are not. However, precast concrete members certainly could be directly reused if connections are studied with that goal in mind.

Figure 22-9
Palazzo Vecchio in Verona by Carlo Scarpa.

Market structure

While the odd warehouse selling salvaged stained glass windows and architectural ornamentation is occasionally available in major urban areas, what is needed is a broad new construction industry similar to the salvaged car parts industry. Salvage and resale of fundamental structural components should be common in all major cities. Structural designers must be prepared by their schooling, personal inclination, and creative imagination to exploit the reuse of this material. Some rebuilding and remanufacture of major structural parts is also a possibility, but will add to both the energy and financial budget attached to them.

Distribution issues

Reuse of salvaged structural parts presents both geographic and temporal problems. If a specific set of structural parts is available in a New Jersey yard, but needed for a small project in Oregon, it may not be known or useful. The Internet has a few web sites that are initiating this market, but they should grow to relieve the first problem. It would be an easy thing to establish a single shared national database containing all currently available salvage building parts. Unfortunately most structural parts are not currently salvaged. On one web site that specializes in building salvage only 7 of 235 transactions involved significant reuse of structural components.

The more restrictive problem is one of timing and predictability. The salvaged structural component must not only be geographically within reach, but also must be available at the time when it is needed. Use of "salvage options" similar to land options must be developed. For this reason the timing of demolition and construction must become the subject of much closer coordination.

AESTHETIC ISSUES

Architects find their basis for the aesthetic appearance in many places, too many for discussion in this work. However, the basis for each individual project must be understood in order to evaluate the role that the structure may play in that expression. The role that the structure should play may be large or small, but it is a significant consideration in the selection of the structural system.

URBAN SETTING

Urban design has a body of knowledge that is too extensive to explore in this text, but it is useful to invite the attention of the structural designer to the built context in which his or her structure will be placed. Perhaps a single example will indicate such a need. The Chicago skyline is dominated by tall buildings with flat roofs, while the New York skyline is thought to have more pointed roofs. Therefore, in New York we might select a somewhat different structural system for that same high rise if built in Chicago, all other things being equal.

INTEGRATION WITH OTHER BUILDING SYSTEMS

One of the architect's most important roles in the design process is to weave the various building systems together into one harmonious whole. This is done by coordinating the contributions of the many professional consultants such as structural, mechanical, and electrical engineers, and by assuring that this human coordination results in a physical building whose systems are equally well integrated. Some of the systems that must be integrated with the structure are briefly discussed below (Fig. 22-10).

Passive energy

Passive energy concerns must be balanced against structural concerns. In a cold climate, the general building proportions will often be developed so that the long axis of the building is exposed to the sun in order to collect heat. In a hot climate a different configuration is ideal. However, such solar considerations ignore structural needs such as lateral stability. Passive solar buildings also often call for large windows on a single wall, or large skylights cut into the roof system. These perforations can represent clear violations of structural integrity (wholeness). These can result in problems in global torsion of the total building, or produce unwanted stress concentrations in a particular structural surface.

Figure 22-10
Mechanical and electrical systems in the Munich central railroad station.

Illumination

Openings for daylighting

Holes cut into the structure for daylighting share many of the same challenges with holes that are cut for passive solar warming. In both cases appropriate openings can be coordinated to meet both illumination and structural needs. Michelangelo's dome at St. Peter's cathedral is a successful example of such coordination.

Support for lighting fixtures and equipment

The placement of light fixtures is dictated by the functions that they are to illuminate. These fixtures must have structural support. For example, library stacks need to have illumination over the parallel aisles that occur at a predictable interval. Structural coordination would call for coordination of structural modules with these lighting intervals.

Heating, ventilation, and air conditioning (HVAC)

Space and support for ducts

Coordination of major structural members with major heating and cooling ducts is an absolute essential. Both are large, so they are often run on parallel, rather than perpendicular paths. In multifloor buildings this is done to reduce floor-to-floor distance, which profoundly reduces building costs. Structural support for these ducts is also an issue, but it can often be resolved with less difficulty than the spatial needs.

Openings and continuity for ducts and pipes

Continuity of load propagation in the structure can come into conflict with continuity of airflow in HVAC ducts. Holes must often be cut into floor plates and the structural core of a building structure in order to provide routes for these ducts. These openings also represent a serious threat to fire protection of the structural system.

Support for heavy machine loads

The HVAC system has several very heavy machine loads. Typical examples include centrifugal chillers, pumps, and air handling units. These loads usually present concentrated point loads to the structural system. Their placement must be closely coordinated and controlled. Reciprocal chillers must also be evaluated as resonating loads on the structure.

Electrical

Electrical wiring is sufficiently small not to threaten a structure in the same way as the HVAC ducts. The electrical system does, however, present the need for structural support for some heavy equipment such as transformers. In addition, some electrical equipment must be isolated for both security and as a fire threat. For example, building codes normally require that electrical transformers must be placed in very substantial "vaults". In such cases strong walls will surround such a vault, even if the rest of the building is post and beam.

Water

Heavy storage tank loads

Many larger buildings must have a very large water storage tank on their roof to supply the fire sprinkler system. Since water weighs 62.4 pounds per cubic foot, this is a very heavy point roof load on the structure. In tall residential buildings large storage tanks may also be required to supply the domestic cold and hot water systems for showers and the like. These are also often located on the roof of the building, and present similar point loads on the structure.

Altered loads due to fire suppression

When fire suppression sprinklers are operated the water will soak into carpets, furniture, and the other contents of the room. Water might even pond temporarily in a room. This room weighs a great deal more than it did when it was dry. In very large buildings, drains through the building skin are sometimes provided so that some of this water can drain out of the building during a fire.

Drainage, waste, and venting

Vertical continuity for vents and stacks

Drains from restrooms, vents, and stacks are often grouped together in a building into a single vertical plumbing chaise. In a tall building this requires that a series of holes be cut through all floors. While individual holes in a single floor plate may be acceptable if they are kept fairly small, it is worth noting that when all of these holes line up vertically in every floor plate, it causes a global weakening to the structure that should be studied.

Slope continuity

Sanitary sewer lines inside of the building must have a "positive slope". This means that horizontal waste water pipes must be sloped downward at about 1/4 inch per foot. So, every 4 feet the pipe will drop an inch. If horizontal runs for this pipe become long, drops of 24 inches or more can develop. This is a functional problem if waste water pipes start to extend below ceilings in the story below. For this text it is more important that such pipes may want to punch through beams that run perpendicular to them in order to maintain the necessary slope. On one occasion the author encountered a well-intentioned plumbing subcontractor warming up his cutting torch to burn a path for his pipe through one of the major steel beams in a high-rise building.

Acoustics

Sound and vibration isolation

Fans associated with the HVAC system can introduce unwanted vibration into the structural system. The structural system may then transport this vibration to spaces where it appears as an acoustical problem. It may be necessary to design a break in the structural system to overcome this problem. Other sources of unwanted vibration include traffic in attached parking facilities, or even external road traffic. If the structure cannot be broken for structural reasons, the interior wall surfaces may have to be isolated from the structure by resilient clips in order to keep them from acting as "sound boards" for the structure born vibrations.

Reconciling of organic and geometric form

The optimum internal acoustical shape for an auditorium is quite organic, and is based on the path that sounds will follow in the space. Unfortunately the structural shape will usually be quite geometric. This conflict of form is made structurally more difficult to resolve since an auditorium usually demands very long structural spans.

BUILDING ENVELOPE

Modular support of/for the building skin

As noted in an earlier chapter the structural module should be coordinated with the module of the skin that will be placed over it. If the building skin and the structure are one and the same (i.e., brick bearing wall), then the natural module of that material must be respected. With brick this is a 4-inch nominal module (Fig. 22-11).

Figure 22-11
Brick cathedral in Santa Cruz, Bolivia.

Thermal expansion and contraction

In large buildings thermal expansion and contraction can become a significant consideration. For example, an interior column in a high rise will maintain its length if its temperature is kept at about 72 degrees Fahrenheit, while exterior columns will shrink and lengthen depending upon the outside temperature. Such differential expansion and contraction in internal and external columns produces bending in the beams that connects them. This bending force occurs in addition to other internal loads that may already bear on these beams.

Accommodation of other types of movement

Remember that other conditions such as differential soil settlement and seismic loading may produce other types of movement that must be addressed by the structure.

Detailing ease

In general, structural designs that leave abundant space around joints will be easier to detail, and easier to fabricate. As previously mentioned limiting the number and diversity of joints in a structure will also ease the detailing required.

OTHER

Support, openings, and continuity for elevators and escalators

If plumbing chaises present horizontal discontinuities in the floor plate, elevators are worse because they are greater in size. Elevator shafts must be fire isolated; therefore, shafts are often constructed of reinforced concrete. This can not only overcome the discontinuity problem generated by punching a hole in the floor plates, but it can also serve as a useful means of lateral support for the total building. This advantage cannot be extended to holes punched to generate a large interior atrium. Such an atrium profoundly compromises the horizontal diaphragm action of the floor plates, making the building vulnerable to such lateral loads as earthquakes. These holes also lead to serious stress concentrations within the floor plates, particularly at the corners of the openings.

Vertical continuity for roof drainage

If the roof of a building is to be drained internally as opposed to shedding the storm water directly off its sides by scuppers, such pipes will present similar structural problems to domestic waste water systems.

Safety

Structures should be designed not only to protect the occupants once it is finished, but also to minimize risks for the workmen who will bring the structure into reality.

Serviceability

A structure should be fulfilled in its use, not destroyed by it.

Designability

The structural choice should not make the designers' work any more difficult than it justifiably must be.

Realizability

Dreams are good, but completed buildings are better. Dream to the edge, and then take one step back. Get it built.

Durability

Just as a person's life is hard, so is the life of a building. Design in extra structural strength, stiffness, and stability for the things that will inevitably occur as an unpleasant surprise during its long life.

Vocabulary		
Value	Fire egress	Floor-to-floor height
Precast concrete	Air rights	HVAC
Easements	Catchment area	Cost/profit ratio
Life cycle cost	Financing window	DWV

REVIEW QUESTIONS

1. How might a change of occupancy affect the structure of an existing building?
2. Why are hallways usually required to carry a heavier occupant load than the rooms that feed people into the hallway?
3. Describe one or two ways that zoning ordinances can affect structural design?
4. Briefly describe the relationship between structural design and the life cycle cost of a building.
5. What types of structural systems would lead to the greatest salvage rewards?
6. Of all the other building systems, which one will probably have the greatest impact on the layout of the structural system?
7. What types of coordination is particularly important between the design of the structure and the design of its envelope?
8. Briefly discuss one or two issues that relate the fire suppression system to the design of the structure.
9. What affect would the design of an atrium bring to the design of the building's structure?

Figure 23-1
Roof top law office remodel in Vienna by Coop Himmelblau.

23 Structural Creativity

ALTERNATIVE FORMS OF THOUGHT

Design is a tale of two minds. Both the rational mind and the intuitive (or creative mind) are used in design. *Rational thought* is dominantly verbal and numeric. It progresses along lines of probable success, is subservient to previously defined constraints, and can produce on a schedule. While it is quite useful in evaluating alternatives, narrowing possibilities, and focusing on a single idea; it is not normally the best approach at raising new ideas, alternatives, and possibilities. Rational methods are therefore referred to as "convergent" thought.

In contrast, *creative thought* is referred to as "lateral" thinking, and is dominantly visual. It shoots off in all directions, not necessarily along paths that are promising or probable. Creative thinking is powerful in raising lots of ideas, alternatives, and possibilities. To do this it is normally best to separate "ideation" (coming up with ideas) from judging ideas in order to "converge" on a single relevant solution. All of the ideas that the creative mind raises may not be relevant, useful, cost effective, or even feasible; however, it is inappropriate to condemn ideas while you are raising them.

Neither rational nor creative inherently means "good", just different. No structure is ever totally rational or creative. They are all some blend of both. A successful designer should be competent to use both methods of relevance and innovation.

GETTING THE RIGHT MIND SET

Dismiss, for the moment, all previous preconceptions involving client demands, project budgets, feasibility in construction, physical gravity, and all other preconceived design constraints. Discard any preconceived set of priorities, or hierarchy of importance that you may have attached to various issues involved either in the specific design project or in your typical approach to all projects. Isolate the generation of innovative structure in a "design vacuum" and prepare to engage in "free play."

Research indicates that creative people are difficult employees, rule breakers, and untimely. Appropriate immediate attitudes and emotions at the moment of creative design are *boldness* to the point of audaciousness or brashness, and *lightheartedness*. By lighthearted we don't mean happy. If your spouse leaves you, you lose your job, and the doctor says you have cancer; then if you can have a light heart, that is what is needed. In Japan lightheartedness is occasionally defined as "filled with vitality." Avoid fear. Creativity is defeated by fear. Fear of failure, of inadequacy, of what others will think or say, or that good ideas won't come forth, are all common killers of creativity. Judgment kills creativity. You must want innovation more than acceptance. Courage is the first prerequisite of creativity. Forget taboos. Sacred cows may not graze in the same land as innovative thought. Reject all willingness to passively "settle" for a conventional solution. One must be ready to crash and burn in glorious defeat, rather than to "settle" with a whimper (Fig. 23-2).

Habits also kill creativity. If we listen to comments like "we don't do it that way in this office," or "we have never done it that way," we are finished before we start. Too often it is the designer's own personal design habits that get in the way of creative thought. If a designer draws up in pride and speaks of his or her "design approach," a look in the mirror is probably warranted. Cultural tradition is such a habit. Inappropriate schooling may be the source of such destructive habits. The highest goal of schooling is not to homogenize.

Figure 23-2
A student design showing that radical appearance is sometimes possible even with conventional structural behavior.

SETTING THE SCENE

If your creative work doesn't make you laugh right out loud, embarrass you in front of more reasonable people, offend many, and shock the rest; then you are not pursuing appropriately *creative goals*. Most people have one time of day, place, or circumstances in which most of their "hot ideas" appeared. Give it that time. Seek that place. Generate those circumstances. The creative mind speaks softly, and it speaks on the subject just once. Be ready to listen. Listen to it, and don't interrupt it.

SOME SELECTED CREATIVE DESIGN METHODS

First thoughts: Often when a designer is first confronted with a problem, a creative insight may come immediately in a single blinding flash. Don't try to suppress it, it is a spontaneous gift. Are they correct, complete, valid, or relevant? Keep an open mind. Immediately record the insight, and get on with designing the structure.

Incubation: If the rational mind can solve a problem it will. If it cannot, frustration will set in, and the creative mind will be triggered to engage the problem. Frustration is your creative friend. So at the start of the synthesis phase the designer knows the facts, what the data means, what the goals and priorities of a good solution should be for the project. Typically the designer then generates a few rational alternatives, and things don't fit. Frustration sets in, and the creative mind goes into action. This is an appropriate moment for "incubation." Step away from the project. Let the problem cook for a while, and do something else. With luck innovation may strike you like lightening, perhaps while you are shaving. Leave time in your design schedule for this to happen (Jones 1980).

A CREATIVE STRUCTURAL DESIGN PROCESS

Step #1: Isolate the development of an innovative structure from all the other constraints of a specific project. The reason for this isolation has been discussed above.

Step #2: The next step in the process offered by the author is to find a source of a significant structural theme or idea. It is the *seed idea* from which the structure can grow. One may use traditional sources for structural ideas such as significant historical buildings, bridges, towers, or other structures. You might review the traditional types of superstructure and foundations discussed in this book for ideas, or you might imagine the shape of the functions, with load propagation flowing around it like water. Unfortunately, traditional seeds like these do not lead to innovative structures. Let's look at a more creative list of sources. You might use anthropometric elements (i.e., human hands, spines, etc.), images from poetry and literature, children's toys, common objects (i.e., combs, grocery bags, etc.), appliances (i.e., fans, vacuum cleaner, etc.), zoomorphic forms (i.e., parts of any living creature), botanic forms (i.e., parts of any plant), nautical forms (i.e., any sailing vessel or its parts), clothing items (i.e., hats, suspenders, etc.), musical instruments (i.e., drums, violins, etc.), vehicles (i.e., hot air balloons, airplanes, etc.), or a myriad other sources.

Step #3: Abstract the essential structural idea: The dictionary defines "essence" as "the simplest and most basic constituent". It comes from a Greek word, meaning to waste down to the bones. Remember now that "structure" is the ordered flow of force. Therefore, this step calls for the designer to abstract and isolate a single structural idea in its simplest, most minimal form. Here is the structural essence of a violin (Fig. 23-3).

Step #4: Forced Manipulations: Now the abstracted structural idea is put through a wide (and arbitrary) series of "forced manipulations." These manipulations include action words such as mirror, fragment, invert, explode, stretch, and tumble. It is appropriate to treat this as a child's play. The best way to pursue these manipulations is with a series of small "thumbnail" study models (Fig. 23-4). The goal is to evolve lots of truly innovative new structures.

Step #5: Develop the concept using a combination of larger models and drawings (Figs. 23-5 and 23-6).

Figure 23-4
Student thumbnail (2 inch) model of a variation on the essence of violin by Breah Page.

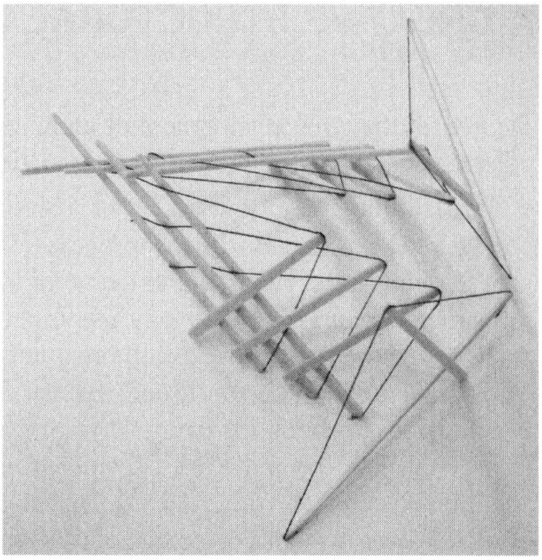

Figure 23-3
Structural essence of a violin.

column
cable
beam

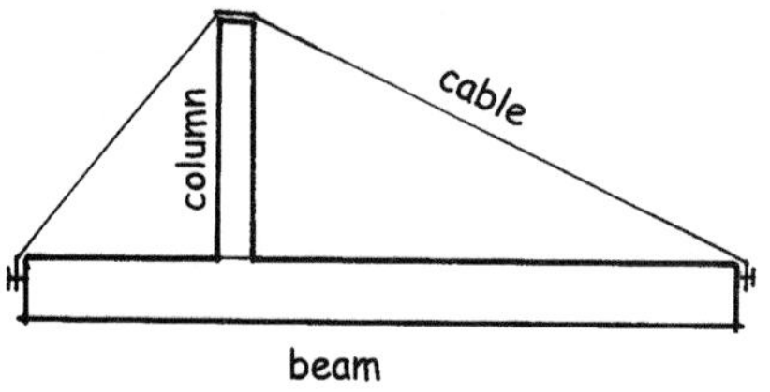

Figure 23-5

Larger scale (about 10 inches) student design development model of the violin theme by Skyler Fike.

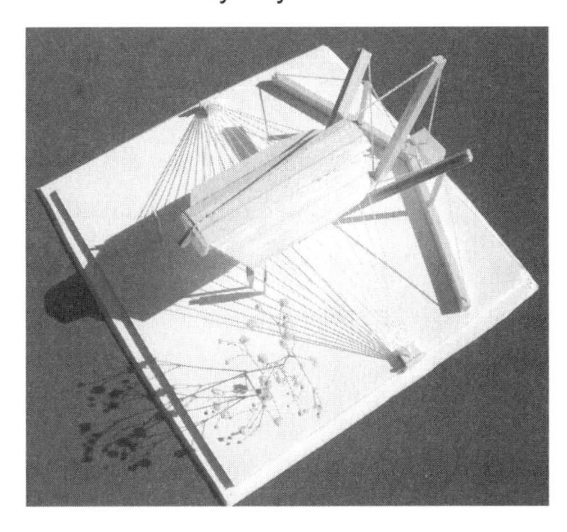

Figure 23-6

Design by Adam Lanman using the method described below and a caterpillar as a starting point.

Vocabulary		
Seed idea	Lateral thought	Convergent thought
Forced manipulations	Incubation	

REVIEW QUESTIONS

1. What conditions favor innovation and creative design?
2. What recurring personality characteristics are often found in creative people?
3. List several types of design strategy and explain when they might be useful.
4. What type of activities should be engaged when a designer is conducting incubation?
5. Why are "ideation" and "judgment of ideas" best kept as separate activities?
6. What is the difference between "good" and "creative"?

Figure 24-1
Nils Ericson Bus Station in Gothenburg Sweden by Nils Torp.

24 Quality Assurance

BACKGROUND

Industrial quality assurance programs

Most industrial corporations (i.e., auto and aerospace) are divided into standardized operational components. Examples of such operational divisions include management and administration, research and design, engineering and product development, procurement, production, *quality assurance*, marketing or vending, and product distribution. The most aggressively developed quality assurance (QA) programs in manufacturing are directed at life support systems (i.e., oxygen supply in a lunar module, or air bags in your car).

Quality in the building industry

In the highly fragmented building design and construction industry such coherent organizational divisions may not even exist, let alone be coherently integrated under a single corporate leader. While the building industry is the largest in the nation, it has lagged seriously behind industrial manufacturing in establishment of effective formal QA programs. It is rare to find even a single person dedicated to QA in a firm, let alone a QA corporate division. One reason for this condition is that the process of building design and production of a single building is widely dispersed between multiple firms. No single authority or control is exerted over all personnel, materials, and activities in direct pursuit of quality in either design or production.

Single matching quality responsibility/authority

While legal assignment of single *responsibility* for product quality on a given building project might one day be coerced organizationally, matching single *authority* over product quality would have to be simultaneously granted over all participating corporate entities. This has not been pragmatically feasible in the building construction industry. In the past, architects were empowered by the client with the responsibility and authority to pursue overall building quality on their behalf. However, the current education, corporate organization, business practice, professional compensation, and standard marketplace contracts do not assure that the architect can or will exercise comprehensive control over QA.

MOTIVATION

The primary reasons to assure the quality of the building structure are to protect life, prevent injury, and to protect property. An urgent, but lesser, reason is client satisfaction. Structure is a *life support system*. A death caused by a failed building structure may receive less media coverage than the death of an astronaut in a failed space mission, but it is no less grave to those suffering the loss. If the building construction industry cannot coherently address QA in any other aspect, it must successfully guarantee the building structure because it is a life support system (Fig. 24-2).

Definitions

Within conventional manufacturing (i.e., auto and aerospace industries) a standardized vocabulary has evolved. For the sake of this brief chapter, the introduction of a few basic terms is helpful. *Quality* means "fitness for use," "conformance to requirements," or "the degree to which the product or services satisfy the wants of a particular user." It is usually divided into quality of design

Figure 24-2
The London Eye by Julia Barfield and David Marks.

and quality of conformance. *Design quality* is the degree to which the design will satisfy the previously established *requirements. Quality of conformance* is the degree to which a specific product conforms to a design or specification. *Quality function* includes all aspects of a firm through which *fitness* is achieved. While *quality control* involves those activities focused on quality conformance intended to achieve established standards, *quality assurance* is the broader term that includes all activities used to pursue quality to include design. QA must be embraced by both labor and management at all levels and be applied to design, fabrication, procurement, and assembly. A *quality characteristic* is any dimension, property, or behavior that contributes to fitness. This is the basic building block for the QA program. It may be visual, functional, effect reliability, maintainability, cost, or any other requirement that the client, government officials, or users may specify (Juran and Gryna 1970).

TWO TYPES OF QUALITY

Design quality

A completed building design and all of the activities that led to it may be evaluated for fitness. Design activities are evaluated for *quality as a service.* Selection and configuring of a structural system, selection of material grades, and specification of particular construction methods or performance are examples of this service. Unlike the aerospace industry, few architects and structural engineers have an independent person or department dedicated to the quality function. If present, QA may be viewed as one of many management duties. Specifically, a designer's drawings and specifications will usually be checked by their immediate supervisor. Separate QA is not normally specifically designated, not uniquely tasked, not formally empowered, and not specifically and adequately funded. In an aerospace firm no design engineer would normally be asked, or allowed, to evaluate the quality of his or her own design service. The conflict of interest and inherent absence of objectivity is too clear.

Quality of conformance

Once the design has been completed, it must be fabricated and erected. Final product quality will then be measured by conformance to the design. If the design is adequate and appropriate, and the construction true to that design, then user needs should be well met.

PLANNING AND ORGANIZATION FOR QUALITY

Planning

Adequate specific *funding* must be earmarked and delivered in order to establish and maintain quality assurance. One reasonable measure of the funding appropriate to the QA program is to predict all of the probable costs that will inevitably arise from multiple deaths in a structural collapse in the absence of this program. A limited number of clearly stated, measurable, and obtainable quality *goals* must be defined. Based upon these announced goals and the changing needs of current projects a series of written *operational policies* and *standard operating procedures* should be initiated and continuously updated. Quality assurance activities must be included in all design and production *schedules*. The placement and structure of the QA personnel must be identified and integrated into all corporate *organization* charts. This QA organization must then be *staffed* with appropriately educated and experienced personnel. Specialized *training* in QA will need to be developed, instructors obtained, and training executed. QA training is not directed at management, QA personnel, designers, and every worker down to the lowest level must know their roles and be committed to final product quality. At one well-known automobile plant, any worker on the assembly line may immediately stop production upon detecting a significant quality defect. They currently produce the best selling car in America. At all levels each individual in the firm (not just QA personnel) must know what they are to do to achieve acceptable quality, and specifically what to do when defects are identified. Comprehensive *quality characteristics* and *standards* must be developed, written, and disseminated for both design and conformance. In the construction industry the construction drawings and specifications are the most common expression of these characteristics; however, they are not the only ones (Rosen 1974). Once QA activities are initiated they will include control, analysis, and correction. *Control* is all activities directed at achieving quality characteristics and standards. *Analysis* identifies patterns of defects, appropriate resolution, and prevention of future occurrences. While most QA activities seek to prevent defects, identification and *correction* of defects is also a critical role. Correction is best accomplished by a clearly established *response system*, not by isolated ad hoc corrective actions. Specialized measurement, testing, and analysis *equipment* will be needed in order to initiate and sustain a QA program. *Testing* seeks to determine quality *reliability* by the use of *statistical sampling*. Both *destructive* and *non-destructive* tests will normally be involved. A destructive test breaks, destroys, or damages the thing being tested so that it cannot be used in the final building or building component. QA *methods* and *techniques* must be coordinated with all other design and production activities necessary to produce the completed building. Quality in marketing, vending, and delivery of the final product is part of the picture. After the building has been occupied by the client for a period of time, some architects will conduct a *post construction evaluation* and a *client satisfaction study.* This is an important part of the quality function. These studies must be analyzed and *lessons learned* systematically cycled back into operations to improve ongoing, and future corporate design and production (Juran and Gryna 1970).

Organization

The single most critical organizational issue is the complete equality and independence of the QA division with other corporate activities. It is best established as a separate activity at the corporation level equal in importance and influence with research and design, engineering, or production. Quality is not a part-time activity under the control of a project manager. The project manager has an inherent conflict of interest by being required to meet clearly stated time deadlines and reducing costs within clearly stated budgets. These goals are inconsistent with product quality as a goal. Establishing QA as a separate and equal activity with design and production allows a system of checks and balances to defend quality against the forces of budget and time (Wahl 2006).

DEFECTS MAY ONLY BE A SYMPTOM

If a defect in design, fabrication, or erection of a structure is found, two general types of remedial action may be taken. If the normal procedures are good and a temporary lapse has taken place, it may only be necessary to restore the status quo. A more serious situation is one that requires the standard operational procedure itself to be modified or improved. If a structural joint or member failed that may only be a symptom, not a cause. Without finding the true cause, subsequent failures are likely. In the building industry this issue becomes emotionally charged since defects in conformance will usually rest with the constructor, and defects in design quality will rest with the architect and engineer. Finger pointing is a poor substitute for rapid and effective problem resolution. *Risk analysis* has become an important part of defining the significance of defects in both design and conformance.

FINISH GOODS ACCEPTANCE

Quality conformance

A final acceptance inspection by the architect and his or her consulting engineers is a traditional part of current building industry operations. A "punch list" will be compiled by the architect of all shortcomings that require correction by the contractor before the building is turned over to the client. If a system of ongoing quality inspections is in place, that list should be fairly short. Errors and defects are usually more expensive to correct in a completed building than in a partially constructed building. Skilled trades may have to be recalled to the site, other work torn out to get at the defects, and corrections can conflict or damage other completed work. It is better to identify and correct defects at the earliest possible time.

Design quality

This is true of design as well. Design decisions build one upon another. If a faulty design decision is made, it may invalidate many subsequent design decisions that are based upon it. It is therefore best to find any faulty design decision immediately.

SPECIFIC QA ACTIVITIES

Quality surveys

A wide range of variables such as equipment, personnel, materials, management, standards, and procedures affect the final quality of a building or any other product. In conventional manufacturing a *source surveyor* is usually sent out to the home factories and offices of prospective suppliers and subcontractors to ascertain if they have the trained personnel, necessary equipment, and quality procedures to qualify them to bid on a given project. It is primarily a matter of systematic prequalification of the quality capabilities and assets of prospective bidders prior to contracting with them. There is currently no systematic equivalent in the building design and construction industry (Wahl 2006).

Quality inspections

This is different than quality inspection. Inspections are done after contracts have been drafted and accepted. Inspections are directed at specific design and production work and products. Inspection offers ongoing assurance that the quality potential identified during the quality survey becomes a quality reality during execution of the project (Clyde 1979) (Fig. 24-3).

Having another person look over your shoulder is not a welcome experience. However, consistent, planned, systematic, comprehensive inspection by objective competent observers is at the heart of any QA program. If those to be inspected are clear on the standards against which their work will be measured before the arrival of the inspector, the process will go much better. It is common

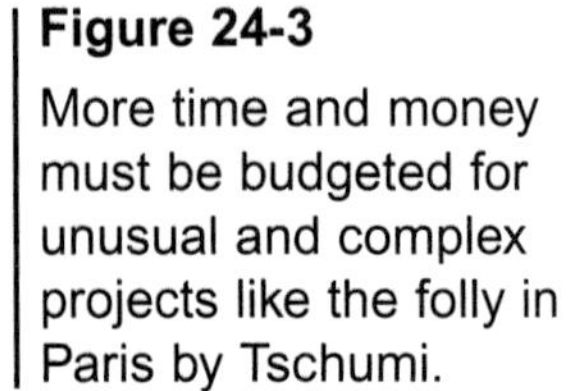

Figure 24-3
More time and money must be budgeted for unusual and complex projects like the folly in Paris by Tschumi.

in government and manufacturing operations to provide the same *checklists* that will guide the inspector to those that will be observed. When inspectors stop work, require expensive corrective actions, or cite safety issues, emotionally charged situations may develop even in the best of circumstance. *Rejection of work* is based on deviation from a clear measurable pre established standard, not on opinions or past experience (Juran and Gyrna 1970).

Quality audits

QA managers and inspectors will look not only at finished products but also the total process that brings the product into being. A *quality audit* is conducted after contracting is completed and work is in progress. Quality audits are conducted both periodically and when special needs surface. Even periodic audits do not occur on a specifically anticipated date in order to get a more authentic picture of ongoing work. Quality audits inspect all design and production processes, records, and products. The total QA program itself is also reviewed. In conventional manufacturing quality audits within the primary contractor, all subcontractors, and all suppliers are conducted under a single QA authority. Six consistent causes of quality problems are listed in "Quality Auditing." The list includes lack of organization, training, discipline, adequate resources, time, and support of top management. Therefore, quality audits normally address all of these subjects (Sayle 1988).

QUALITY ACCOUNTABILITY

In an industry such as aerospace, systematic records are kept that identify all quality defects that were found, who made decisions related to any defect, what was done to correct the defect, and what was done to prevent any similar future occurrence. Such records include management decisions, all design activities, and track all production activities. This system of accountability is sobering for all who must "sign off" on a defect. Such a continuous and comprehensive QA record is not systematically kept in the building construction industry. Iver William Wahl, Fellow in the American Society of Quality Control, has suggested that this "QA history" for each building project might be made a permanent attachment to the title of that property when delivered to the client. The client would then need to be required to continue this QA documentation for all subsequent building modifications. Stiff fines could then be imposed if the complete, continuous, and currently updated QA history documentation was not attached to the title at the time of any subsequent property transfer (Wahl 2006).

BARTERING QUALITY

Management of the trade-off between quality, cost, and time of delivery is a necessary, unavoidable, continuous process. It will normally require considerable negotiation, collaboration, and compromise. Generally, the architect, constructor, and client engage in this process. In issues concerning the building structure, the structural engineer will play a pivotal role. In the construction industry, cost is normally clearly defined in the building's budget. Time of delivery is also usually very specifically defined for a building. Unfortunately, quality characteristics are not usually equally clearly defined within the building industry. In the absence of clear, previously defined quality characteristics, quality may easily become the most negotiable aspect. To negotiate structural quality, is to flirt with disaster. Don't do it. Find money and time elsewhere in the project.

QUALITY IMPROVEMENT

In general, quality may be improved in two ways. *Prevention* takes place before problems surface. Prediction and planning are critical to prevention. It is always cheaper to get it right the first time. *Elimination* takes place after the problem erupts. Elimination may involve changes in people, technology, methods, procedures, values, and attitudes. Such changes should only be based on clearly defined standards. It can be difficult for a project architect to be objective if he or she is also responsible for the design, production schedule, and budget (Juran and Gyrna 1970).

REWARDS FOR QUALITY

Immediate, significant, appropriate, well-publicized personal rewards are an important part of changing the quality "culture" in a firm. A system of consistent recognition and tangible individual rewards for quality design and conformance is essential to wide spread acceptance of QA at every level in a firm. Do the most reliable cars sell better? Yes. Then how does the individual manager or worker share in those increased profits? It is harder to achieve "zero defects" than to allow defects. What are the individual rewards for taking that harder path? There must be such rewards, or that harder path will not be taken. The first reward on that harder path is continued employment in a firm that is successful and growing because of its quality work (Fig. 24-4).

City building inspectors will review your drawings, specifications, and actual construction for conformance to the building code. While these inspectors bring objectivity in these reviews, are you really willing to have them define the quality and safety for your projects? Are you really willing to place your firm's reputation and future solely in their hands?

QUALITY SUMMARY

The most significant, enduring, and recurring problems of QA are people problems. "The value, concern, commitment, and discipline of all the people

Figure 24-4
Carefully designed and executed detail in the Innsbruck train station at a scale where it is seen often, and in detail.

involved in a project are the most important determinates of quality" (Wahl 2006). If people at every level, and in all activities, are apathetic, appropriate quality is unattainable. In a life support system like structures an apathetic attitude is more than difficult to understand. If negligence becomes extreme, it is criminal.

Vocabulary		
Quality	Quality control	Quality characteristics
Design quality	Quality of conformance	Standard operational procedures
Destructive testing	Nondestructive testing	Reliability
Statistical sampling	Post construction evaluation	Lessons learned
Life support system	Quality survey	Quality inspection
Quality audit	Punch list	Building inspector

REVIEW QUESTIONS

1. Briefly describe the difference between design quality and quality of conformance.
2. Briefly describe the difference between quality surveys, quality inspections, and quality audits.

3. What are two good reasons not to leave quality problems until final acceptance inspections?
4. What are the six consistent causes of quality problems?
5. What are the major components of a typical comprehensive QA program?
6. How many of these components are missing in the current building design and construction industry?
7. Why is a single integrated comprehensive quality control program missing in most current building design and construction projects?
8. What conflicts of interest exist if a project architect or project engineer checks the design quality of his/her project?
9. What are the conflicts of interest if the prime contractor verifies conformance quality in the construction of a building?
10. What are the benefits and liabilities of placing city building inspectors in charge of the QA function of your design and construction projects?
11. In the trade-off negotiations between cost, time, and quality why is it so common to sacrifice quality?
12. What are the immediate feasible steps that an architect or engineer can take toward improving quality control?
13. Why is it important to get quality right on building structure even if it is beyond possibility in other areas?

Bibliography

SOURCES, END NOTES, AND RECOMMENDED READINGS

Allen, E. *Fundamentals of Building Construction Materials and Methods*. New York: John Wiley and Sons, 2004.

Allen, E. *Architect's Studio Companion.* New York: John Wiley and Sons, 2002.

Ambrose, J. *Simplified Design of Building Foundations*. New York: John Wiley and Sons, 1981.

Ambrose, J, and D. Vergun. *Simplified Building Design for Wind and Earthquake Force*. New York: John Wiley and Sons, 1995.

American Institute of Architects, and J. A. Demkin, ed. *Architect's Handbook of Professional Practice*. 13th ed. New York: John Wiley and Sons, 2001.

AIA Research Corporation and National Science Foundation. *Architects and Earthquakes.* Washington, DC: National Science Foundation and AIA Research Corporation, 1975.

American Institute of Steel Design. *Manual of Steel Construction, Allowable Stress Design*. 9th ed. Chicago, IL: American Institute of Steel Construction Inc., 1989.

Amrehein, J. E., ed. *Masonry Design Manual of the Colorado Masonry Institute.* 2d ed. San Francisco, CA: Masonry Industry Advancement Committee, 1972.

Benjamin, B. S. *Structural Evolution, An Illustrated History*. Lawrence, KA: A. B. Literary House, 1990.

Billington, D. P. *Thin Shell Concrete Structures*. New York: McGraw-Hill, 1982.

Borrego, J. *Space Grid Structures*. Cambridge, MA: MIT Press, 1968.

Butler, M. *London Architecture*. London: Metro Publications, 2004.

Butler, R. B. *Standard Handbook of Architectural Engineering*. New York: McGraw-Hill, 1998.

Breyer, D. E., K. J. Fridley, and K. E. Cobeen. *Design of Wood Structures ASD.* 4th ed. New York: McGraw-Hill, 1999.

Callender, J. H., ed. *Time Saver Standard for Architectural Data.* 5th ed. New York: McGraw-Hill, 1974; 6th ed. 1982.

Canadian Wood Council. *Wood Reference Handbook*. Ottawa, Ontario: Canadian Wood Council, 1991.

Carpenter, J., ed. *Handbook of Landscape Architectural Design.* Washington, DC: Landscape Architecture Foundation Inc., 1976.

Carson, A. B. *Foundation Construction*. New York: McGraw-Hill, 1965.

Cerver, F. A. *The World of Contemporary Architecture.* Cologne, Germany: Konemann Verlagsgesellshaft mbH, 2000.

Ching, F. D. K. *Building Construction Illustrated*. 3d ed. New York: John Wiley and Sons, 2001.

Christensen, H. E. "Procurement Quality Control." Thesis, Colorado State University, Fort Collins, CO, 1971.

Clyde, J. E. *Construction Inspection: A Field Guide to Practice*. New York: John Wiley and Sons, 1979.

Corkill, P. A., H. Puderbaugh, and H. K. Sawyers. *Structures and Architectural Design.* 2d ed. Iowa City, IA: Sernoll Inc., 1974.

Crosby, P. B. *Quality is Free*. New York: Mentor Books, 1979.

Cowan, H. J., and F. Wilson. *Structural Systems*. New York: Van Nostrand Reinhold, 1981.

Dent, R. *Principles of Pneumatic Architecture*. London: Architectural Press, 1971.

Drew, P. *Frei Otto Form and Structure*. Boulder, CO: Westview Press, 1976.

Engel, H. *Structural Systems*. New York: Van Nostrand Reinhold, 1971.

Faber, J., and B. Johnson. *Foundation Design Simply Explained*. 2d ed. London: Oxford University Press, 1979.

Fairweather, V. *Expressing Structure, the Technology of Large Scale Buildings*. Boston, MA: Birkhauser-Publishers of Architecture, 2004.

Fletcher, B., Sir. *History of Architecture*. 18th ed. New York: Charles Schribner's Sons, 1975.

Foster, J. S. *Structure and Fabric*. Part 1. London: Mitchell's Building Series, Batsford Academic and Educational Ltd., 1983.

Francis, A. J., *Introducing Structures*. Oxford: Pergoman Press, 1980.

Frisch, K. V. *Animal Architecture*. New York: Harcourt Brace Jovanovich, 1974.

Frohlich, B. *Concrete Architecture Design and Construction*. Berlin: Birkhauser Publishers for Architecture, 2002.

Gaylord, E. H., C. N. Gaylord, and J. E. Stallmeyer. *Structural Engineering Handbook*. 4th ed. New York: McGraw-Hill, 1997.

Geiger, D. "Low-Profile Air Structures in the USA. Building Research and Practice. March/April 1975, pp. 80–87. www.columbia.edu/cu/gsapp/BT/DOMES/OSAKA/o-lowpro.html

Glover, J. A. *Becoming a Morre Creative Person*. Englewood Cliffs, NJ: Prentice-Hall, 1980.

Gordon, J. E. *Structures*. New York: Plenum Press, 1978.

Gordon, J. E. *Structures, or Why Things Fall Down*. New York: Plenum Press, 1978.

Gwilt, J. *The Encyclopedia of Architecture*. New York: Bonanza Books, 1982.

Halprin, D. A. *Statics and Strength of Materials*. 2d ed. New York: John Wiley and Sons, 1981.

Herzog, T. *Pneumatic Structures*. New York: Oxford University Press, 1976.

Hilson, B. *Basic Structural Behavior via Models*. New York: John Wiley and Sons, 1972.

Hodgkinson, A., ed. *Architects Journal Handbook of Building Structure*. 2d ed. London: Architectural Press, 1982.

Holgate, A. *The Art of Structural Design*. Oxford: Clarendon Press, 1986.

Houghton, E. L., and N. B. Carruthers. *Wind Forces on Buildings and Structures*. New York: John Wiley and Sons, 1976.

Huntington, W. C., and R. E. Mickadeit. *Building Construction Materials and Types of Construction*. 4th ed. New York: John Wiley and Sons, 1975.

Huxtable, A. L. *Pier Luigi Nervi*. New York: George Braziller, 1960.

International Code Council. *International Building Code*. Falls Church, VA: International Code Council, 2000.

Nicolas Jansberg's "*Structurae*" website. http://en.structurae.de/structures.

Jensen, A., and H. H. Chenoweth. *Statics and Strength of Materials*. 4th ed. New York: McGraw-Hill, 1983.

Jones, J. C. *Design Methods, Seeds of Human Futures*. New York: Wiley and Sons, 1980.

Juran, J. M., and F. M. Gryan, Jr. *Quality Planning and Analysis*. New York: McGraw-Hill, 1970.

Kenner, H. *Geodesic Math and How to Use It*. Berkley, CA: University of California Press, 1976.

Ketchum, M. and Ketchum M. S. . *Structural Engineers' Handbook*. 2d ed. New York: McGraw-Hill, 1918.

Ketchum M., Concrete Shell Structures website, http://www.ketchum.org/ShellTandF/index.html, 2006.

Kidder, F. E., and H. Parker. *Architects' and Builders' Handbook*. 11th ed. New York: John Wiley and Sons, 1949.

Koberg, D. *Universal Traveler*. New Horizons ed. Los Altos, CA: Crisp Publications, 1991.

Lawson, B. *How Designers Think*. 2d ed. Oxford: Butterworth Architecture, 1990.

Levy, M., and M. Salvadori. *Why Buildings Fall Down*. New York: W. W. Norton and Company, 1992.

Liu, C., and J. B. Evett. *Soil and Foundations*. Englewood Cliffs, NJ: Prentice Hall, 1981.

MacDonald, A. *Wind Loads on Buildings*. New York: John Wiley and Sons, 1975.

Mark Ketchum's Concrete Shell Page. *Types & Forms of Concrete Structures*. 2006. http://www.ketchum.org/ShelTandF/index.html

Margolius, I. *Architects + Engineer = Structures*. Chichester, England: Wiley Academy, 2002.

Martin, R. *Hartford, Civic Center Arena Roof Collapse*. http://www.eng.uab.edu/cee/reu_nsf99/hartford.htm

Martin, R. and N. Delatte *Another Look at the Hartford Civic Center Coliseum Collapse*. ASCE Journal of Performance of Constructed Facilities, Vol. 15, No. 1, 2001.

Mays, G. C., and P. D. Smith. *Blast Effects on Buildings*. London: Thomas Telford Services Ltd., 1995.

McHale, J. *Buckminster Fuller*. New York: George Braziller, 1962.

Merriman, T., and T. H. Wiggin. *American Civil Engineers Handbook*. 5th ed. New York: John Wiley and Sons, 1942.

Merritt, F. S., ed. *Standard Handbook for Civil Engineers*. 1st ed. New York: McGraw-Hill, 1968; 3rd ed. 1986.

Mills, C. B. *Designing with Models*. New York: John Wiley and Sons, 2000.

Moore, F. *Understanding Structures*. New York: McGraw-Hill, 1999.

Morgan, W. *Elements of Structure*. 2d ed. London: Pitman Publishing Inc., 1977.

Motro, R. *Tensegrity Structural Systems of the Future*. London: Kogan Page Science, 2003.

Nervi, P. L. *Structures*. New York: F.W. Dodge Corporation, 1956.

Nervi, P. L. *Buildings, Projects, Structures 1953-1963*. New York: Frederick A. Praeger, 1963.

O'Brian, J. J. *Construction Inspection Handbook*. New York: Van Nostrand Reinhold, 1974.

Otto, F. *Tensile Structures*. Vol. 2. Cambridge, MA: MIT Press, 1969.

Powell, K. *City Reborn*. London: Merrell Publishing Ltd., 2004.

Pugh, A. *An Introduction to Tensegrity*. Berkley, CA: University of California Press, 1976.

Pugh, A. *Polyhedra a Visual Approach*. Berkley, CA: University of California Press, 1976.

Ramsey, C. G., and H. R. Sleeper, eds. *Architectural Graphic Standards*. 10th ed. New York: John Wiley and Sons, 2000.

Robinson, M. *Kiting: The Journal of American Kitefliers Association*. Vol. 23, No. 4. Fall 2001.

Roland, C. *Frei Otto Tension Structures*. New York: Praeger Publishers, 1970.

Rosen, H. J. *Construction Specification Writing*. New York: John Wiley and Sons, 1974.

Salvadori, M., and R. Heller. *Structure in Architecture*. Englewood Cliffs, NJ: Prentice Hall, 1963.

Salvadori, M., *Why Buildings Stand Up*. New York: W.W. Norton and Co., 1990.

Salvadori, M., and M. Levy. *Structural Design in Architecture*. 2d ed. Englewood Cliffs, NJ: Prentice-Hall, 1981.

Salewski, W., and E. Allen. *Shaping Structures, Statics*. New York: John Wiley and Sons, 1998.

Sayle, A. *Quality Auditing*. 2d ed. New York: McGraw-Hill, 1988.

Seelye, E. E. *Design*. New York: John Wiley and Sons, 1960.

Schaeffer, R. E. *Building Structures Elementary Analysis and Design*. Englewood Cliffs, NJ: Prentice-Hall, 1980.

Schueller, W. *The Vertical Building Structure*. Van Nostrand Reinhold. New York: Van Nostrand Reinhold, 1990.

Schodek, D. L. *Structures*. Englewood Cliffs, NJ: Prentice Hall, 1980.

Slaby, Steve M. and Herbert I. Tyson. *Statics and Introduction to Strength of Materials*. New York: Harcourt, Brace, and World Inc., 1969.

Smith, C. B. *Builders in the Sun*. New York: Architectural Book Publishing Co., 1967.

Sowers, G. B., and G. F. Sowers. *Introductory Soil Mechanics and Foundations*. New York: Macmillan, 1970.

Stok, T. L. *The Worker and Quality Control*. Ann Arbor, MI: Bureau of Industrial Relations, 1965.

Taiyo Kogyo Company. *The Tent, Soft Shell Structures at Expo '70*. Tokyo: Taiyo Kogyo Co., 1970.

Tang, S., *Tanguage, a Primer of design, Planning, Evaluation, and Management:* Stephen S.Y. Tang, Eugene, Oregon, 1978.

Teng, W. C. *Foundation Design*. Englewood Cliffs, NJ: Prentice-Hall, 1962.

Trautwine, J. C., and J. C. Trautwine, Jr. *Civil Engineers Reference Book*. Ithaca, NY: Tautwine Company, 1937.

Truss-Frame. *Design Terms*. 2006. http://www.truss-frame.com/design-common.html

Underwood, R., and M. Chiuini. *Structural Design A Practical Guide for Architects*. New York: John Wiley and Sons, 1998.

U.S. Department of Agriculture., "Soil Texture Calculator NRCS Soils," http://soils.usda.gov/technical/investigations/texture/triangle.

Wahl, I. W. (Fellow in the American Society of Quality Control) in multiple discussions with the author between 14 January 2006 and 10 May 2006.

Winterkorn, H. F., and H. -Y. Fang. *Foundation Engineering Handbook*. New York: Van Nostrand Reinhold, 1975.

Zalewski, W., and E. Allen. *Shaping Structures, Statics*. New York: John Wiley and Sons, 1998.

Zannos, A. *Form and Structure in Architecture*. New York: Van Nostrand Reinhold, 1987.

Illustration Credits

The University of Oklahoma, College of Architecture kindly released student work to be used for the following illustrations: Figures 11.2, 13.2, 13.29, 14.20, 14.27, 15.34, 16.12, 16.20, 17.16, 19.39, 19.42, 20.12, 20.14, 22.2, 22.3, 22.8, 23.2, 23.4, 23.5

All photographs within this book are by the author except the following:

Figure	Source
18.17	Courtesy of Terry Patterson
23.6	Courtesy of Adam Lanman

With the exception of any student work listed above, all of the drawings in this book are by the author. The following sources were used as a basis for those individual drawings. (See Bibliography for complete citations)

Figure	Source
3.2	Slaby & Tyson, 1969
4.1	With permission of Dr. Quaas, Cenepred
4.2	Butler, 1998
5.2–5.9	NSF/AIA Research Corp., 1975
5.21	Ambrose & Vergun, 1995
5.22	Ambrose & Vergun, 1995
5.29–5.33	Ambrose & Vergun, 1995
5.38	Ambrose & Vergun, 1995
5.41	Schueller, 1990
5.42	Ambrose & Vergun, 1995
5.43	Schodek, 1980
5.44	Ambrose & Vergun, 1995
5.45	Schodek, 1980
5.46	Ambrose & Vergun, 1995
6.2	Seeyle, 1960
6.3	U.S. Department of Agriculture, 2006
7.2	Hodgkinson, 1982
7.4–7.6	Faber & Johnson, 1979
7.7	Ambrose, 1981
7.9	Ambrose, 1981
7.11	Corkill, Puderbaugh, & Sawyers, 1974
7.13	Winterkorn & Fang (Joseph E. Bowles), 1975
7.15	Winterkorn & Fang (H.Q. Golder), 1975
7.16	Allen, 1985
7.17–7.18	Huntington & Mickadeit, 1975
7.19	Ambose, 1981
7.23	Ambrose, 1981
7.25	Ambrose, 1981
7.29	Teng, 1962
7.31	Ambrose, 1981

7.32	Carson, 1965
7.33	Winterkorn & Fang (Joseph E. Bowles), 1975
7.34–7.36	Ambrose, 1981
7.41–7.45	Winterkorn & Fang (Bengt B. Broms), 1975
7.53–7.54	Ambrose, 1981
7.60–7.62	Winterkorn & Fang (G.M. Cornfield), 1975
8.5	Moore, 1999
8.7	Schodek, 1980
8.9	Moore. 1999
8.10–8.11	Engel, 1971
8.13	Moore, 1999
8.15	Moore, 1999
8.16	Roland, 1970
8.17	Merritt (John J. Kozak & James E. Roberts), 1986
8.18	Salvadori & Heller, 1963
8.20–8.21	Salvadori & Heller, 1963
8.24–8.25	Moore, 1999
8.26	Merritt, 1986
9.7	Merriman & Wiggin, 1942
9.8	Zalewski and Allen, 1998
9.9	Schodek, 1980
9.18	Merriman & Wiggin, 1942
9.22	Fletcher, 1975
9.23	Corkill, Puderbaugh, & Sawyers, 1974
9.24	Gordon, 1978
9.26	Gaylord, Gaylord, & Stallmeyer (Thomas C. Kavenaugh & Robert C. Y. Young), 1997
9.27	Schodek, 1980
9.28	Corkill, Puderbaugh, & Sawyers, 1974
9.29	Colorado Masonry Institute, 1972
9.30	Francis, 1980
9.32–9.34	Kidder & Parker, 1949
9.35	Merritt, 1986
9.40–9.41	Merriman & Wiggin, 1942
9.42–9.44	Trautwine, 1937
10.12	Allen, 1985
10.15	Kidder & Parker, 1949
10.22–10.23	Schodek, 1980
10.32	Salvadori & Heller, 1963
10.34–10.36	Salvadori & Heller, 1963
10.39	Salvadori & Heller, 1963
10.41	Jensen & Chenoweth, 1983
10.55	American Institute of Steel Construction, 1989
11.6	Salvadori & Heller, 1963
11.9	Salvadori & Heller, 1963
11.10–11.11	Moore, 1999
11.12	Gaylord, Gaylord, & Stallmeyer (Thomas C. Kavenaugh & Robert C.Y. Young), 1997
11.14	Schodek, 1980
11.17–11.18	Schodek, 1980
11.21	Salvadori & Heller, 1963

11.22–11.23	Schodek, 1980
11.24	Salvadori & Heller, 1963
11.25	Schodek, 1980
11.26	Salvadori & Heller, 1963
11.30	Salvadori & Heller, 1963
11.32–11.35	Salvadori & Heller, 1963
12.7–12.14	Salvadori & Heller, 1963
12.15	Morgan, 1977
12.17	Merritt, 1968
12.21–12.23	Corkill, Puderbaugh, & Sawyers, 1974
13.15	Ketchum, 1918
13.16	Cowan & Wilson, 1981
13.17	Schaeffer, 1980
13.18	Cowan & Wilson, 1981
13.20	Moore, 1999
14.23–14.25	Martin, 1999
15.7–15.9	Ketchum, 2006
15.10	Corkill, Puderbaugh, & Sawyers, 1974
15.12–15.18	Ketchum, 2006
15.22	Huntington & Mickadeit, 1975
15.23	Morgan, 1977
15.24	Cowan & Wilson, 1981
15.27	Merritt, 1968
15.30–15.31	Morgan, 1977
15.32	Schodek, 1980
16.11	Moore, 1999
16.13	Corkill, Puderbaugh, & Sawyers, 1974
16.16	Callender (Seymour Howard), 1974
16.17	Salvadori & Heller, 1963
17.8	Merriman & Wiggin, 1942
17.11–17.12	Pugh, 1976
17.15	Callender (Seymour Howard), 1974
17.18	Gaylord, Gaylord, & Stallmeyer (David P. Billington & Julian A. Dumitrescu), 1997
17.27	Fletcher, 1975
18.5	Ketchum, 2006
18.10	Callender (Seymour Howard), 1974
18.12	Callender (Seymour Howard), 1974
18.16	Jansberg (Yoshito Isono), 2006
18.17	Courtesy of Terry Patterson
18.20	Salvadori & Heller, 1963
19.10	Kogyo, 1970
19.11	Engel, 1971
19.14	Moore, 1999
19.17	Drew, 1976
19.18	Roland, 1970
19.19	Drew, 1976
19.27	Roland, 1970
19.32	Roland, 1970
19.33	Drew, 1976
19.34	Roland, 1970

20.3	Kogyo, 1970
20.6	Herzog, 1976
20.10	Herzog, 1976
20.13	Herzog, 1976
20.15	Dent, 1971
20.16	Herzog, 1976
20.19–20.22	Herzog, 1976

Index